The Shrubs and Woody Vines of Florida

The Shrubs and Woody Vines of Florida

A Reference and Field Guide

Gil Nelson

Drawings by R. Marvin Cook, Jr.
Photographs by the Author

Pineapple Press, Inc.
Sarasota, Florida

Dedicated to my good friends Joseph and Marcella Nemec
of Key Largo, whose enthusiastic suggestion first inspired me
to take this project on.

Inquiries should be addressed to:

Pineapple Press, Inc.
P.O. Box 3889
Sarasota, Florida 34230
www.pineapplepress.com

Library of Congress Cataloging-in-Publication Data

Nelson, Gil, 1949–
   Shrubs and woody vines of Florida / by Gil Nelson. – 1st ed.
      p. cm.
   Includes bibliographical references (p.) and indexes.
   ISBN 1-56164-106-5 (hardcover : alk. paper). – ISBN 1-56164-110-3 (pbk. : alk. paper)
   1. Shrubs—Florida—Identification. 2. Climbing plants—Florida—Identification. I. Title.
QK154.N435   1996
582.1'7'09759—dc20

                                                    96-21970

First Edition
10 9 8 7 6 5 4 3

Printed in the United States of America

TABLE OF CONTENTS

ACKNOWLEDGMENTS

First, I would like to offer a special thanks to Marvin Cook, whose outstanding drawings grace many of the pages that follow. His agreement to take on a second project like this was much appreciated and gave me the confidence and reassurance to continue. His drawings add a dimension to the book that no description or color photograph can surpass. I hold both his work and friendship in high regard.

Several people stand out as having made significant contributions to the content of this book. Foremost among them are Joseph and Marcella Nemec of Key Largo, Angus K. Gholson Jr. of Chattahoochee, Roger Hammer of Homestead, and Dr. Bobby Hattaway of Tallahassee.

Joseph and Marcella Nemec, to whom the volume is dedicated, provided the initial encouragement which led to the decision to take this project on. Their knowledge of the flora of the Florida Keys, enthusiastic field demeanor, willingness to collect and ship numerous specimens of sample material to me, and dedicated review of and comments on the manuscript were valuable assets to the work's completion. I owe a great debt to both of them.

Angus Gholson, highly regarded north Florida field botanist, sought-after field trip leader, and owner/curator of the AKG Herbarium, an outstanding private collection of nearly 17,000 specimens, spent many hours with me in the field, allowed me to use his herbarium and reference material when needed, was always ready to provide a location for even the rarest of north Florida's plants, and never failed to provide enjoyable and stimulating company and conversation. His immense knowledge of the flora of north and northwest Florida coupled with his willingness to share it freely have added much to my knowledge and I am deeply grateful.

Roger Hammer's knowledge of the flora of tropical Florida and his willingness to share his knowledge with me contributed significantly to my understanding of the south Florida flora and to the book's coverage of this important plant assemblage. His willingness to apprise me of additions to this rapidly expanding flora, to provide location data, to take me places I otherwise would have never found, to collect specimens for illustrations, and to diligently review the manuscript and its art for accuracy and completeness are much appreciated and were essential to the book's completion.

Bobby Hattaway's detailed review and comments on the manuscript were also very instructive and helpful. His expertise in sorting out the key diagnostic characters of the various plant families, his knowledge of woody plants from many parts of the eastern United States, his keen interest in both the north and south Florida flora, his help in providing directions to some difficult-to-find specimens, and his good company and expertise in the field are all highly regarded and much appreciated.

I also owe a debt to Tammera Race, Curator of Endangered Plant Species at Bok Tower Gardens. Tammera provided me with much information about the mint family as well as the extremely rare *Ziziphus celata*. She also allowed me to visit and photograph Bok Tower Gardens' collection of special plants, and graciously reviewed, commented on, and made several corrections to my treatment of Labiatae.

In addition to those above, a number of other individuals offered their help in numerous ways ranging from providing resources, field assistance, and location data to offering their yards, gardens, and nurseries as photographic locations. These include Dr. Loran Anderson, Guy Anglin, Dr. Dan Austin, Wilson Baker, Keith Bradley, Barbara Cook, Eleanor Deitrich, Rick Holder, Dr. Ann Johnson, Gary Knight, Donna Legare, Maureen MacLaughlin, Chuck Salter, Jody Walthall, Dick Workman, Dr. Richard P. Wunderlin, Scott Zona, and the many staff members of Florida's state and national parks and forests who have been eager to share what they know about the natural resources which they have been charged to manage on our behalf.

I would like to thank David and June Cussen of Pineapple Press for agreeing to publish the book. Their personal attention to detail, collaborative attitude, and commitment to quality always make working with them and their staff both refreshing and enjoyable.

Finally, but far from least, I offer my sincere appreciation and love to my wife, Brenda, and daughter, Hope. Both are consistent sources of inspiration and encouragement. I am confident that I would have never completed this book without their love and support.

INTRODUCTION

On a crisp October morning about two decades ago, my partner and I were making our way into the magnificent woodlands of the Bradwell Bay Wilderness Area in northwest Florida's Apalachicola National Forest. We had just emerged from the knee-deep waters of a luxuriantly vegetated bay swamp and were standing in the dense, thigh-high ground cover of fetterbushes, staggerbushes, gallberry, and wax myrtle. As we surveyed the expansive sea of greenery my companion remarked, "How would anyone ever learn all this stuff?" Indeed, there were few readily available plant guides in those days, and none that focused solely on native shrubs. Those of us interested in woody plants either had to make do with a rather limited selection of popular wildflower field guides, or schedule regular visits to the stacks of professional journals at one of the university libraries.

In many ways, the current volume is the result of a project begun on that field trip to Bradwell Bay. Though the decision to write the book was not made then, the decision to learn the native woody vines and shrubs was. Since then, several books have been published that focus on the woody plants of various regions of Florida and the southern United States. Some of these are popular pictorial works designed for amateur plant lovers. Others are technical botanical manuals directed primarily to professional botanists. None encompasses the entire state of Florida or brings together all of the state's woody shrubs and vines into one volume. This book attempts to fill this void.

How to Use This Book

The book is organized alphabetically by class, family, genus, and species. Professional botanists, experienced observers, and others who are acquainted with the diagnostic characters of the several plant families will appreciate the ease with which they can turn to particular families and genera. Beginning plant enthusiasts might at first find the alphabetical presentation somewhat perplexing, but will soon come to appreciate the design and its ease of use.

My decision to present all species alphabetically by family was not made haphazardly. Implicit in the design is my desire to help those just starting out to develop a working concept of plant families, while simultaneously offering more experienced observers a ready reference and easily usable handbook. Those new to plant study will learn the ways in which one family and its member genera and species compare to those of another, and how to recognize such differences in the field. This will encourage familiarization with the specialized characteristics of particular plant families, an indispensable tool for efficient field identification. Being able to make an educated guess about the family or genus to which an unknown species belongs narrows the search for the plant's specific identity and fosters a sense of accomplishment when sorting out the identities of the many plant species that clothe our landscape.

All descriptive entries follow a general format which includes a description of each plant's form, leaves, flowers, fruit, distinguishing marks, and distribution. Many of the descriptions rely heavily on measurements of leaves, flowers, and fruit. These measurements are intended to be used as guides to identification. In general I have tried to use reasonable measurements that encompass the normal range of variability for a particular species. In some instances I have used the size of leaf, fruit, or flower as a dependable character for distinguishing between two similar species. In such cases I have attempted to clearly describe the distinction and the degree of its dependability. In some species the size of fruit, flower, or leaf is quite variable over a broad range. In these latter cases I have attempted to provide the most inclusive extremes. Nevertheless, readers may encounter individual specimens that exceed the stated limits. This is particularly likely for poorly situated specimens or for sucker shoots that have developed from old root systems. Suffice it to say that the size of a plant's leaves, flowers, or fruits should normally be used only in conjunction with other characteristics of the plant in making a positive identification.

For many entries a notation is included about the species' suitability for landscape use and its requirements under cultivation. As might be expected, gardening is a popular activity in Florida due to the ease with which many plants can be cultivated. Many species have been introduced to the state strictly for horticultural purposes and have become sought-after ornamentals. However, at least some of these introduced species have taken hold in the state's natural landscape and, in a number of cases, have become noxious, unwanted weeds that threaten our native flora and fauna. This has led the Florida Department of Agriculture, the Florida Department of Environmental Protection, and the U. S. Department of Agriculture to develop lists of pest plants that should not be cultivated in the state. According to Florida's Exotic Pest Plant Council, Category I plants are those that are currently invading and disrupting native plants; Category II plants are those that have shown potential to invade and disrupt. Plants that appear on these lists or that are otherwise known to have a weedy nature are specifically identified in the descriptions that follow, and their use in landscape design should be avoided whenever possible.

Most entries also include a comment section that highlights such items as the plant's historical or medicinal uses, notes about the derivation of its name, its status as endangered, threatened, or commercially exploited, or a brief treatment of other, nonnative members of its family with which the reader may be familiar. Such final remarks provide a context which helps readers develop a keener appreciation of individual plants and add depth to what might otherwise be an essentially sterile description.

In addition to the more than 550 plants which are fully described within the text, a considerable number of additional species are mentioned or only partially described. Part of this results from an attempt at completeness. Another part results from a desire to help readers learn to distinguish our native and naturalized shrubs from closely similar herbs or trees.

To use this guide most effectively, read and study it at home before embarking on a field excursion. This is especially true if you are new to plant study. It is also a good idea to list those plants that you might see on your trip based upon the habitat you plan to visit and the time of year. By studying the descriptions and illustrations of your listed plants diligently before you leave home, you will more likely recognize the plants you find in the field. When new plants are found, jot down personal observations in the book's margins that will help you remember their identities.

It should be noted that you will probably not be able to identify all of the plants you find on every field trip. This is normal. Some species require the presence of flowers or fruit to make an accurate identification or to accurately distinguish between two physically similar or closely related species. Even with flowers or fruit present it is sometimes difficult to tell some species apart.

What Is a Shrub?

Answering the question "What is a shrub?", then using the answer to decide what to include in this book, has been a bewildering challenge. There are few authorities that address this question clearly, and no widely accepted definitions. Some authors include in their definition plants that are predominantly herbaceous, but take on a bushy, shrublike appearance. Others include only plants that have above-ground woody stems. A few include species that arise from a woody caudex (a thickened, woodlike base), even though the caudex is not visible. A single species might be described by one author as suffrutescent (or shrublike), by another as a woody herb, by yet another as a subshrub, and by still another as a perennial herb. To make matters worse, some plants are herbaceous in some parts of the state and woody in others.

Given the above explanation as a premise, my aim has been to include all woody or somewhat woody perennial plants that are vinelike, or that are shrubby and have either multiple or single trunks that do not normally exceed about 4 m in height. However, my own rule of thumb notwithstanding, there are a number of typically shrubby plants that also approach or reach treelike stature, and a number of tree species that retain a shrublike form, or that flower and fruit when of a shrublike stature. In at least a few cases, I have chosen to include plants of this latter category. It is likely that some will question the "shrubbiness" of some of the included species. As a defense, I have chosen to err on the side of inclusion rather than exclusion.

Although the flora of Florida is well-known from the research of several centuries of naturalists and botanists, what the state's flora includes is anything but static. New species are regularly recognized, either as newly established escapes or new species of naturally occurring plants, or as rediscovered plants that have not been found in many years. The constant advance of botanical science, continuing search for new plants, and a climate that is conducive to the establishment of nonnative introductions will render this book, or any book like it, out of date shortly after publication. As a result, I encourage you to make notes in the book as plant names change and new discoveries are made.

Nomenclature and Botanical Terminology

The naming of plants is a precise activity governed by an elaborate set of internationally-agreed-upon rules. Though space does not permit a complete discussion of these rules, at least a few remarks will help readers understand the importance of this system.

All plants which have been validly described to science are referred to by a three-part, Latinized name that includes, in order, the genus name, specific epithet, and the authority who described and named the plant. For example, the scientific name for the common lantana is *Lantana camara* L. The genus name, in this case *Lantana*, may be the same for a large group of related plants. The specific epithet (*camara*) may also be used by other species in different genera. However, no two plants in the same genus can have the same specific epithet. Hence, every scientific name is unique to a specific plant. In this example, "L." at the end stands for Linnaeus.

For a plant to be validly named, it must have been validly described in writing and published in an acceptable publication. The name associated with the earliest valid publication of a plant following the year 1753 is the one that is accepted as valid. Those described prior to 1753 are attributed to Carl Von Linne, or Linnaeus. Hence, the plant *Torreya taxifo-*

lia Arn. (known also by the common name torreya) was named by George Arnott, while the common coontie, *Zamia pumila* L., is attributed to Linnaeus.

Sometimes more than one authority's name follows the species name. The name for the Florida yew, *Taxus floridana* Nutt. ex Chapm., is a good example. It was described by A. W. Chapman with credit given to Thomas Nuttall. The name for switchcane, *Arundinaria gigantea* (Walt.) Muhl., is another example. It was named first by Thomas Walter, then reassigned to another genus (but with the same specific epithet) by Gotthilf Henry Ernest Muhlenberg.

In addition to Latinized plant names, botanical terminology also comprises a rich and varied vocabulary used for describing plants. While somewhat daunting to those new to botany, this highly specialized language is indispensable to effective communication. Though I have attempted to keep the use of technical terms to a minimum in the descriptions that follow, it would be a disservice to eliminate them entirely. The following glossary and descriptive drawings should prove useful in learning botany's specialized terms as well as the morphology of plants.

Glossary of Common Botanical Terms

Actinomorphic. Said of a flower that is radially symmetrical, or having the symmetry of a wheel with spokes.

Acuminate. Tapering to a pointed apex, the sides of the taper concave in shape.

Alternate leaves. Leaves that arise singly from the stem rather than in pairs or whorls; a type of leaf arrangement with only one leaf at a node.

Anaerobic. Generally used to refer to soils that lack free oxygen.

Anther. The pollen-bearing portion of a stamen.

Anthesis. The time at which a flower is open and in full bloom.

Apex. Used to refer to the distal tip of a leaf.

Apices. Plural of apex.

Appressed. Pressed flat, or nearly so, against another structure.

Aril. Pulpy and often colorful appendage to a seed.

Ascending. Said of a plant or appendage that is curving or pointing upwards at an angle of less than 90 degrees.

Axil. The angle formed where two plant parts are joined; commonly used in reference to the angle between leaf and stem.

Axillary. In or arising from an axil.

Biennial. A plant whose life cycle is completed in two years.

Bipinnate. Doubly pinnate; twice cut.

Bloom. A waxy, whitish covering sometimes found on leaves, stems, or other plant parts, i.e., glaucous.

Bract. A typically (but not always) reduced, leaflike structure that is normally situated at or near the base of a flower.

Calyx. The sepals of a flower when referred to collectively.

Cambium. Layer of soft tissue between the bark and the wood which adds width to a trunk or branch.

Campanulate. Said of a flower that has joined petals and is bell-like in shape.

Carpel. One of the female reproductive organs of a flower consisting of an ovary with at least one ovule, as well as the stigma and style.

Catkin. A spikelike inflorescence bearing small unisexual flowers; often hangs pendantlike from a branch.

Caudex. A thickened, woodlike base, stem, or erect rhizome, often below or at the surface of the ground.

Cauline. Said of leaves that occur along a stem rather than basally.

Ciliate. Having hairs along the margins of a leaf or other structure.

Clasping. Said of a leaf whose base partially encircles the stem.

Complete. A flower that contains all basic parts, including sepals, petals, stamens, and pistil.

Compound leaf. A leaf divided into leaflets along a common axis.

Conspecific. Said of two plants belonging to the same species.

Cordate. Said of a structure (usually a leaf) that is heart-shaped at the base.

Corolla. The petals of a flower when referred to collectively.

Crenate. Said of a leaf margin with rounded teeth which give a scalloped appearance.

Crenulate. Finely crenate.

Cuneate. Wedge-shaped.

Cuspidate. With a short, sharp apex.

Cyme. A flower structure in which the distal or apical flowers bloom first.

Cymose. Arranged in a cyme.

Deciduous. Trees or shrubs that shed their leaves each year; opposite of evergreen; some plants are described as "tardily deciduous," meaning that the leaves fall late in the season.

Decumbent. Reclining or lying flat with tips ascending.

Dentate. Having teeth that are perpendicular to, rather than angled from, the supporting margin.

Dioecious. Said of plants that have unisexual male and female flowers on separate plants.

Disc flower. The central-most flowers in the head of a composite flower; like the dark center of a sunflower or black-eyed Susan.

Distal. Generally used to denote the point that is farthest from the point of attachment, as in the distal end (apex) of a leaf.

Drupe. Fleshy fruit in which the inner wall is hardened into a pit and surrounds the seed or seeds.

Ecotone. The transition zone between two different plant communities.

Endemic. Restricted or peculiar to a particular locality.

Entire. Said of a margin which is smooth rather than toothed.

Epiphytic. Said of a plant that grows on the bark of another plant but does not obtain food from and, therefore, is not parasitic on, its host; such plants are called epiphytes.

Equisetum-leaved. Having leaves reduced in size and reminiscent of members of the genus *Equisetum*.

Evergreen. Trees and shrubs that remain green in winter or do not lose all leaves at the same time; opposite of deciduous.

Exserted. Extending beyond, as in a flower with stamens that extend or project beyond the petals.

Fascicle. Bundle or tightly bound cluster, such as a fascicle of pine needles.

Filiform. Threadlike and slender; usually rounded in cross-section.

Foliaceous. Having leaflike foliage.

Follicle. A dry fruit splitting along a single suture.

Glabrous. Lacking pubescence.

Glaucous. Covered with a whitish bloom that can be removed by rubbing.

Globose. Rounded.

Habit. Overall appearance or growth form of a plant.

Halophyte. A plant which grows in salty or alkaline conditions, such as plants of the salt marsh.

Head. A crowded cluster of flowers at the tip of a single flower stalk, as in a sunflower.

Herbaceous. Not woody.

Inflorescence. Used variously to refer to the flowering portion of a plant; to the type of flower arrangement; or to a flower cluster.

Irregular. Said of a flower with bilateral symmetry, meaning that it can be cut through the center in only one way to form equal halves; like the flower of a violet.

Lanceolate. Lance shaped, wider at the base and tapering toward the apex, entire structure appearing narrow.

Leaflet. An individual segment of a divided or compound leaf.

Lepidote. Covered with small scales; often used to describe a leaf surface.

Locular. Said of an ovary or fruit which has compartments or cavities (locules).

Monoecious. Said of plants having unisexual flowers with both male and female flowers borne on the same individual.

Node. Place on a stem where leaves or their scars appear.

Oblanceolate. Reverse of lanceolate; widest portion near the apex rather than the base.

Obovate. Opposite of ovate; shaped like an egg but widest toward the apex.

Opposite leaves. With leaves arising from the stem in pairs opposite one another.

Orbicular. Circular in outline.

Ovate. Shaped like an egg; widest toward the base.

Palmate. Radiating from a single point like the fingers of a hand, as in palmately compound leaves or palmate venation.

Panicle. A loosely branched, compound inflorescence with stalked flowers.

Pedicel. The stalk of a flower.

Peduncle. Stalk of an inflorescence or flower.

Peltate. Stalked from the center rather than the edge like an umbrella.

Perennial. Plants that live and flower beyond two years and that persist through the winter or dormant season; such plants are often woody.

Perfect. Said of a flower with both stamens and pistils.

Petal. A whorl of flower parts separating the sepals from the stamens in a perfect flower; usually, but not always, showy.

Petiole. The stalk of a leaf.

Pinna. A leaflet or other major division of a pinnately compound leaf.

Pinnae. Plural of pinna.

Pinnate leaf. A compound leaf with leaflets along opposite sides of a central stalk (or rachis).

Pistil. The ovary, style, and stigma collectively; female portion of a flower.

Pith. The soft tissue in the center of a stem.

Pome. A fleshy fruit in which the ovarial portion of the flower becomes surrounded by an enlarged floral tube, such as an apple or pear.

Prop root. Said of the aerial roots of a red mangrove (*Rhizophora mangle*) that extend to the ground from the lower trunk and branches and provide stability to the tree.

Pubescent. Covered with hairs.

Punctate. With small, depressed, sometimes colored dots on the surfaces (punctations); dotted.

Raceme. An inflorescence with a single axis in which the basal flowers open first.

Rachis. The main axis of a compound leaf.

Ray flower. One of the many typically showy, petallike flowers near the periphery in the head of a composite flower; the typical "petals" of a sunflower.

Receptacle. The terminal, sometimes thickened end of a flower stalk that bears a flower or flower head.

Reticulate. Netted, as is the venation of many leaves.

Revolute. With rolled-under margins; usually said of a leaf.

Rhizome. An underground, horizontal stem.

Rhombic. Having the outline of a rhombus; diamond shaped.

Riparian. Said of a plant that is typically situated along the banks of a river or other body of water.

Rosette. A radiating cluster; often refers to leaves radiating from the base of a plant.

Rotate. Said of a flower that spreads radially and in one plane.

Ruderal. Said of highly disturbed habitats such as roadsides, vacant lots, and fields.

Rugose-veiny. With a roughened, veiny surface; usually refers to the surface of a leaf.

Samara. Winged fruit.

Scabrid. Said of a structure that is rough to the touch due to stiff hairs.

Scandent. Climbing or vinelike.

Sepal. Member of the outermost whorl of flower parts (calyx).

Serrate. Said of a margin that is toothed, with teeth pointing toward the tip.

Sessile. Without a stalk; typically said of a leaf, flower, or fruit.

Spatulate. Having the shape of a spatula.

Specific epithet. The species designation, or second word, in a binomial scientific name; specific name.

Stamen. The anther and filament collectively; the male portion of a flower.

Steephead. A steep-sided ravine located along a natural gradient created by the seepage of ground water near the base of the ravine.

Stellate. Star shaped; often refers to leaf hairs that radiate in a starlike pattern.

Stilt root. Same as prop root.

Stipe. The stalk that supports a fruit or pistil.

Stipule. A leaflike appendage at the base of a leaf or petiole.

Tepal. Said of petals and sepals when not easily distinguishable from one another.

Terete. Rounded in cross-section.

Terminal. Referring to an appendage that is situated at the apex of a structure.

Tomentose. Densely covered with short, matted, or woolly hairs.

Trifoliolate. Said of a compound leaf with three leaflets.

Tripinnate. Said of a compound leaf with a central axis, one to several secondary axes, with the leaflets attached to the secondary axes.

Truncate. Having a flat or squared-off apex or base.

Two-ranked. Typically said of leaves that are arranged in two vertical ranks alternating along either side of the stem.

Unifoliolate. Said of a compound leaf with a single leaflet.

Zygomorphic. Bilaterally symmetrical or asymmetrical (see irregular flower above).

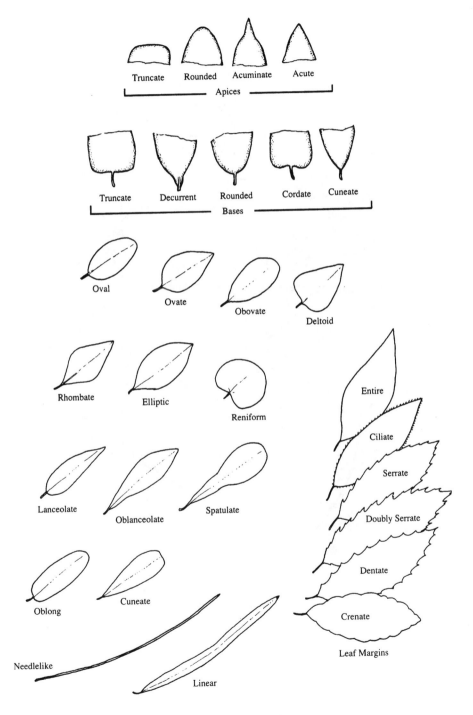

Leaf Shapes

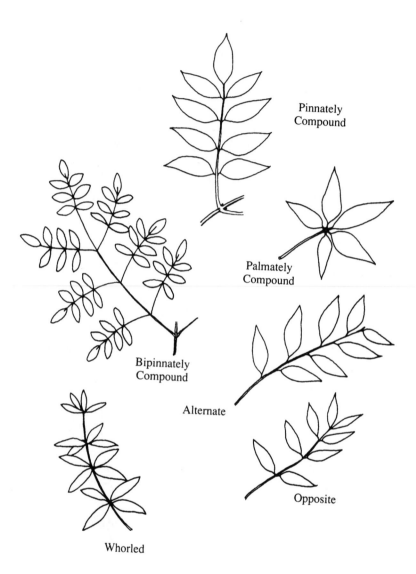

Pinnately Compound

Palmately Compound

Bipinnately Compound

Alternate

Opposite

Whorled

Leaf Arrangements

The Shrubs and Woody Vines of Florida

Following are descriptions of more than 550 of Florida's woody vines and shrubs. Included are all the woody shrubs and vines that are native to or naturalized in Florida, as well as some of the state's more common exotics. Each entry includes a description of the species' salient morphological characteristics, hints about how to recognize the plant in the field and distinguish it from similar plants, and a note about the plant's distribution in the state. Also included are the flowering times for each species.

Many species are illustrated with line drawings or color photographs, sometimes both. Extremely similar species may be represented by an illustration of only one of the similar plants. In these cases, discussions of how the similar plants differ are included in the descriptions. In all descriptions, Page refers to the page on which a line-drawn illustration of the species may be found, and Photo refers to the number of a photograph in the color section of the book.

Most descriptions offer a range of measurements for the particular species' height, leaf length, flower size, and fruit. These measurements generally represent maximum and minimum dimensions and are intended only as guides. Field observers might occasionally find plants that exceed the stated extremes. In addition, all measurements are metric. Some descriptions detail characteristics that may be seen or measured only with magnification. A 10x hand-held magnifier and a 15 cm ruler are recommended.

GYMNOSPERMS

TAXACEAE — YEW FAMILY

The yew family is represented by two species in Florida, both of which are confined to the central Panhandle and are exceedingly rare. Both are also relic species that date from pre-glacial times. Though neither species is common, the existing populations of Florida yew (*Taxus floridana*) are the healthier of the two. As noted below, the several remaining populations of the torreya (*Torreya taxifolia*) are in serious decline.

Florida Yew

Photo 1

Taxus floridana Nutt. ex Chapm.

Form: Shrub or small evergreen tree to about 8 m tall, with irregular branching, a bushy appearance, and scaly bark.

Leaves: Dark green, needlelike, not exceeding about 2.5 cm in length and 2 mm in width, tips pointed but pliable and not sharp to the touch.

Distinguishing Marks: Similar in appearance to the torreya tree (*Torreya taxifolia*), distinguished from it by the yew's shorter, less lustrous, flexible leaves with soft-pointed tips and irregular branching.

Distribution: Found chiefly on bluffs and in ravines along the eastern edge of the upper Apalachicola River from just north of Bristol northward to Flat Creek and its tributaries, which lie a few miles north of Torreya State Park.

Landscape Use: This is a difficult plant to maintain. For skillful horticulturists, the Florida yew makes a nice pruned shrub or background plant. Due to its scarcity, specimens should never be taken from the wild; it may be difficult to find specimens at native plant nurseries.

Comment: This plant is listed as endangered by the Florida Department of Agriculture; only a few specimens are extant. One good place to see this species is along the trails at Torreya State Park. Two of the best locations are along the trail to the Rock Creek primitive camp and near the old stone bridge constructed by the Civilian Conservation Corps. Ask park staff for directions.

Torreya, Stinking Cedar, Gopherwood

Photo 2

Torreya taxifolia Arn.

Form: Shrub to small evergreen tree, formerly to about 10 m tall, branches borne in whorls along the trunk.

Leaves: Needlelike, glossy green, typically 2 - 5 cm long; apices sharply pointed and piercing to the touch.

Distinguishing Marks: Distinguished from Florida yew (*Taxus floridana*) by whorled branching and by leaves being longer, less pliable, and with sharply pointed tips.

Distribution: Occurring naturally in the bluffs and ravines area of the upper Apalachicola River in the Panhandle, in ravines of extreme southwestern Georgia, and in a small population of several sprouts on Dog Pond near Shady Grove in southeastern Jackson County.

Comment: This is one of Florida's most endangered woody plants and is listed as endangered by both the Florida Department of Agriculture and the U. S. Fish and Wildlife Service. A disease that probably first attacked the plant in the 1930s has all but eliminated the species, and no mature specimens remain in native habitat. Old-timers report that the torreya was once so abundant that it was regularly cut for use as Christmas trees. Today's population consists chiefly of saplings and sprouts. *Torreya taxifolia* has the distinction of being the first member described for its genus. It was first discovered by Hardy B. Croom, a well-to-do North Carolinian who, in the early 1800s, owned a plantation near Aspalaga Landing on the eastern side of the Apalachicola River and later settled near Tallahassee. Croom probably first saw the plant in 1833 and, recognizing it as distinctive, sent samples to Thomas Nuttall and later to John Torrey, both of whom are well known in the history of botany. The latter conferred with George Arnott who officially described the plant to science and named the genus for Torrey.

Today, the genus *Torreya* is represented by five species worldwide, including one in California, one in Japan, and two in southeastern China. Like their Florida cousin, most of these other species are also rare. According to a report by Schwartz and Hermann (1993), the first report of disease in the Florida population was probably in 1938, followed by a second report only in 1955, at which time perhaps no adult plants remained in the wild. Today, Schwartz and Hermann continue, the population is probably in the range of 800 to 1500 (perhaps 2000) individuals. No reproductive adult females have been observed in the wild for at least 15 years, meaning that no new plants have germinated from seed in at least that long. (It should be noted, however, that a pair of trees consisting of a male and female are in private cultivation at a home on the banks of the lower Apalachicola River. These two individuals are approximately 10 m tall and quite impressive. Both bear flowers each year, and the female bears at least a few fruits annually. Why these two trees remain healthy and vital is unclear.) Many members of today's population are beset with needle spots, needle necrosis, and stem cankers, leading to the assessment that we may be witnessing this species' decline toward extinction.

It is interesting to note that Dr. A. W. Chapman, an early Florida plantsman, first sounded the alarm for the *Torreya* in an 1885 article in the *Botanical Gazette*. In his reminiscence he expressed concern about the unbridled harvesting of the plant for a variety of uses, including "posts, shingles, and other exposed constructions." The tiny country church at Rock Bluff, at the intersection of state roads 270 and 270-A, not far from Torreya State Park, still has a pulpit made from the wood of this species.

ZAMIACEAE (CYCADACEAE) — CYCAD FAMILY

The cycads constitute an ancient family of about 100 species in 10 genera of mostly tropical distribution and as old as the conifers and *Ginkgo*. According to Corner (1964), from outward appearances they may seem to the average observer to be halfway between the conifers and the ferns because they look like tree ferns but have cones reminiscent of the pines. The genus *Zamia* is the family's only representative in the United States. Their antiquity, which dates to the Mesozoic, has made the genus extremely interesting to botanists, plant ecologists, and those interested in the evolution, diversity, and expansion of the plant kingdom.

Coontie, Arrowroot, Comfortroot, Compties, Contis, Seminole Bread

Photo 3

Zamia pumila L.

Form: Low-growing, fernlike shrub, with a below-ground stem; entire plant usually not exceeding 2 - 3 m tall, often much shorter.

Leaves: Borne from the crown of the stem, dark shiny green, arching, pinnately compound, 3 - 16 cm long; leaflets stiff, evenly distributed on either side of the rachis, numbering 20 - 60 per leaf, each leaflet 8 - 20 dm long, 3 - 15 mm wide, margins rolled under; petioles usually long and conspicuous.

Cones: Large, reddish brown, borne at ground level; male cones lance shaped, 5 - 8 cm long, female cones more rounded; male and female cones borne on separate plants.

Distinguishing Marks: The arching, dark green, fernlike leaves, short, erect, subterranean stems, and distinctive fruiting cones distinguish the species.

Distribution: Well-drained sites, especially those areas where the limestone is covered by only a thin layer of soil; from about Taylor County eastward and southward to the southern peninsula.

Landscape Use: The low stature, dark green, palmlike evergreen leaves, and interesting fruiting cones make this an attractive and sought-after landscape plant. It does best in partial shade and works well in borders. It should never be transplanted from natural habitat (mostly due to declining numbers, but also because it often does not survive transplantation and can be readily obtained from many native plant nurseries).

Comment: As treated here, *Z. pumila* is the only member of its genus in Florida and the only cycad native to the conterminous United States. It encompasses a number of synonymous names, including *Z. angustifolia*, *Z. integrifolia*, *Z. silvicola*, and *Z. umbrosa*, all of which were described by Small (1933) and several others. The plant is best known for its historical use as a primary source of starch for Seminole Indians. The rootlike stem of the plant was harvested, chopped into small bits, crushed into a powder, then washed and strained. The residue was left to dry into a yellowish flour (hence one of the common names). According to Hammer (1995), eating the stem raw can be lethal, and it is not precisely known when the first humans learned to transform the poisonous stem into an edible product. The plant is listed by the Florida Department of Agriculture as commercially exploited.

ANGIOSPERMS — MONOCOTS

MONOCOTYLEDONS, or monocots, take their name from the number of seed leaves, or cotyledons, contained in their embryos; they have only one. For practical purposes, however, determining whether an individual plant is a monocot can be most easily accomplished by examining the plant's leaf venation, as well as the number of its flower parts. Monocots usually have parallel rather than netted leaf venation, which means that the leaf veins tend to run parallel with the central leaf axis rather than angling away from it. Monocots also typically (though not always) have flower parts in threes or multiples of three. Together, these two characters are generally diagnostic.

It is probably misleading to include the monocots in a book about woody plants. In the true sense of the word (see explanation of dicotyledons, p. 21), monocots do not develop wood. Essentially, a monocot stem is composed of a large number of vascular bundles (food and water transporting tissue), each surrounded by a layer of thin- to occasionally somewhat thick-walled cells. Thickening of the stem results primarily from the formation of new vascular bundles rather than from the development of wood. In defense of their inclusion here, the stems of at least a few monocots become hard and rigid, and take on a somewhat "woody" appearance. Some also reach arborescent stature.

AGAVACEAE — AGAVE FAMILY

The Agavaceae are succulent-leafed perennials native to arid regions of both North and South America. Their stems are generally thick and hardened. As suggested above, it is probably questionable whether they belong in a book about woody shrubs. However, their evergreen, shrublike stature, popularity as landscape plants, and inclusion in many books and guides that focus on shrubby plants seem to justify the inclusion here. In addition to the two species described below, at least three other *Agave* species have been reported in Florida: the wild century plant (*A. neglecta* Small), the American century plant (*A. americana* L.), and *A. demettiana* Jacobi.

Century Plant or False Sisal
Agave decipiens Baker

Form: Tropical shrub to about 3 m tall, with basal leaves and a thickened base.

Leaves: Borne in dense, basal rosettes; each leaf simple, lanceolate, dark green, deeply concave, to about 1 m long and 10 cm wide; margins with sharp spines; apices brownish and tipped with a sharp, needlelike point.

Flowers: Greenish yellow, borne in clusters on short branches off a woody, fibrous scape that may reach 8 m in height; typically appearing fall through winter.

Fruit: An ellipsoid capsule to about 4 cm long; splits at maturity to expose a collection of thin, flattened seeds.

Distinguishing Marks: Distinguished from *A. sisalana* by having concave rather than flattened leaves and by having sharp spines along the leaf margins.

Distribution: Shell mounds, coastal hammocks; southernmost peninsula and the Keys.

Landscape Use: Century plants, of which there are more than 300 species, are popular landscape plants where a tropical aspect is desired. They grow best in full sun but also tolerate shade. They are particularly suited for seaside conditions but will do well in any location with well-drained soil and year-round warm temperatures. They are most commonly used in southern Florida, but are also planted in north Florida.

Comment: This species was probably introduced from Mexico.

Century Plant or Sisal   Photo 4
Agave sisalana Perrine

Form: Tropical shrub with a dense rosette of basal leaves that may reach 1.5 m in height.

Leaves: Borne in dense, basal clusters; each leaf simple, lanceolate, flat, grayish to dark green, to about 1.5 m long and 10 cm wide; apices with a sharp, needlelike point.

Flowers: Greenish, to about 7 cm wide, borne on a tall, branching scape that may reach 9 m or a little more in height; typically appearing spring through summer.

Fruit: Egg-shaped capsule, splitting at maturity and releasing black seeds.

Distinguishing Marks: Distinguished from *A. decipiens* by having flattened rather than conspicuously concave leaves and smooth leaf margins.

Distribution: Coastal strands; southernmost counties and the Keys.

Landscape Use: See *A. decipiens*.

Comment: Introduced to the Keys from the Yucatan in 1836 by Henry Perrine. Listed as a Category II pest plant by the Florida Exotic Pest Plant Council.

Spanish Dagger, Spanish Bayonet, Aloe Yucca   Photo 5
Yucca aloifolia L.

Form: Evergreen, clump-forming shrub with an erect, densely leafy stem and overlapping leaves.

Leaves: Rigid, stiff, simple, dark green (except grayish near the tips and bases), daggerlike in shape, 2 - 6 dm long, 2 - 5 cm wide; margins with sharp outgrowths; apices with a sharp, needlelike tip.

Flowers: White, conspicuous, borne in a dense, terminal cluster 5 - 6 dm long and about 2 dm wide; each flower pendent on a stalk about 2 cm long; appearing late spring and early summer.

Fruit: Fleshy, leathery berry to about 13 cm long and 3 cm wide; black at maturity.

Distinguishing Marks: Likely to be confused only with the relatively uncommon *Y. gloriosa*; distinguished from the latter by having predominantly dark green rather than bluish-green leaves and by the flower cluster being at least partially seated within the terminal leaves rather than conspicuously raised above them.

Distribution: Native in dune fields and along the edges of salt marshes; throughout the state.

Landscape Use: This is a common landscape plant, especially near the coast. It is excellent as a foundation plant, or for barriers or enclosures. It requires well-drained soil and does well in full sun or shade.

Beargrass, Silkgrass, Adam's Needle

Photo 6

Yucca flaccida Haw.

Form: Low-growing shrub with a dense basal rosette of overlapping leaves.

Leaves: Grayish green, entire, simple, lanceolate, to about 8 dm long and 4 cm wide, at first rigid but becoming flexible; margins with peeling, threadlike fibers; apices sharp-pointed.

Flowers: White, borne in a conspicuous, branching cluster terminating a stalk that may be up to 2 m tall; each flower borne on a stalk 1.5 - 2 cm long; appearing late spring and early summer.

Fruit: An erect capsule about 4 cm long and 2 cm wide; black seeds.

Distinguishing Marks: Distinguished by flower clusters held as much as 2 m above the basal leaves, by the flexible leaves, and by having fibrous threads along the leaf margins.

Distribution: Pine–scrub oak ridges, open sandy and secondary woods, coastal sands; throughout north Florida southward to about Palm Beach County.

Landscape Use: The low-growing leaf rosette lends itself to use in large planters, as a tropical border, or for a foundation in conjunction with century plants (*Agave* sp.).

Comment: The common name beargrass should not be confused with species of *Nolina*, a nonwoody monocot genus which is not included in this treatment.

Spanish Bayonet or Mound-Lily Yucca

Yucca gloriosa L.

Form: Evergreen shrub with an erect, densely leafy stem with overlapping leaves.

Leaves: Rigid, stiff, simple, bluish green, daggerlike in shape, mature leaves 6 - 10 dm long, 5 cm wide; margins smooth or with sharp outgrowths; apices with a sharp, needlelike tip.

Flowers: White, conspicuous, borne in a dense, terminal cluster 7.5 - 12 dm long and 4.5 dm wide; cluster usually raised 3 - 5 dm above the terminal leaves.

Fruit: A pendent, leathery berry, 5 - 6 cm long.

Distinguishing Marks: Very similar in appearance to *Y. aloifolia*; separated from it by having bluish rather than predominantly dark green leaves and by flower clusters usually raised above the terminal leaves rather than being partially covered by them.

Distribution: Coastal dunes; northeast and Panhandle Florida.

Landscape Use: See *Y. aloifolia*; not used as often in landscaping as this latter plant.

GRAMINEAE (POACEAE) — GRASS FAMILY

This is a large, mostly herbaceous family that offers considerable challenge to the amateur botanist. Only two woodlike species occur in Florida.

Cane or Switchcane
Arundinaria gigantea (Walt.) Muhl.

Page 9

Form: Stiff, bamboolike perennial with hollow, woodlike stems to about 8 m tall and 3.5 cm in diameter; branched or unbranched; typically growing in dense stands.

Blades: Narrow, lanceolate, flexible, 10 - 30 cm long, those on basal shoots and main stems short, sessile or essentially so; those toward the ends of shoots much longer and having petioles.

Flowers: Borne in loosely branched clusters, chiefly from the main stem or primary branches; appearing in spring.

Distinguishing Marks: Most easily distinguished as the plant from which "cane fishing poles" are fashioned, though the stem of some plants are much longer and much larger in diameter than the typical fishing pole.

Distribution: Typically in low, wet woodlands or moist areas including river and stream banks, in bogs and bays, and on the edges of sloughs and bayous; throughout north Florida, southward to about Osceola County.

Wild Bamboo, Small Cane, Florida Tibisee
Lasiacis divaricata (L.) Hitchc.

Page 9

Form: A tall, woodlike grass with spreading branches; main stem (culm) to about 4 m tall and 6 mm in diameter; sometimes arching and then vinelike; secondary shoots often strongly zigzag.

Blades: Alternate, narrowly lanceolate, 5 - 20 cm long, 5 - 15 mm wide.

Flowers: Borne in terminal, branching, few-flowered clusters; clusters 5 - 20 cm long and appearing summer and fall.

Fruit: A small, shiny black seed.

Distinguishing Marks: The bamboolike appearance, rigid stem, and shiny black seeds set this species apart from most other south Florida plants.

Distribution: Hammocks and hammock edges; southernmost counties and the Keys.

Cane or Switchcane
Arundinaria gigantea

Wild Bamboo, Small Cane or Tibisee
Lasciacis divaricata

PALMAE (ARECACEAE) — PALM FAMILY

The palm family contains perhaps 3,000 species worldwide and more than 230 genera. Most of these are found in the warmer regions of the world; only a few are native to the United States. Four shrubby species are found in Florida, along with seven additional species that are generally considered to be trees. All of the shrubs treated below are native to the state.

Silver Palm, Florida Silver Palm, Biscayne Palm, Seamberry Palm

Photo 7

Coccothrinax argentata (Jacq.) Bailey

Form: Small, slender, straight-trunked shrub, or short tree, with a smooth trunk; not usually exceeding 6 m in height.

Leaves: Fan shaped, deeply divided almost to the point of attachment with the petiole, about 60 cm wide; segments shiny green above, conspicuously silvery white beneath; petioles unarmed, slender, flexible, to about 1 m long.

Flowers: White, fragrant, borne in long clusters; appearing in spring.

Fruit: Rounded, purplish-black to black, 1 - 2 cm in diameter.

Distinguishing Marks: Distinguished from most other palms with fan-shaped leaves by the silvery white undersurfaces of the leaf segments, from Key thatch palm (*Thrinax morrisii*) by its smaller stature, by leaves being more deeply divided with solid, nonsplitting bases, by being darker green above, by having more narrow leaf segments, and by dark rather than white fruit.

Distribution: Coastal dunes and rocky pinelands; from north Palm Beach County southward, including the Keys; the state champion for this species is found at Bahia Honda State Recreation Area.

Comment: Listed as commercially exploited by the Florida Department of Agriculture.

Needle Palm

Photo 8

Rhapidophyllum hystrix (Pursh) Wendle. & Drude

Form: Low-growing, leafy, evergreen palm; central stem often below-ground and not evident, eventually extending above the ground to as much as 1.5 m and exhibiting conspicuous masses of sharp needles; because of the retention of old needles and leaf bases, trunks of older specimens may appear to be as much as 6 dm in diameter.

Leaves: Fan shaped, dark green above, scaly-pubescent and silvery below, divided into 14 - 24 segments, each segment typically 5 - 8 dm long, 2 - 5 cm wide; petioles slender, stiff, smooth, to about 6 dm long.

Flowers: Small, borne in many-flowered clusters among the spines; appearing in spring and summer.

Fruit: A red to brownish, spherical drupe to about 2 cm in diameter and covered with long, tawny hairs.

Distinguishing Marks: The sharp needles along the main stem are diagnostic (but see *Sabal minor*).

Distribution: Bluffs, ravine slopes, wooded floodplains and bottoms, calcareous hammocks; disjunctively distributed in Florida, from Walton to Liberty Counties in the Panhandle, and Clay County southward to Highlands County in the central peninsula.

Landscape Use: An attractive foundation shrub on rich, shady sites; should never be transplanted from natural habitats.

Comment: Listed as commercially exploited by the Florida Department of Agriculture. The needle palm may be the world's most cold-hardy palm and has been reported to survive temperatures just below zero degrees Fahrenheit with little or no damage (Clancy and Sullivan, 1990). Though still limited in numbers, it is now thought to be more common than once believed and is restricted almost exclusively to five southern states of the coastal plain, including Alabama, Florida, Georgia, Mississippi, and South Carolina.

Scrub Palmetto
Sabal etonia Swingle ex Nash

Form: Evergreen shrub with an S-shaped, normally subterranean trunk; trunk rarely aboveground to about 2 m tall.

Leaves: Fan shaped, leaf segments to about 6.5 dm long, divided into 20 - 50 segments, usually not more than about five living leaves per crown; petioles 2.5 - 5.5 dm long, to about 2 cm wide.

Flowers: White, fragrant, individually small, but borne on long, many-flowered stalks; flowering is episodic for this species and is most prolific following a fire (Abrahamson, 1995).

Fruit: A fleshy, globose, bluish-black, single-seeded berry, about 1.5 cm in diameter.

Distinguishing Marks: Most easily confused with young specimens of the tree sabal palm (*S. palmetto*); distinguished from the latter generally by habitat, but also by having most fruit approaching or equaling 1.5 cm in diameter. (The fruit of the sabal palm is typically less than 1.2 cm in diameter.)

Distribution: Sand pine–oak and dune scrub; predominantly along the central sand pine scrub ridge from Clay and Columbia Counties southward to Highlands County, also in outlying patches of scrub along the coast from Volusia County to Greynolds Park in Dade County, as well as in Citrus, DeSoto, Hernando, Manatee, Okeechobee, and Seminole Counties.

Comment: Endemic to Florida; listed as threatened by the Florida Department of Agriculture.

Sabal miamiensis Zona

Form: Shrub, similar in general respects to *S. palmetto*, but with an underground stem.

Leaves: Fan-shaped, yellow-green blades with 35 - 65 segments, each one 50 - 75 cm long and 1.5 - 3.5 cm wide.

Flowers: White, unstalked, individually small but borne in showy, branching clusters.

Fruit: A shiny, black, rounded, fleshy, one-seeded berry to about 2 cm in diameter.

Distinguishing Marks: Similar to both *S. etonia* and *S. palmetto*, distinguished from each by the larger fruit.

Distribution: Rocky ridges and pinelands of the Everglades keys; Dade and Broward Counties.

Comment: This plant was first described in 1985, though its distinctively large fruit was likely noted by several of Florida's earlier botanists. According to Scott Zona (1985), who described it, many of its characters seem to be intermediate between *S. etonia* and *S. palmetto*, and the plant may have originated as a hybrid of these two. Zona also remarks that the habitat of *S. miamiensis* is quickly disappearing due to the Miami area's extensive urban development, and that the species is in danger of extinction unless its habitat is preserved or it is brought into cultivation.

Dwarf Palmetto, Bush Palmetto, Blue-Stem
Photo 9

Sabal minor (Jacq.) Pers.

Form: Evergreen shrub with a leafy crown and subterranean stem.

Leaves: Fan shaped, green, typically to about 7 dm long and 12 dm wide, divided into about 30 segments; segments to about 3 cm wide at the base, usually lacking fibers along their margins or in the sinuses between segments; lower surfaces of segments often covered with a whitish coating (not silvery as in *Rhapidophyllum hystrix)*; petioles smooth, to about 15 dm long, 1 - 2 cm wide.

Flowers: Flowers small, borne in branching clusters near the end of a long stalk; distance between the base of the stalk and the first flowers often reaching or exceeding 1 m; appearing spring to fall.

Fruit: A shiny, black, globose drupe, 6 - 10 mm in diameter.

Distinguishing Marks: Most easily confused with young specimens of *Rhapidophyllum hystrix*; easily distinguished from it and other shrubby palms by the combination of smooth petiole, elongated flower stalk, subterranean trunk without needlelike appendages, and lack of fibers along the edges of the leaf segments.

Distribution: Lowland woods, bluffs, ravine slopes, bottomlands; northern two-thirds of the state.

Comment: Listed as threatened by the Florida Department of Agriculture.

Cabbage Palm or Sabal Palm

Sabal palmetto (Walt.) Lodd. ex J. S. Schult. & J. H. Schult.

Form: Most often seen as a straight-trunked tree to about 25 m tall; often found as a shrubby plant in fire-prone, pine rockland areas of southern Florida.

Leaves: Fan shaped, 1 - 2 m long and wide, deeply divided and conspicuously V-shaped; segments usually numbering 40 - 90, shiny green above, gray-green below, with numerous threads suspended from the segment margins; petioles smooth, to about 2 m long.

Flowers: Greenish-white, individually small, but borne in conspicuous, long-stalked, often drooping clusters; appearing spring and summer.

Fruit: Round, black, 1 - 1.5 cm in diameter, borne in long, drooping clusters.

Distinguishing Marks: The V-shaped leaf is diagnostic for identification.

Distribution: Native throughout the state.

Comment: This is the state tree of both Florida and South Carolina. Early Florida Indians and later settlers were known to harvest the large leaf buds from the top of this plant. Said to have the look and taste of cabbage, these growing tips were relished as a food source. However, removing the bud kills the tree and should never be attempted today. Wildlife is known to feed on the berries.

Saw Palmetto   Photo 10
Serenoa repens (Bartr.) Small

Form: Typically a low, prostrate shrub with most of the trunk more or less buried, but sometimes upright and having the dimensions of a small tree.

Leaves: Fan shaped, deeply divided into numerous segments, yellowish-green to green; petioles 5 - 10 dm long, armed with sharp, curved spines reminiscent of a saw blade.

Flowers: Greenish-white, 5 - 6 mm long, borne in spikelike clusters from among the leaves; flowering is episodic for this species and is usually most prolific following fire, especially in spring (Abrahamson, 1995).

Fruit: An oblong drupe, yellowish at first but turning black at maturity, 15 - 25 mm long, 12 - 15 mm in diameter.

Distinguishing Marks: This is the common palmetto that ranges across much of Florida; most easily distinguished by the hard, sharp, typically recurved prickles that line both edges of the petiole.

Distribution: Sandy prairies, dunes, flatwoods, scrub oak ridges, and cabbage palm hammocks; throughout the state.

Comment: Saw palmetto is likely an extremely long-lived plant. Based on research at Archbold Biological Research Station near Lake Placid, botanist Warren Abrahamson (personal communication) suggests that many of the plants included in his studies probably exceed 700 years old. He has noted the exceedingly low natural mortality and slow growth rate as evidence for his theory.

The fruit of the saw palmetto is also of interest. Current medical research, especially in Europe, suggests that the plant's yellowish drupes might be beneficial in the treatment of prostate cancer. Another interesting attribute is the belief, at least by some in the Far East, that the plant's fruit is a powerful aphrodisiac with extraordinary sexual powers (Associated Press, 1995). These latter two uses have led to a thriving international trade for saw palmetto fruit. According to the Associated Press story cited above, during 1995 the price per pound of saw palmetto drupes soared from 10 cents to $3.50 per pound, allowing some south Florida gatherers to gross as much as $300.00 per day for their summer harvest.

Key Thatch Palm, Brittle Thatch Palm, Key Palm, Small Fruited Thatch Palm
Thrinax morrisii Wendl.

Form: A shrubby palm, often with a short, erect trunk, or a small tree not normally exceeding about 7 m tall; trunk smooth gray and encircled by conspicuous leaf scars.

Leaves: Fan shaped, to about 1 m wide; segments green above, paler and whitish below; petioles unarmed, slender, to about 1.2 m long.

Flowers: Small, white, turning to yellow.

Fruit: Rounded, white at maturity, 4 - 7 mm in diameter, borne essentially stalkless.

Distinguishing Marks: Distinguished from silver palm (*Coccothrinax argentata*) by white fruit and by leaf segments being wider and divided only about halfway to the leaf base. (The Florida thatch palm [*Thrinax radiata* Lodd. ex J. S. Schult. & J. H. Schult], a tree not described here, is similar but lacks the whitish leaf undersurface and stalked fruit of the present species.)

Distribution: A commercially exploited species that occurs in Florida only along the edges of hammocks and in pinelands of the Keys; readily seen on much of Key Deer National Wildlife Refuge.

SMILACACEAE — SMILAX FAMILY

There are ten species of "woody" smilax in Florida. All are climbing vines with conspicuous tendrils, and all are noted for their sharp thorns. Several species are quite similar and are not often discriminated by the casual observer. Leaf variation from plant to plant of the same species is also common; precise identification of particular plants can be difficult. Most often the members of this genus are considered weeds in the suburban landscape due to their aggressive growth habit. However, several species can be trained to trellises and bear attractive fruiting clusters.

Leaf dimensions are given for most of the species presented below. It should be noted that all of these measurements are based on the average for typical plants. Leaves on particular individuals may exceed the stated extremes.

Catbrier or Greenbrier   Page 15, Photo 11

Smilax auriculata Walt.

Form: Evergreen, climbing vine with scattered prickles; typically scrambling over low shrubs; lower portions of mature leader shoots are pinkish.

Leaves: Alternate, simple, entire, typically oblong in shape but sometimes ovate to lanceolate, also sometimes with a widened base, 3 - 12 cm long, 1 - 5 cm wide; midvein and lateral veins on lower surface somewhat raised above the surface; marginal veins often so close to one another as to form a narrow groove; apices generally bearing a tiny point; both surfaces green, the upper surface somewhat darker than the lower.

Flowers: Small, green to greenish-yellow, borne in clusters; appearing primarily in May in the north, year-round farther south.

Fruit: A glaucous berry that is reddish at first, purple at maturity, about 6 - 13 mm in diameter; borne in clusters.

Distinguishing Marks: The apparent groove along the leaf margins, slightly raised veins on the lower surfaces of the leaves, and the pinkish color of the lower stems combine to help distinguish this species from other species of *Smilax*.

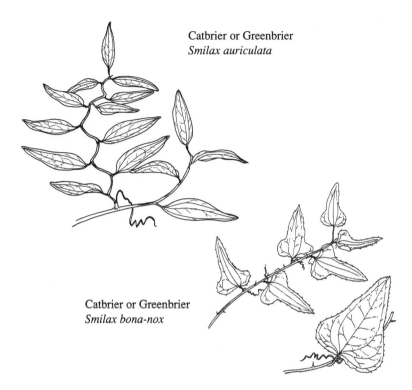

Catbrier or Greenbrier
Smilax auriculata

Catbrier or Greenbrier
Smilax bona-nox

Distribution: Typically in deep sands of scrub oak ridges and sandy sites along the coasts, also sometimes in flatwoods, wet woodlands, and hammocks; common from north Florida southward, including the Keys.

Catbrier or Greenbrier   Page 15

Smilax bona-nox L.

Form: Semievergreen vine with numerous sharp, brownish prickles; lowermost stem and prickles copiously covered with scales and conspicuously roughened to the touch.

Leaves: Alternate, simple, ovate to distinctly widened at the base and fiddle shaped, 5 - 14 cm long, 1 - 12 cm wide; margins thickened, entire or with conspicuous, small prickles; upper surfaces shiny green, lower surfaces paler; bases often heart-shaped; apices with a tiny point; midveins on lower surfaces often with evident prickles.

Flowers: Small, white, borne in clusters; appearing March and April in the north, nearly year-round farther south.

Fruit: Shiny black berries, 6 - 8 mm in diameter, borne in tight, globular clusters.

Distinguishing Marks: The brownish, roughened scales on the lower stems and prickles, in conjunction with the prickles on the margins of at least some leaves, usually distinguish this plant (but see *S. havanensis*, below).

Distribution: Common in a variety of uplands and lowlands, including wet pinelands, hammocks, yards, and fields; from north Florida southward, nearly throughout the state.

Wild Sarsaparilla

Photo 12

Smilax glauca Walt.

Form: Semievergreen vine with slender prickles.
Leaves: Alternate, ovate, simple, entire, typically 4 - 10 cm long; upper surfaces green, lower distinctly grayish-glaucous.
Flowers: Small, borne in clusters; appearing in spring.
Fruit: Berry, glaucous at first, typically shiny black at maturity, 6 - 8 mm in diameter; borne in clusters.
Distinguishing Marks: The distinctly grayish-white cast to the undersurfaces of the leaves sets this species apart from all other species of *Smilax*.
Distribution: Common in a variety of uplands and lowlands, including pine flatwoods, hammocks, yards, and fields; throughout north Florida, southward to about the central peninsula.

Smilax havanensis Jacq.

Form: Evergreen vine with angled stems bearing short, stout, brown-tipped, somewhat recurved prickles.
Leaves: Alternate, simple, oval or elliptic to ovate, 3 - 8 cm long, 1 - 6 cm wide; margins wavy, entire, or with tiny spines; midvein on lower surfaces often bearing conspicuous spines.
Flowers: Small, borne in clusters.
Fruit: A rounded to egg-shaped black berry, 5 - 6 mm in diameter, 5 - 8 mm long.
Distinguishing Marks: Similar in leaf shape to *S. laurifolia*, but leaves much shorter; the spines on the leaf margins and midveins of the lower surfaces of leaves distinguish this species from most members of the genus; most quickly distinguished from *S. bona-nox*, which also has spines on the leaf margins, by never having the widened leaf base characteristic of at least some leaves on the latter species.
Distribution: Hammocks and pinelands of the everglades and the Keys.

Bamboo-Vine or Blaspheme-Vine

Photo 13

Smilax laurifolia L.

Form: Evergreen, high-climbing vine with stems to about 1.5 cm in diameter and numerous prickles.
Leaves: Alternate, simple, entire, leathery, oblong to lanceolate, 5 - 15 cm long; midvein of lower leaf surfaces prominently raised, lateral veins on lower surface not at all raised and often not evident.
Flowers: Small, greenish-white, borne in clusters; appearing late spring and summer.
Fruit: Shiny black berry (at maturity), 5 - 8 mm in diameter; borne in loose clusters.
Distinguishing Marks: The oblong leaves with raised midveins and obscure lateral veins on the lower surfaces help distinguish this species; most similar to *S. auriculata* in overall leaf shape.

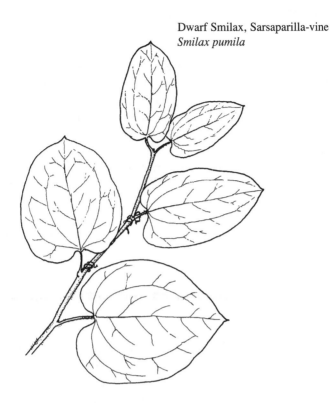

Dwarf Smilax, Sarsaparilla-vine
Smilax pumila

Distribution: Wet and dry pinelands, bay swamps, stream banks, generally in rather wet areas; from north Florida southward, nearly throughout the state.

Dwarf Smilax, Sarsaparilla-vine   Page 17

Smilax pumila Walt.

Form: Typically a low-growing, trailing vine with underground runners; sometimes climbing but often not; not usually exceeding about 5 dm tall, often much shorter.

Leaves: Simple, alternate, entire, ovate to oblong, mostly 4 - 10 cm long, 3 - 5 cm wide, bases heart-shaped, apices often terminated by a small point, upper surfaces dark green, lower surfaces grayish with dense pubescence.

Flowers: Small, borne in clusters; appearing spring, summer, and fall.

Fruit: Ovate berries borne in clusters along the stem; bright red at maturity.

Distinguishing Marks: The densely compact pubescence on the lower surfaces of the leaves sets this species apart from all other "woody" smilaxes.

Distribution: Moist to dry woodlands, including sand pine–oak scrub; from north Florida southward to at least Highlands and Sarasota Counties in the west, less farther south in the east.

Bullbrier, Horsebrier, Common Greenbrier
Smilax rotundifolia L.

Page 19

Form: Semievergreen, high-climbing vine, usually with numerous prickles scattered between the leaf nodes; prickles to about 8 mm long and with a reddish or brownish point.
Leaves: Alternate, simple, entire, ovate, to about 10 cm long, and about 15 cm wide, those on leader shoots usually wider than long; bases conspicuously heart-shaped; apices often pinched to a sharp point; petioles typically reddish.
Flowers: Small, borne in clusters.
Fruit: Glaucous, bluish-black (sometimes reddish-brown) berry, 6 - 8 cm in diameter; borne in clusters.
Distinguishing Marks: The wider than long leaves on leader shoots, reddish petioles, and thin leaf margins generally characterize this species (but see *S. walteri*).
Distribution: Rather uncommon in moist to dry woods, on river banks, and along pond and lake margins; north Florida.

Jackson-Vine, Jackson-Brier, Lanceleaf Greenbrier
Smilax smallii Morong.

Page 19

Form: Evergreen, high-climbing vine with sharp prickles; stems to about 2 cm in diameter.
Leaves: Alternate, simple, entire, chiefly lanceolate, 4 - 10 cm long, 1 - 3 cm wide; dark green above, paler below; apices tapering to an acute point.
Flowers: Small, yellowish green, borne mostly in clusters of 5 to 10; appearing in summer.
Fruit: Glaucous, dull-red to brownish-red berry, 5 - 8 mm in diameter; borne in clusters.
Distinguishing Marks: The predominately narrow, lanceolate leaves set this species apart from other members of the genus.
Distribution: Rich woods, hammocks, and well-drained places; northern Florida southward to about Highlands County but less common in the southern part of this range.
Comment: Though not currently listed, many observers consider this species threatened.

Bristly Greenbrier
Smilax tamnoides L.

Page 19

Form: Semievergreen vine bearing thin, dark, needlelike, sharp-pointed prickles that are about 1 cm long, the latter more evident on the lower stem.
Leaves: Alternate, simple, entire (with magnification some leaves appearing very finely toothed due to tiny outgrowths), ovate to fiddle-shaped, 5 - 15 cm long; apices usually with a short point; bases typically truncate to heart-shaped; both surfaces distinctly green.
Flowers: Small, borne in clusters; appearing March and April.
Fruit: A rounded, black berry, 6 - 8 mm in diameter.
Distinguishing Marks: Most similar to *S. glauca* (with which it often grows), distinguished from it and most other members of the genus by lower surfaces of leaves being green in conjunction with nearly black, needlelike prickles on the lower stem.

Bullbrier, Horsebrier, Common Greenbrier
Smilax rotundifolia

Jackson-Vine, Jackson-Brier,
Lanceleaf Greenbrier
Smilax smallii

Bristly Greenbrier
Smilax tamnoides

Distribution: Uplands, old fields, clearings, stream banks (often in association with *S. bona-nox* and *S. glauca*); throughout north Florida, southward to at least the vicinity of Lake Okeechobee.

Coral Greenbrier

Page 20, Photo 14

Smilax walteri Pursh.

Form: Deciduous vine with slender stems and few prickles; usually clambering over low shrubs but also into trees; often growing in dense thickets.

Leaves: Alternate, simple, entire, ovate to oblong, 4 - 14 cm long, 2 - 6 cm wide, with reddish petioles; bases rounded to truncate; apices often with a small point.

Flowers: Small, borne in clusters; appearing March and April.

Fruit: A bright, coral-red berry (hence the common name), 6 - 8 mm in diameter; typically maturing in early winter after the leaves have fallen.

Distinguishing Marks: The bright red berries, deciduous leaves, and inundated wetland habitat distinguish this species; most similar to *S. rotundifolia*, which also has red petioles.

Distribution: Marshes, cypress swamps, pineland depressions; throughout north Florida southward to Highlands County.

Coral Greenbrier
Smilax walteri

ANGIOSPERMS — DICOTS

Like the monocotyledons, the dicotyledons (dicots for short) take their name from the number of seed leaves, or cotyledons, contained in their embryos; they have two. Determining whether an individual plant is a dicot, however, can be most easily accomplished by examining the plant's leaf venation and the number of its flower parts. Dicots usually have netted rather than parallel leaf venation and flower parts that typically (though not always) number four or five.

Dicot stems also have a different internal structure than do those of monocots (see p. 5) and are the only plants to develop true wood. The stem of an herbaceous dicot is characterized by three layers of cells: the epidermis and cortex (at and just below the surface, respectively), the primary food- and water-conducting cells (the primary phloem and xylem) just below the cortex, and the pith at the stem's center. In herbaceous stems, growth is terminal, or lengthwise, leading to the elongation of the stem (a process called primary growth); very little lateral growth occurs. In woody stems, on the other hand, growth is both terminal and lateral. As the stem ages, the food-conducting tissues of the xylem and phloem grow laterally (a process commonly referred to as secondary growth) which leads to hardening of the tissue known as secondary xylem which surrounds the pith. It is this secondary xylem, a tissue found only in dicots, that develops into true wood.

ANACARDIACEAE — SUMAC OR CASHEW FAMILY

The sumac family is best known for its wide range of both edible and poisonous species. Some of its most famous edible representatives include the cashew, pistachio, and mango; poisonous species include poison ivy, poison oak, poison sumac, and the poisonwood tree (*Metopium toxiferum* [L.] Krug & Urban).

Few avid outdoorspeople or native plant gardeners are unfamiliar with the popular quip "leaves of three, let it be." Though only poison oak and poison ivy have trifoliolate leaves (poison sumac and poisonwood have compound leaves with more than three leaflets), the adage is a good one. Few other Florida vines have similar leaves, and none are likely to cause such a severe itching and burning rash.

Fragrant Sumac
Rhus aromatica Ait.

Form: Nonpoisonous, aromatic, upright, deciduous, typically thicket-forming shrub to about 2.5 m tall.

Leaves: Alternate, compound, trifoliolate, similar in general appearance to leaves of poison oak; leaflets ovate, obovate, to elliptic, 2.5 - 8 cm long, terminal leaflet typically larger than the lateral pair; margins of leaflets with large, blunt to rounded teeth.

Flowers: Yellowish green, small, borne February through June in small but conspicuous clusters.

Fruit: A bright red, conspicuously hairy, rounded drupe, 3 - 8 mm in diameter; surface hairs long and whitish.

Distinguishing Marks: The shrubby stature, trifoliolate leaves, hairy red fruit, and leaflets with crenate margins set this species apart.

Distribution: Dry, rocky woodlands; uncommon in the westernmost Panhandle.

Landscape Use: Used outside of Florida as a low-growing shrub, especially along roadsides, on slopes, and in fill areas to reduce erosion. The colorful fall leaves and interesting fruit make this plant an interesting possibility for native landscaping.

Comment: The leaves of this species are pleasantly aromatic if bruised. However, care should be taken to insure that a particular specimen has not been confused with either poison ivy or poison oak, described below, before handling the foliage.

Winged Sumac or Shining Sumac

Page 23, Photo 15

Rhus copallina L.

Form: Deciduous shrub or small, slender tree to about 8 m tall.

Leaves: Alternate, pinnately compound with a winged rachis, to about 30 cm long; leaflets 9 to 23 in number, lanceolate to elliptic, 3 - 8 cm long, 1 - 3 cm wide, margins typically entire but sometimes with a few teeth, lower surfaces pubescent, upper surfaces mostly glabrous except for a few scattered hairs along the main veins.

Flowers: Tiny, greenish yellow, borne in summer in conspicuous clusters.

Fruit: A flattened drupe, each 3 - 5 mm in diameter, pubescent, dull reddish, borne in conspicuous clusters, mostly in the fall.

Distinguishing Marks: Similar in appearance to smooth sumac (*R. glabra*) but distinguished by having a winged rachis; distinguished from similarly leaved Brazilian pepper (*Schinus terebinthifolius*) by leaflets of the latter usually numbering less than nine, and fruits glabrous rather than hairy, from the tropical soapberry (*Sapindus saponaria*), which also has a winged rachis, by the latter typically having nine or fewer leaflets.

Distribution: Uplands and disturbed sites; statewide except the Keys.

Landscape Use: Good for brilliant fall color, winter fruit clusters, and showy summer flowers in large shrub beds or as an accent specimen; easy to care for, easy to transplant; requires open, sunny, well-drained sites.

Smooth Sumac

Page 23, Photo 16

Rhus glabra L.

Form: Slender deciduous shrub or small tree to about 7 m tall and very similar in general appearance to shining sumac (*R. copallina*).

Leaves: Alternate, pinnately compound, to about 50 cm in overall length; leaflets numbering 9 - 31, lanceolate, 5 - 14 cm long, 1 - 4 cm wide, upper surfaces bright green, lower surfaces grayish, margins toothed.

Flowers: Tiny, yellowish-green, borne in large clusters at the tips of branches; appearing in early summer.

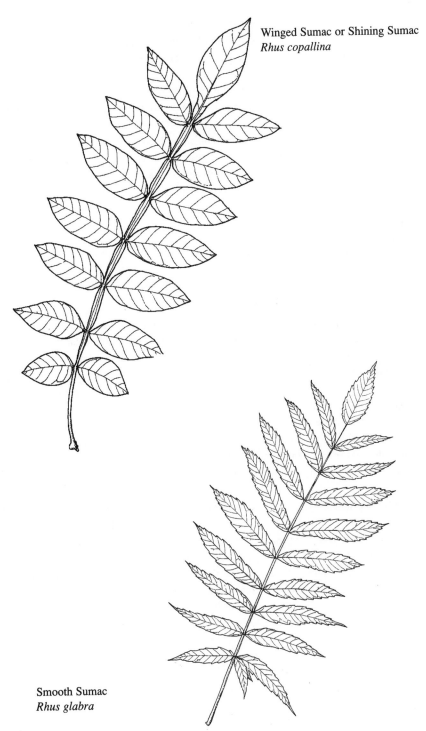

Winged Sumac or Shining Sumac
Rhus copallina

Smooth Sumac
Rhus glabra

Fruit: Berrylike, rounded, borne in large, conical clusters at the tips of branches.

Distinguishing Marks: Similar to the shining sumac, distinguished from it by lacking a winged leaf rachis and by the lower surfaces of leaflets having a grayish, waxy bloom.

Distribution: Woodland borders and disturbed sites; central Panhandle from about Jefferson to Jackson Counties.

Landscape Use: Valued as a wildlife food as well as for its attractive fruit and fall color; reaches the stature of a small tree, making it good for patios. It is also tolerant of harsh growing conditions. Though common along roadsides in the southern Appalachians, this plant is not common in north Florida in the wild or in manicured landscapes.

Comment: This and related species were used medicinally by American Indians and in dyeing and tanning by the early colonists. Some report that a lemonadelike drink may be made from its berries. American Indians ate the raw young sprouts, and birds and mammals still feed on the bright red berries.

Brazilian Pepper or Pepper Tree

Photo 17

Schinus terebinthifolius Raddi

Form: Evergreen shrub or small, attractive tree to about 8 m tall.

Leaves: Alternate, pinnately compound, to about 18 cm in overall length, with a narrowly winged rachis; leaflets typically numbering three to nine (rarely 11), lanceolate to elliptic, to 8 cm long, margins sometimes entire but often toothed; crushed foliage gives off a distinctive turpentine aroma.

Flowers: Small, white, borne in conspicuous clusters at the leaf axils; appearing most prolifically in spring; male and female flowers borne on separate plants.

Fruit: A bright red drupe, borne in conspicuous clusters (on female plants), typically appearing from about November to February, but evident at almost any time of year.

Distinguishing Marks: Distinguished from winged sumac (*Rhus copallina*) by leaflets usually numbering fewer than nine and by fruits glabrous and bright red, rather than hairy and dark red.

Distribution: Brazilian pepper is a troublesome weed in many habitats throughout central and southern Florida and the Keys. (It has also been reported as such in Hawaii.)

Landscape Use: Brazilian pepper is listed as a Category I pest plant by the Florida Exotic Pest Plant Council. The plant was first introduced into the United States in 1898 by the U. S. Department of Agriculture and was distributed widely. Its compatibility with the south and south-central Florida landscape has now made it a dangerous threat to our native flora. Though it is attractive in both bloom and fruit, it is not a plant to be encouraged. Its introduction, possession, movement, or release is illegal in Florida.

Comment: This plant causes a skin irritation similar to poison ivy (*Toxicodendron radicans*) in some people and is also reported to produce respiratory difficulties in some people when it is in bloom.

Poison Ivy

Photo 18

Toxicodendron radicans (L.) Kuntze.

Form: A trailing to somewhat erect vine, rarely shrublike, more often climbing on support-ing trees or other shrubs; sometimes rooting on walls and trees.

Leaves: Alternate, compound, trifoliolate; leaflets ovate, entire or, more typically, with lobes or blunt teeth on one or both sides, varying in size, 3 - 20 cm long, to about 12 cm wide; peti-oles reddish, usually shorter than the blades, terminal leaflet stalked; apices of leaflets taper-ing to a rather sharp point; upper surfaces of leaflets dark green, lower surfaces paler.

Flowers: Small, white, borne spring through summer in loosely branched clusters near the base of the petioles.

Fruit: A grayish-white drupe, 4 - 7 mm in diameter.

Distinguishing Marks: Easily distinguished from most vines by alternate, trifoliolate leaves with coarsely toothed leaflets; difficult to distinguish from *T. toxicarium* at first glance, gen-erally differs from the latter by having petioles usually shorter than the blades, by leaflets being thinner with apices more sharply pointed, by typically (but not always) having tufts of hairs in the vein axils on the lower surfaces of leaflets, and by being found in wetland as well as upland habitats.

Distribution: Found in a variety of habitats from uplands to wetlands; throughout north Florida, southward to southernmost Florida, including the Keys.

Landscape Use: Even though this plant is poisonous to the touch for most people, it is an attractive vine with attractive flowers and berries, and its foliage turns a beautiful orange in late fall.

Comment: This and the next two plants are quite poisonous to those who are allergic; do not touch any of these species if you are not sure of your reaction. Washing with soapy water or alcohol, then rinsing thoroughly immediately after contact will help ward off the irritating rash that can be caused by these plants. The active poisonous ingredient in all three members of this genus in Florida is urushiol, a derivative of catechol, which is itself a white, crystalline derivative of benzene and is used in photography. It may also be listed, particularly in older literature, by the synonym *Rhus radicans* L.

Eastern Poison Oak

Toxicodendron toxicarium (Salisb.) Gillis

Form: A low shrub to about 1 m tall; similar in general appearance to *T. radicans* (the latter is more vinelike).

Leaves: Alternate, compound, trifoliolate; leaflets ovate, 4 - 12 cm long, entire, or more typ-ically lobed with blunt teeth on one or both sides, apices blunt to rounded, terminal leaflet stalked; petioles typically as long, longer, or nearly as long as the blades.

Flowers: Greenish-white, borne March through April in loosely branched clusters near the base of the leaf stalk.

Fruit: A rounded drupe, similar to *T. radicans*.

Distinguishing Marks: Easily distinguished from most plants by alternate, trifoliolate leaves; quite similar to *T. radicans* at first glance, may be distinguished from the latter by having petioles usually longer than the blades, by leaflets being blunt tipped, by lower surfaces of leaflets lacking tufts of hairs in the vein axils (though otherwise generally pubescent), and by the plant's more shrubby stature.

Distribution: Pinelands, scrub areas, generally dry sites; throughout north Florida southward to about Levy and Marion Counties.

Landscape Use: See comment for *T. radicans.*

Comment: See comment for *T. radicans.* This plant may also be listed, particularly in older literature, by the synonym *Rhus toxicodendron* L.

Poison Sumac
Toxicodendron vernix (L.) Kuntze

Page 26, Photo 19

Form: Erect, slender, sparingly branched deciduous shrub or small tree to about 7 m tall; main stem tan colored with many small, dark spots about the size of a pinpoint.

Leaves: Alternate, pinnately compound, 18 - 35 cm long, held at about a 45-degree angle from the main stem, main stem leaves much larger; leaflets numbering 7 - 15, ovate to elliptic, 3.5 - 10 cm long, 2 - 5 cm wide, smooth, entire but somewhat wavy and irregular, shiny green above, much paler below, sometimes wider on one side of the central leaflet vein than the other; leaf rachis and leaflet stalks often reddish.

Flowers: Tiny, yellowish, borne in large, branching clusters from the leaf axils; appearing spring through summer.

Fruit: A grayish-white, rounded drupe, typically about 6 mm in diameter but sometimes to about 1 cm.

Distinguishing Marks: The compound leaves with reddish petioles, well-spaced leaflets, asymmetrical leaflet blades, and tan-colored stems set this plant apart from all other wetland species in northern Florida.

Distribution: Uncommon in wet woodlands, bogs, and swamps throughout the Panhandle, eastward and southward to about Marion County.

Comment: See comment for *T. radicans.* The grayish-white, milky sap that runs from the leaf stem when picked turns black upon exposure to air.

Poison Sumac
Toxicodendron vernix

ANNONACEAE — PAWPAW AND CUSTARD APPLE FAMILY

Most members of this large family are found in the tropical regions of the world, but a few are found in more temperate climes. They are sometimes confused with the monocots because their flower parts are in threes rather than fours or fives. Three genera are native to the United States, all of which are found in Florida. All of Florida's shrubby species are characterized by relatively large, yellow to yellowish-green fruits that are quite distinctive. Members of the family are also noted for the presence of ethereal oil cells (as are many of the closely related genera of the order Magnoliales) which give their leaves a distinctive, though not always pleasant, aroma when crushed.

Pond Apple

Photo 20

Annona glabra L.

Form: Densely branched shrub, or small- to medium-sized evergreen tree, normally not exceeding about 6 m tall.

Leaves: Alternate, simple, entire, two-ranked, shiny green, leathery, 7.5 - 15 cm long, 3 - 7 cm wide, apices pointed, blade often reflexed upward in the shape of a V from the central axis.

Flowers: Hanging pendently on short stalks, with six cream-white to pale-yellow petals in two sizes, outermost petals 1.6 - 2 cm long, opening from a distinctive triangular bud, typically appearing March to August.

Fruit: Edible but astringent to the taste, large, 7 - 13 cm long, egg- or heart-shaped, pale yellow with brown spots.

Distinguishing Marks: Similar to some species of the genus *Ficus* (not described here) but distinguished from them by the generally reflexed leaves and distinctive flowers.

Distribution: Banks of freshwater ponds and streams and wet hammocks; from about Brevard County southward; sparsely distributed in the Keys, especially on Big Pine and Lignum Vitae Keys.

Comment: Only two members of this genus are found in the United States, both of which are found only in southern Florida. The pond apple is the more common and more widely known of the two. The sugar apple (*A. squamosa*) is an introduced species that was originally imported for its sweet-tasting fruit and persists in the Keys only from cultivation.

Sugar Apple

Annona squamosa L.

Form: Tropical shrub or small tree to about 4 m tall, with branches that often droop toward their tips.

Leaves: Similar to pond apple in being alternate, two-ranked, simple, and entire, but more lance-shaped, 5 - 13 cm long, less than 5 cm wide; petioles 5 - 14 cm long.

Flowers: Outer petals 1.6 - 2.6 cm long, the entire flower appearing longer and less rounded than pond apple; appearing in summer.

Fruit: Rounded, yellowish-green, 6.5 - 10 cm in diameter, knobby, very sweet to the taste and quite different in appearance from that of the pond apple.

Distinguishing Marks: The knobby fruit is diagnostic.

Distribution: Introduced and persistent from cultivation, found only in the Keys.

Comment: This plant is included here for historical purposes and with some misgiving. Though it is present in cultivation in the Keys, it is probably not well established nor truly naturalized; young plants are usually found only in conjunction with planted specimens. See also *A. glabra*, above.

Flag Pawpaw or Polecat Bush

Page 29, Photo 21

Asimina incarna (Bartr.) Exell.

Form: Tardily deciduous, stiffly branched shrub to about 1.5 m tall; young wood reddish brown and covered with a dense covering of whitish hairs, older wood gray or grayish brown.

Leaves: Alternate, simple, entire, leathery, elliptic to ovate or oblong, 4 - 10 cm long, 2 - 6 cm wide; apices bluntly angled to rounded, sometimes with a small notch; margins wavy; upper and lower surfaces of young leaves with a dense covering of tan to whitish hairs, the latter usually persisting on the lower surfaces but quickly disappearing from the upper surfaces.

Flowers: Fragrant, hanging pendently from the branch; outer petals 3 - 7 cm long, yellowish white to white, oblong in shape; inner petals to about 3 cm long, deltoid, lower inside portion of inner petals with a deep yellow spot; flower stalks 2 - 3.5 cm long and copiously covered with whitish hairs; appearing most prolifically in midspring.

Fruit: Large, yellowish-green, bulging berry typical of the pawpaws, to about 8 cm long.

Distinguishing Marks: The combination of leathery, sometimes wavy-edged leaves, dense pubescence on young leaves, and deep yellow lower portions of the three inner flower petals distinguish this species from the other pawpaws.

Distribution: Sandy, well-drained soils, pine–scrub oak hills, pine flatwoods; from the central Panhandle eastward and southward to about Lee County.

Comment: There has been disagreement about the correct scientific name for this species. William Bartram, who first described the plant, ascribed it to the genus *Annona*, giving it in one place the specific epithet *incana*, in another *incarna*. Kral (1960), who revised the genus, used the name *Asimina speciosa* Nash and went to lengths to explain his position. Still others, including Godfrey (1988), awarded the name *Asimina incarna*, presumably since Bartram used this species name in his journals.

When not in flower the pawpaws are some of the more difficult to identify of Florida's native shrubs. All species of the genus can be divided into two groups based upon the color and aroma of their flowers. Those with maroon flowers, like the dog banana and small-flowered pawpaw, exhibit a fetid odor somewhat like the scent of rotting meat. Those with white flowers, like the two flag pawpaws, exhibit a pleasant fragrance. The reason for the association between the color and aroma of pawpaw flowers is not well understood, but may have to do with the varying preferences of the several beetle species that pollinate the plants.

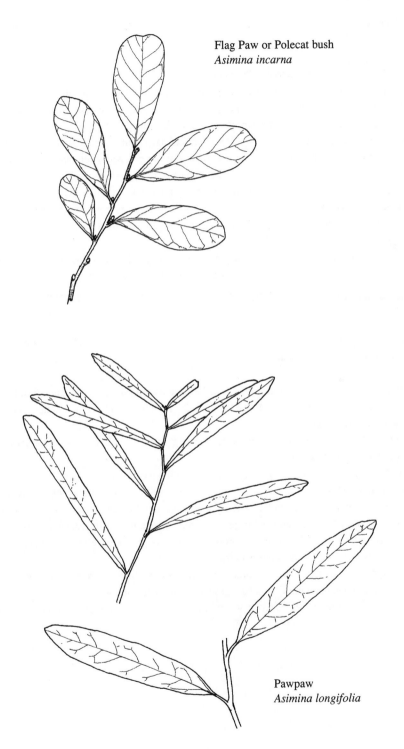

Flag Paw or Polecat bush
Asimina incarna

Pawpaw
Asimina longifolia

Pawpaw

Page 29, Photo 22

Asimina longifolia Kral

Form: Deciduous shrub to about 1.75 m tall.

Leaves: Alternate, simple, entire, leathery, linear to spatulate (see comment below), 5 - 20 cm long, 0.5 - 3 cm wide; apices sharply pointed to rounded, sometimes slightly notched; upper surfaces dark green, lower surfaces paler; margins rolled under.

Flowers: Fragrant, hanging pendently from the leaf axils, outer petals white (rarely pale pink), 3 - 8 cm long; inner petals white, the lower third tinged with deep purple, to about 4 cm long, generally about 1/3 the length of the outer petals; appearing April through June.

Fruit: Large, oblong, bulging, yellowish-green berry typical of the pawpaws, 4 - 10 cm long.

Distinguishing Marks: The linear leaves distinguish this species from all other pawpaws.

Distribution: Sandy pinelands, pine flatwoods, pine–scrub oak woodlands; Walton County eastward and southward to about Lake County.

Comment: There are two varieties of this species, *A. longifolia* var. *longifolia* Kral and *A. longifolia* var. *spatulata* Kral. These are distinguished from each other rather easily by leaf shape. The leaves of the former are linear, those of the latter obovate to spatulate.

Flag Pawpaw

Page 31, Photo 23

Asimina obovata (Willd.) Nash

Form: Deciduous shrub that occasionally reaches treelike proportions, to about 4.5 m tall.

Leaves: Alternate, simple, entire, 4 - 12 cm long, 2 - 4 cm wide, oblong to oval in shape but somewhat narrowed near the base.

Flowers: White, fragrant, 6 - 10 cm wide, hanging from the tips of new shoot growth; appearing most prolifically in midspring.

Fruit: A large, fleshy berry, 5 - 9 cm long, typical of the pawpaws.

Distinguishing Marks: Distinguished from other pawpaws by occurring only on coastal dunes and inland sand ridges and in coastal hammocks, and by young twigs, petioles, veins on lower surfaces of leaves, and peduncles conspicuously clothed with reddish pubescence.

Distribution: Coastal dunes, sand pine–scrub oak woods of eastern Florida; ranging from the northeastern to the southeastern peninsula.

Landscape Use: The large size and large, attractive flowers make this species a good shrub for sandy locations, particularly as a background plant along solid fences.

Comment: The common name, pawpaw, actually derives from a corruption of the name for the papaya, a tropical fruit tree.

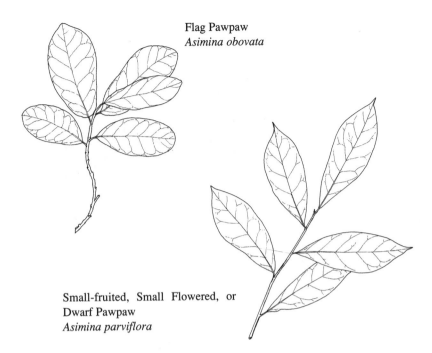

Flag Pawpaw
Asimina obovata

Small-fruited, Small Flowered, or
Dwarf Pawpaw
Asimina parviflora

Small-Fruited, Small-Flowered, or Dwarf Pawpaw

Page 31, Photo 24

Asimina parviflora (Michx.) Dunal

Form: Shrub or small deciduous tree to about 6 m tall.

Leaves: Alternate, simple, entire, 6 - 15 (sometimes 20) cm long, reddish hairy on the lower surfaces when young, becoming sparsely reddish hairy on the veins when mature; new leaves on flowering branches often held somewhat erect and only marginally resembling mature leaves.

Flowers: Maroon with a fetid aroma, small, less than 2 cm wide, not at all conspicuous, appearing February to April.

Fruit: A fleshy berry, greenish-yellow, 3 - 7 cm long.

Distinguishing Marks: Similar to dog banana (*A. triloba*), differing from the latter mainly by having shorter leaves, smaller flowers, smaller fruits, and a generally smaller stature.

Distribution: Mesic woodlands, floodplains, and coastal hammocks; throughout the Panhandle and northern Florida, extending down the eastern peninsula to about Orange and Brevard Counties.

Landscape Use: This is a good species for shaded areas. Though its flowers are small and somewhat inconspicuous, the large pawpaw fruit adds an interesting aspect to the garden.

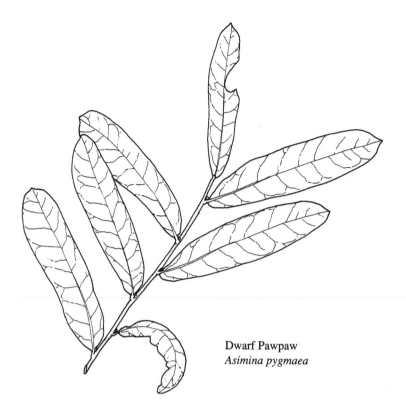

Dwarf Pawpaw
Asimina pygmaea

Dwarf Pawpaw
Page 32

Asimina pygmaea

Form: Low, deciduous shrub with reddish-brown bark, 2 - 3 dm tall.

Leaves: Alternate, simple, entire, leathery, obovate, oblanceolate, to oblong, 4 - 11 cm long, 1 - 4 cm wide; apices rounded or bluntly angled, sometimes with a small notch; upper surfaces pubescent with reddish hairs when young, dark green and without pubescence at maturity; petioles twisted so that all leaves appear to be held erect along the branch.

Flowers: Maroon, with a fetid aroma, hanging pendently on slender stalks to about 4 cm long; outer petals 1.5 - 3 cm long, pinkish with purple streaking; inner petals about 1/2 to 2/3 as long as the outer, deep maroon; appearing April through May.

Fruit: A yellowish-green berry, 3 - 5 cm long, typical of the pawpaws.

Distinguishing Marks: The combination of low stature, flower petals streaked with maroon, and the flowers opening after the appearance of new leaves help distinguish this species from the other pawpaws.

Distribution: Sandhills, dry pinelands, pine–palmetto flatwoods; from just west of the Suwannee River eastward and southward to Lee County.

Landscape Use: The attractive reddish to pinkish flowers of this small shrub make a nice addition to dry, sandy gardens or lawns.

Pawpaw

Photo 25

Asimina reticulata Shuttlw. ex. Chapm.

Form: Deciduous, stiffly and many-branched shrub to about 1.5 m tall; young wood reddish brown and sometimes pubescent, older wood brownish gray; very young shoots reddish with reddish pubescence near the tips.

Leaves: Alternate, simple, entire, leathery, elliptic to oblong, 5 - 8 cm long, 1 - 3 cm wide; apices rounded or notched; margins rolled under, sometimes distinctively so; upper surfaces pale green, lower surfaces so pale as to appear grayish; veins on lower surfaces reddish brown.

Flowers: Fragrant, one to three hanging pendently from the axils of the uppermost leaves; stalks 2 - 3.5 cm long and with orange hairs; outer petals 3 - 7 cm long, white, sometimes with orange markings along the outside veins; inner petals 1/3 to 1/2 the length of the outer, white or pink, with deep purple markings near the base inside; appearing most prolifically in midspring.

Fruit: An oblong to globular, yellowish-green berry, 4 - 6 cm long, typical of the pawpaws.

Distinguishing Marks: The combination of relatively low stature, leathery leaves, flowers being borne before new leaf growth, and the deep purple markings on the inside of the inner petals distinguish this species from the other pawpaws.

Distribution: Common in pine flatwoods and coastal scrub; northeast Florida southward to Lee County.

Landscape Use: The large, white flowers of this species make it a nice shrub for spring color. It should be incorporated in somewhat open shrub beds to allow for full flowering.

Opossum Pawpaw or Four-Petaled Pawpaw

Asimina tetramera Small

Form: Tall, strongly scented shrub to about 3 m tall with one to several relatively smooth, arching, reddish-brown to grayish stems; twigs often with reddish hairs.

Leaves: Alternate, oblong to oblanceolate, 5 - 13 cm long, margins rolled under; lower surfaces pale green with raised veins.

Flowers: Maroon, appearing in late spring, typically with six petals in two sets of three each, or sometimes one set with four petals (hence the specific epithet), mature flower 2 - 3 cm wide; sepals typically four in number, sometimes three or five, triangular, green, with lines of reddish hairs.

Fruit: A large, greenish-yellow berry to about 9 cm long, containing shiny, dark brown seeds.

Distinguishing Marks: Most easily distinguished by flowers with four sepals (at least some flowers on any given plant displaying this characteristic), and by being the tallest of the pawpaws in the southeastern peninsula.

Distribution: Sand scrub and old inland dunes, generally inland from the coast; endemic to Martin and Palm Beach Counties.

Comment: Listed as endangered by both the Florida Department of Agriculture and the U. S. Fish and Wildlife Service; only a few small populations of this plant are extant; found

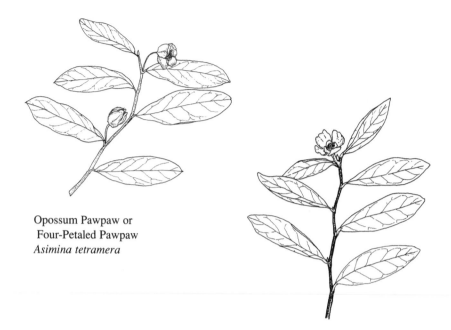

Opossum Pawpaw or
Four-Petaled Pawpaw
Asimina tetramera

chiefly in association with Florida rosemary (*Ceratiola ericoides*), saw palmetto (*Serenoa repens*), fetterbush (*Lyonia* sp.), and several scrub oak species.

Dog Banana or Indian Banana   Photo 26
Asimina triloba (L.) Dunal

Form: Deciduous shrub or small tree to about 14 m tall.

Leaves: Alternate, simple, entire, 15 - 30 cm long (many on a given plant over 15 cm), widest at the tip then tapering to a narrowed base; pungently aromatic when bruised; apices mostly acuminate.

Flowers: Maroon, with a fetid aroma, 2 - 5 cm wide when opened, their stalks 1 cm long or more, appearing in May and June.

Fruit: Oblong, 5 - 15 cm long, greenish yellow.

Distinguishing Marks: Leaves similar in general outline to dwarf pawpaw (*A. parviflora*), pictured on p. 31, differing from the latter by flowers generally greater than 2 cm wide and leaves usually greater than 15 cm long.

Distribution: Mesic woodlands; limited to the central Panhandle from Okaloosa to Liberty Counties.

Landscape Use: This species grows to larger proportions than the similar *A. parviflora* but its landscape value is similar to that described above for this latter species.

Comment: This plant was first discovered in 1543 by members of the DeSoto expedition on their travels in the lower Mississippi River valley region. Its fruit is tasty and edible and has sometimes been used medicinally as a laxative. The fruit is also a food source of wildlife.

Angus Gholson Jr. (personal communication), an expert on north Florida's flora, questions whether the plants ascribed to this species in Florida are correctly identified; they may, in fact, be large-leaved specimens of *A. parviflora*. His reservations are based on his observations of the length of the pedicels of those ascribed to this species in Florida; he maintains that they are always shorter than 1 cm.

Asimina x *nashii* Kral

Form: Shrub with intermediate characteristics between *A. incarna* and *A. longifolia*, with numerous primary shoots; older stems with reddish-brown bark.
Leaves: Alternate, simple, entire, oblong, 4 - 15 cm long, 1 - 3 cm wide; upper surfaces dark green, lower surfaces paler.
Flowers: Fragrant, borne nearly erect on reddish to orange-red stalks; outer petals white or pale pink, 3 - 10 cm long; inner petals 1/2 to 1/4 the length of the outer, white to maroon, with deep purple markings near the base on the inside.
Fruit: A large berry, 3 - 9 cm long, sometimes with a wrinkled surface.
Distinguishing Marks: Distinguished from *A. incarna* by having deep purple rather than deep yellow markings near the bases of the inner petals, from *A. longifolia* by having oblong rather than linear leaves.
Distribution: Fairly common in association with mixed populations of *A. incarna* and *A. longifolia*, on pine–oak hills and ridges and in other well-drained sandy places; from about the Suwannee River eastward and southward to Levy and Marion Counties.

White Squirrel-Banana or Beautiful Pawpaw   Photo 27
Deeringothamnus pulchellus Small

Form: Similar in form to yellow squirrel-banana (*Deeringothamnus rugelii*), stems to about 3 dm tall.
Leaves: Alternate, bright green or blue green, leathery, oblong to spatulate, 3 - 11 cm long; upper surfaces without hairs (except when young), lower with scattered but persistent hairs on the midrib; apices rounded to notched.
Flowers: White or pale pink with linear, conspicuously recurved petals, fragrant; borne singly in the leaf axils; appearing late April and May.
Fruit: Yellow-green berry, similar to others of the family.
Distinguishing Marks: Distinguished from the pawpaws (*Asimina* sp.) by flowers having flattened rather than globose receptacles, from yellow squirrel-banana (*D. rugelii*) by having white flowers.
Distribution: Slash pine (*Pinus elliottii* Engelm.) woodlands and disturbed sites; endemic to a limited region along the southwest peninsula, especially Lee and Charlotte Counties but with outlying populations in Orange County; found mostly in sites where the canopy has been burned off or removed mechanically, such as along power line easements.
Comment: A rare species listed as endangered by both the Florida Department of Agriculture and the U. S. Fish and Wildlife Service.

Yellow Squirrel-Banana or Rugel's Pawpaw

Photo 28

Deeringothamnus rugelii (Robins.) Small

Form: Deciduous, aromatic, sparsely branched shrub with slender, arching, brown stems potentially to about 5 dm tall, but usually much shorter than this and not exceeding about 2 dm.

Leaves: Alternate, leathery, oblong to obovate, 1 - 7 cm long (more often toward the low end of this measurement); margins entire but somewhat revolute; apices blunt.

Flowers: Lemon yellow, fragrant, with 6 - 15 fleshy petals and three greenish sepals, borne on slender stalks in the leaf axils, usually nodding; petals to about 1.5 cm long; appearing midspring.

Fruit: Yellow-green berry typical of the family, 3 - 6 cm long.

Distinguishing Marks: Distinguished from the pawpaws (*Asimina* spp.) by flowers having flattened rather than globose receptacles, from white squirrel-banana (*D. pulchellus*) by having yellow flowers.

Distribution: Poorly drained flatwoods, generally in conjunction with tar-flower (*Befaria racemosa*), fetterbush (*Lyonia* sp.), and gallberry (*Ilex* sp.); endemic to northeastern peninsula Florida, especially Volusia and Seminole Counties.

Comment: Rare species, listed as endangered by both the Florida Department of Agriculture and the U. S. Fish and Wildlife Service.

APOCYNACEAE — OLEANDER FAMILY

The oleander family is best known in Florida for a wide assortment of attractive ornamental species, none of which are native to the state and none of which are described below. Many of these ornamentals produce colorful and conspicuous flowers that are widely recognized. These include the oleander (*Nerium oleander* L.), confederate jasmine (*Trachelospermum jasminoides* Lem.), crape-jasmine (*Ervatamia coronaria* [Jacq.] Stapf.), frangipani (*Plumeria sp.*), heralds-trumpet (*Beaumontia grandiflora* [Roxb.] Wallich), lucky nut (*Thevetia peruviana* [Pers.] K. Schum.), and several species of allamanda of the genera *Allamanda* and *Mandevilla*. Many members of this family, which is known for its milky sap, are noted for their medicinal value, while others are highly toxic if consumed.

By contrast, Florida's native Apocynaceae are relatively few in number and consist chiefly of vines, shrubs, and herbs. As might be expected, most are attractively flowered and easy to identify when in bloom, and most are confined to the state's more tropical regions.

Pineland Allamanda

Photo 29

Angadenia berterii (A. DC.) Miers

Form: An evergreen, typically erect, suberect, or ascending shrub, but sometimes with reclining stems that exude a milky sap when injured.

Leaves: Opposite, simple, entire, leathery, ovate to oblong, 1 - 3 cm long; margins rolled under; bases rounded.

Flowers: Bright yellow to cream colored, showy, bell shaped with spreading petals; 3 - 4 cm across when fully opened; appearing year-round.

Fruit: An erect, slender, cylindrical follicle, 5 - 10 cm long.

Distinguishing Marks: Flowers and leaves quite similar to those of wild allamanda (*Urechites lutea*); however, the latter plant is a twining vine, not a shrub; otherwise, the distinctive yellow flowers set this species apart from all other south Florida pineland plants.

Distribution: Pinelands; southernmost Florida and the Keys.

Comment: This plant is native to the West Indies.

Natal-Plum

Page 37

Carissa macrocarpa (Ecklon) A. DC.

Form: An evergreen shrub with milky sap, stout, branched thorns, and dark gray branches.

Leaves: Opposite, simple, entire, leathery, oval, very dark green above, paler below, 1 - 7 cm long; apices with a small but distinct point.

Flowers: Fragrant, white, star shaped with five thin petals which overlap to the left at their bases, to about 5 cm wide; appearing in spring.

Fruit: A scarlet, egg-shaped, edible berry, to about 5 cm in diameter; the fruit has a cranberrylike flavor.

Distinguishing Marks: The distinctive scarlet fruit in conjunction with the very dark green opposite leaves and forked, very sharp spines distinguish the species.

Distribution: Native to Africa, escaped along the edges of hammocks; southern Florida.

Landscape Use: This is a very popular shrub in sandy sites in southern Florida; it is salt tolerant and often used near the coast; fruiting is most prolific in full sun.

Comment: This species is sometimes seen listed as *C. grandiflora* (E. H. Mey.) A. DC.

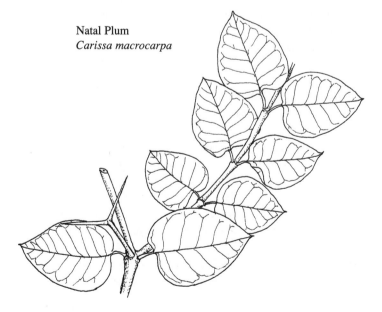

Natal Plum
Carissa macrocarpa

Devil's Potato or Rubber Vine

Photo 30

Echites umbellata Jacquin

Form: Evergreen, smooth-stemmed, twining vine; stems exuding a milky sap when injured.
Leaves: Opposite, simple, entire, ovate, 5 - 9 cm long, the plane of the midvein often curving downward at both ends, individual blades often reflexed upward and V-shaped from the midvein; apices with a tiny point.
Flowers: White, very showy, 2 - 6 cm long, tubular below then spreading into five ornate petals that are twisted clockwise; appearing year-round.
Fruit: Long, cylindrical follicles, curving to form a nearly complete circle when young, standing straight out from the base when mature, 15 - 20 cm long.
Distinguishing Marks: The showy white flowers which appear year-round, set this species apart.
Distribution: Pinelands, margins of hammocks, disturbed sites; southernmost Florida and the Keys.
Landscape Use: This plant makes an attractive climbing vine along fences and on trellises.

Mangrove Rubber Vine or Rubber Vine

Photo 31

Rhabdadenia biflora (Jacq.) Muell. Arg.

Form: Erect, sparsely branched shrub or climbing vine, stems smooth.
Leaves: Opposite, entire, varying from narrowly lanceolate to oblong, 5 - 9 cm long, veins conspicuous and parallel, apices with a small but obvious point; petioles pinkish orange.
Flowers: Funnelform, white with a yellow throat, 5 - 6 cm long; appearing year-round.
Fruit: Several-sided follicles, 12 - 15 cm long.
Distinguishing Marks: Most easily recognized by the white, funnellike flowers with yellow throats in conjunction with the small points at the leaf tips.
Distribution: Coastal hammocks and mangrove swamps, rarely in freshwater wetlands; south Florida and the Keys.

Climbing Dogbane

Page 39

Trachelospermum difforme (Walt.) A. Gray

Form: Deciduous, twining vine (often twining on itself); new shoots herbaceous, becoming woody; woody portions of the stem reddish purple; stem with milky sap.
Leaves: Opposite, simple, entire, typically 4 - 10 cm long but sometimes to about 14 cm and about 8 cm wide, but typically much narrower, widely variable in shape (even on the same plant) from relatively short and broadly ovate, elliptical, or even obovate to much longer and narrowly lanceolate; apices of some leaves abruptly pinched to a point; upper surfaces dark green, lower pale green.
Flowers: Small, less than 1 cm long, borne in stalked clusters from the leaf axils, yellow to greenish yellow and streaked with brown; appearing in spring and summer.

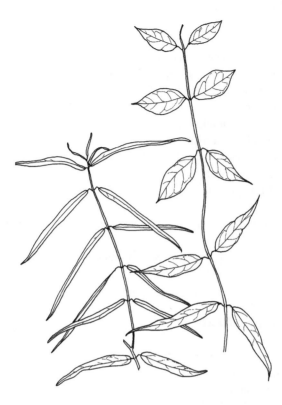

Climbing Dogbane
Trachelospermum difforme

Fruit: A slender, cylindrical follicle, 1 - 2 dm long, splitting to expose angled seeds with conspicuous tufts of silky hairs.

Distinguishing Marks: Leaves on some plants somewhat similar in shape to those of the two species of yellow jessamine (*Gelsemium sempervirens* and *G. rankinii*) but may be distinguished from both by breaking a leaf petiole. Petioles of *T. difforme* will exude milky sap, the latter two species will not.

Distribution: Wet woods, river banks, marshes, swamps; northern Florida southward to Levy and Marion Counties.

Comment: This plant is closely related to the well-known ornamental, confederate jasmine (*T. jasminoides* Lem.). The latter is a smooth-stemmed vine with milky sap that is often used to decorate mailboxes, trellises, and fences, and is said to be escaped from cultivation in some parts of the state. Though often erroneously assumed to derive its common name from the Confederacy of the old south, it is actually named for the Federation of Malay States, to which it is native.

Wild Allamanda

Photo 32

Urechites lutea (L.) Britton

Form: Vine or scrambling shrub; stems with milky sap.

Leaves: Opposite, entire, oblong to nearly elliptic, typically strongly revolute (particularly on younger plants) but sometimes broad and more flattened, 5 - 7 cm long, upper surfaces shiny, lower surfaces pubescent.

Flowers: Showy, funnelform, bright yellow, to about 5 cm wide, borne in loose, one- to several-flowered clusters; appearing year-round.

Fruit: A distinctive, narrow, elongated follicle, 8 - 20 cm long, 4 - 5 mm in diameter, splitting at maturity to expose cottony seeds.

Distinguishing Marks: The bright yellow flowers and strongly revolute, shiny green leaves set this species apart.

Distribution: Coastal hammocks, pinelands, mangrove wetlands; south Florida and the Keys.

Landscape Use: This attractive vine blooms year-round and makes an attractive addition to fences and trellises.

Pearl Berry or Tear Shrub

Photos 33, 34

Vallesia antillana Woodson

Form: Typically an evergreen shrub to about 4 m tall, sometimes obtaining the stature of a small tree; bark pale and furrowed.

Leaves: Alternate, simple, entire, elliptic to obovate, to about 8 cm long.

Flowers: Small, star shaped with five thin, white petals that spread laterally at the terminus of a tube-shaped corolla, borne in branched clusters that arise opposite a leaf; appearing essentially year-round.

Fruit: A glossy, white, nearly translucent, pear-shaped drupe to a little more than 1 cm in length.

Distinguishing Marks: Both the fruits and the flowers may be seen on the plant throughout the year (sometimes in combination) and aid in identifying the plant.

Distribution: Hammocks and hammock edges of south Florida and the Keys.

Landscape Use: The attractive flowers and pearly-white fruit make this an interesting specimen plant in native gardens.

Comment: As described here, this species includes *V. glabra* (Cav.) Link, which is considered to be a distinct species by some authorities. Long and Lakela (1971) separate the two based upon the length of the flower stalk; those of *V. antillana* are less than 5 mm long, those of *V. glabra* are longer than 5 mm.

AQUIFOLIACEAE — HOLLY FAMILY

The holly family consists of three genera and about 400 species worldwide, at least 350 of which are classified in the genus *Ilex*. The family is characterized by having simple, alternate, petiolate leaves with minute stipules at the point at which the leafstalk joins the branch.

The hollies are dioecious plants, meaning that most male and female flowers are borne on separate trees. The flowers are typically quite small and usually arise in small clusters at the leaf axils. They are white to green in color and appear in profusion in early spring.

Hollies bear rounded drupes for fruits. With the exception of the sometimes purplish drupes of the tawnyberry holly (*I. krugiana*) or the shiny black fruits of the two gallberries (*I. coriacea*, *I. glabra*), the fruits of most holly species are typically either red, orange, or reddish-orange. Holly berries appear late in the season and are a favorite and important fall forage for a variety of animals and songbirds. Holly fruits are also useful to humans when attempting to identify the plants. Several of the more similar species may be separated, at least partly, on the basis of the size and color of their berries.

Carolina or Sand Holly

Page 41

Ilex ambigua (Michx.) Torr. var. *ambigua*

Form: A low, dioecious, deciduous shrub with light gray bark; occasionally reaching treelike proportions to about 6 m tall.
Leaves: Alternate, simple, with crenate to serrate margins, 1.5 - 8 cm long and 1 - 5 cm wide, marginal teeth generally only present from about the middle of the leaf upward.
Flowers: Male flowers borne in clusters, female flowers solitary; appearing late spring.
Fruit: Drupe, green at first, turning red with maturity, relatively large, 4 - 9 mm in diameter.
Distinguishing Marks: Distinguished from other deciduous hollies by having flower and fruit stalks less than 4 mm long, and by its dry habitat (see especially *I. verticillata*).
Distribution: Upland mixed woods and sand ridges; throughout northern Florida and south to Lee County.

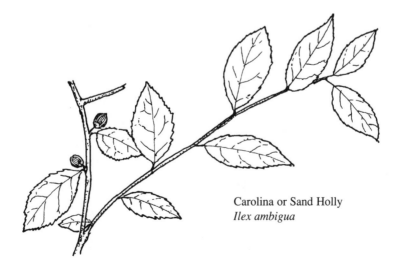

Carolina or Sand Holly
Ilex ambigua

Comment: Listed as threatened by the Florida Department of Agriculture. A variety of this plant, variously known as *I. ambigua* var. *monticola* (A. Gray) Wunderlin & Poppleton or *I. montana* T. & G. (the latter of which is also listed as threatened by the Florida Department of Agriculture), typically has larger leaves than the present species and barely reaches north Florida along the northernmost extent of the Apalachicola River near Chattahoochee.

Sarvis Holly or Serviceberry Holly   Page 42
Ilex amelanchier M. A. Curtis in Chapm.

Form: Typically a deciduous shrub but sometimes treelike to about 5 m tall.
Leaves: Alternate, simple, oblong, 5 - 9 cm long, 1.5 - 4.5 cm wide, margins entire to minutely serrate, lower surfaces of leaves copiously shaggy pubescent.
Flowers: Tiny, borne in small clusters at the leaf axils; appearing in spring.
Fruit: Dull red, rounded drupe, 5 - 10 mm in diameter.
Distinguishing Marks: Distinguished from black-alder (*I. verticillata*) and possum-haw (*I. decidua*), the other two wetland hollies, by having leaves with margins entire, or with only a few minute teeth, and by having pubescent leaves; very similar in appearance to downy serviceberry (*Amelanchier arborea*) but generally found in wetter habitats and retaining pubescence on the lower surfaces of leaves into maturity.
Distribution: Restricted to wetland habitats, including gum and creek swamps and floodplain forests; known in Florida from Escambia to Liberty Counties; populations of this plant are scattered, making the plant only locally common.
Comment: Listed as threatened by the Florida Department of Agriculture.

Sarvis Holly or Serviceberry Holly
Ilex amelanchier

Dahoon

Photo 35

Ilex cassine L.

Form: Typically a dioecious evergreen tree to about 12 m tall with smooth, light gray bark; sometimes flowering and fruiting when of shrublike stature.

Leaves: Alternate, simple, 3 - 14 cm long, with mostly entire margins (a few to many on any specimen with marginal teeth), apices tipped with a small bristle.

Flowers: White, small, with four petals; appearing most prolifically in late spring

Fruit: Yellow to orange when young, typically maturing to bright red, 5 - 9 mm in diameter.

Distinguishing Marks: The smooth, light-gray bark, bright red fruit, and bristle-tipped leaves help set this species apart.

Distribution: Chiefly occurring close to the coast in the Panhandle but found throughout the peninsula, south nearly to Flamingo in Monroe County and to the Ten Thousand Islands in Collier County, not present in the Keys; often associated with cypress ponds and flatwoods depressions in the peninsular locations.

Landscape Use: A very good plant to insure bright color near the Christmas season; does well in wet, boggy soil and low light or bright sun; tolerates a variety of conditions when cultivated and established; not readily available from many native plant nurseries.

Comment: Listed as commercially exploited by the Florida Department of Agriculture; specimens should not be removed from the wild.

Large Sweet Gallberry

Page 44

Ilex coriacea (Pursh) Chapm.

Form: Typically an evergreen shrub; sometimes to about 5 m tall and taking on arborescent qualities.

Leaves: Alternate, simple, 3.5 - 9 cm long, 1.5 - 4 cm wide, with black dots on undersurfaces (requires magnification), margins entire or with a few spreading, short, bristlelike teeth.

Flowers: Small, borne in clusters at the leaf axils; appearing in spring.

Fruit: A shiny black drupe, 6 - 10 mm in diameter.

Distinguishing Marks: Distinguished as one of two widely distributed Florida hollies with black fruits; distinguished from the gallberry (*I. glabra*) by a few leaves that have at least a few marginal teeth below the leaf's midsection rather than only above the leaf's midsection, by the teeth on the latter species being appressed-crenate rather than spreading, and by the latter's smaller fruit.

Distribution: Commonly inhabiting bogs and wet areas from the western Panhandle south to about Polk County; often in the wettest of such places.

Landscape Use: See comments for *I. glabra*, below.

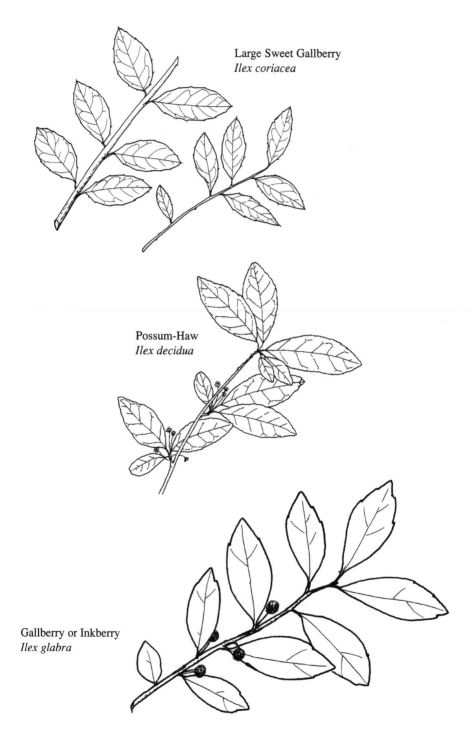

Large Sweet Gallberry
Ilex coriacea

Possum-Haw
Ilex decidua

Gallberry or Inkberry
Ilex glabra

Possum-Haw

Page 44, Photo 36

Ilex decidua Walt.

Form: Small, deciduous, understory shrub or tree to about 10 m tall.

Leaves: Alternate (but sometimes crowded and appearing opposite toward the tips of branchlets), simple, spatulate to obovate in shape, usually widest above the middle but sometimes elliptic, typically 2.5 - 8 cm long, 0.8 - 4.5 cm wide, margins obscurely to obviously crenate, each marginal tooth tipped with a tiny gland that is visible with magnification; bases cuneate.

Flowers: Male and female flowers borne in the leaf axils on separate plants.

Fruit: Red, yellow, or orange, 4 - 9 mm in diameter with a conspicuous stalk up to 2 cm long.

Distinguishing Marks: Superficially similar to yaupon holly (*I. vomitoria*) but distinguished from it by being deciduous rather than evergreen and by having longer, more pliable leaves; from black-alder (*I. verticillata*) and sarvis holly (*I. amelanchier*) by crenate leaf margins; also similar to Walter viburnum (*Viburnum obovatum*) but distinguished from it by having alternate rather than opposite leaves.

Distribution: Floodplains, secondary woods; throughout the Panhandle eastward to the Suwannee River and southward to DeSoto County.

Landscape Use: Most enjoyed in winter after the leaves have fallen and the bright red berries have matured; fruit is a good wildlife food and is relished by birds.

Comment: Listed as threatened by the Florida Department of Agriculture.

Gallberry or Inkberry

Page 44

Ilex glabra (L.) A. Gray

Form: Evergreen shrub, 2 - 3 m tall.

Leaves: Alternate, simple, 2 - 5 cm long; upper surfaces dark green, lower pale green with scattered reddish glands (requires magnification); margins thickened, sometimes entire, more often toothed or notched toward the apices (the teeth blunt, usually not exceeding six in number, and always above the center of the blade); petioles with a powdery pubescence; apices usually with a tiny point.

Flowers: Male and female flowers borne in the leaf axils on separate plants, individual flowers small, white, with six petals; appearing March to May.

Fruit: A shiny black, rounded drupe, 5 - 8 mm in diameter; often persistent through the winter.

Distinguishing Marks: The black drupes and dark green leaves with several blunt teeth toward the apices distinguish this species, but see *I. coriacea*.

Distribution: Common in flatwoods, bogs, wet woodlands, prairies; throughout northern Florida, southward to the lower peninsula, not found in the Keys.

Landscape Use: Good hedge plant in landscapes emphasizing native plants; shade to full sun and moist acid soil are best.

Myrtle-Leaved Holly

Photo 37

Ilex myrtifolia Walt.

Form: Dioecious evergreen shrub with gray bark; sometimes assumes the stature of a scrubby tree to about 8 m tall.

Leaves: Alternate, simple, stiff, entire, leathery, short, very narrowly elliptic, 0.5 - 3 cm long, 3 - 8 mm wide; apices with a small, but distinctive point.

Flowers: Borne in the leaf axils; appearing late spring.

Fruit: Typically red but sometimes orange or yellow, 5 - 8 mm in diameter.

Distinguishing Marks: Most easily distinguished by its hollylike appearance in combination with its short, very narrow leaves.

Distribution: Commonly associated with cypress-gum ponds, savannas, flatwoods depressions, bay swamps, and open wetlands throughout the Panhandle and south to about Union and Bradford Counties.

Scrub Holly or Sand-Loving American Holly

Ilex opaca Ait. var. *aenicola* (Ashe) Ashe

Form: Shrub or small tree, reaching heights of about 5 m; stems smooth, pale gray, with thin bark.

Leaves: Alternate, simple, oblong to obovate, to about 6 cm long and 2.5 cm wide; margins typically with 3 - 4 pairs of sharp spines, rarely entire; margins conspicuously rolled under; upper surfaces shiny, yellowish green, lower surfaces more strongly yellowish.

Flowers: Small and borne in small clusters from the leaf axils; appearing in spring.

Fruit: A deep red to reddish-orange, rounded drupe, to about 1 cm in diameter when mature, easily the largest fruit of our native hollies.

Distinguishing Marks: Very similar to *I. opaca* Ait. var. *opaca* (not included here); most easily distinguished from the latter by narrower, more yellowish leaves with more revolute margins (the leaves of *I. opaca* var. *opaca* typically exceed 3.5 cm in width).

Distribution: Well-drained sands of the central peninsula sand pine–scrub oak highlands; from about Marion County southward to Highlands County.

Landscape Use: A sought-after landscape plant due to its tolerance of well-drained sandy soils and its large, red, showy fruit.

Comment: This species is listed as commercially exploited by the Florida Department of Agriculture; specimens should not be removed from native habitats.

Black-Alder or Common Winterberry

Ilex verticillata (L.) A. Gray

Form: Dioecious deciduous shrub or small tree to about 8 m tall.

Leaves: Alternate, simple, elliptic to oval, typically 4 - 10 cm long, 1.5 - 5 cm wide, apices acuminate.

Flowers: Small, with four petals, borne in the leaf axils; appearing in late spring.

Fruit: Round, usually red, 5 - 8 mm in diameter.

Distinguishing Marks: Distinguished from the Sarvis holly (*I. amelanchier*) and possum-haw (*I. decidua*), which also inhabit wetland communities, by having leaf margins with small but sharp teeth. It should also be noted that distinguishing between this plant and *I. ambigua* is extremely difficult. In general the latter plant is not known to inhabit wetlands. However, at least one observer has reported it from such locations. Other observers (Duncan and Duncan, 1988) distinguish the two when in fruit by their nutlets: those of *I. ambigua* are ribbed on the back, those of *A. verticillata* smooth on the back.

Distribution: Generally limited and local in distribution, and uncommon; confined to wetlands, including swamps, bogs, floodplains, and wet woodlands of the western Panhandle, eastward to Liberty County.

Landscape Use: Not common in Florida but used farther north as a native shrub in naturalistic settings; the red fruit is attractive to birds and other wildlife. A number of horticultural varieties are available but are used mostly in areas north of Florida.

Comment: Listed as threatened by the Florida Department of Agriculture.

Yaupon

Page 48, Photo 38

Ilex vomitoria Ait.

Form: Dioecious evergreen shrub or small bushy tree to about 8 m tall.

Leaves: Alternate, simple, dark green on the upper surfaces, stiff, elliptic to oval, 0.5 to 3 cm long, 0.5 - 2.5 cm wide (occasional plants with leaves much larger than this); margins crenate.

Flowers: White, small (but conspicuous), appearing in spring and borne in the leaf axils.

Fruit: Round, bright red, averaging 5 - 7 mm in diameter; appearing in fall and winter.

Distinguishing Marks: Distinguished as the only evergreen holly with leaves having crenate edges throughout their lengths; somewhat similar to both *Ilex decidua* and *Viburnum obovatum* by having leaves with crenate edges, but distinguished from the former by having generally shorter, stiffer leaves, from latter by leaves being alternate rather than opposite.

Distribution: Widespread and common in a variety of situations in northern Florida south to Sarasota County on the west coast, Brevard County on the east coast; a disjunct population once stood at a single location just east of Naples and was probably cultivated by the Seminoles.

Landscape Use: Widely used as a hedge or background shrub for its dark green, evergreen foliage and bright red berries; requires well-drained soil and is tolerant of shade. Both male and female plants must be planted to insure the showy, bright-red berries. A number of cultivars and horticultural varieties are available in the nursery trade.

Comment: This is the plant made famous by the American Indians, who used it in ceremonial and religious rituals. Early explorers learned to brew "black drink" from its leaves. Some reports suggest that this beverage was widely used in place of more expensive teas imported from Europe (Mell, 1922). In sufficient quantities the drink acts as a purgative, hence its scientific name.

Yaupon
Ilex vomitoria

ARALIACEAE — GINSENG FAMILY

The Araliaceae, or ginseng family, is a relatively large grouping of between 55 and 60 genera and nearly 800 species worldwide. Less than five of these genera are represented in Florida. The devil's walking stick (*Aralia spinosa*) is the only shrubby or treelike species of the family native to the Sunshine State. The common and well-known schefflera (*Brassaia actinophylla* Endl.), a beautiful species with large, palmately compound leaves, a graceful stature, and huge, deep red inflorescences that stand above the foliage in long, armlike appendages, is also a member of the ginseng family and has escaped in the southern parts of the state. However, because it is nonnative and not naturalized, the latter plant is not described below.

Devil's Walking Stick   Page 49, Photo 39

Aralia spinosa L.

Form: Deciduous shrub or small, single-trunked tree to about 10 m tall; trunk armed with short, stout, sharp-pointed thorns; most leaves extending from the upper portions of the trunk in umbrellalike fashion.

Leaves: Alternate, bipinnately or tripinnately compound, triangular in overall outline, very large, 0.5 - 1.5 m long, arising from and clasping the main trunk; leaflets numerous, ovate, 3 - 10 cm long, margins serrate; petioles to about 3 dm long.

Flowers: Tiny, whitish, borne in summer in long, showy, densely branched clusters, each inflorescence up to 1.2 m long.

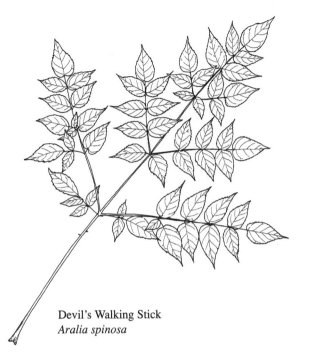

Devil's Walking Stick
Aralia spinosa

Fruit: A rounded, purplish to purplish-black drupe, 5 - 8 mm in diameter.

Distinguishing Marks: Distinguished from all other north Florida shrubs and trees by large, triangular, bipinnately to tripinnately compound leaves and thorny stems (but see *Nandina domestica*).

Distribution: Understory in upland and lowland woods in the northern third of the state.

Landscape Use: This is an outstanding background plant and is a much better choice where an erect stature is needed than is the nonnative and weedy nandina (*Nandina domestica*). The plant does well in poor situations, in shade or sun. The flowers and fruit are very showy, and the leaves are often borne umbrellalike at the top of the erect main stem. It also propagates easily from late fall cuttings or from sucker shoots.

Comment: The thorny trunk of this plant suggests its common name.

ARISTOLOCHIACEAE — BIRTHWORT FAMILY

Worldwide, this family consists primarily of lianas, most of tropical origin. Two genera of the family, *Aristolochia* and *Hexastylis*, are found in Florida. Two members of the former are described below but several others are used ornamentally in the southern parts of the state. The single member of the other genus in Florida is wild ginger or heartleaf (*H. arifolia* [Michx.] Small), a threatened herb found sparingly on bluffs and in hammocks from the central Panhandle eastward to Jefferson County.

The common name for the genus *Aristolochia*, as well as for the family, is birthwort. There are about 300 species in the genus, most of which have exceedingly unique flowers that are considered ugly or grotesque by some observers. The flowers often exhibit an obnoxious odor. Members of the genus are often seen under cultivation in botanical gardens.

Aristolochia pentandra Jacq.

Form: Twining or decumbent vine.
Leaves: Alternate, simple, entire, ovate, thick, 4 - 10 cm long.
Flowers: Nearly erect, pubescent, greenish to purplish.
Fruit: A rounded, six-angled, drooping capsule to about 2 cm long.
Distinguishing Marks: The fleshy leaf blades and globular fruit help distinguish this species from others in its genus.
Distribution: Hammocks; doubtfully present in the southern peninsula and the Keys, currently known only from Elliott Key.
Comment: The more showy dutchman's pipe (*A. maxima* Jacq.) with large, purple, variegated, deeply curved flowers is an exotic, cultivated species in southern Florida that has escaped into hammocks of Dade County (most noticeably at the Charles Deering Estate); it has oblong to oblong-obovate leaves which are 6 - 12 cm long and 3 - 7 cm wide; its very large ribbed capsule, which is 10 - 15 cm long and 7 - 10 cm wide, is a distinctive field mark.

Woolly Dutchman's Pipe, Woolly Pipe Vine, Pipe Vine

Page 51

Aristolochia tomentosa Sims.

Form: Deciduous, high climbing, twining vine, often extending far into the tree tops; main stems soft-woody.
Leaves: Alternate, simple, entire, heart shaped, 5 - 15 cm long; lower surfaces grayish, velvety pubescent to the touch; petioles long to nearly the length of the leaf blades, softly pubescent.
Flowers: Borne singly adjacent to a leaf, somewhat reminiscent in shape to a miniature version of Sherlock Holmes' pipe (hence the common name), to about 5 cm long, greenish yellow with a purple orifice; appearing in spring.
Fruit: A ribbed, oblong capsule, 4 - 8 cm long.
Distinguishing Marks: The only north Florida vine with such large, heart-shaped leaves and long petioles; the catalpa (*Catalpa bignonioides*) has similarly shaped leaves and overlaps in range, but is a shrub or tree with opposite or whorled leaves.
Distribution: Stream and creek banks, bottomland woods along alluvial rivers, floodplains; restricted to the Panhandle from Bay and Holmes Counties to Liberty County.
Landscape Use: The large leaves, interesting flowers, and climbing aspect makes this species good for use on trellises or other structures where climbing vegetation is appropriate.

Wooly Dutchman's Pipe, Wooly Pipe Vine, Pipe Vine
Aristolochia tomentosa

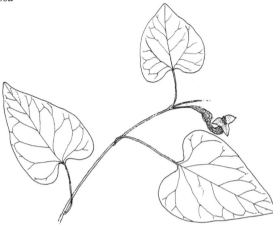

ASCLEPIADACEAE — MILKWEED FAMILY

The Asclepiadaceae are very closely related to the Apocynaceae; both have opposite, simple, entire leaves, and milky latex. The family is well-represented in Florida by several genera of which most species are herbaceous. Only one woody species is described below.

Pink Allamanda or Indian Rubber Vine

Cryptostegia grandiflora R. Brown

Form: Stout, woody vine to about 6 m long; stems with a milky sap characteristic of the milkweed family.

Leaves: Opposite, simple, entire, dark shiny green, elliptic, ovate, or broadly lanceolate, leathery, 6 - 10 cm long, to about 6 cm wide, apices rounded.

Flowers: Corolla pink, rose to lilac purple, or white, bell shaped, to about 5 cm across when open; conspicuous and showy.

Fruit: Pointed pods to about 5 cm long, borne in pairs; splitting at maturity to expose seeds borne on long, silky, white hairs.

Distinguishing Marks: The woody stem, milky sap, and showy, funnel-shaped flowers set this species apart.

Distribution: Shell mounds, disturbed sites, hammocks; south Florida and the Keys.

Landscape Use: This tropical vine has been used in sandy, well-drained soils in southern Florida. It is sometimes pruned and trained to be a free-standing shrub, but is more typically used as a cover for fences or small buildings. However, it is listed as a Category II pest plant by the Florida Exotic Pest Plant Council and should no longer be incorporated into planted landscapes.

Comment: A native of Africa that has become naturalized in southern Florida.

AVICENNIACEAE — BLACK MANGROVE FAMILY

The black mangrove is one of four Florida species commonly referred to as mangroves. It, along with the red mangrove (*Rhizophora mangle*), white mangrove (*Laguncularia racemosa*), and buttonwood (*Conocarpus erectus*), is a common constituent of southernmost Florida's coastal zone. Though these species are not closely related to each other and do not belong to the same family, they are often thought of as being grouped together ecologically because of their tolerance of a saltwater environment.

Black Mangrove

Photo 40

Avicennia germinans (L.) L.

Form: Bushy evergreen shrub or, more commonly, a tree of tidal flats and other shallow saltwater areas, usually not exceeding about 10 m tall in Florida.

Leaves: Opposite, simple, elliptic to lanceolate, 5 - 12 cm long, 2 - 4 cm wide, upper surfaces green, lower surfaces copiously covered with grayish pubescence, often with salt crystals evident on one or both surfaces.

Flowers: White, tubular, with four petals, borne in dense, conical heads at almost any time of year.

Fruit: A flat, shiny green pod, 3 - 5 cm long, asymmetrical in shape, apices pointed.

Distinguishing Marks: Distinguished from other mangroves by leaves with grayish undersurfaces, by green, flattened fruits, by dark to blackish bark, and by the presence of numerous short breathing roots, or pneumatophores, projecting from the ground in dense thickets below and around the plant.

Distribution: By far the most wide-ranging mangrove in Florida; most common on the lower southwest coast and the Keys; found sparingly at least as far north as Shell Island off Panama City on the west coast and St. Johns County on the east coast; the Shell Island plants are often small, typically not exceeding 3 dm tall, even after several years of warm winters.

BASELLACEAE — MADEIRA VINE FAMILY

This is a mostly tropical family that is represented in Florida by a single, nonnative, questionably woody species that has escaped cultivation in southern Florida.

Madeira Vine

Anredera leptostachys (Moq.) Steenis

Form: Slender-stemmed vine.

Leaves: Alternate, simple, entire, elliptic to ovate, succulent, 2 - 7 cm long, tapered to an acute or pinched point.

Flowers: Borne on a long, slender, distinctive, curving raceme; appearing primarily in the summer.

Fruit: A small, multilocular capsule.

Distinguishing Marks: The showy racemes help set this species apart.

Distribution: Roadsides, hammocks, pinelands; south-central and southern Florida.

Landscape Use: This plant is valued horticulturally for its bright green leaves and fragrant flowers. It is not native but has been widely cultivated in south Florida and has now escaped and become established.

BATACEAE — SALTWORT FAMILY

The saltwort family contains only the single genus *Batis* with only two species. One of these species, *B. argillicola* van Royen, is known primarily from northeastern Australia and southern New Guinea. The other, *B. maritima*, which is described below, ranges along the east coast of the Americas from about North Carolina southward (including both coasts of Florida) to Brazil, as well as along the west coast of the Americas from southern California to northern Peru. The family has no close relatives and botanists have tended to place it high in taxonomic rankings. Some have placed the family in its own order; others in its own subclass. Both species are especially well-known for their high degree of salt tolerance. The seeds of at least *B. maritima* have been reported to maintain their vitality even after several months of floating in salt water.

Saltwort

Photo 41

Batis maritima L.

Form: Evergreen, dioecious, sprawling, small shrubs with grayish, succulent stems; young stems herbaceous, older stems woody; rarely more than about 1 m tall; often growing in thick patches that are so sprawling as to appear almost vinelike.

Leaves: Opposite, simple, entire, succulent, 1 - 3 cm long; without petioles.

Flowers: Yellow, small, borne on a fleshy conelike structure (actually a spike) in the leaf axils, appearing from April throughout the summer, mostly near the beginning of this time period.

Fruit: Green, fleshy, rounded, cylindrical, rough-surfaced.

Distinguishing Marks: The salty habitat, grayish stem, and opposite, succulent leaves are enough to distinguish this species.

Distribution: Muddy tidal banks, mangrove swamps, salt marshes, mud and salt flats; statewide along both coasts, including the Keys.

Landscape Use: This plant could be an excellent ground cover in coastal locations, particularly in salt-rich areas. It is probably seldom used.

Comment: This species can tolerate long periods of waterlogging and a wide range of salinity. It easily colonizes areas near the edges of marshes and mangroves and is known in Florida as one of the major colonizers after loss of mangroves due to hurricanes.

BERBERIDACEAE — BARBERRY FAMILY

The barberry family consists of 10 - 12 genera worldwide and 300 - 600, mostly woody, species. A single species in each of five genera is native to the eastern United States. Florida's only woody member of the family, *Nandina domestica*, is not among these native plants and is considered a serious weed in most locations, especially in northern Florida.

Nandina or Heavenly Bamboo   Page 54, Photo 42
Nandina domestica Thunb.

Form: Evergreen, sparsely branched, upright shrub to 3 m tall, with leaves usually borne near the ends of branches and stems; wood distinctly yellowish.

Leaves: Alternate, large, bi- to tripinnately compound, to about 5 dm long, 8 dm wide overall with a purplish-red rachis; leaflets ovate to lanceolate, entire, dark shiny green above when mature (much paler and soft when young), 2 - 7 cm long, 1 - 2 cm wide; lateral veins of leaflets depressed on the upper surfaces, at least near the central vein (a feature that is sometimes somewhat obscure); apices of leaflets tapered to a longish point.

Flowers: Small, but borne in large, branched, conspicuous, showy, whitish clusters at the ends of branches and stems; appearing in late spring.

Fruit: Bright red (at maturity), rounded berry, borne in branched clusters, very conspicuous, each berry 6 - 12 mm in diameter; appearing fall and winter.

Distinguishing Marks: The large compound leaves and bright red fruit set this species apart; potentially confused only with devil's walking stick (*Aralia spinosa*) but lacking the latter's toothed leaflets and sharp thorns.

Distribution: Native to China and Japan, often used as an ornamental and naturalized near homes and in neighborhoods; northern Florida.

Nandina or Heavenly Bamboo
Nandina domestica

Landscape Use: This species is listed as a Category I pest plant by the Florida Exotic Pest Plant Council and is not recommended for landscaping. Nevertheless, it is widely used as a background shrub or in clusters of 2 - 3 around the trunks of pine trees. It is preferred primarily for the color of its fall fruit and seems to do best in the Panhandle. See the entry for devil's walking stick (*Aralia spinosa*) for an acceptable landscaping alternative.

Comment: The fruit of this species is relished by birds. Homeowners often report finding nandina seedlings that have apparently been sewn with bird droppings. Unfortunately, birds have also encouraged this plant to spread into natural plant communities. If left unchecked, it is likely to become an extremely troublesome weed.

BETULACEAE — BIRCH FAMILY

The birch family consists of six genera and about 150 species. Most are found in the cooler climates of Asia, Europe, and North America, or the mountainous regions of Mexico, Central America, and northern Argentina. They belong to the same botanical order as the beeches and oaks (which also share wind-pollinated flowers that are often borne in tassellike arrangements called catkins or aments) and are generally believed to be rather closely allied with these latter plants. The family is relatively small, but a number of its members are well-known and dominant components of temperate forest communities.

The family constitutes a very old collection with a fossil record extending at least as far back as 70 million years ago. The origin of the family is not precisely known. Some believe its ancestors to be from the oak family; others have suggested that both the oaks and birches might have derived separately from a common ancestor. In either event, it is clear that all of the family's present-day species reach far back in time to very ancient stock.

Hazel Alder

Page 56

Alnus serrulata (Ait.) Willd.

Form: Deciduous shrub or small tree to about 10 m tall with a crooked trunk and young twigs bearing dense, brown pubescence.

Leaves: Alternate, simple, elliptic to obovate, 5 - 10 cm long, 2 - 5 cm wide, upper surfaces green, lower surfaces brownish, margins slightly wavy and unevenly toothed; veins conspicuously depressed on the upper surfaces of leaves and protruding on the lower.

Flowers: Male flowers tiny, borne in conspicuous, pendulous catkins, 4 - 8 cm long; female flowers borne in tiny, conelike catkins to about 1 cm long; appearing mid- to late fall.

Fruit: Borne in a structure reminiscent of a tiny pine cone, 7 - 12 mm long.

Distinguishing Marks: Distinguished from all other Florida shrubs by the tiny "cones," some of which commonly persist on the plant year-round. [The river birch (*Betula nigra* L.), a scaly-barked tree, also has such cones but differs from the alder by both its bark and its distinctly doubly serrate leaves.]

Distribution: Swamps, rivulets, wet woods, alluvial streambanks and similar places; irregularly distributed throughout the Panhandle and northernmost Florida.

Hazel Alder
Alnus serrulata

BIGNONIACEAE — BIGNONIA FAMILY

The bignonia family is a large and varied family of about 100 genera with a wide assortment of species that are well-known in the tropics. One of the family's most distinctive features, which is characteristic of four of the five woody species found in Florida, is the opposite, compound leaves, often with only a few leaflets. Members of the family are sometimes confused with the legumes because of their typically long, beanlike fruit, but differ from legumes by having winged seeds.

Cross-Vine or Trumpet-Flower

Page 57, Photo 43

Bignonia capreolata L.

Form: Evergreen, woody, high-climbing vine.

Leaves: Opposite, compound, with two leaflets, and a single tendril arising between the leaflets; leaflets oblong or elliptic to lanceolate, entire, 5 - 15 cm long, 2 - 8 cm wide, apices pinched to a point, bases rounded to heart shaped.

Flowers: Large, showy, tubular, with five petals; tube reddish orange to orange outside, yellow to red inside, about 5 cm long and 2 cm across the open petals; appearing in spring.

Fruit: A flattened, conspicuous, beanlike capsule, 1 - 2 dm long, 2 - 2.5 cm wide, containing winged seeds to about 3 cm long each.

Distinguishing Marks: The compound leaves with two leaflets, and tubular orange flowers with yellow to reddish markings inside the tube distinguish the species; the flowers are superficially similar to those of trumpet creeper (*Campsis radicans*), but the leaves of the latter plant have seven or more leaflets, never just two.

Cross-Vine or Trumpet-Flower
Bignonia capreolata

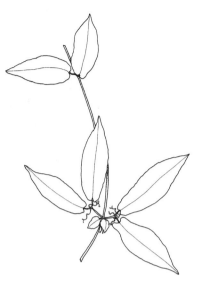

Distribution: Floodplains, lowland woods, upland mixed woods, shrub bogs; throughout northern Florida, southward to the southern peninsula.

Landscape Use: Not often used but an excellent vine for trellises and fences; the showy, tubular flowers are equaled only by those of the trumpet creeper. Cross-vine is an aggressive species that can get out of control if not pruned regularly.

Comment: The name cross-vine comes from the cross-shaped appearance of the stem tissue when it is cut in cross section.

Trumpet-Creeper or Cow-Itch-Vine

Page 58, Photo 44

Campsis radicans (L.) Seem. ex Bureau.

Form: Deciduous, trailing to high-climbing woody vine with shredding, buff-colored bark; stems potentially to 10 cm or more in diameter; climbing by aerial rootlets.

Leaves: Opposite, compound, with at least seven leaflets (sometimes up to 15); leaflets ovate to broadly lanceolate, serrate, tapering to a pinched point, to about 8 cm long and 4 cm wide.

Flowers: Showy, tubular, red to orange, 6 - 8 cm long, borne in clusters; appearing in spring and summer.

Fruit: A long, conspicuous, beanlike capsule, 10 - 20 cm long, containing many flat, winged seeds.

Distinguishing Marks: The compound leaves with serrated leaflets and red to orange, tubular flowers set this species apart (but see *Bignonia capreolata*, above).

Distribution: Upland and lowland woods, thickets; throughout northern Florida, southward to the southern peninsula.

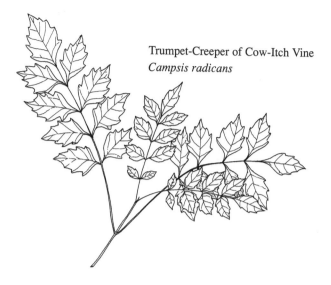

Trumpet-Creeper of Cow-Itch Vine
Campsis radicans

Landscape Use: Very good for trellises or fences; can be detrimental to trees if allowed to encircle the trunk and grow to full maturity.

Comment: Some uninformed and quite casual observers regard this species as poison oak (*Toxicodendron toxicarium*), though the current species is not at all poisonous to the touch.

Catalpa, Southern Catalpa, Catawba Tree, Caterpillar Tree, Indian Bean

Photo 45

Catalpa bignonioides Walt.

Form: Shrub or small deciduous tree to about 15 m tall, with a slender, grayish, somewhat scaly trunk.

Leaves: Opposite or whorled, simple, entire, heart shaped, 10 - 26 cm long, bases 8 - 18 cm wide, petioles conspicuously long.

Flowers: White with conspicuous yellow and purple markings, bell shaped with fringed margins, borne in many-flowered, widely branched clusters; appearing in March and April.

Fruit: A long, brown, narrow pod, 10 - 38 cm long.

Distinguishing Marks: The only north Florida shrub with large, opposite, heart-shaped leaves (but see *Aristolochia tomentosa*).

Distribution: Occurring naturally on floodplains and riverbanks of the Panhandle; often planted and frequently naturalized in urban locations at least as far south as Citrus County.

Landscape Use: This plant is often found in yards, particularly near the dwellings of freshwater fishing enthusiasts. The caterpillar that feeds on this plant is an excellent fish bait (but can completely defoliate the tree). In addition to its practical utility, the attractive flower clusters that adorn this plant in early summer make it a good choice for landscaping. The plant is fast growing but short-lived.

Comment: This is the only woody bignonia in Florida that lacks compound leaves. Its wood is strong, resistant, and is used as fence posts in some parts of its range. The plant has also been used medicinally in the treatment of snakebites, in pulmonary disorders, and as an antiseptic for cuts and bruises.

Cat's Claw Vine

Macfadyena unquis-cati (L.) A. Gentry

Form: Evergreen or deciduous (in the northern parts of the state), high climbing vine, with woody stems; stems to at least 6 cm in diameter.

Leaves: Opposite, compound, with two leaflets, the central leafstalk extending beyond the leaflets as a three part tendril (hence the name "cat's claw"); leaflets ovate to lanceolate, 3 - 7 cm long, with entire margins.

Flowers: Tubular, yellow with orange lines, showy, with five petals; to about 8 cm long and 2 cm wide across the open petals; appearing in spring.

Distinguishing Marks: The yellow, tubular flowers and opposite, compound leaves with only two leaflets distinguish the species.

Distribution: Native to tropical America and used ornamentally, escaped from cultivation in all parts of the state; an unwanted exotic pest plant in southern Florida.

Landscape Use: Though this is an attractive vine for fences and trellises, tolerates a wide assortment of soils, and does well in full sun or part shade, it is a troublesome weed in the southern parts of the state and is not recommended. It is currently listed as a Category I pest plant by the Florida Exotic Pest Plant Council.

Yellow Elder

Photo 46

Tecoma stans (L.) Juss.

Form: Evergreen shrub or small tree to about 8 m tall with furrowed, light gray bark.

Leaves: Opposite, pinnately compound, 10 - 25 cm long; leaflets typically 5 - 13 (sometimes 3) in number, lanceolate to elliptic, 4 - 12 cm long, margins serrate.

Flowers: Bright yellow, conspicuous and very showy, bell shaped, most about 5 cm long; appearing year-round.

Fruit: A slender pod to about 20 cm long.

Distinguishing Marks: Distinguished as the only shrub in southern Florida with opposite, pinnately compound leaves with more than seven leaflets.

Distribution: Roadsides and hammock edges; naturalized in the Keys and lower peninsula; native to the West Indies and tropical America.

Landscape Use: The attractive clusters of tubular yellow flowers make this nonnative shrub an often-used ornamental.

Comment: A second member of this genus (*T. gaudichaudii* DC.) is reportedly naturalized in the Dry Tortugas (Long and Lakela, 1971), but has been more recently reported escaped along the edges of a pineland in Dade County (Roger Hammer, 1995, personal communication). It differs from *T. stans* by having simple leaves, though it also has tubular, yellow flowers.

BORAGINACEAE — BORAGE FAMILY

The borage family is a large, mostly herbaceous family of about 100 genera and more than 2,000 species worldwide. About 10 genera represent the family in Florida, four of which contain definitely woody species. At least one genus, *Heliotropium*, contains several perennials, the main stems of which emanate from woody caudexes and are considered shrubby by at least some observers. The most common of these include the white-flowered and somewhat showy scorpion-tail (*H. angiospermum* [Murr.] Brit.), the succulent-leaved seaside heliotrope (*H. curassavicum* L.), the purple-flowered *H. amplexicaule* Vahl., and the white- to yellow-flowered *H. polyphyllum* Lehm. All are characterized by tiny flowers that are borne in a row along only one side of an extended flower stalk.

Sea Lavender, Beach Heliotrope, Bay Lavender   Photo 50
Argusia gnaphalodes (L.) Britt.

Form: Evergreen, much-branched shrub with densely leafy, dark gray to almost black stems; to about 2 m tall.

Leaves: Alternate, narrow, fleshy to succulent, simple, entire, linear to spatulate, whitish to silvery gray, densely pubescent, 4 - 11 cm long; borne in dense whorls, especially near the ends of the branches.

Flowers: Small, white, with five petals, borne densely clustered on one side of a curving spike; appearing winter and spring.

Fruit: Rounded, black drupe; about 5 mm long.

Distinguishing Marks: Most easily distinguished by the dense clusters of silvery gray leaves; most similar to the pale-green-leaved bay cedar (*Suriana maritima*), especially in characters of the bark.

Distribution: Coastal dunes, beaches; south Florida and the Keys.

Landscape Use: An excellent shoreline erosion plant and attractive shrub, but difficult to grow.

Comment: Listed as endangered by the Florida Department of Agriculture; this plant is often seen listed under the scientific synonyms *Mallotonia gnaphalodes*, (L.) Britt. or *Tournefortia gnaphalodes* (L.) R. Br. ex Roemer & J.A. Schultes.

Smooth Strongbark, Little Strongbark, or Strongback
Bourreria cassinifolia (A. Rich.) Griseb.   **Photo 47**

Form: Low, evergreen, many-branched shrub to about 3 m tall.

Leaves: Alternate, elliptic to ovate, simple, entire, rough to the touch, 1 - 3 cm long; apices rounded.

Flowers: White, solitary, tubular, with five lobes, 1 - 1.5 cm wide, very similar to other species of *Bourreria*; appearing almost any time of year.

Fruit: Rounded, pale-orange, one- to several-seeded drupes, to about 7 mm in diameter, similar to other species of *Bourreria*.

Distinguishing Marks: The small leaves and white, five-petaled flowers help distinguish the species; the leaves of this species are always smaller than the other Florida representatives of its genus.

Distribution: Rare in pinelands, in only a few locations (about 11 as of this writing) in southern Dade County and one population on Big Pine Key in Monroe County.

Landscape Use: When cared for in the garden this plant will develop into a large, bushy shrub that responds well to cultivation.

Comment: Listed as endangered by the Florida Department of Agriculture. The common name "strongback" derives from a Bahamian folk custom which holds that a tea made from the plant gives men a strong back. The name "strongbark" is probably a corruption of the former name.

Bahama Strongbark, Strongbark, or Strongback   Photo 48

Bourreria ovata Miers

Form: Bushy, evergreen (leaves at least persistent) shrub or small tree to about 12 m tall with reddish-brown, scaly bark.

Leaves: Alternate, simple, oval, entire, apices often notched, 6 - 12 cm long, 4 - 8 cm wide, yellowish green above, paler below.

Flowers: White, campanulate, to about 1.3 cm wide, borne in terminal clusters; appearing late summer and fall.

Fruit: A rounded, one- to several-seeded fleshy drupe, to about 1.2 cm in diameter, green when new, turning reddish orange to orange at maturity.

Distinguishing Marks: Similar to rough strongbark (*B. radula*) but having glabrous and generally longer leaves; young leaves of this species are noticeably rough to the touch, becoming smooth only with age, which has probably led to its misidentification as *B. radula*, and to inaccurate reports of the latter's range.

Distribution: Hammocks and hammock margins in the Keys and the extreme southern peninsula.

Landscape Use: The small white flowers and particularly the orange fruit, the latter of which remains on the tree throughout the winter and early spring, make this species a viable candidate for adding a touch of color to south Florida lawns.

Rough Strongbark

Bourreria radula (Poir. in Lam.) G. Don

Form: Evergreen shrub or small tree to about 12 m tall with reddish-brown, scaly bark.

Leaves: Alternate, simple, entire, elliptic, 2.5 - 6.5 cm long, 1.2 - 3.5 cm wide, dark green above, paler below, apices either notched or rounded.

Flowers: White, campanulate, borne in terminal clusters.

Fruit: A rounded drupe to about 1.4 cm in diameter, turning red at maturity.

Distinguishing Marks: Very similar to the Bahama strongbark (*B. ovata*), pictured in Photo 48, but differing by having generally shorter leaves that are densely pubescent and rough to the touch.

Distribution: Very rare in the Lower Keys (three locations are currently reported by the Florida Natural Areas Inventory); perhaps close to extirpation in the wild. Previously reported from pinelands and hammocks in south Florida and the Keys, which may have been misidentifications of *B. ovata*.

Bloodberry
Cordia globosa (Jacq.) HBK

Page 62

Form: Evergreen, much-branched shrub to about 3 m tall.
Leaves: Alternate, simple, ovate to lanceolate, coarsely serrate, softly pubescent with a grayish cast, 2 - 4 cm long; apices long, tapering to a point; venation on upper surfaces conspicuous.
Flowers: White, small, borne in clusters, each flower less than 1 cm long.
Fruit: A conspicuous, red, rounded drupe.
Distinguishing Marks: The softly hairy leaves with coarse dentations in conjunction with the clusters of white flowers are characteristic.
Distribution: Hammocks and sandy soils; southernmost Florida and the Keys.
Landscape Use: This is an attractive, bushy shrub that does well in open sun and can be used to soften the corners of fenced yards, or as an isolated shrub in the lawn.
Comment: Another member of this genus, granny bush (*C. bahamensis* Urban) was collected in Dade County pinelands by George Avery and later seen by Roger Hammer; however, no recent reports of the plant have been made, and it may be extirpated in southern Florida.

Bloodberry
Cordia globosa

Geiger Tree

Photo 49

Cordia sebestena L.

Form: Evergreen shrub or small, straight-trunked tree to about 9 m tall; with very dark bark and green, pubescent twigs.

Leaves: Alternate, simple, stiff, ovate, 10 - 25 cm long, 5 - 13 cm wide, margins entire to irregularly toothed toward the apices, bases of at least some leaves cordate; upper surfaces of leaves dark green and rough to the touch due to a covering of short, stiff hairs; lower surfaces paler and also hairy; the blades of many leaves often appear tattered and in poor shape.

Flowers: Orange red, showy, tubular or funnel shaped at the base but spreading into wavy-edged petals, 1 - 1.5 cm long, borne in compact, flattened, terminal clusters, appearing at almost any time of year.

Fruit: Egg shaped but completely enclosed in the enlarged, white calyx, 2 - 5 cm long.

Distinguishing Marks: Most easily recognized by large, scabrid, cordate leaves and large, attractive flower clusters.

Distribution: Occurs naturally but sparingly in hammocks and coastal scrub of the Florida Keys. According to Roger Hammer, a single plant is located on Chicken Key in Biscayne Bay, as well as on Key Biscayne, a sand barrier island. Some authorities consider this plant native; others suggest that it was imported.

Landscape Use: This plant is often used for landscaping but is very cold sensitive; it does best in full sun but tolerates partial shade and prefers sandy, alkaline soil. Cultivated specimens are common in the Keys.

Comment: The Geiger tree is listed as endangered by the Florida Department of Agriculture. Its common name was reportedly bestowed by John James Audubon in honor of John Geiger, a pilot and wrecker who lived in Key West and hosted Audubon on his visit to Florida. The Geiger tree is also the host plant for the Geiger beetle, a small, multicolored to golden-flecked insect that feeds only on this species. These insects are easy to find on the leaves of most specimens and account for their tattered appearance.

Tournefortia hirsutissima L.

Form: Erect shrub to about 2 m tall or a partly woody to woody, sometimes high-climbing vine to at least 6 m long; with pubescent branches.

Leaves: Alternate, simple, entire, ovate to broadly elliptic, 10 - 15 cm long, to at least 8 cm wide, surfaces with conspicuous shaggy hairs; apices gradually tapering or pinched to a point.

Flowers: Small (2 - 3 mm long), white, fragrant, borne on one side of a many-flowered, curved spike; appearing year-round.

Fruit: A soft, white, rounded drupe, 4 - 5 mm in diameter.

Distinguishing Marks: The curved spike with flowers only on one side establish this species as a member of the borage family; the much larger leaves set it apart from the other boraginaceous woody vine, *T. volubilis*.

Distribution: Hammocks; south Florida, not the Keys.

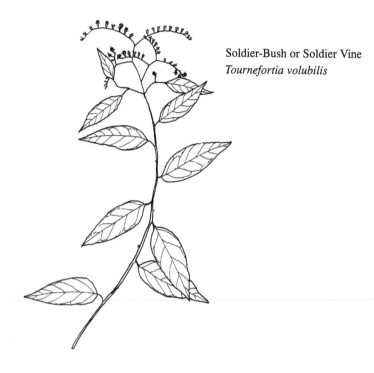

Soldier-Bush or Soldier Vine
Tournefortia volubilis

Soldier-Bush or Soldier Vine   Page 64

Tournefortia volubilis R & S

Form: Slender, woody vine to about 3 m long.

Leaves: Alternate, simple, entire, ovate to lanceolate or oblongish, 3 - 7 cm long, to about 4 cm wide; apices varying from acuminate to sharply angled.

Flowers: Greenish white, borne on a single side of a slender spike, each spike 3 - 4 cm long; appearing spring and summer.

Fruit: A rounded drupe, 2 - 3 mm in diameter.

Distinguishing Marks: The several, slender, one-sided flowering spikes establish this species as a member of the borage family; its smaller leaves set it apart from the other boraginaceous woody vine, *T. hirsutissima*.

Distribution: Hammocks; southern Florida and the Keys.

CALYCANTHACEAE — STRAWBERRY SHRUB FAMILY

This is a small family of trees and shrubs, most of them with simple, opposite, aromatic leaves and flowers with numerous tepals. There are three genera with nine species occurring in eastern Asia and North America. Florida's flora includes only one member of the family.

Sweet Shrub

Photo 51

Calycanthus floridus L.

Form: Deciduous, aromatic shrub to 3 m tall with reddish-brown bark.

Leaves: Opposite, simple, entire, elliptic to oval, 5 - 18 cm long, dark green and veiny above, somewhat whitish below, aromatic when bruised; apices pinched to a point.

Flowers: Sweetly fragrant (hence the common name), reddish to purple-brown, showy, with many, ribbonlike tepals; appearing mid- to late spring.

Distinguishing Marks: The opposite, aromatic leaves and distinctive flowers set this species apart.

Fruit: A fleshy, pendent, rough-textured structure bearing many one-seeded nutlets.

Distribution: Ravines, river banks, rich woods; Panhandle, eastward to about the Ochlockonee River.

Landscape Use: The clonal nature of the sweet shrub makes it a good hedge or garden border plant. It prefers sun to the north of Florida, but within Florida seems to do best in shade. It is prized primarily for its interesting flowers and its variably fruity fragrance which has been described as resembling a range of fruit from strawberry and banana to pineapple and grapefruit.

Comment: Listed as threatened by the Florida Department of Agriculture.

CANELLACEAE — WILD CINNAMON FAMILY

The Canellaceae, or wild cinnamon family, is a small family with only a few genera. Found intermittently throughout the West Indies, Brazil, and Venezuela as well as East Africa, Madagascar, and southern Florida, its rather spotty distribution and limited number of species are probably indicative of the family's ancient origin. Florida has only one member of the genus among its woody flora.

Cinnamon Bark

Photo 52

Canella winterana (L.) Gaertn.

Form: A shrub flowering when only 2 - 3 m tall, or a small evergreen tree to about 10 m tall.

Leaves: Alternate, obovate, deep green, lustrous, entire, 7 - 13 cm in length, 1 - 5 cm wide, apices rounded.

Flowers: Small, with five deep red petals, borne in spring in dense clusters.

Fruit: A red berry, about 1 cm in diameter.

Distinguishing Marks: Distinguished by the cinnamonlike aroma of the inner bark of mature trees and by the spicy (described by some as fiery) taste of its leaves.

Distribution: Hammocks of extreme southern Florida, especially near Cape Sable in Everglades National Park; more common in the Keys.

Comment: The plant's scientific name is derived from the root word *canella*, which is the Latin term for cinnamon. Both its common and scientific names refer to the cinnamonlike aroma of its inner bark. The plant is widely distributed in the West Indies and has been used throughout history variously as a spice, aromatic stimulant, and tonic. The spicy, fiery taste of the leaves provides a good trait for identifying the plant.

CAPPARACEAE — CAPER FAMILY

The caper family is a relatively large collection of nearly 1000 species and over 45 genera found mostly in the tropics. The family is probably best known for *Capparis spinosa* L., a species native to the Mediterranean region. The flower buds of this spiny deciduous shrub are pickled and sold as capers, a pungent condiment that is used as a garnish or seasoning.

Only two shrubby members of the family occur in Florida, both of which are restricted to the coastal zone of the southernmost peninsula and the Keys. The Jamaica caper (*Capparis cynophallophora*) and bay-leaved or limber caper (*C. flexuosa*) are evergreen shrubs that also sometimes reach treelike proportions in the Keys. The latter species is often so sprawling that it appears almost vinelike.

Both of Florida's capers have ornate, fragrant flowers characterized by masses of long stamens that extend well beyond the flower petals. In the Jamaica caper the flower petals are white and the stamens purple; in the limber caper the petals are sometimes pinkish in the morning but are clear white by night. The capers are pollinated by night-flying moths, and their flowers open just after dark. The long stamens brush against the moth as it approaches the nectar, and the pollen is then deposited on the stigma of the next plant the moth visits. The moths are attracted to the plants by the strong fragrance of the flowers, which can be detected from a long distance.

Jamaica Caper

Page 67, Photo 53

Capparis cynophallophora L.

Form: Evergreen, upright shrub or small tree to about 6 m tall with reddish-brown bark.
Leaves: Alternate, simple, elliptic, slightly leathery, entire, quite variable in size, 5 - 10 cm long, 1.5 - 3.5 cm wide, apices blunt or commonly notched.
Flowers: White, becoming pinkish to purplish with age, spreading, with clusters of long, brushlike stamens, inflorescence borne in clusters near the ends of branchlets, appearing in the evening in spring and summer.
Fruit: A pod with a long stalk, total structure 10 - 30 cm long and narrow between the seed cavities; seeds elliptic, shiny, brown.
Distinguishing Marks: Similar to the limber caper (*C. flexuosa*), distinguished from it as well as other south Florida trees and shrubs with notched leaves by lower surfaces of leaves having a dense covering of scales which imparts a distinctive sheen.
Distribution: Coastal hammocks, shell middens; Brevard and Pinellas Counties southward and throughout the Keys.
Landscape Use: The arresting flowers and interesting fruit make this and the next species interesting plants to include in south Florida native gardens.

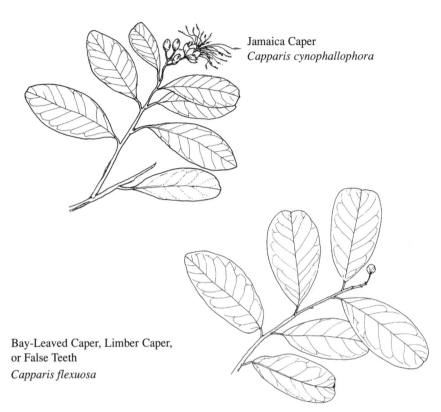

Jamaica Caper
Capparis cynophallophora

Bay-Leaved Caper, Limber Caper,
or False Teeth
Capparis flexuosa

Bay-Leaved Caper, Limber Caper, or False Teeth

Page 67, Photo 54

Capparis flexuosa L.

Form: Evergreen, usually sprawling shrub or small tree to about 8 m tall.

Leaves: Alternate, simple, varying from oblong to elliptic to almost linear, leathery, entire, two-ranked, apices blunt or notched, pale green, predominately 4 - 10 cm long, 1 - 5 cm wide.

Flowers: Fragrant with white sepals, spreading white to yellow or pink petals, and clusters of white, threadlike spreading stamens, appearing in summer in loose terminal clusters, opening late in the day and in the evening, closing in the morning.

Fruit: A brown pod, 3 - 22 cm long, about 1.3 cm in diameter; very showy at maturity, splitting to expose several white seeds against the pod's bright red inner lining, hence the name "false teeth."

Distinguishing Marks: Distinguished from Jamaica caper (*C. cynophallophora*) by lower leaf surface lacking a dense covering of scales.

Distribution: Coastal hammocks and shell middens from Brevard and Lee Counties southward along the coast and throughout the Keys.

CAPRIFOLIACEAE — HONEYSUCKLE FAMILY

The family Caprifoliaceae constitutes a diverse collection of trees, shrubs, and vines represented by 18 genera and perhaps 500 species. Members of the family are found worldwide in both temperate and tropical climatic regions. Four genera, including nine shrubby species, are found in Florida.

Japanese Honeysuckle
Lonicera japonica Thunb.

Page 68

Form: High-climbing twining or trailing, evergreen vine.

Leaves: Opposite, simple, entire, elliptic to ovate; apices with a tiny point at the tip; margins often bearing tiny hairs (requires magnification).

Flowers: White to cream colored or yellowish, slender, tubular, fragrant, 3 - 5 cm long, abruptly spreading into two lips and exposing several curving stamens; appearing from April to August.

Fruit: Roundish, black berry, 5 - 6 mm in diameter.

Distinguishing Marks: The white to cream-colored honeysuckle flowers distinguish the species.

Distribution: Native to Asia but widely naturalized throughout northern Florida, southward to about the central peninsula.

Landscape Use: This is an often-used vine for trellises and fences. However, it is listed as a Category I pest plant by the Florida Exotic Pest Plant Council, is potentially difficult to control due to its weedy nature, and may be detrimental to native flora.

Comment: There are about 180 species of *Lonicera* worldwide, almost all of which are deciduous.

Japanese Honeysuckle
Lonicera japonica

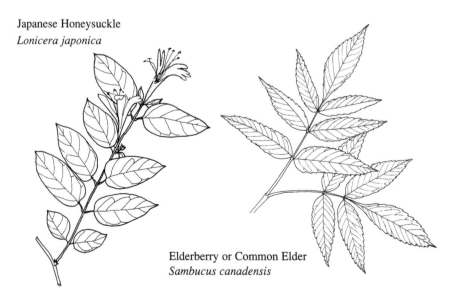

Elderberry or Common Elder
Sambucus canadensis

Coral Honeysuckle or Trumpet Honeysuckle

Photo 55

Lonicera sempervirens L.

Form: Trailing or twining, deciduous vine.

Leaves: Opposite, simple, entire, mostly elliptic to narrowly obovate, 3 - 7 cm long, some leaves (especially those nearest the ends of the branches) appearing to clasp or completely surround the stem; undersurfaces with a whitish cast.

Flowers: Red exteriorly, often yellow interiorly, tubular, 4 - 6 cm long, borne in clusters, very attractive; appearing spring through summer.

Fruit: A red, somewhat rounded berry.

Distinguishing Marks: The red and yellow honeysuckle flowers, in conjunction with the terminal leaves usually surrounding the stem, are diagnostic.

Distribution: Uplands, well-drained and moist woodlands; throughout north Florida southward to the southernmost peninsula.

Landscape Use: This plant is a much better choice for trellises and fences than the Japanese honeysuckle (*L. japonica*). It is native, not weedy, easy to control, much more attractive than Japanese honeysuckle, enjoys full sun, will grow in poor soil, and is generally available at native plant nurseries. Hummingbirds are attracted to the flowers and songbirds enjoy the red berries.

Elderberry or Common Elder

Page 68, Photo 56

Sambucus canadensis L.

Form: Deciduous (perhaps evergreen in southern Florida) shrub or very small tree to about 4 m tall.

Leaves: Opposite, pinnately (or occasionally bipinnately) compound, 15 - 25 cm long overall; leaflets 5 - 15 cm long, lanceolate, five to seven in number, opposite except the terminal one, giving off a rank odor when crushed, margins serrate.

Flowers: Small, white, arranged in showy clusters and appearing in late spring and early summer.

Fruit: Purplish black and juicy, appearing in mid- to late summer.

Distinguishing Marks: Most easily recognized by opposite, compound, rank-smelling leaves and showy flower clusters; distinguished from Brazilian pepper (*Schinus terebinthifolius*) by black rather than red fruit, from *Rhus copallina* by lacking the latter's winged rachis, from both by having opposite leaves.

Distribution: Found naturally in open wet areas and along the edges of wet woodlands, also in ditches, canals, wet roadsides, and in other disturbed sites throughout the state.

Landscape Use: This is a rapidly growing shrub that prefers wet or rich areas. It produces very showy flowers which are attractive to butterflies, and fruit which is attractive to birds. It is probably best to cut large specimens back every two to three years to keep them under control.

Comment: *Sambucus* berries have long been used in the production of wines, jellies, jams, and pies, and have enjoyed a long history as the source of a variety of popular homemade recipes. Wildlife biologists also recognize them as an important food source for a large number of songbirds as well as for some of the state's more important mammals.

Coralberry or Indian Currant
Symphoricarpos orbiculatus

Maple-Leaved Arrow-Wood or
Maple-Leaved Viburnum
Viburnum acerifolium

Arrow-Wood
Viburnum dentatum

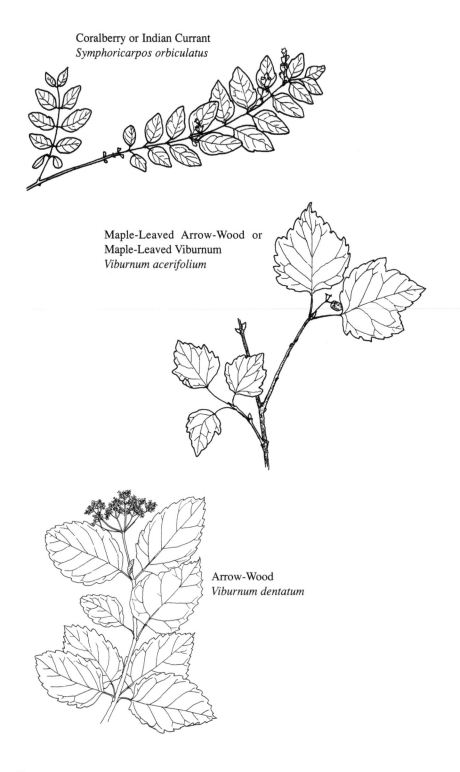

Coralberry or Indian Currant

Page 70

Symphoricarpos orbiculatus Moench.

Form: Deciduous, erect, much-branched shrub, 1 - 2 m tall, young branchlets purplish and densely gray pubescent, older stem light brown, lower stem typically exfoliating in thin strips.

Leaves: Opposite, simple, entire, oval to ovate, blunt to rounded at both ends, 1 - 5 cm long, 1 - 3 cm wide.

Flowers: Small, greenish to pinkish, borne in the fall in dense clusters in the axils of upper leaves.

Fruit: Roundish to ellipsoid, red to pinkish drupe, 4 - 5 mm long.

Distinguishing Marks: Similar to *Ligustrum sinense*, differing mostly by its lower stature, and by the brownish rather than gray-green color of the lower stem.

Distribution: Limestone bluffs; restricted in Florida primarily to the vicinity of Marianna in the central Panhandle.

Landscape Use: This species enjoys only marginal ornamental use somewhat north of Florida.

Comment: This plant is most easily seen along the trails at Florida Caverns State Park, particularly along the concrete trail that leads from the visitor center to the entrance of the caverns.

Maple-Leaved Arrow-Wood or Maple-Leaved Viburnum

Viburnum acerifolium L. Page 70

Form: Deciduous shrub to about 2 m tall with copiously pubescent stems.

Leaves: Opposite, simple, three-lobed and maplelike in general form, to about 8 cm both long and wide; margins coarsely toothed; lower surfaces with miniature black dots.

Flowers: Small, creamy white, but borne in conspicuously branched clusters at the ends of branches; clusters up to 9 cm across; appearing in spring.

Fruit: A purplish-black drupe, 5 - 9 mm long.

Distinguishing Marks: The opposite, maplelike leaves distinguish this species in its relatively narrow Florida range.

Distribution: Moist woodlands, ravines, bluffs; western and central Panhandle.

Landscape Use: A nice, shade-tolerant shrub with colorful fall foliage; not regularly used but appropriate for northwestern Florida.

Arrow-Wood

Page 70, Photo 57

Viburnum dentatum L.

Form: Slender-trunked deciduous shrub or potentially small tree, seldom exceeding 3 m tall.

Leaves: Opposite, simple, generally ovate but terminal pair sometimes more nearly lanceolate, 3 - 12 cm long, 2 - 8 cm wide, margins generally dentate with coarse teeth, each tooth serving as the termination point for a lateral vein, both upper and lower surfaces somewhat rough to the touch.

Flowers: White, borne in showy spreading clusters; appearing April to July.

Fruit: Green at first, turning blue black with maturity.

Distinguishing Marks: Distinguished from other *Viburnum* species and most other Florida shrubs and trees by its coarsely dentate leaves; potentially confused with maple-leaved viburnum (*V. acerifolium*) but lacking the three-lobed leaves.

Distribution: Found in a variety of situations, mostly in areas that are poorly drained such as the edges of rivers, bogs, bays, and flatwoods but sometimes also in well-drained woods; throughout the Panhandle and eastward to the counties of the west-central peninsula.

Landscape Use: This is a good hedge plant that will tolerate a wide range of soil conditions; the fruit is attractive to birds.

Possum-Haw
Photo 58

Viburnum nudum L.

Form: Deciduous shrub or small tree to about 6 m tall.

Leaves: Opposite, simple, lanceolate to elliptic, long-elliptic, or ovate, usually 10 - 15 cm long, but sometimes much shorter, upper surfaces dark, shiny green, lower surfaces copiously covered with tiny glandular dots, apices pinched to an abrupt point, margins typically entire but sometimes finely crenate to serrate and slightly revolute; petioles inconspicuously and narrowly winged.

Flowers: Small, white, borne in showy, spreading clusters, each cluster to about 15 cm wide, appearing in March and April.

Fruit: Ellipsoid, initially red to pink but turning deep blue.

Distinguishing Marks: Distinguished from rusty haw (*V. rufidulum*) by punctate dots on lower leaf surfaces, from Walter viburnum (*V. obovatum*) by much larger and typically ovate leaves, from wax-leaf ligustrum (*Ligustrum lucidum*) by the slightly winged petiole; one of two species with the common name "possum-haw", the other, *Ilex decidua*, can be distinguished from this species most quickly by its alternate, rather than opposite, leaves.

Distribution: Swamps, bay heads, and wet woodlands; throughout northern Florida, southward to about DeSoto County.

Landscape Use: This is an excellent understory or background shrub in naturalistic settings; its flowers are very showy and its fruit is attractive to birds.

Walter or Small Viburnum
Photos 59, 60

Viburnum obovatum Walt.

Form: Sometimes a shrub but often a small, deciduous to semi-evergreen tree to about 9 m tall.

Leaves: Opposite, simple, 2 - 5 cm long, 1 - 3 cm wide, margins entire or irregularly and minutely toothed, especially toward the apices, lower surfaces copiously covered with small brown dots.

Flowers: Small, white, borne in flat-topped clusters, each cluster 4 - 6 cm wide, appearing February to March, thus the earliest flowering *Viburnum*.

Fruit: An ellipsoid drupe, 6 - 10 mm long, red at first, turning black with maturity.

Distinguishing Marks: Distinguished from possum-haw (*V. nudum*) by generally smaller leaves that are typically widest above the middle; similar to *Ilex decidua* and *Ilex vomitoria* in leaf structure but distinguished from them by having opposite, rather than alternate, leaves.

Distribution: More common in wet areas such as flatwoods, streambanks, swamp margins, and hammocks, but also in dry uplands underlain by limestone; from about Washington County eastward and southward to about Hendry County.

Landscape Use: The early flowering period and attractive fall fruit make this a good shrub for naturalistic settings.

Rusty Haw or Southern Black Haw   Page 73
Viburnum rufidulum Raf.

Form: Deciduous shrub or small tree with blocky bark that resembles both common persimmon (*Diospyros virginiana*) and flowering dogwood (*Cornus florida* L.).

Leaves: Opposite, simple, 4 - 8 cm long, 3 - 6 cm wide, margins finely toothed, upper surfaces shiny green, lower surfaces exhibiting patches of shaggy, rusty pubescence, especially along the midvein.

Flowers: White, small, borne in spreading clusters, each cluster 5 - 10 cm wide; borne in early to midspring

Fruit: Purple, ellipsoid, 10 - 15 mm long, borne in spreading clusters.

Distinguishing Marks: Distinguished from Walter viburnum (*V. obovatum*) and possum-haw (*V. nudum*) by patches of rusty pubescence on the lower surfaces of leaves and lack of punctate dots.

Distribution: Upland, well-drained woods; throughout the Panhandle, eastward and southward to about Hernando County.

Landscape Use: This is another native *Viburnum* that has much to offer in the landscape. Its dense clusters of bright white flowers and dark green leaves are attractive additions to background shrubbery.

Rusty Haw or Southern Black Haw
Viburnum rufidulum

CELASTRACEAE — STAFF-TREE FAMILY

The Celastraceae include a widely diverse group of plants with affinities to several related families, including the hollies. Depending upon the taxonomic scheme chosen to represent this complex group of dicotyledons, the family may contain up to 60 genera and more than 800 species. At least five genera are represented in Florida, each of which includes at least one shrub-sized species.

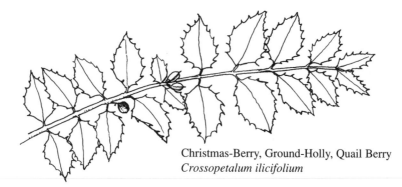

Christmas-Berry, Ground-Holly, Quail Berry
Crossopetalum ilicifolium

Christmas-Berry, Ground-Holly, Quail-Berry   Page 74

Crossopetalum ilicifolium (Poir.) Kuntze

Form: Low, essentially prostrate, evergreen, sprawling shrub with pubescent stems.
Leaves: Opposite to whorled, simple, elliptic to ovate, 1 - 2 cm long; margins spiny or sharply toothed.
Flowers: Red, tiny, borne in short clusters at the leaf axils.
Fruit: A rounded, red to orange-red drupe, 3 - 4 mm long.
Distinguishing Marks: Similar to *C. rhacoma*, differing from the latter by being primarily prostrate in growth form, and by the much smaller leaves with sharply toothed or spiny margins.
Distribution: Hammock edges and pinelands; southern Florida and the Keys.
Landscape Use: Sometimes used as a ground cover.

Rhacoma or Florida Crossopetalum   Photo 61

Crossopetalum rhacoma Crantz

Form: An evergreen shrub but sometimes a small, short-trunked, much-branched tree to about 6 m tall.
Leaves: Opposite, alternate, or whorled, simple, obovate to elliptic, 1 - 4 cm long, 0.5 - 2 cm wide, yellow green in color, margins crenate with shallow, rounded teeth, or sometimes entire.

Flowers: Very small, petals reddish, borne in long-stalked clusters from the leaf axils; appearing year-round, mostly in conjunction with new stem growth.

Fruit: A rounded, red to reddish-purple drupe, 5 - 7 mm in diameter.

Distinguishing Marks: Distinguished from other hammock species by small, primarily opposite leaves that are definitely toothed or notched along the edges; but see *C. ilicifolium*.

Distribution: Sun-loving species of southern Florida and the Keys; more common in pinelands, occasional in hammocks.

Hearts-A-Bustin'-With-Love or Strawberry Bush

Page 75, Photos 62, 63

Euonymus americanus L.

Form: Tardily deciduous shrub to about 2 m tall; with green stems and spreading, sometimes arching or ascending branches.

Leaves: Opposite, simple, varying from lanceolate to elliptic in overall shape; margins minutely and finely serrate; petioles absent or very short.

Flowers: Yellowish green, petals 5 in number and nearly triangular in outline, borne at the end of long stalks; typically appearing in March and April.

Fruit: A showy, red, somewhat rounded capsule with a strawberrylike appearance (hence one of the common names), splitting open at maturity to expose bright red seeds which first hang on the capsule, then eventually fall to the ground (hence the other common name).

Distinguishing Marks: The dull red, typically knobby capsules and bright red seeds provide the easiest means for separating this plant from all others; distinguished from *E. atropurpureus* by leaves lacking a distinctive petiole and by having numerous branches that are green rather than brown; both of these plants are inconspicuous and easily overlooked when not in flower or fruit.

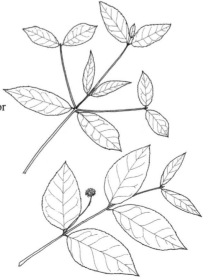

Heart's-A-Bustin'-With Love or
Strawberry Bush
Euonymus americanus

Distribution: Moist or rich woods, floodplains, stream banks; throughout northern Florida, southward to about the central peninsula.

Landscape Use: The fruit of this species is very attractive. The plant fruits best in sunny or partly sunny locations but will tolerate deep shade (where it is most often found in nature). Since it is deciduous, it serves best when mixed with evergreen species or placed in the back of flower beds.

Eastern Wahoo or Burning Bush   Page 76, Photo 64

Euonymus atropurpureus Jacq.

Form: Ordinarily a deciduous shrub in Florida, potentially a small, erect tree to about 8 m tall, often branching close to the ground; new twigs angled.

Leaves: Opposite, simple, elliptic, 5 - 12 cm long, 2 - 5 cm wide, margins finely serrate; leaf stalks 1 - 1.5 cm long.

Flowers: Maroon to purple in color, borne in few-flowered clusters on long, slender stalks, petals four in number and only about 4 mm long, individual flowers about 10 mm wide when fully open; appearing in spring.

Fruit: A pinkish to tan, four-winged capsule that splits at maturity; seeds brownish to bright red, sometimes inconspicuous and remaining hidden in the capsule until falling, other times conspicuous and dangling on a threadlike aril.

Distinguishing Marks: Most readily identified by its opposite, finely serrate leaves that are long tapering at both the apices and bases; easily distinguished from hearts-a-bustin'-with-love (*E. americanus*) by the distinctly petiolate leaves and by having only a few branches that are greenish toward the tips.

Eastern Wahoo or Burning Bush
Euonymus atropurpureus

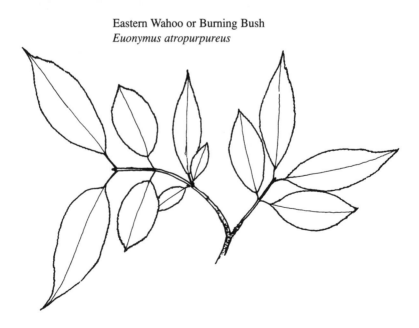

Distribution: Infrequent along streambanks, bluffs, and ravines, generally in conjunction with limestone soils; a tree of more northern distribution confined in Florida to the northern Panhandle from about Jefferson County westward.

Landscape Use: Appropriate as a background plant fronted by low herbs or shrubs, but not widely used.

Comment: The bark of this species was once ground into a powder and used as a purgative, especially by the American Indians and early colonists. However, the internal damage that sometimes results from high dosages and overuse led the U. S. Food and Drug Administration to label the plant as unsafe for medicinal purposes. The specific epithet, *atropurpureus*, is Latin for "dark purple", a reference to the color of mature fruit.

False Boxwood or Falsebox

Photo 65

Gyminda latifolia (Sw.) Urban

Form: Large evergreen shrub or small tree to about 8 m tall with gray to reddish-brown bark; twigs angled or squared.

Leaves: Opposite, simple, light green in color, elliptic to obovate, 3.8 - 5 cm long, 2 - 3 cm wide, margins entire to slightly crenate near the apices, sometimes revolute, apices rounded, veins inconspicuous.

Flowers: Small, white, borne in few-flowered clusters; appearing year-round but less prolifically in winter.

Fruit: Blue to black, rounded to ovoid, 5 - 8 mm in diameter.

Distinguishing Marks: Most easily recognized by the combination of square twigs and opposite leaves.

Distribution: Uncommon and restricted to only a few hammocks of the lower Florida Keys.

Florida Mayten, Mayten, Gutta-Percha Mayten

Page 78, Photo 66

Maytenus phyllanthoides Benth.

Form: Evergreen shrub or small tree to about 6 m tall with a short trunk and smooth, gray bark.

Leaves: Alternate, simple, fleshy, leathery, oblong to elliptic, 2.5 - 4 cm long, 1.2 - 2 cm wide, margins entire but often wavy, apices blunt or notched.

Flowers: Greenish-white, small, borne singly or in few-flowered clusters from the leaf axils, appearing primarily January to May.

Fruit: A bright red, four-angled, egg-shaped capsule, 6 - 12 mm long, may be seen on the tree at almost any time of year.

Distinguishing Marks: Most easily recognized by light green, fleshy leaves with notched apices and minute marginal scales.

Distribution: Coastal scrub and hammock edges; from Levy County (where it is not common) southward along the west coast, Miami southward along the east coast, throughout the Keys.

Florida Mayten, Mayten, Gutta-Percha Mayten
Maytenus phyllanthoides

Florida Boxwood or Yellowwood
Schaefferia frutescens

Florida Boxwood or Yellowwood

Page 78

Schaefferia frutescens Jacq.

Form: Evergreen shrub or small tree potentially to about 12 m tall with dark bark and angled, green twigs; often shrubby and less than 3 m tall.

Leaves: Alternate, simple, leathery, elliptic to oval, 4 - 7 cm long, 1.2 - 2.5 cm wide, margins entire, usually revolute, apices with a small point.

Flowers: Greenish-white, tiny, borne in clusters at the leaf axils; appearing March to May.

Fruit: A rounded, fleshy, red drupe, 5 - 8 mm in diameter.

Distinguishing Marks: The green, angled twigs and stiff leaves help set this species apart.

Distribution: Hammocks of the Keys and, to a lesser extent, of the southern peninsula.

CHRYSOBALANACEAE — COCO-PLUM FAMILY

The coco-plum family is a mostly tropical collection of 17 genera and more than 400 species. Two genera, each with a single species, are found in the United States. The coco-plum (*Chrysobalanus icaco*) is an attractive shrub that sometimes becomes arborescent. The other species is the gopher apple (*Licania michauxii*), a low, clonal shrub distributed from the lower Florida peninsula northward to at least South Carolina and westward to Louisiana. The Chrysobalanaceae were formerly classified with the Rosaceae but are now considered by most taxonomists to constitute a clearly definable and quite natural family unit.

Coco-Plum

Photo 67

Chrysobalanus icaco L.

Form: Evergreen shrub or small bushy tree to about 5 m tall.

Leaves: Alternate, simple, leathery, dark green, shiny, oval to nearly round, 2 - 8 cm long, 1 - 6 cm wide, two-ranked on the stem but often borne erect so that all leaves appear to be on the same side of the branch, apices slightly notched; often with two glands on the undersurface at the base near the petiole.

Flowers: White, bell shaped, small, 5 - 7 mm long; appearing year-round.

Fruit: A rounded, one-seeded, dark purple to yellowish (rarely white) drupe, 1 - 4 cm in diameter; plants with reddish new growth typically produce purple fruit, those with greenish-white new growth typically produce yellowish-white fruit.

Distinguishing Marks: The rounded, erect, two-ranked leaves in conjunction with the dark purple fruit that is evident at almost any time of year is diagnostic for identification.

Distribution: Low hammocks, beaches, sand dunes, cypress heads, and other wet habitats, primarily along the coastal zone but occasionally in inland swamps; Brevard and Charlotte Counties southward and throughout the Keys.

Landscape Use: A very attractive and often-used landscape plant, especially for hedges or borders, or to line walkways; the fruit is edible.

Comment: The sweet taste of this species' fruit probably made it an important part of the diet of the earliest Floridians. More recently the fruits have been canned as an export item for several Caribbean basin countries. White-fruited specimens were once considered a distinct species but are now recognized as conspecific with dark-fruited plants.

Gopher Apple or Ground Oak

Page 80, Photo 68

Licania michauxii Prance.

Form: Very low evergreen shrub, to about 4 dm tall but typically much shorter, spreading by underground stems; often found in large colonies due to the plant's clonal habit.

Leaves: Alternate, simple, elliptic to almost spatulate, oaklike in general appearance, 2 - 10 cm long, 1 - 4 cm wide, leaves of the midstem larger than those at top and bottom; margins entire to slightly wavy.

Flowers: White, borne in terminal clusters that commonly extend beyond the uppermost leaves; appearing from about April throughout the summer.

Fruit: An elliptical drupe, 2 - 3 cm long.

Distinguishing Marks: The low stature of this plant sets it apart from all but very young oak seedlings; however, the latter never display the gopher apple's conspicuous, terminal flower clusters.

Distribution: Sandhills, pine ridges, roadsides, old coastal dunes; throughout northern Florida, southward to the southern peninsula.

Landscape Use: The conspicuous flowers, extended flowering period, and low stature of this evergreen make it suitable for a low ground cover in sandy soils.

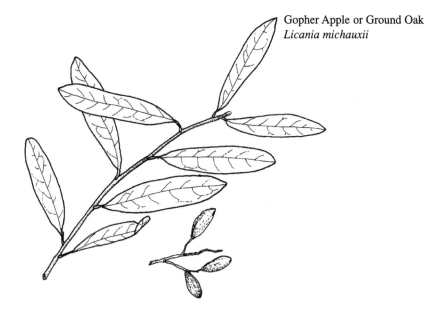

Gopher Apple or Ground Oak
Licania michauxii

CLETHRACEAE — WHITE ALDER FAMILY

The Clethraceae is a small family with a single genus of about 40 species. Most members of the genus are limited to the tropics and subtropics. A single species is found in Florida. Most authorities agree that the family is closely related to members of the Ericaceae or heath family.

Sweet Pepperbush or Summersweet

Page 81, Photo 69

Clethra alnifolia L.

Form: Deciduous shrub potentially to about 3 m tall but generally only about half this height.

Leaves: Alternate, simple, with conspicuous lateral veins, elliptic to widest above the middle, to about 8 cm long and 4 cm wide but typically smaller; margins serrate from about the middle of the blade toward the tip.

Flowers: Bright white, very conspicuous, borne in terminal racemes beyond the leaves; appearing throughout the summer.

Fruit: A small, darkened, rounded capsule to about 3 mm in diameter.

Distinguishing Marks: The combination of bright white flowering racemes and leaves serrated outwardly from the middle set this plant apart from all other flatwoods and wetland plants; often confused with Virginia willow (*Itea virginica*) but easily distinguished by the latter's leaves having margins serrated from base to tip.

Distribution: Flatwoods, swamps, savannas; throughout northern Florida southward to about the central peninsula.

Landscape Use: The fragrant flowers of this species attract butterflies and bees and are quite beautiful. It does best in low, wet soils and requires little care once established. However, it also responds well to pruning if keeping its size under control is desirable; works well as a hedge or background plant.

Sweet Pepperbush or Summersweet
Clethra alnifolia

COMBRETACEAE — COMBRETUM FAMILY

The Combretaceae, or combretum family is a primarily tropical collection of about 500, mainly woody species native to Central and South America. Five species in four genera are found in Florida. Only three of these are typically shrublike; all are considered native by most observers, though the native status of spiny bucida is doubted by some. The other of Florida's established woody Combretaceae, both of which are nonnative trees, include the sea almond (*Terminalia catappa* L.) and black olive (*Bucida buceras* L.)

Spiny Bucida or Ming Tree

Bucida spinosa Jennings

Form: Typically a flat-topped, evergreen tree to about 8 m tall; most often found in the wild in south Florida as a slow-growing shrub or shrubby tree with thorny stems.

Leaves: Alternate, simple, entire, elliptic to obovate, small, 1.5 - 2 cm long.

Flowers: White, borne in short, densely flowered spikes at the leaf axils.

Fruit: Small, rounded, to about 3 mm in diameter.

Distinguishing Marks: The thorny stems, relatively small leaves, and densely flowered spikes help distinguish this species.

Distribution: Hammocks; rare in the southern Florida peninsula, also recently reported from Key Largo.

Landscape Use: The twisted, thorny appearance of this species makes it an interesting specimen plant for native south Florida gardens; it is almost certain to be a conversation starter with other gardeners.

Comment: This plant is assumed to be native by some observers; others consider it only sparingly naturalized. Roger Hammer (1995, personal communication) reports a sizable population of this plant in a remote area east of Homestead as well as a recent discovery on Key Large, and believes that the plant has been overlooked by earlier authors. Several tree-sized specimens can be found along the trails at Fairchild Tropical Garden.

Buttonwood   Photo 70

Conocarpus erectus L.

Form: Evergreen shrub or tree to about 20 m tall.

Leaves: Alternate, simple, leathery, 2 - 10 cm long, 1 - 4 cm wide, apices often with a tiny point; typically with a pair of glands at the point of attachment of the blade and petiole.

Flowers: Tiny, green, borne in dense, rounded, compact heads (hence the name "buttonwood"), appearing from about March to September.

Fruit: Tiny, flattened, scalelike, borne in conspicuous conelike collections that are 1 - 2 cm in diameter and may be seen at almost any time of year.

Distinguishing Marks: Distinguished from all other south Florida shrubs and trees by its buttonlike flowers and fruit; distinguished from the silver buttonwood (*C. erectus* var. *sericeus* Griseb.) by the latter having leaves conspicuously covered with a distinctive, silvery-gray pubescence.

Distribution: Generally coastal in distribution, normally found along the landward edge of the mangrove zone and along the edges of hammocks bordering the transition zone; southern Florida and the Keys, but also found in smaller numbers northward to Hernando County on the west coast and Merritt Island on the east.

Comment: This is one of the plants that is often referred to as a mangrove since it is often found near saltwater on the inland side of the mangrove fringe. In the strictest sense it is not a mangrove and does not tolerate as much salt as do the black, white, and red mangroves. This species was once a source of charcoal in the lower Everglades, especially in the vicinity of Florida Bay.

White Mangrove   Page 83
Laguncularia racemosa (L.) Gaertn. f.

Form: Evergreen shrub or, more typically, a small tree to about 13 m tall.

Leaves: Opposite, thick, leathery, smooth, succulent, oval, 2.5 - 8 cm long, 2.5 - 3 cm wide, apices often notched, both upper and lower surfaces light green with obscure veins; petioles with two conspicuous glands just below the base of the leaf blade.

Flowers: Tiny, white, velvetlike to the touch, borne in branched clusters at the tips of branches or in leaf axils; appearing in spring and early summer.

Fruit: Greenish to reddish, narrow at the base and widening toward the apex, 1 - 1.5 cm long, with ten distinctive, lengthwise ribs, appearing in fall.

Distinguishing Marks: The two glands on the petiole in combination with the smooth, thick, oval leaves are diagnostic field marks; specimens of this tree may be separated from the other two strictly mangrove species by the light green color of both leaf surfaces and by the generally oval shape of the blades.

Distribution: Coastal zone from about Brevard and Hernando Counties southward and throughout the Keys.

White Mangrove
Laguncularia racemosa

Comment: The white mangrove is typically the more landward member of the true mangroves (see *Avicennia germinans*, *Rhizophora mangle*, and *Conocarpus erectus*) but is often found in mixed associations with the black mangrove (*A. germinans*). Like the black mangrove, it has the propensity to develop breathing roots, or pneumatophores, although such appendages are not nearly so commonplace with the white mangrove and are not always present.

COMPOSITAE — COMPOSITE, SUNFLOWER, OR ASTER FAMILY

The composites constitute a morphologically advanced group of plants that is probably best known for its numerous, low-growing, herbaceous species that burst into flower throughout the spring, summer, and fall. The family's inflorescences are typically borne in complex, showy heads that contain both ray and disk flowers that are subtended by numerous, small, leaflike bracts or phyllaries. The many members of this family make it a favorite among avid wildflower enthusiasts. As might be expected, only a few of its members are woody.

Climbing Aster   Photo 71

Aster carolinianus Walt.

Form: Sprawling, scrambling or climbing, much-branched shrub with woody, buff-colored stems and herbaceous branches; climbing to about 4 m tall.
Leaves: Alternate, simple, entire, elliptic to lanceolate, 2 - 6 cm long, to about 1.5 cm wide; bases of leaves often clasping the stems.
Flowers: A many-flowered head with numerous, showy, lavender to bluish ray flowers and yellow disc flowers; ray flowers to about 1.5 cm long; appearing in late fall in the northern part of the state, almost all year in the lower peninsula.
Fruit: Small, hard, dry, single seeded.
Distinguishing Marks: The clasping leaves and lavender, asterlike flowers set this species apart from all other native shrubs.
Distribution: Wet woods, stream banks, spring edges; from the easternmost Panhandle generally eastward and southward to the southern peninsula.
Landscape Use: Widely used in native plant landscapes; the fall flowering period of this species and its sprawling nature make it an excellent backdrop around decks, along fences, or in corners.

False-Willow or Saltbush   Page 85

Baccharis angustifolia Michx.

Form: Much-branched, evergreen to tardily deciduous shrub to about 4 m tall; young stems dark green, older stems more nearly tan colored.

False-Willow or Saltbush
Baccharis angustifolia

Leaves: Alternate, simple, linear to needlelike, 2 - 8 cm long, dark shiny green; margins usually entire, sometimes slightly toothed.

Flowers: Borne in compact heads; appearing in summer and fall.

Fruit: Fruits and fruiting heads whitish, similar in appearance to the bristle end of an artist's paint brush; often appearing cottony from a distance.

Distinguishing Marks: The linear, dark green leaves and typically near-coastal habitat is usually enough to identify this species.

Distribution: Edges of saltmarshes, coastal hammocks, shores of estuaries, brackish marshes; throughout north Florida, southward to the southern peninsula and the Keys.

Baccharis dioica Vahl

Form: A multi-branched shrub to about 3 m tall.

Leaves: Alternate, simple, entire, fleshy, spatulate to ovate, 1 - 3 cm long.

Flowers: Yellowish-green, borne in compact, many-flowered heads.

Fruit: Dry, smooth, with ten ribs.

Distinguishing Marks: Distinguished from the other two wide-leaved members of the genus by having entire rather than toothed leaves.

Distribution: Coastal areas along Biscayne Bay, previously reported as being in hammocks and the Everglades keys; southern Florida.

Comment: This plant has not been reported in recent years and may be extirpated in Florida.

Groundsel Tree

Photo 72

Baccharis glomeruliflora Pers.

Form: Bushy, evergreen to tardily deciduous shrub to about 4 m tall.

Leaves: Alternate, simple, often coarsely toothed along the margins, surfaces without conspicuous punctate glands.

Flowers: Borne in tightly compact heads; appearing in summer and fall.

Fruit: Fruits and fruiting heads whitish, similar in appearance to the bristle end of an artist's paint brush; often appearing cottony from a distance.

Distinguishing Marks: Most similar to, and often confused with, *B. halimifolia*; distinguished from the latter plant by having sessile flower heads and by lacking fine, amber-colored punctations on the leaf surfaces.

Distribution: Edges of fresh and brackish marshes, wet coastal hammocks; throughout north Florida, southward to the southern peninsula.

Saltbush, Groundsel Tree, Sea Myrtle

Page 86

Baccharis halimifolia L.

Form: Freely branched evergreen shrub or small tree to about 4 m tall.

Leaves: Alternate, thick, pale green, 4 - 7 cm long, 1 - 4 cm wide, margins sometimes entire but often widely serrate with a few coarse teeth, particularly toward the apices; surfaces finely dotted with many pale punctations.

Flowers: Small, greenish to white, borne in conspicuous heads; appearing in early fall; similar to those of *B. glomeruliflora*, pictured in photo 72, except stalked rather than sessile.

Fruit: Small but with a mass of hairlike bristles that become very conspicuous as the fruit matures and makes the entire plant look like a conglomeration of cottony or flossy appendages, even at some distance.

Saltbush, Groundsel Tree, Sea Myrtle
Baccharis halimifolia

Distinguishing Marks: Similar to, and often confused with, *B. glomeruliflora*; distinguished from it by the stalked flower heads and by having pale amber punctations on the leaf surfaces.

Distribution: Coastal areas such as the upper edge of marshes, along swales, and extending into sandy areas but also found in disturbed sites far inland; throughout the state, including the Keys.

Landscape Use: A useful background shrub, particularly in seaside locations; also grows well in more inland locations. The flosslike seeds that cover female plants in early fall are very attractive. Often seen along roadsides, though perhaps not planted there.

Sea-Oxeye

Photo 73

Borrichia arborescens (L.) DC.

Form: Evergreen shrub to about 1.5 m tall.

Leaves: Opposite, simple, thick, fleshy (almost succulent), oblanceolate to spatulate, 3 - 8 cm long; light green in color; apices with a small point.

Flowers: Flowering head to about 2.5 cm across; borne at the ends of branches; ray flowers bright yellow, to about 1 cm long, disc flowers darker yellow; appearing most profusely in spring and summer; apices of the leaflike bracts below the flower blunt or only slightly pointed.

Fruit: Small, dry, hard.

Distinguishing Marks: Very similar to *B. frutescens*, distinguished from the latter by the apices of the leaflike bracts that subtend the flower being rounded or only slightly pointed rather than bearing sharp spines, and by slightly larger leaves that are green rather than grayish.

Distribution: Shores, sand dunes, edges of brackish marshes; southernmost peninsula and the Keys.

Landscape Use: Useful as a flowering shrub in maritime locations in the southernmost portions of the state.

Comment: *Borrichia* x *cubana*, of southern Florida, is often listed as a natural hybrid of this species and the next.

Sea-Oxeye or Sea-Daisy

Photo 74

Borrichia frutescens (L.) DC.

Form: Low, erect, little-branched, evergreen shrub; potentially to about 1.2 m tall but usually shorter; often spreading profusely by underground stems.

Leaves: Opposite, simple, thick, fleshy (almost succulent), elliptic to oblanceolate, 2 - 6 cm long; margins typically entire, sometimes with coarse teeth; surfaces grayish in color from dense pubescence; apices with a small point.

Flowers: Flowering head to about 2 cm across; borne at the ends of branches; ray flowers bright yellow, to about 1 cm long, disc flowers darker yellow; appearing in spring and summer; apices of the leaflike bracts below the flower bearing sharp spines.

Fruit: Dry, angled, grayish, to about 4 mm long.

Distinguishing Marks: Very similar to *B. arborescens*, distinguished from the latter by the leaflike bracts that subtend the flower terminating in sharp spines and by having grayish leaves.

Distribution: Tidal marshes, mangrove edges, shores of estuaries, always in maritime habitats; throughout Florida, including the Keys.

Landscape Use: Useful as a low flowering shrub in maritime situations; salt tolerant.

Woody Goldenrod

Photo 75

Chrysoma pauciflosculosa (Michx.) Greene

Form: Low, evergreen, densely branched shrub, with ascending leafy branches and conspicuous flowering and fruiting branches that normally extend well beyond the leafy branches.

Leaves: Alternate, simple, entire, elliptic to oblong, grayish to grayish green, 2 - 6 cm long, without petioles.

Flowers: Bright yellow; borne in clusters of numerous heads at the ends of conspicuous flowering branches that extend well beyond the leafy branches; appearing chiefly in the late summer and fall.

Fruit: Hard, dry, pale in color, with numerous bristles.

Distinguishing Marks: The bushy habit, long flowering branches with yellow flowers, and gray-green leaves generally distinguish this species in its preferred habitat.

Distribution: Coastal dunes, barrier islands, sand pine–oak scrub, inland scrub oak ridges; from about Franklin County westward across the Panhandle.

Eupatorium villosum Sw.

Page 89

Form: A semiwoody to woody shrub with densely hairy stems (requires magnification); 0.5 - 2 m tall.

Leaves: Opposite to whorled, simple, ovate to deltoid, with two prominent veins diverging on either side of the midrib when viewed from below, 1.5 - 8 cm long, predominantly more than 1.5 cm wide; margins entire to obscurely sinuate.

Flowers: White to pinkish white, small, to about 3 mm long; borne in compact heads.

Fruit: Small, dry nutlet, 1 - 2 mm long.

Distinguishing Marks: There are many species of *Eupatorium* in Florida, many of which are quite similar in general aspect. The current species, as well as the bitter bush (*E. odoratum* L.), are the only ones that normally become woody. *E. villosum* may be distinguished from south Florida's other members of the genus by the combination of its shrublike stature, its upper leaves being predominantly wider than 1.5 cm, its leaf shape being ovate and heart shaped at the base, and its leaf margins being entire to obscurely sinuate.

Distribution: Hammocks and pinelands; south Florida and the Keys.

Landscape Use: This plant makes a large, attractive shrub when planted alone. It also serves well to soften fence corners.

Eupatorium villosum

Marsh-Elder, Sump-Weed, Highwater-Shrub
Iva frutescens

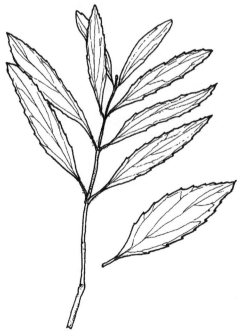

Garberia heterophylla (Bartr.) Merrill & F. Harper   **Photo 76**

Form: Bushy-branched, semi-evergreen shrub, 1 - 2.5 m tall.

Leaves: Alternate, simple, entire, grayish-green, obovate to almost rounded, 1 - 3.5 cm long, held erect on the stem and appearing to overlap each other; surfaces covered with sticky hairs and minute, variously colored glands (the latter require magnification to see clearly).

Flowers: Pink to lavender, to about 1 cm long; borne in clusters of compact heads; appearing primarily in October and November; plant very showy when in full bloom.

Fruit: Dark gray, dry, 10-ribbed, to about 8 mm long.

Distinguishing Marks: The erect, sticky, dull grayish, nearly rounded leaves set this species apart in the sand pine–oak scrub.

Distribution: Sand pine–oak scrub and sandy ridges; northeast Florida, southward to at least Highlands County.

Comment: Listed as threatened by the Florida Department of Agriculture, primarily because it is endemic to the state's disappearing sand scrub regions; this plant is often seen listed by the synonym *G. fruticosa* (Nutt.) A. Gray.

Marsh-Elder, Sump-Weed, Highwater-Shrub   Page 89

Iva frutescens L.

Form: Many-branched, tardily deciduous shrub to about 3.5 m tall; branches arising from near the base; woody below, mostly herbaceous above; with prominent lines along the stem between the leaf nodes.

Leaves: Opposite (except those nearest the branch ends), simple, fleshy and nearly succulent, lanceolate to long elliptic, 4 - 10 cm long; margins serrate toward the base and sometimes toward the apices.

Flowers: Borne terminally in short, rounded heads; appearing in summer and fall.

Fruit: Very small, dry, hard, angled.

Distinguishing Marks: Distinguished from *I. imbricata* by most leaves being opposite rather than alternate, and by leaves being at least partially serrate rather than entire; otherwise unique in its maritime habitat.

Distribution: Shores and coastal marshes; Atlantic and Gulf Coasts, throughout north Florida southward to the southern peninsula.

Dune Sump-Weed or Beach Elder

Iva imbricata Walt.

Form: Bushy-branched shrub to about 1 m tall, often much shorter; branches arising from the base.

Leaves: Alternate (except for the lowermost, which are opposite), simple, entire, fleshy and nearly succulent, oblong to nearly linear, but widest near the tips, 2 - 5 cm long.

Flowers: Borne in heads among leafy bracts near the ends of branches; appearing in summer and fall.

Fruit: Hard, dry, reddish brown.

Distinguishing Marks: Distinguished from *I. frutescens* by leaves being predominantly alternate rather than opposite, and by having mostly entire leaves; otherwise easily distinguished from other coastal dune plants.

Distribution: Coastal dunes on both the Atlantic and Gulf Coasts; north Florida (including the Panhandle), southward to the southern peninsula and the Keys.

Landscape Use: This is a good dune building plant and is recommended for coastal beach habitats, especially where erosion control is important. Seedlings are readily transplanted and cuttings root easily.

Bushy Fleabane

Pluchea symphytifolia (Mill.) Gillis

Page 91

Form: Bushy, evergreen, much-branched shrub, 1 - 3 m tall.

Leaves: Alternate, simple, entire to obscurely serrate, broadly lanceolate to elliptic, 7 - 15 cm long, surfaces covered with a fine, grayish pubescence; petioles 1 - 1.5 cm long; with a pungent odor when crushed.

Flowers: Small, pale pink to lavender, borne in conspicuous terminal clusters; appearing winter and spring.

Fruit: Small, dry, hard, single-seeded.

Distinguishing Marks: The grayish pubescence, dense terminal clusters of pink to lavender flowers, and pungently scented leaves distinguish this species.

Distribution: Mostly seen in disturbed sites or on the edges of hammocks; southern Florida and the Keys.

Comment: This plant is sometimes considered native but was probably introduced from Mexico. The somewhat similar marsh fleabane (*P. odorata* [L.] Cass.), not described here, is occasionally referred to as a shrub but is a deep-rooted, robust annual.

Bushy Fleabane
Pluchea symphytifolia

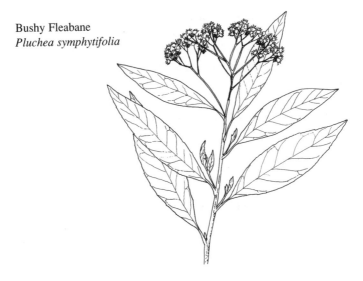

CONVOLVULACEAE — MORNING GLORY FAMILY

The Convolvulaceae is a worldwide family of about 50 genera and 2,000 species; about ten genera are represented in Florida. It is best known in Florida for the large number of attractively flowered, herbaceous morning glories that are found across the state. Only one genus of Florida's native Convolvulaceae is commonly considered to contain woody species, and even some of these are questionable. Of the five *Jacquemontia* species in Florida (there are about 70 additional species found throughout the tropics), only three are considered woody or semiwoody, all of which are vines. The common and widespread *J. tamnifolia* (L.) Griseb., a twining annual with distinctive pale blue flowers that appear summer through fall, is not included here because it is neither woody nor perennial. The other genus included below contains one native and one nonnative species; only the nonnative species is regularly considered woody.

Though not described below, two other species bear mention. The first is the large-blossomed moon flower (*Ipomoea alba* L.), a south Florida species that occurs in coastal hammocks. It has entire leaves and large, white, morning-glory-like flowers which are up to 15 cm long and have a yellow center. Moon flower is native to the state and difficult to misidentify.

The second species is the trailing morning glory (*Turbina corymbosa* [L.] Raf.). This high-climbing or trailing, herbaceous, perennial vine has alternate, simple, entire, ovate leaves that are heart shaped at their bases. The flowers are bell-shaped, tubular and in general appearance look like those of other morning glories but are white with green bands. *T. corymbosa* was used by the Aztecs as a narcotic in religious practices, as well as a medicine and magical ingredient in ointments.

Pineland Jacquemontia or Jacquemontia   Page 93
Jacquemontia curtissii Peter ex Hallier f.

Form: Semiwoody, prostrate, reclining, or erect vine; to about 1 m long.
Leaves: Alternate, simple, elliptic, entire, 1 - 2 cm long, reflexed upward from the midrib, soft green in color; apices of at least some leaves sharply pointed.
Flowers: White or blushed with purplish pink, with five petals, 2 - 3 cm across the open corolla; appearing spring, summer and fall; calyx at least 4 mm long.
Fruit: Capsule, 5 - 6 mm long.
Distinguishing Marks: Similar to *J. havanensis*, pictured in photo 77, distinguished from it by having larger flowers; also very similar to *J. reclinata*, distinguished by the calyx being at least 4 mm long.
Distribution: Pine rocklands; endemic to southern Florida, not found in the Keys.

Jacquemontia havanensis (Jacq.) Urb.   **Photo 77**

Form: Twining vine; stems with woody bases and herbaceous tips and often covered with dense starlike pubescence.
Leaves: Alternate, simple, entire, linear to elliptic or ovate, 5 - 15 mm long; apices often with a tiny point.

Pineland Jaquemontia or Jaquemontia
Jacquemontia curtissii

Wood Rose
Merremia tuberosa

Flowers: White, with five petals, to about 1 cm across the open corolla; appearing from September to May.

Fruit: An erect, somewhat rounded capsule, 4 - 6 mm long.

Distinguishing Marks: Similar to *J. curtissii* and *J. reclinata*, distinguished from both by having smaller flowers.

Distribution: Margins of hammocks and coastal strand vegetation; Florida Keys, primarily Key Largo and Bahia Honda.

Jacquemontia   Photo 78

Jacquemontia pentantha (Jacq.) G. Don

Form: A pubescent, twining and trailing vine to about 1 m long; with herbaceous stems and woody rootstock.

Leaves: Alternate, simple, ovate to lanceolate, 3 - 5 cm long; apices pointed; bases rounded to heart shaped.

Flowers: Showy, light blue, to about 2 cm long; appearing in the fall; usually closing by midafternoon.

Fruit: A capsule.

Distinguishing Marks: The blue flowers and trailing habit help set this species apart.

Distribution: Roadsides, hammocks; southernmost Florida and the Keys.

Landscape Use: A common garden plant in southern Florida; dense, fast growing, delicate, especially suited for trellises; prefers a well-drained site in full sun.

Jacquemontia reclinata House

Form: Prostrate, reclining, or ascending vine with densely hairy stems to at least 2 m long.

Leaves: Alternate, simple, entire, elliptic to ovate, 2 - 3 cm long; apices rounded or notched.

Flowers: White, with five petals, 2 - 3 cm across the open corolla; appearing fall to spring; calyx less than 4 mm long.

Fruit: A rounded capsule to about 5 mm long.

Distinguishing Marks: Similar to *J. havanensis*, pictured in photo 77, distinguished from it by having larger flowers; also very similar to *J. curtissii* (pictured on p. 93), but distinguished by the calyx segments being less than 4 mm long.

Distribution: Coastal dunes; southernmost southeastern Florida.

Comment: Listed as endangered by the Florida Department of Agriculture; also proposed for endangered classification by the U. S. Fish and Wildlife Service.

Wood Rose   Page 93

Merremia tuberosa (L.) Rendle

Form: Woody, semiwoody, or herbaceous, twining vine.

Leaves: Alternate, simple, to about 15 cm long with five to seven lobes, each lobe lance shaped and tapering to a pinched point.

Flowers: Yellow, tubular with flaring petals (like a morning glory), 3 - 4 cm long, about 5 cm wide across the open petals, borne in few-flowered clusters; appearing spring through fall.

Fruit: A woody, roselike capsule, 3 - 4 cm wide.

Distinguishing Marks: The yellow, morning glory-like flowers and simple, five- to seven-lobed leaves are diagnostic.

Distribution: Native to tropical America; naturalized in disturbed sites and hammocks in southern Florida.

Landscape Use: This plant is listed as a Category II pest plant by the Florida Exotic Pest Plant Council. It is extremely invasive, especially in Dade County, and is not recommended for cultivation. This weedy nature notwithstanding, it is often propagated by seed or cuttings, is available from many nurseries, and is used often as a screening plant.

Comment: The fruit of this species is often used in dried arrangements. The miniature wood rose or Alamo vine (*M. dissecta* [Jacq.] Hallier f.), a native member of the genus found throughout the state, is a twining, chiefly herbaceous vine. The latter species also has deeply lobed leaves, but the lobes are distinctively dissected (hence the scientific name); the flowers, which are like a morning glory, are white with a reddish to maroon center. The *Merremia* genus includes about 80 tropical species. Members of the genus are often confused with the several species of morning glories of the genus *Ipomoea*. The two genera can be distinguished from each other by examining the pollen grains with a 20x hand lens. Those of *Merremia* are smooth; those of *Ipomoea* spiny.

CORNACEAE — DOGWOOD FAMILY

The Cornaceae include about 5 genera and less than 100 species worldwide; most members of the family are trees or shrubs. Florida's shrubby dogwoods encompass three species, all from the genus *Cornus*. Although all of these species are showy when in flower or fruit, their typically out-of-the-way habitats make them much less widely known than the flowering dogwood (*C. florida* L.)—which is not described here—one of the state's most attractive and extensively planted native trees. The other member of the genus found in Florida is the alternate-leaved or pagoda dogwood (*C. alternifolia* L. f.), an uncommon tree of the central Panhandle that is listed as threatened by the Florida Department of Agriculture. All members of the genus *Cornus* exhibit strands of mucilage within their veins that are easily visible when the leaf is slowly pulled apart lengthwise. This is often referred to as the "*Cornus* test."

Swamp Dogwood, Silky Dogwood, Silky-Cornel   Photo 79
Cornus amomum Mill. subsp. *amomum*

Form: Spreading, deciduous shrub with several erect or leaning stems; to about 5 m tall; main stem olive green to reddish brown or red; new branches reddish and densely silvery or rusty pubescent.

Leaves: Opposite, simple, entire, ovate to oblong, 3 - 10 cm long, 2 - 8 cm wide; both leaf surfaces soft green, with shaggy gray or brown pubescence.

Flowers: White, small, borne in showy, branched clusters near the ends of branches; appearing in spring.

Fruit: Pale blue drupe with cream-colored spots, 5 - 10 mm in diameter.

Distinguishing Marks: The opposite leaves, multi-branched habit, showy flower clusters, and relatively large, spotted fruit help distinguish this species; leaves are wider overall than either *C. foemina* or *C. asperifolia*, but otherwise similar.

Distribution: Edges of streams, marshes, and swamps; westernmost Panhandle, eastward to about Jackson and Gadsden Counties.

Landscape Use: A beautiful shrubby dogwood for low, moist sites.

Rough Leaf Cornel Page 96
Cornus asperifolia Michx.

Form: Deciduous shrub, sometimes a small tree to about 5 m tall, with hairy twigs.

Leaves: Opposite, simple, entire, elliptic to lanceolate, 2 - 8 cm long, 1 - 4 cm wide, both surfaces pubescent, the upper surfaces of some leaves bearing stiff hairs that are conspicuously rough to the touch.

Flowers: Small, whitish, five petaled, borne in the spring in conspicuous, flat-topped clusters.

Fruit: A light blue drupe to about 8 mm in diameter.

Distinguishing Marks: Similar in general appearance to the stiff cornel (*C. foemina*), differing from it by at least some of the leaves having upper surfaces that are rough to the touch, and by typically occurring in well-drained rather than wetland habitats.

Distribution: Upland mixed woods generally on calcareous soils; throughout the Panhandle southward to the central peninsula.

Landscape Use: Does well in rich soils and is valued for its purple color in fall and for its attractiveness to wildlife; relatively easy to grow and care for.

Rough Leaf Cornel
Cornus asperifolia

Stiff Cornel Dogwood

Cornus foemina Mill.

Form: Deciduous shrub or small tree to 8 m tall.

Leaves: Opposite, simple, lanceolate to elliptic, 2 - 10 cm long, 1 - 4 cm wide, margins entire, but wavy.

Flowers: Small, cream colored, borne in spreading clusters, each cluster 3 - 7 cm wide; appearing in spring and early summer.

Fruit: Globular, blue, 4 - 6 mm in diameter.

Distinguishing Marks: Most similar to rough leaf cornel (*C. asperifolia*) but distinguished from it by having smooth rather than rough leaf surfaces.

Distribution: Wet areas such as riverbanks, marshy shores, and swamp borders; throughout north Florida and southward to at least Collier and Hendry Counties, including Fakahatchee Strand State Preserve.

Stiff Cornel Dogwood
Cornus foemina

CYRILLACEAE — TITI FAMILY

The titi (pronounced tie-tie) family, or Cyrillaceae, includes two shrubby trees of the swamps and bays of northern and central Florida as well as the adjacent states along the southeastern coastal plain. The family contains a total of only three genera and about 14 species world-wide. The two genera that occur in Florida have but one species each, both of which are common components of their wetland habitats. The family was long considered to be closely related to both the Celastraceae and Ericaceae. It is now believed that the family may be most closely related to the Clethraceae. The family is also thought to be quite old. Pollen grains from members of the family have been preserved in the fossil record at least as far back as the Upper Cretaceous period, or about 70 million years ago.

Black Titi   Photo 80

Cliftonia monophylla (Lam.) Britt. ex Sarg.

Form: Medium-sized evergreen tree to about 8 m tall, with dark, sometimes blackish bark.
Leaves: Alternate, simple, entire, 2.5 - 10 cm long, normally sessile, rarely with short peti-oles; mature leaves dark green, young leaves on fruiting branches pale, bluish green.
Flowers: White, fragrant, appearing in early spring and borne in conspicuous, upright clus-ters.
Fruit: Four winged, golden amber in color, borne in conspicuous clusters.
Distinguishing Marks: Most easily recognized by its winged, buckwheat-type fruit, the darkened remains of which can be found on most specimens year-round; distinguished from swamp titi (*Cyrilla racemiflora*), with which it is frequently found, by the veins on the lower surfaces of leaves not at all conspicuous.
Distribution: Bay swamps and edges of pine flatwoods; throughout the Panhandle eastward to about Jefferson County (an outlier population is also known from northeast Florida).
Landscape Use: Good, easy to grow, hardy shrub for low, moist, acidic sites where early spring flowers are desired; attractive to bees and butterflies.

Swamp Cyrilla or Titi   Page 99

Cyrilla racemiflora L.

Form: Small, often twisted, thicket-forming shrub or small tree to about 8 m tall, tardily deciduous and appearing evergreen.
Leaves: Alternate, simple, entire, quite variable in size from 1 - 10 cm long, 0.5 - 2.5 cm wide, individual plants having leaves predominately tending toward one of these extremes or the other.
Flowers: Appearing in late spring and early summer, borne in elongated, cylindrical clusters; trees with longer leaves also have longer flower clusters.
Fruit: A small, inconspicuous, dry drupe.
Distinguishing Marks: Most easily recognized by flowers in long clusters and by the remains of these clusters being present on the tree nearly year-round; distinguished from

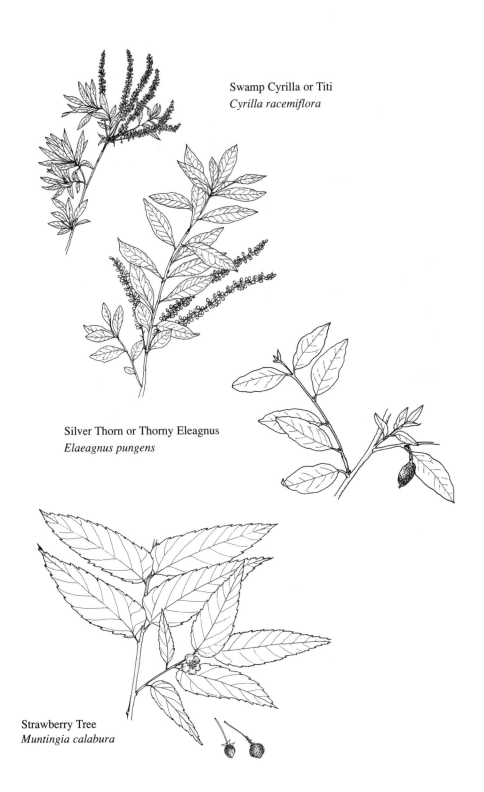

Swamp Cyrilla or Titi
Cyrilla racemiflora

Silver Thorn or Thorny Eleagnus
Elaeagnus pungens

Strawberry Tree
Muntingia calabura

black titi (*Cliftonia monophylla*) by the veins on the lower surfaces of leaves being at least somewhat visible rather than not at all conspicuous.

Distribution: Swamps and wetlands; throughout north Florida and south to about Highlands County; more common in the northern part of its range.

Landscape Use: Grows best in wet soils, even in standing water; easy to grow and attractive to bees; should be more often used in naturalistic landscapes. Titi does not tolerate competition and should be planted so as not to be overcome by more aggressive shrubs or trees.

Comment: The two leaf sizes in this species once led taxonomists to regard the little-leaved form as *C. parvifolia* Raf., or little-leaved cyrilla. Today the two forms are considered to be geographic variations of the same species. The two forms are easily distinguished in the field.

EBENACEAE — EBONY FAMILY

The ebony family is best known for *Diospyros ebenum* Koenig, an Asian tree that is by far the family's most notable species. The hard, black, highly acclaimed heartwood of this important tree is well known for its use in manufacturing piano keys. The common persimmon (described below) is Florida's only member of the family.

Common Persimmon

Photo 81

Diospyros virginiana L.

Form: The common persimmon is actually a medium-sized deciduous tree to about 20 m tall; however, the low-growing young specimens that are common in sandy pinelands (especially where frequently burned) sometimes look like shrubs and can be confusing to some observers.

Leaves: Alternate, simple, entire, ovate to elliptic with rounded bases and acuminate tips, 7 - 15 cm long, 3 - 8 cm wide; lower surfaces of leaves with a whitish cast.

Flowers: Male flowers tubular, borne in clusters; female flowers white to greenish yellow, to about 2 cm long; appearing April and May.

Fruit: Orange (when ripe), round, 4 - 5 cm in diameter.

Distinguishing Marks: Distinguished from other low shrubs by elliptic leaves with whitish lower surfaces.

Distribution: Wide ranging in a variety of habitats and communities throughout the state, except the Keys.

Landscape Use: Though this plant is included here, its chief value in landscape design is as a fruit tree. Its fruit is attractive to wildlife.

Comment: The persimmon has several uses. Its fruit has been fashioned into delectable puddings and jellies and its wood is particularly tough and has been used in the fabrication of golf club heads and kitchen utensils. The fruit is not edible until fully ripe. The genus name, *Diospyros*, means "fruit of the gods."

ELAEOCARPACEAE — FALSE OLIVE FAMILY

This is a family of about 400 species primarily of the tropics and subtropics. It is represented in Florida's shrub flora by a single cultivated and now naturalized species.

Strawberry Tree   Page 99
Muntingia calabura L.

Form: Typically a small, evergreen tree to about 6 m tall in its native locations outside the U. S.; often a large woody shrub in southern Florida.

Leaves: Alternate, simple, lanceolate, 5 - 14 cm long, to about 5 cm wide; margins irregularly toothed; upper surfaces smooth and green, lower grayish white and covered with star-shaped clusters of hairs (requires magnification); bases typically asymmetrical on either side of the midvein.

Flowers: White, with five petals, borne in clusters of one to three, with many stamens.

Fruit: A reddish berry, 1 - 1.5 cm in diameter.

Distinguishing Marks: The lanceolate, irregularly toothed leaves in conjunction with the spreading flowers with five white petals, and the rounded berry distinguish this species from most others.

Distribution: Hammocks and pinelands; native to parts of South America as well as Cuba; planted and naturalized in southern Florida.

Landscape Use: Cultivated for its large size, bright white flowers, and edible, sweet-tasting fruit.

ELAEAGNACEAE — OLEASTER FAMILY

The oleaster family is best known for a relatively few ornamental species, but also includes about 40 additional species worldwide. Only a few species occur naturally in North America. Florida's two members of the family belong to the genus *Elaeagnus* and are both native to Asia; both are also commonly used as landscape plants but are only sparingly naturalized.

Silverthorn or Thorny Elaeagnus   Page 99
Elaeagnus pungens Thunb.

Form: Thorny, evergreen, tangled shrub with long, limber shoots; to about 6 m tall if not pruned; branches sometimes appearing vinelike.

Leaves: Alternate, simple, elliptic to oval, 3 - 10 cm long, 2 - 5 cm wide; margins mostly entire to slightly undulate; lower surfaces of mature leaves copiously covered with silvery scales that impart a distinctive sheen.

Flowers: Tiny, brown, about 1 cm long, borne in clusters in the leaf axils, appearing in fall and early winter.

Fruit: Oblong, drupelike, changing from green to pinkish brown and covered with fine dots, to about 1.5 cm long, borne on a short stalk, 5 - 8 mm long.

Distinguishing Marks: The silvery scales on mature leaves and long, pliant branches distinguish this species from most other species; the evergreen leaves and thorns in the leaf axils of young branches distinguish it from the closely similar *E. umbellata*.
Distribution: Naturalized in scattered locations.
Landscape Use: Widely used as an attractive, evergreen, garden shrub throughout the state; particularly tolerant of sandy soil, full sun, and salt; tends to be weedy if not monitored.

Autumn Olive
Elaeagnus umbellata Thunb.

Form: Deciduous, much-branched shrub to about 3 m tall.
Leaves: Alternate, simple, elliptic to oval, 1 - 8 cm long, 1 - 3 cm wide; lower surfaces copiously covered with silvery scales.
Flowers: Yellow, fragrant, about 1 cm long, borne in clusters at the leaf axils; appearing primarily in spring.
Fruit: Drupelike, red, 5 - 8 mm long, borne on stalks to about 1 cm long.
Distinguishing Marks: The metallic-silvery scales on the undersurfaces of leaves help distinguish this species from most plants; the deciduous habit and lack of thorns distinguishes it from *E. pungens*.
Distribution: Naturalized in scattered locations.
Landscape Use: Planted for wildlife food and cover, also as an ornamental shrub; tolerant of a wide variety of soil conditions.

EMPETRACEAE — CROWBERRY FAMILY
The crowberry family is a small collection of less than five species typically ranging in the temperate regions of the world. It is represented in Florida by a single, quite unique and interesting species.

Rosemary

Photo 82

Ceratiola ericoides Michx.

Form: Bushy, evergreen shrub with numerous erect branches arising from near the base; typical form is distinctly rounded.
Leaves: Opposite but often appearing whorled, simple, strongly revolute so as to appear needlelike, dark green, 8 - 12 mm long, about 1 mm wide.
Flowers: Very small, stalkless, brownish to yellowish, unisexual, male and female flowers borne in the leaf axils on separate plants; appearing in spring, summer, and fall.
Fruit: Small greenish-yellow drupe, 2 - 3 mm in diameter.
Distinguishing Marks: This plant's opposite, dark green leaves in four rows, greenish-yellow fruit, rounded form, and chiefly coastal or deep sand habitat set it apart.
Distribution: Mature coastal dunes, old inland dunes or sandy hills, scrub; throughout northern Florida and southward to the south-central peninsula, then more sparingly to the southernmost peninsula.

ERICACEAE — HEATH FAMILY

The Ericaceae constitute a large and widely distributed family of about 80 genera and 2000 species worldwide. About 35 genera occur in North America, at least 10 of which are found in Florida. The family includes a wide variety of trees, shrubs, and vines, but is probably best known for its enchanting assortment of showy rhododendrons as well as its several varieties of delectable blueberries. The family is closely related to the Clethraceae, Cyrillaceae, and Empetraceae, all of which are classed in the order Ericales, and all of which are represented among Florida's native shrubs. Members of the family are known for their preference for acidic habitats.

Some members of the heath family can be difficult to distinguish in the field, particularly for the beginning plant enthusiast. Several of the blueberries (*Vaccinium* spp.) and dangleberries (*Gaylussacia* spp.) are sometimes confused, as well as several members of the genera *Lyonia* and *Leucothoe*. Attention to detail is important when learning to identify the members of this family.

Agarista or Fetter-Bush

Agarista populifolia (Lam.) Judd

Photo 83

Form: Relatively tall evergreen shrub with arching to leaning branches; to about 4 m tall; often somewhat arborescent; with a chambered pith.

Leaves: Alternate, simple, bright green, lanceolate to ovate, 2.5 - 10 cm long, 1 - 4 cm wide; margins entire or sometimes serrate; apices long tapering.

Flowers: White, narrowly urn-shaped, 7 - 8 mm long, appearing in late spring and borne in many-flowered clusters at the leaf axils; plant very showy when in bloom.

Fruit: A rounded capsule, 4 - 5 mm long, 5 - 6 mm wide.

Distinguishing Marks: Taken together, the arching stature, arborescent habit, and white, urn-shaped flowers help distinguish this species; the very similar members of the genus *Leucothoe* may be distinguished by having a solid, rather than chambered, pith.

Distribution: Moist woodlands, lower slopes of rich ravines, near springs and spring runs; north-central peninsula.

Landscape Use: This is an outstanding ornamental shrub that is widely sold by native plant nurseries. It does particularly well in moist, acid soils, especially in shaded sites and along streams. Agarista's dark green, drooping foliage adds as much to the garden as its flowers.

Tar-Flower or Fly-Catcher

Befaria racemosa Vent.

Photo 84

Form: Slender, sparsely branched, evergreen shrub with hairy twigs and stiff, erect branches; to about 2.5 m tall.

Leaves: Alternate, simple, entire, elliptic to ovate, 2 - 4 cm long, 0.5 - 2 cm wide; typically held erect and often twisted along the branch so that the whitish-green to pinkish lower surfaces are more visible than the upper.

Flowers: Sticky, bright white, often tinged with pink, sometimes entirely pink toward the ends, fragrant, very distinctive, with conspicuous stamens and seven narrow petals, each petal 2 - 3 cm long; borne on stalks 1 - 3 cm long; quite conspicuous from late spring into midsummer.

Fruit: Rounded, sticky capsule, 6 - 8 mm in diameter.

Distinguishing Marks: The erect leaves with whitish-green to pinkish lower surfaces and distinctive flowers are diagnostic.

Distribution: Moist to wet flatwoods and sand scrub; from about the Suwannee River eastward and southward to the southern peninsula, formerly to Dade County where it is now extirpated.

Comment: This plant takes its name from its flowers and fruit which are sticky to the touch; often traps insects, hence one of its common names.

Spotted Wintergreen or Pipsissewa   Photo 85
Chimaphila maculata (L.) Pursh.

Form: A low, evergreen, single-branched subshrub typically not exceeding about 2 dm tall.

Leaves: Alternate, simple, narrowly to broadly lanceolate, leathery, 2 - 6 cm long, 0.6 - 2.3 cm wide; margins serrate to sharply dentate; upper surface green suffused with white along the central vein and major lateral veins (hence one of the common names).

Flowers: White, fragrant, nodding, borne in loosely branched, few-flowered, terminal clusters; very distinctive; appearing in late spring and early summer.

Fruit: An erect capsule.

Distinguishing Marks: The thick green leaves with whitish mid- and lateral veins, and distinctive flower set this species apart.

Distribution: Rich pine or hardwood woodlands.

Comment: This plant is not well-known in Florida and has been reported in only a few locations. It is common farther north, particularly in rich mountain woodlands and pine hardwood forests of northern Georgia and North Carolina. The plant has long been used as a medicinal herb in the Appalachians and was once an official drug. North Florida plant enthusiasts would do well to be on the lookout for this species and to report it to the curator of one of the state's several university herbaria if found.

Trailing-Arbutus   Photo 86
Epigaea repens L.

Form: A trailing, evergreen, prostrate subshrub with slender, underground stems; leaves barely rising above the leaf litter.

Leaves: Alternate, simple, entire, elliptic to oblong, 2 - 9 cm long, 1.5 - 6 cm wide; bases rounded to heart shaped; margins and surfaces with relatively long, rusty hairs; petioles 2 - 5 cm long, visibly covered with long, rust-colored hairs.

Flowers: White to pinkish, tubular at the base, opening into five spreading petals, borne in the leaf axils; appearing in spring.

Dwarf Huckleberry
Gaylussacia dumosa

Fruit: A small, rounded capsule copiously covered with rust-colored hairs.

Distinguishing Marks: The low stature, rusty, hairy leaf stems, leaf surfaces, and fruits set this species apart from most species in its rather limited range and habitat. It often grows in close proximity to *Smilax pumila*, with which it could be confused. The leaf margins of *Epigaea* are more undulate than the latter species, the lower surfaces of the leaves are not so densely pubescent, and the leaf bases are not quite so heart shaped.

Distribution: Wooded slopes and ravines; from about Liberty County westward in the Panhandle; this plant reaches the southern limits of its range in northern Florida.

Comment: Listed as endangered by the Florida Department of Agriculture.

Dwarf Huckleberry

Page 105

Gaylussacia dumosa (Andr.) A. Gray

Form: Tardily deciduous shrub, 1 - 5 dm tall.

Leaves: Alternate, simple, entire, oblanceolate to elliptic, larger leaves 2 - 3 cm long, to about 2 cm wide; margins and lower surfaces of leaves usually pubescent, lower surfaces also with amber dots.

Flowers: White to pinkish, bell shaped, 6 - 9 mm long; appearing mid- to late spring and borne in several-flowered clusters, each cluster to about 4 cm long.

Fruit: A shiny black drupe covered with short hairs, 6 - 8 mm in diameter.

Distinguishing Marks: The larger leaves with amber dots on the lower surfaces help distinguish this species from *Vaccinium darrowii* and *V. myrsinites*, the two blueberries of similar stature; similar in many respects to *G. mosieri*, but distinguished by being generally shorter in stature, by having short, curly hairs on the flower tube, rather than longish, spreading ones, and by having comparatively short, gland-tipped hairs on the newer branchlets rather than long, gland-tipped hairs.

Distribution: Dry pinelands and pine–oak woods; throughout northern Florida, southward nearly to the southern peninsula.

Landscape Use: The three species of *Gaylussacia* described here are probably more deserving of landscape use than their present use suggests; though they are all deciduous, they flower profusely in spring and can provide a nice accent to a shrub garden.

Mosier's Huckleberry   Photo 88
Gaylussacia mosieri (Small) Small

Form: Deciduous shrub, 0.3 - 1.5 m tall.

Leaves: Alternate, simple, entire, elliptic to oblanceolate, 3 - 6 cm long.

Flowers: Bell shaped, similar to those of *G. dumosa*, except with long, straight hairs rather than short, curly ones; appearing in spring.

Fruit: A hairy (hairs longer and more conspicuous than those of *G. dumosa*), black drupe, 8 - 10 mm in diameter.

Distinguishing Marks: Similar in many respects to the description of *G. dumosa*, generally distinguished from it by the larger growth form; the present species also has long hairs on the flower tube, rather than short, curly ones as in the former species, and comparatively long, gland-tipped hairs on newer branchlets rather than short, gland-tipped hairs.

Distribution: Generally found in seasonally wet areas such as bogs, wet savannas, bays, and moist flatwoods, sometimes in the scrub; restricted in Florida to the Panhandle.

Landscape Use: See comment above for *G. dumosa*.

Dangleberry
Gaylussacia nana (A. Gray) Small

Form: Small, deciduous to tardily deciduous shrub to about 6 dm tall, often shorter; with relatively short, often upright branches that give the plant a somewhat narrow, compact appearance.

Leaves: Alternate, simple, entire, oval to elliptic, leathery, to about 4 cm long; veins on both surfaces distinct; lower surfaces with raised veins, moderately to strongly glaucous, only sparsely hairy, and covered with tiny resinous glands (the latter two characters require 10x magnification to see clearly).

Flowers: Greenish white, slenderly bell shaped, 2 - 3 mm long, borne in small, loosely branched clusters; appearing in spring.

Fruit: A glaucous blue drupe, 6 - 7 mm in diameter.

Distinguishing Marks: The upright branching, conspicuously grayish-white (glaucous) undersurfaces of the leaves, and glaucous blue fruit help in identifying this species in its habitat; distinguished from *G. tomentosa* by lower surfaces of leaves being strongly glaucous rather than densely tomentose.

Distribution: Moist to well-drained woods and pinelands; throughout the Panhandle, southward to the central peninsula.

Landscape Use: See comment above for *G. dumosa*.

Comment: Some authorities, for example Godfrey (1988) and Clewell (1985), treat this species and *G. tomentosa* as varieties of *Gaylussacia frondosa* (L.) T. & G., to wit, *G. frondosa* var. *nana* A. Gray and *G. frondosa* var. *tomentosa* A. Gray (though Godfrey questions the validity of this treatment). Other authorities, for example Duncan and Brittain (1966) and Wunderlin (1982), treat them as separate species. In addition, Duncan and Brittain maintain that *G. frondosa* does not occur in Georgia (and presumably, therefore, not in Florida). Given Duncan and Brittain's assessment, and the fact that the two are quite distinguishable in the field, they are treated as distinct species here.

Dangleberry

Photo 87

Gaylussacia tomentosa (A. Gray) Small

Form: Small, deciduous to tardily deciduous shrub to a little more than 1 m tall with spreading branches; branchlets copiously tomentose (hence the specific name).

Leaves: Alternate, simple, entire, oval to elliptic, to about 6 cm long; lower surfaces with raised veins, dense, brownish hairs, and tiny resinous glands (the latter two characters require 10x magnification to see clearly).

Flowers: Greenish white, slenderly bell-shaped, 2 - 4 mm long, borne in small, loosely branched clusters; appearing in spring.

Fruit: A glaucous blue drupe, 6 - 7 mm in diameter; often appearing to be borne paired, with one of the pair more lightly colored than the other; appearing in spring.

Distinguishing Marks: The spreading branches, conspicuously tomentose lower surfaces of leaves, and glaucous blue fruit help in identifying this species in its habitat; distinguished from *G. nana* by lower surfaces of leaves being tomentose rather than glaucous.

Distribution: Moist to well-drained woods and pinelands; throughout the Panhandle, southward to the central peninsula.

Landscape Use: See comment above for *G. dumosa*.

Comment: See *G. nana*.

Hairy Wicky or Wicky

Photo 89

Kalmia hirsuta Walt.

Form: Low, bushy, evergreen shrub normally not exceeding about 6 dm tall, sometimes to 10 dm.

Leaves: Alternate, simple, elliptic to oval or oblanceolate, very small, 5 - 15 mm long, 2 - 8 mm wide; margins entire and usually bearing small hairs (better seen with magnification); petiole essentially absent.

Flowers: Borne solitary in two- to three-flowered clusters, especially near the ends of branches; showy, cup shaped, pink to white, with ten stamens, each held under tension in one of the tiny, reddish pouches that form a circle on the petals; appearing from spring to early fall.

Fruit: A rounded capsule, 2 - 3 mm in diameter.

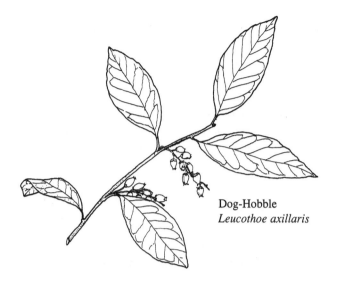

Dog-Hobble
Leucothoe axillaris

Distinguishing Marks: The distinctive flowers distinguish this species from all other low shrubs; without flowers the plant can be easily overlooked or misidentified; differs from mountain laurel, which has similar flowers, by the much smaller leaves and smaller stature. **Distribution:** Flatwoods and the edges of wet areas in pinelands; throughout northernmost Florida and the Panhandle.

Mountain Laurel, Calico-Bush, Mountain Ivy Photo 90
Kalmia latifolia L.

Form: A relatively large, many-stemmed shrub, sometimes a small evergreen tree to about 9 m tall.
Leaves: Very closely alternate, thick, firm, simple, entire, 2 - 10 cm long, 2.5 - 5 cm wide, elliptic to lanceolate.
Flowers: Borne in branched clusters, showy, cup shaped, pink to white; ten stamens, each held under tension in one of the tiny, reddish pouches that form a circle on the petals; appearing in spring.
Fruit: A small, five-lobed capsule containing tiny seeds.
Distinguishing Marks: The flowers distinguish this plant from all others except *K. hirsuta*; distinguished from the latter by having much larger leaves and a larger stature.
Distribution: Along woodland streams, wooded bluffs, and shady woodlands in the northern reaches of the Panhandle from Escambia to Leon counties; one outlier population exists near the Suwannee River; the southern limits of its range in the United States is in northern Florida.
Landscape Use: Mountain laurel is a prized landscape plant but sometimes difficult to grow. It is best left alone after becoming established. It prefers dry soils and is easily over watered. It does well in the shade, but prefers at least a few hours of sun per day. When in bloom, it is a conversation piece that is unsurpassed. A number of horticultural varieties are available.

Fetter-Bush
Leucothoe racemosa

Comment: Listed as threatened by the Florida Department of Agriculture. This plant is considered highly toxic and the leaves are known to be poisonous to livestock and presumably deer. Honey made from the flowers is also said to be toxic. The stamens are "spring loaded". When a bee ventures into the flower, the stamens spring forward, spreading pollen over the insect's back.

Dog-Hobble **Page 108**

Leucothoe axillaris (Lam.) D. Don

Form: Loosely branched, evergreen shrub to about 1.5 m tall.

Leaves: Alternate, simple, leathery, shiny green above, paler below, elliptic to oval, 5 - 14 cm long, 1.5 - 5 cm wide; upper surfaces without pubescence; margins entire to variably serrate; petioles to about 1 cm long.

Flowers: White, often tinged with pink, urn shaped, 6 - 8 mm long, borne in conspicuous racemes at the leaf axils; racemes to 7 cm long and appearing in spring.

Fruit: A dark brown, rounded capsule, lighter colored at the sutures; about 5 mm in diameter.

Distinguishing Marks: The short racemes of urn-shaped flowers and dark green, evergreen leaves help distinguish this species; similar to several other members of the family, including species of *Agarista* (see entry above) and *Lyonia*; most readily distinguished from *Leucothoe racemosa* by the current species' leathery, evergreen leaves that lack pubescence on the upper surfaces.

Distribution: Wet woods, swamps, floodplain woods; occurs chiefly in the Panhandle but also reported as uncommon in Marion County.

Landscape Use: This plant is an excellent species to use in naturally wet areas, such as along streams. Its shiny, evergreen leaves are borne on arching branches and are attractive year-round, and its flowers are typically borne in profusion, making the plant quite showy during its March blooming season.

Fetter-Bush   **Page 109**
Leucothoe racemosa (L.) Gray

Form: Tardily deciduous shrub to about 4 m tall.

Leaves: Alternate, simple, elliptic to oval, 1 - 5 cm long, 0.5 - 3 cm wide; both surfaces usually at least somewhat pubescent, even at maturity; margins obscurely crenate to serrate.

Flowers: White, tinged with pink, cylindrical, about 8 mm long, borne in racemes 2 - 10 cm long; appearing in April and May.

Fruit: A dark brown, rounded capsule with lighter colored sutures; 4 - 5 mm in diameter.

Distinguishing Marks: Similar to several other members of the heath family; distinguished from *L. axillaris* by having deciduous, membranous leaves with at least some pubescence on their upper surfaces.

Distribution: Swamps, bogs, wet depressions, wettest portions of pine flatwoods; throughout the Panhandle, eastward to the north-central peninsula; also reported from Volusia County.

Landscape Use: This species, like *L. axillaris*, does well in wet areas and has showy flower clusters; its deciduous nature makes its less suitable for year-round use.

Stagger-Bush or Poor-Grub
Lyonia fruticosa

Stagger Bush or Rusty Lyonia

Photo 91

Lyonia ferruginea (Walt.) Nutt.

Form: Typically an evergreen shrub with several crooked trunks; sometimes to about 9 m tall and taking on treelike proportions.

Leaves: Mature leaves alternate, simple, 1 - 9 cm long, 0.5 - 3 cm wide, dark green above, paler and lightly pubescent below, margins entire, sometimes wavy and often revolute; lower surfaces of young leaves copiously covered with rust-colored scales of two sizes and pubescence.

Flowers: White and urn shaped, appearing in spring, typical of many genera of the Ericaceae; borne on wood of the previous season.

Fruit: A five-angled, pubescent capsule, 3 - 6 mm long, borne on a relatively long stalk.

Distinguishing Marks: Distinguished from *L. fruticosa* by having most leaves with revolute margins (although these two species are quite similar in south Florida and this distinction is less diagnostic), by the flowers being borne on twigs of the previous season, and by the lower surfaces of leaves of rusty lyonia bearing scales of two sizes (requires magnification) rather than a single, uniform size as in *L. fruticosa*.

Distribution: Wet pine flatwoods as well as dry sand pine–scrub oak woods from about Bay County southward to the northern edges of Lake Okeechobee in the central peninsula, much farther south along the coasts.

Landscape Use: Serves well massed or as individual plants; the fruit is a good wildlife food.

Maleberry or He-Huckleberry
Lyonia ligustrina var. *foliosiflora*

Stagger-Bush or Poor-Grub

Page 110

Lyonia fruticosa (Michx.) G. S. Torr. in Robbins.

Form: An evergreen shrub with erect, rigid branches; usually not exceeding about 2 m tall, but potentially taller.

Leaves: Alternate, simple, entire, oval to elliptic, 0.5 - 5 cm long, 0.3 - 2.8 cm wide; surfaces of young leaves covered with rust-colored scales, scales on lower surface of a single, uniform size (requires magnification); margins generally flat, only rarely revolute; lower surface of mature leaves usually grayish and easily spotted at some distance due to their ascending growth pattern, especially those along the lower portions of the main stem.

Flowers: White, nearly rounded, 2.5 - 5 mm long, arising during spring and early summer on long stalks in clusters in the axils of new leaves; borne on new wood rather than on wood of the previous season as in *L. ferruginea*.

Fruit: A cylindric, five-angled capsule, to about 5 mm long.

Distinguishing Marks: Distinguished from most other members of the heath family by having rusty scales on the leaves; from the very similar *L. ferruginea* by flowers being borne on twigs of the current season, by scales on lower surfaces of leaves being of a single, uniform size, by the leaf margins only rarely being revolute, and by the terminal leaves typically being smaller than the stem leaves.

Distribution: Wet pine flatwoods, bogs, wet depressions in flatwoods; from about Liberty and Franklin Counties eastward and southward to the southernmost peninsula.

Landscape Use: Landscape use is similar to *L. ferruginea*, above.

Stagger-bush
Lyonia mariana

Maleberry or He-Huckleberry

Page 111

Lyonia ligustrina (L.) DC. var. *foliosiflora* (Michx.) Fern.

Form: Deciduous shrub to about 4 m tall.

Leaves: Alternate, simple, lanceolate to elliptic or oval (but quite variable in shape and size), 2 - 9.5 cm long, 1 - 5 cm wide; apices with a tiny tooth; lower surfaces and petioles copiously pubescent; margins minutely serrate (best seen with magnification).

Flowers: Small, rounded, less than 5 mm in diameter, white, sometimes tinged with pink, borne in clusters at the leaf axils; appearing in spring.

Fruit: A rounded capsule, 2.5 - 3 mm long.

Distinguishing Marks: The clusters of small, rounded flowers and deciduous, pubescent leaves help distinguish this plant.

Distribution: Wet pinelands, streamside thickets, swamps, bogs, and bays; throughout northern Florida, southward to the south-central peninsula.

Fetterbush, Stagger-Bush, Hurrah-Bush, Shiny Lyonia

Lyonia lucida (Lam.) K. Koch **Photo 92**

Form: An evergreen shrub to about 4 m tall; generally much shorter than this; often only a few dm tall.

Leaves: Alternate, leathery, simple, dark shiny green, mostly broadly elliptic (but sometimes narrowly so), 2 - 8 cm long, 1 - 4 cm wide; margins entire but closely paralleled by a distinctive and conspicuous vein.

Flowers: Varying from pale to deep pinkish or almost red, cylindric, borne in clusters at the leaf axils, quite showy during the plant's spring flowering period.

Fruit: A rounded to urn-shaped capsule, to about 5 mm long.

Distinguishing Marks: The distinctive vein that parallels the leaf margin and reddish to deep pink flowers are diagnostic for this plant in its habitat.

Sourwood
Oxydendrum arboreum

Distribution: Bogs, bays, swamp borders, wet pine flatwoods, scrub; throughout northern Florida southward to the southernmost peninsula.

Landscape Use: Distributed by native plant nurseries; a particularly good species for wet, acidic areas due its evergreen foliage and showy flowers; tolerant of a wide range of soil conditions.

Stagger-Bush
Page 112

Lyonia mariana (L.) D. Don.

Form: Low, colonial, tardily deciduous shrub; potentially to about 2 m tall but often much shorter.

Leaves: Alternate, simple, entire, elliptic to oblong, 4 - 10 cm long, 1.5 - 4.5 cm wide.

Flowers: White to pinkish, cylindric, 7 - 14 mm long; tips of petals curving outward; borne in distinctive, nodding, many-flowered clusters from the leaf axils; appearing in spring.

Fruit: A somewhat rounded to urn-shaped capsule, 5 - 7 mm long.

Distinguishing Marks: The nodding clusters of comparatively large (for *Lyonia*), cylindric flowers help distinguish this species.

Distribution: Flatwoods, edges of pineland depressions and bogs, well-drained mixed woodlands; throughout northern Florida, southward to the central peninsula.

Sourwood
Page 113

Oxydendrum arboreum (L.) DC.

Form: At maturity a slender, medium-sized deciduous tree to 18 m tall; often flowering and fruiting when of shrubby stature, particularly in dry, sandy areas.

Leaves: Alternate, simple, elliptic, 12.5 - 18 cm long, 2.5 - 7.5 cm wide, margins finely serrate, upper surfaces medium dark green, lower surfaces much paler, blades turning orange or scarlet-red in the fall and becoming quite obvious; apices often curved to one side.

Flowers: White, urn shaped, borne in long, narrow racemes that extend beyond the leaves at the tip of the branches and appear from May to July; each inflorescence is actually a collection of several racemes extending spraylike from a single axis.

Fruit: Borne in small capsules.

Distinguishing Marks: Distinguished from most other shrubs by the long, elliptic, finely serrate leaves with slightly curved apices.

Distribution: Bluffs, ravines, well-drained hills; found chiefly in the northern half of the Panhandle from about Escambia to Jefferson Counties.

Landscape Use: Sourwood flowers (often profusely) in summer when little else is blooming, making it an excellent choice for extending the flowering season; its brilliantly colored fall leaves are also a favored attraction in autumn. Plant sourwood in good sun for best performance. Bear in mind that this plant becomes a tree.

Comment: This is the plant from which comes the famous sourwood honey of the southern Appalachian Mountains. Its common name derives from the sour taste of its leaves.

Climbing Heath, Climbing Pieris, Vine Wicky

Photo 93

Pieris phillyreifolius (Hook.) Small

Form: Weakly erect, nonparasitic, evergreen shrub or, more commonly, extending upward by sending leafless stems just under the bark of cypress (*Taxodium* spp.), Atlantic white cedar (*Chamaecyparis thyoides* [L.] B.S.P.), or particularly old titi (*Cyrilla racemiflora*) trees.

Leaves: Alternate, simple, stiff and leathery, dark green above, elliptic to long elliptic, 1.5 - 7 cm long, 0.5 - 2 cm wide; margins entire to sparingly toothed and conspicuously revolute.

Flowers: Urn shaped, white, similar to those of many members of the heath family, borne in clusters in the leaf axils, often toward the ends of branches; appearing in early spring.

Fruit: A five-parted capsule.

Distinguishing Marks: The revolute leaves and climbing nature of this plant distinguish it.

Distribution: Cypress depressions and the wet edges of pinelands and moist woodlands; throughout north Florida, southward to about Lake and Marion Counties.

Landscape Use: Pieris can be trained to grow as a low shrub in moist soils and provides an attractive and interesting addition to a native plant garden or landscape.

Comment: The specimens growing under the bark of the Atlantic white cedars in the Morman Branch Scenic area of the Ocala National Forest are particularly noteworthy and provide excellent examples of the climbing nature of this species; many are evident and pro-truding through the bark to several meters above the ground. Similar places occur near the edges of cypress ponds in north Florida and the Panhandle, where the supporting trees also include pond cypress (*Taxodium ascendens* Brongn.). In a few places in the Florida Big Bend, particularly in the Bradwell Bay Wilderness Area in the Apalachicola National Forest, climbing heath is found growing under the bark of especially old titi trees (*Cyrilla race-mosa*). In other places it has been found climbing under the bark of longleaf pine (*Pinus palustris* Mill), slash pine (*P. elliottii* Englem), and even near the base of the trunk of sand live oak (*Quercus geminata*).

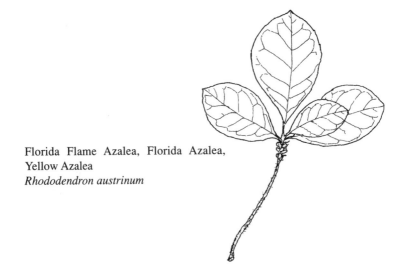

Florida Flame Azalea, Florida Azalea, Yellow Azalea
Rhododendron austrinum

115

Alabama Azalea

Photo 94

Rhododendron alabamense Rehd.

Form: Deciduous shrub to about 4 m tall.

Leaves: Alternate, simple, entire, elliptic to oblanceolate, 2.5 - 7.5 cm long, 1 - 3.5 cm wide, exhibiting a distinctive odor when crushed; margins and usually midveins bearing short hairs; petioles 2 - 6 mm long; apices sometimes with a tiny point.

Flowers: White, usually with a yellow spot on one petal, tubular, flaring into five spreading petals, 2.5 - 4 cm long, mildly scented, stamens and pistil extending well beyond the flower tube; appearing in spring.

Fruit: A cylindric capsule, 1.5 - 2 cm long.

Distinguishing Marks: Flowers and leaves similar to *R. canescens* but flowers white with a yellow spot rather than pink; distinguished from all other native species of *Rhododendron* by combination of deciduous leaves, white flowers with a yellow blotch, and flowers appearing before or with new leaf growth.

Distribution: Rare in Florida, occurring naturally perhaps only in Leon County.

Landscape Use: A frequently sold landscape plant, particularly in the western Panhandle; requires sandy soil, light shade, regular watering, and semiannual fertilization. Native plants in Alabama are known to hybridize regularly, resulting in a range of flower colors. No species of *Rhododendron* should be removed from the wild.

Comment: Listed as endangered by the Florida Department of Agriculture.

Florida Flame Azalea, Florida Azalea, Yellow Azalea

Page 115, Photo 95

Rhododendron austrinum (Small) Rehd.

Form: Loosely-branched, deciduous shrub with red-brown twigs; 3 - 6 m tall.

Leaves: Alternate, simple, elliptic to obovate, 3 - 11 cm long, 1.5 - 4.5 cm wide, apices with a tiny point; margins minutely dentate; petioles to about 1.5 cm long; both surfaces conspicuously pubescent, the lower copiously so.

Flowers: Orange to yellow, or red orange, fragrant, tubular, 2.5 - 4.5 cm long, stamens and pistil extending well beyond the flower tube; appearing in spring just before or with new leaf growth.

Fruit: A cylindric capsule to about 2.5 cm long.

Distinguishing Marks: The bright orange to yellow flowers set this species apart in Florida.

Distribution: Sandy, acid soils of bluffs and slopes, and in rich woods along small streams; Panhandle from about Leon County westward.

Landscape Use: This is one of Florida's showiest and easiest to grow native azaleas and is an often-used landscape plant, despite its deciduous nature. Its sweet-scented flowers are excellent for adding the first touch of color to the coming spring. No species of *Rhododendron* should be removed from the wild.

Comment: Listed as endangered by the Florida Department of Agriculture.

Pinxter Bloom, Pinxter Azalea, Hoary Azalea, Piedmont Azalea, Bush Honeysuckle, Wild Azalea

Photo 96

Rhododendron canescens (Michx.) Sweet

Form: An erect, branching, deciduous shrub with yellow-brown twigs; to about 5 m tall.

Leaves: Alternate, simple, entire, elliptic to oblanceolate, 2 - 10 cm long; apices with a tiny tooth; margins with short hairs; petioles 2 - 10 mm long.

Flowers: Pink to sometimes white, markedly sweet-scented (hence the common name bush honeysuckle), tubular, 2.5 - 4.5 cm long, spreading into five narrow petals; stamens and pistil extending well beyond the flower tube; appearing in early spring prior to or with new leaf growth.

Fruit: A cylindric, curving capsule, 1 - 3.5 cm long.

Distinguishing Marks: This is the most common of Florida's (and the southeastern United State's) native azaleas; it is most similar to *R. alabamense* but differs from it by having flowers that are generally more pinkish in color and that lack the latter's characteristic yellow spot.

Distribution: Flatwoods, borders of bays and shrub bogs, wet woods, near wooded streams; throughout northern Florida, southward to the north-central peninsula.

Landscape Use: An easily grown, early blooming wild azalea that naturalizes well in moist settings. No species of *Rhododendron* should be removed from the wild.

Comment: Listed as commercially exploited by the Florida Department of Agriculture.

Chapman's Rhododendron

Photo 97

Rhododendron minus Michx. var. *chapmanii* (A. Gray) Duncan & Pullen

Form: An evergreen, rather inconspicuous shrub to about 3 m tall.

Leaves: Alternate, simple, entire, thick, leathery, dark green above, elliptic, to about 10 cm long; lower surfaces conspicuously dotted with rust-colored scales, upper surfaces bearing small, dark spots.

Flowers: Pink, tubular, spreading into five, frilly petals, 1.5 - 3.5 cm long, 3 - 4 cm across; borne in showy clusters, appearing in spring prior to new growth.

Fruit: A cylindric capsule, 0.5 - 1.5 cm long.

Distinguishing Marks: The evergreen habit, frilly, pink to rose-pink flowers, and rust-colored scales on the lower surfaces of leaves distinguish this species from all other native rhododendrons.

Distribution: Flatwoods, edges of bays; central Panhandle and northeast Florida.

Landscape Use: An attractive, evergreen landscape plant with showy flowers. No species of *Rhododendron* should be removed from the wild.

Comment: Listed as endangered by the Florida Department of Agriculture and the U. S. Fish and Wildlife Service.

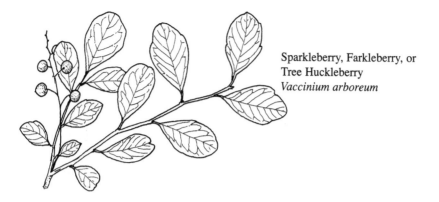

Sparkleberry, Farkleberry, or
Tree Huckleberry
Vaccinium arboreum

Swamp or Clammy Azalea

Photo 98

Rhododendron viscosum (L.) Torrey

Form: Stiff, openly branched, deciduous shrub, 3 - 5 m tall.

Leaves: Alternate, simple, entire, oblong to oblanceolate, 1 - 9 cm long, 1 - 3 cm wide; margins with hairs that curve under the leaf blade; apices with a tiny tooth.

Flowers: White to pink tinted, very fragrant, thinly tubular, spreading into five narrow petals, 1.5 - 2.5 cm long, borne in four- to nine-flowered clusters, typically characterized by a dense covering of cottony pubescence; appearing in summer well after new leaf growth.

Fruit: A lanceolate, densely hairy capsule, 1 - 2 cm long.

Distinguishing Marks: The white, honeysucklelike flowers that appear in summer rather than spring distinguish this species from other wild azaleas; the Japanese honeysuckle (*Lonicera japonica*), which has superficially similar flowers, is a vine.

Distribution: Swamps, wet woodlands, and wet flatwoods; throughout northern Florida, southward to the central peninsula.

Landscape Use: The summer flowering period makes this a good landscape plant and allows the careful gardener to have sweet-scented wild azalea flowers in at least two seasons of the year. No species of *Rhododendron* should be removed from the wild.

Comment: Listed as threatened by the Florida Department of Agriculture.

Sparkleberry, Farkleberry, or Tree Huckleberry

Vaccinium arboreum Marsh.

Page 118, Photo 99

Form: Shrub or small tree, potentially to about 9 m tall, often much shorter and flowering when of relatively low stature; deciduous, but often seemingly evergreen, outer bark scaling and flaking, inner bark smooth and reddish brown, trunk often crooked and leaning.

Leaves: Alternate, simple, oval to broadly elliptic, somewhat stiff, margins entire (but sometimes with tiny serrations), commonly 1.5 - 4 cm long (sometimes to about 7 cm), 0.8 - 3 (sometimes 4) cm wide, apices tipped with an abrupt, short, very small point.

Flowers: Small, white, cup shaped, borne on long stalks; appearing profusely in spring.

Fruit: Typical of other blueberries in shape, green at first, turning black, 5 - 8 mm in diameter, adorned at the apex with the tiny, five-pointed, star-shaped remains of the sepals.

Distinguishing Marks: Most easily recognized in its preferred habitat by its reddish-brown bark, by its leaves with minutely pointed apices and tiny marginal glands, and by the distinctive apices of its berries.

Distribution: Dry woodlands, hammocks, and clearings; throughout north Florida, southward to about Lee County; one population is also known from Fakahatchee Strand State Preserve.

Landscape Use: A very good and easy to care for landscape plant, especially as a border or background. The white flowers appear in April and May and are often borne in dense, showy clusters; the shiny black berries are both beautiful and highly attractive to native birds.

Highbush Blueberry   Photo 100
Vaccinium corymbosum L.

Form: A deciduous, branching shrub (rarely arborescent) to about 5 m tall.

Leaves: Alternate, elliptic to lanceolate or ovate, entire to serrate, to about 8 cm long, 5 cm wide, very variable in size and shape.

Flowers: White, sometimes suffused with pink, cylindrical and similar in shape to those of sparkleberry (*V. arboreum*), borne in clusters; appearing in spring.

Fruit: A dull (sometimes shiny) blue or black berry, 4 - 12 mm in diameter; typically open at the distal end and rimmed with persistent sepals.

Distinguishing Marks: In general, the several species of highbush blueberries are quite variable, not well defined taxonomically, and are often difficult to distinguish from each other; the present species may be distinguished from the deer berry (*V. stamineum*) by lacking the latter's open, bell-shaped flowers with exserted stamens, from the sparkleberry (*V. arboreum*) by lacking the latter's reddish, scaling, and flaking bark, and from the mayberry (*V. elliottii*) by having overall larger leaves and lacking the latter's green woody stems.

Distribution: Swamps, bogs, pinelands, upland woods; throughout northern Florida southward to Collier County.

Landscape Use: This plant is valued for its spring flowers and its shiny black fruit, which are sought after by birds. As with many of the heaths, it seems to do best in acidic soils.

Comment: The highbush blueberries constitute a complex and not easily differentiated group of plants that are not clearly understood. *V. corymbosum* is a highly variable plant that most often expresses itself as a shrub. In the understory of some of northern Florida's woodlands, however, it sometimes grows to proportions that some might call a small tree. As described here, the species *V. corymbosum* encompasses a rather large number of scientific synonyms. In his extensive investigation of this complex, Vander Kloet (1980) lists more than a dozen species that are included within what he considers to be a single, highly variable highbush blueberry classification. Those familiar with Godfrey's (1988) work on north Florida trees and shrubs will note that he tentatively accepts Vander Kloet's work but excludes *V. elliottii*, which he maintains is easily identifiable in the field. With this one exception, Vander Kloet is also accepted for the purposes of this volume, and the latter species is described below. Lyrene (1995) also argues in favor of treating *V. elliottii* as a distinct

119

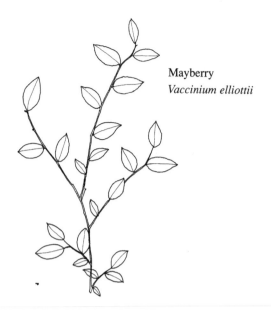

Mayberry
Vaccinium elliottii

species, but also suggests treating *V. ashei* Reade. as a distinct species as well. While his arguments for his taxonomic conclusions are convincing and may eventually be accepted, distinguishing the latter as a species is beyond the scope of the current volume; hence, the latter is not described.

Glaucous Blueberry

Vaccinium darrowii Camp.

Form: Low, evergreen shrub to about 6 dm tall.

Leaves: Alternate, simple, small, elliptic, 5 - 15 mm long, to about 1 cm wide; lower surfaces often markedly glaucous and without pubescence; margins entire or with appressed teeth, sometimes revolute.

Flowers: White to pink, cylindrical and urn shaped, typically 6 - 8 mm long; appearing early to midspring.

Fruit: A glaucous blue berry, 4 - 6 mm in diameter.

Distinguishing Marks: Very similar to *V. myrsinites* (pictured in photo 102) with which it is often found; distinguished by the conspicuously glaucous leaves, fruit, and receptacle, and by lacking the stalked glands prevalent on the undersurfaces of the latter's leaves.

Distribution: Scrubs, pinelands, sandhills, flatwoods; throughout northern Florida, southward to the southernmost peninsula.

Mayberry

Page 120, Photo 101

Vaccinium elliottii Chapman

Form: Bushy, deciduous shrub to about 4 m tall; with green stems.

Leaves: Alternate, simple, shiny green above, elliptic to oval, 1 - 3 cm long, to about 1 cm wide, or a little wider; margins with small teeth.

Flowers: White to pinkish, cylindrical and urn shaped, 5 - 7 mm long, appearing in spring and borne in clusters of 2 - 6.

Fruit: A shiny, black berry, 5 - 10 mm in diameter.

Distinguishing Marks: Most easily distinguished from *V. corymbosum*, the other highbush blueberry, by the tiny serrations on the leaf margins, the green woody stems, and the larger leaves generally not exceeding about 3 cm in length.

Distribution: Both upland and bottomland woods; throughout northern Florida, southward at least to the central peninsula.

Landscape Use: An excellent large native shrub. See also *V. corymbosum*.

Comment: See *V. corymbosum*.

Evergreen Blueberry or Shiny Blueberry

Photo 102

Vaccinium myrsinites Lam.

Form: Low, evergreen shrub to about 6 dm tall; in many respects similar to *V. darrowii*.

Leaves: Alternate, simple, elliptic, 5 - 15 mm long, to 1 cm wide; margins entire but sometimes revolute and with small, appressed teeth; lower surface typically bearing stalked, red glands (requires magnification to see clearly).

Flowers: White to pink, cylindrical and urn-shaped, 6 - 8 mm long; appearing in spring.

Fruit: A black berry, 5 - 8 mm in diameter.

Distinguishing Marks: Very similar to *V. darrowii*, with which it is often found; distinguished from it by the stalked glands on the lower surfaces of leaves, and by the fruit and receptacle not being glaucous.

Distribution: Sandy pinelands, scrub, flatwoods, sandhills; throughout northern Florida, southward to the southernmost peninsula.

Deer Berry

Photo 103

Vaccinium stamineum L.

Form: A deciduous shrub to about 5 m tall; sometimes taking on treelike proportions.

Leaves: Alternate, elliptic to obovate, simple, entire, 2 - 8 cm long, 1 - 3 cm wide, whitish below and often increasing in size toward the tips of the branches, margins with spreading hairs and appearing ciliate.

Flowers: Small, white, cuplike, with a mass of yellowish stamens that extend beyond the petals; appearing in spring.

Fruit: Variously colored from whitish to blue-, reddish-, or purplish-black, 5 - 16 mm in diameter, typical of other blueberries.

Distinguishing Marks: Distinguished from sparkleberry (*V. arboreum*) by stamens extending far beyond the lip of the corolla; most easily recognized by leaves increasing in size toward the tip of the branches and whitish lower surfaces of leaves.

Distribution: Pine woods, mixed uplands, longleaf pine–scrub oak woodlands throughout northern Florida, southward to Martin County.

Landscape Use: Deer berry is a good hedge or background plant but is also attractive as a free-standing shrub.

Comment: The deer berry probably takes its common name from its attractiveness to the white-tailed deer, which browse on the plant's leaves and twigs as well as its fruits.

Dwarf Blueberry
Vaccinium tenellum Ait.

Form: Low, erect, deciduous shrub to about 4 dm tall; often spreading by underground runners.

Leaves: Alternate, simple, obovate to oblanceolate or oblong, pubescent, to about 3.5 cm long; margins with tiny teeth and hairs which may require magnification to see clearly.

Flowers: White to pinkish, cylindrical, 5 - 8 mm long; appearing in spring with the new leaves.

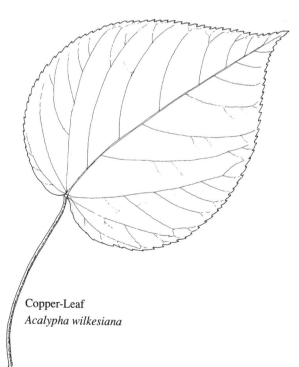

Copper-Leaf
Acalypha wilkesiana

Fruit: A black berry, 5 - 8 mm in diameter.

Distinguishing Marks: Separated from the other two low-growing blueberries (*V. darrowii* and *V. myrsinites*) by being deciduous rather than evergreen.

Distribution: Sandy pinelands and dry woodland borders; uncommon in Florida, known only from northeastern Florida, primarily Clay County.

EUPHORBIACEAE — SPURGE FAMILY

The Euphorbiaceae, or spurge family, is one of the world's largest and most diverse families of flowering plants. Like many primarily tropical families, the spurge family is best known to temperate plant lovers for its wide variety of herbaceous species. However, it also includes a number of woody shrubs and trees among its more than 300 genera and nearly 7000 species. An extensive variety of spurge species occur in Florida, some of which might be considered shrubby by at least some observers but are not described below. The several members of the genus *Chamaesyce*, in particular, sometimes take on shrubby characteristics. However, most, if not all, of these species are herbaceous annuals rather than woody perennials. North Florida's tung tree (*Aleurites fordii* Hemsl.), an exotic species which sometimes flowers and fruits when of quite low stature, might also be considered a shrub by some observers. It is easily distinguished by its large, broadly heart-shaped leaves, showy clusters of reddish- to pinkish-tinged flowers, and large, rounded fruits that hang on long stalks. This latter species is quite weedy and is listed as a Category II pest plant by the Florida Exotic Pest Plant Council.

The spurge family takes its common name from the characteristic way in which a number of species distribute their seeds. The fruit of all members of the family is a distinctive three-lobed capsule. As the capsules dry and reach maturity they rupture, sometimes with a discernible popping sound, and hurl the enclosed seeds up to several yards.

Several characteristics help in recognizing members of the spurge family. These include the three-locular fruit, stipules at the leaf bases, the presence of milky latex in some genera, and, in many species, the distinctive spikelike inflorescence.

Copper-Leaf   Page 122

Acalypha wilkesiana Muell.-Arg.

Form: A large, sprawling, evergreen shrub to about 5 m tall.

Leaves: Alternate, large, simple, heart shaped, coarsely dentate, to about 2 dm long; surfaces often mottled in shades of red, purple, green, and yellow; apices tapered to a point.

Flowers: Reddish, individually inconspicuous, appearing in fall and borne in catkins in the leaf axils; catkins to about 20 cm long.

Distinguishing Marks: The large, mottled, variously colored leaves of copper-leaf are like those of no other Florida plant.

Distribution: Frequently cultivated and rarely escaped in the southern peninsula, chiefly in disturbed sites; native to the Pacific Islands.

Landscape Use: Easy to grow but sensitive to cold; full sun insures the best leaf color, which is the most interesting and attractive part of the plant.

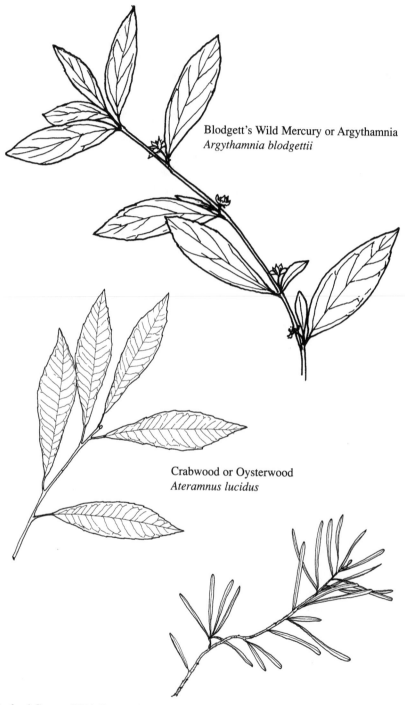

Blodgett's Wild Mercury or Argythamnia
Argythamnia blodgettii

Crabwood or Oysterwood
Ateramnus lucidus

Pineland Croton, Wild Croton, Granny-Bush
Croton linearis

Blodgett's Wild Mercury or Argythamnia

Page 124

Argythamnia blodgettii (Torr.) Chapman

Form: Erect, sparsely branched, evergreen shrub to about 6 dm tall, but usually shorter.
Leaves: Alternate, simple, entire, pubescent, elliptic to ovate or spatulate, 2 - 5 cm long, often with a grayish cast.
Flowers: Small, white, to about 6 mm wide, with five petals.
Fruit: A three-locular capsule, 4 - 5 mm in diameter and characteristic of the spurge family.
Distinguishing Marks: The three-locular fruit marks this species as a member of the Euphorbiaceae.
Distribution: Endemic to south Florida and the Keys; rocky pinelands in Dade County, edges of hammocks and low, moist areas in the Keys.
Comment: Listed as endangered by the Florida Department of Agriculture and as a candidate for federal listing.

Crabwood or Oysterwood

Page 124

Ateramnus lucidus (Sw.) Rothm.

Form: Evergreen shrub or, more typically, a small tree to about 10 m tall.
Leaves: Alternate, simple, widest above the middle, leathery, dark green, 5 - 10 cm long, 1 - 4 cm wide, margins wavy and irregularly blunt toothed toward the apices, each tooth exhibiting a tiny, toothlike gland that is eventually shed; leaf base shouldered and extending minutely beyond the point of attachment with the petiole (auriculate).
Flowers: Appearing in summer but remaining on the tree until the following spring, male flowers borne in yellow-green spikes up to 5 cm long, female flowers solitary on a long stalk.
Fruit: A rounded, multilocular capsule typical of the spurge family, to about 12 mm in diameter.
Distinguishing Marks: Easily distinguished from other south Florida hammock species by leaf base as described above.
Distribution: Hammocks of the extreme southern peninsula and the Keys.
Comment: Also seen listed as *Gymnanthes lucida* Sw.

Pineland Croton, Wild Croton, Granny-Bush

Croton linearis Jacq.

Page 124, Photo 104

Form: A bushy-branched, narrow-leaved, clump-forming, evergreen shrub to about 2 m tall.
Leaves: Alternate, simple, linear, dark green above, yellowish below, to about 8 cm long.
Flowers: Whitish, borne in racemes 4 - 10 cm long; appearing year-round; male and female flowers borne on separate plants.
Fruit: A rounded, yellowish, pubescent, three-locular capsule.
Distinguishing Marks: The linear leaves and typical spurge fruit distinguish this plant within its limited range.

Milkbark or Whitewood
Drypetes diversifolia

Guiana Plum
Drypetes lateriflora

Distribution: Pinelands and coastal areas; southernmost Florida and the lower Keys.

Beach Tea or Silver-Leaf Croton
Croton punctatus Jacq.

Form: Low, erect, branching, perennial herb with a woody base (branches also appearing woody at even a close distance); to about 1.2 m tall.

Leaves: Alternate, simple, entire but often undulate, elliptic, 1 - 6 cm long; lower surfaces (and most other parts of the plant) densely pubescent with clusters of star-shaped hairs, each cluster with a conspicuous red dot in the center (hence the name *punctatus*).

Flowers: Borne singly or in clusters of three at the leaf axils; appearing May to September in the more northern counties, year-round farther south.

Fruit: A green, three-locular, three-seeded capsule characteristic of the spurge family.

Distinguishing Marks: No other beach shrub has pale green leaves with tiny red spots on the lower surfaces of the leaves.

Distribution: Dunes and beaches; sandy portions of the Gulf and Atlantic Coasts, southward to the southern peninsula.

Milkbark or Whitewood   Page 126
Drypetes diversifolia Krug & Urban

Form: Evergreen shrub or small tree to 12 m tall with milk-white bark that is often partially covered with lichens.

Leaves: Alternate, simple, very stiff to the touch, dark green, elliptic to oval, 8 - 13 cm long, 2.5 - 5 cm wide (those of the crown smaller overall than those farther down the trunk), margins of mature leaves entire, margins of leaves on very young plants with sharp teeth (almost hollylike).

Flowers: Small, white, appearing in spring and borne in tight clusters at the leaf axils.

Fruit: An ivory-white, ovoid drupe, 1 - 2.5 cm in diameter.

Distinguishing Marks: This plant is distinguished from other hammock species by its splotchy white bark and stiff, two-ranked leaves.

Distribution: Fairly common in hammocks of the Keys, absent from the mainland.

Guiana Plum   Page 126
Drypetes lateriflora (Sw.) Krug & Urban

Form: Evergreen shrub or small tree to about 10 m tall with smooth, light brown bark.

Leaves: Alternate, simple, entire, leathery, shiny dark green, 8 - 10 cm long, lanceolate, tapering abruptly to a blunt point.

Flowers: White, small, borne in tight clusters in the leaf axils from spring throughout the summer.

Fruit: A round, bright red, fuzzy drupe, about 5 mm in diameter, appearing in early summer.

Distinguishing Marks: Leaves somewhat similar in appearance to lancewood (*Ocotea coriacea*) of the Lauraceae but distinguished from it by lacking the distinctive fragrance that often emanates from the latter's crushed leaves.

Distribution: Uncommon in hammocks of southern Florida, northward to about Brevard County, less common in the Keys.

Manchineel or Poison Guava   Photo 105
Hippomane mancinella L.

Form: Generally found only as a deciduous shrub today, but known to reach a height of 15 m where it has been left undisturbed; known for its poisonous, bright white sap which can produce burnlike skin sores if handled.

Leaves: Alternate, simple, minutely and finely serrate, ovate, shiny, light green, 5 - 10 cm long, with long petioles; petiole with a small gland on the upper surface at the point of attachment with the blade.

Flowers: Individual flowers small and inconspicuous, greenish, borne in terminal spikes characteristic of many members of the family.

Fruit: Rounded, applelike, 2 - 4 cm in diameter, yellowish-green when mature, sometimes tinted with pink on one side, extremely poisonous if ingested.

Distinguishing Marks: The alternate, light green, finely serrate leaves with relatively long petioles set this species apart from all other hammock species; potentially confused with the strangler fig (*Ficus aurea* Nutt.), but with finely toothed, rather than entire, margins.

Distribution: A plant of the seacoast, found naturally in brackish swamps just inside the mangrove zone of southern Florida and the Keys.

Comment: The manchineel is listed as threatened by the Florida Department of Agriculture and is now a rare plant in the wild. It was once widespread and common in the coastal zone. Its bright white sap, which is extremely toxic to the touch, formerly made it the target of human-engineered destruction that reduced its population dramatically. Even a tiny drop of the juicy fluid produces an intense burning sensation in some people and can result in blisterlike sores akin to those resulting from chemical burns. The foliage is also potentially toxic, and ingesting the reportedly pleasant-tasting fruit can cause intense gastric upset. Some even assert that eating the fruit can be lethal. One such account reported by Little and Wadsworth (1964) holds that in the late 1800s, 54 German seaman who landed near Curacao ate the fruit of this tree, resulting in the death of five and severe sickness in others. Although such claims have not always been clearly substantiated, the tree has been the target of much abuse throughout the tropics, including south Florida, and is now only sparsely scattered in the Keys as well as near Flamingo in Everglades National Park. Examples can be seen on Elliott Key, at John Pennekamp Coral Reef State Park and other locations on Key Largo, at Bahia Honda State Recreation Area, at several locations in Key Deer National Wildlife Refuge on Big Pine Key, and at Fairchild Tropical Garden. It is wise to refrain from handling specimens of this plant.

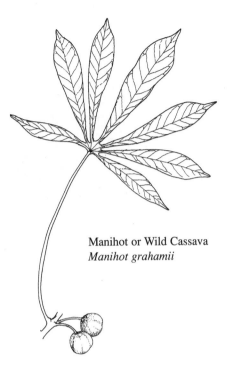

Manihot or Wild Cassava
Manihot grahamii

Manihot or Wild Cassava

Page 129

Manihot grahamii Hook.

Form: Deciduous, monoecious, thicket-forming shrub to about 7 m tall.

Leaves: Alternate, deeply palmately incised into 5 to 11 long, narrow lobes that all originate near the point of the blade's attachment to the petiole, so deeply incised that the lobes take on the superficial appearance of leaflets; lobes 8 - 15 cm in length, the centermost lobes flared toward the apices then narrowing abruptly to a sharp point; petioles to about 20 cm in length.

Flowers: Yellowish green, attractive, appearing in late spring and early summer and borne in conspicuous spreading clusters.

Fruit: A rounded, three-sided capsule characteristic of the spurge family, about 1.5 cm in diameter.

Distinguishing Marks: The large, palmately lobed leaves make this plant unlikely to be confused with any other shrubs in northern Florida.

Distribution: Occasionally cultivated, infrequently escaped; central Panhandle, Tallahassee area, Polk County, perhaps other places.

Landscape Use: This plant is an often-used ornamental. It is not native, but easy to care for. It does best in protected sunny areas and is especially good for drier sites.

Comment: Manihot is native to South America. It was first known in the United States from the New Orleans area, into which it was presumably accidentally imported as part of a ship's cargo. It has now spread, primarily due to cultivation.

Castor Bean or Castor Oil Plant
Ricinus communis

Castor Bean or Castor Oil Plant   Page 130

Ricinus communis L.

Form: A many-branched, bushy, evergreen shrub potentially to about 5 m tall.

Leaves: Alternate, simple, coarse, to about 40 cm wide and divided into 7 - 9 deeply-cut lobes, the lobes coarsely serrate; petiole long and attached near the center of the lower surface.

Flowers: Male and female flowers separate but borne on the same plant in conspicuous, upright spikes; male flowers yellow, female pink to pinkish red; appearing nearly year-round.

Fruit: A red, green, or bluish, spiny, burrlike capsule, 1 - 2 cm in diameter, splitting open at maturity to expose white to tan, attractive, but very poisonous, seeds which can be fatal if ingested.

Distinguishing Marks: The coarse, deeply lobed, star-shaped leaves are diagnostic; perhaps confused with papaya (*Carica papaya* L.), which is not described here, but lacking the latter's large, green to orange fruit.

Distribution: Naturalized along roadsides and in pinelands throughout Florida, more common from the central peninsula southward; native to Africa.

Landscape Use: Widely cultivated as a foundation or background plant, or massed in corners.

Maiden Bush or Bahama Maiden Bush
Savia bahamensis

Corkwood
Stillingia aquatica

Maiden Bush or Bahama Maiden Bush
Page 131

Savia bahamensis Britt.

Form: Low evergreen shrub with erect branches, or rarely a small tree to about 4 m tall.

Leaves: Alternate, simple, entire, ovate, leathery, shiny green with a light-colored central vein, 2 - 5 cm long, 1.5 - 4 cm wide, apices rounded or notched.

Flowers: Small, greenish white, appearing March through June, male flowers borne in dense clusters in the leaf axils, female flowers solitary.

Fruit: A round, three-locular capsule, to about 7 mm in diameter.

Distinguishing Marks: Most easily recognized by combination of upright branches, ovate leaves, and the conspicuous pair of brown stipules at each leaf base; the latter character in conjunction with all leaves being alternate easily separates this species from both blolly (*Guapira discolor*) and black torch (*Erithalis fruticosa*).

Distribution: Generally restricted to coastal thickets of the lower Keys.

Sebastian-Bush
Photo 106

Sebastiania fruticosa (Bartr.) Fern.

Form: A sparsely branched evergreen to tardily deciduous shrub; 1 - 3 m tall.

Leaves: Alternate, simple, entire, elliptic to lanceolate, often long tapered toward the apices, 2 - 7 cm long, 1 - 3 cm wide, widely spaced along the stem; petiole to about 1 cm long.

Flowers: Appearing from midspring to early summer and borne in a cylindrical spike to about 4 cm long; individual flowers small, green to yellowish green, without petals.

Fruit: A rounded, green, three-locular capsule, 4 - 8 mm long; conspicuous.

Distinguishing Marks: Most easily distinguished when in fruit by the distinctive, spurgelike capsule.

Distribution: Slopes, bluffs, mixed calcareous woods, floodplain woods; throughout northern Florida, southward to about Levy and Citrus Counties.

Corkwood
Page 131, Photo 107

Stillingia aquatica Chapman

Form: Single-stemmed, tardily deciduous shrub to about 1.5 m tall; branches essentially herbaceous, reddish, borne primarily near the top of the plant.

Leaves: Alternate, simple, narrowly lanceolate, 3 - 8 cm long, well separated on the lower stem, closely set on the branches, especially near the ends; petioles short, less than 5 mm long; margins with minute teeth.

Flowers: A greenish, yellowish, or reddish, cylindrical spike; conspicuous and borne at the ends of the branches; appearing late spring and early summer.

Fruit: A rounded, three-locular capsule, to about 1 cm in diameter.

Distinguishing Marks: The combination of narrowly lanceolate and minutely serrate leaves borne most abundantly near the ends of the branches, spikelike inflorescence, typically wet-

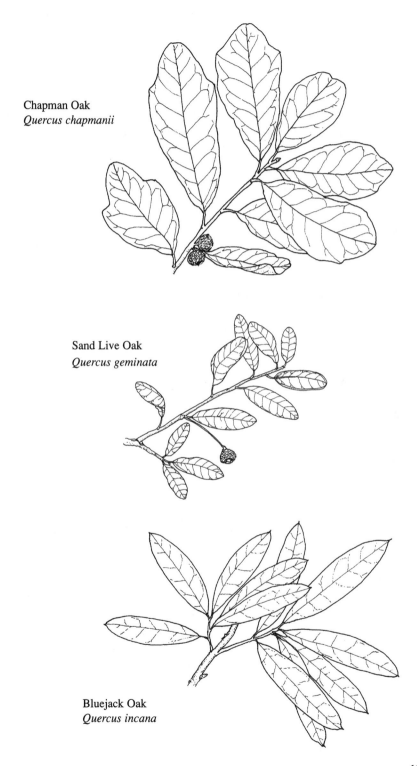

Chapman Oak
Quercus chapmanii

Sand Live Oak
Quercus geminata

Bluejack Oak
Quercus incana

land habitat, and three-locular fruit distinguish this species. This plant is similar in many respects to its close relative, the mostly herbaceous Queen's delight (*Stillingia sylvatica* Garden ex L.). The latter may be distinguished by typically having several herbaceous stems from a central crown rather than a single, upright, woody stem.

Distribution: Generally in shallow waters of flatwoods ponds, open swamps, ditches, grassy ponds; throughout northern Florida, southward to the southernmost peninsula.

Comment: This is one of two shrubs with the common name corkwood. The other species, *Leitneria floridana*, is a threatened member of Florida's flora and is not as easily or commonly found as the current species. Both have exceedingly light wood, hence their common names.

FAGACEAE — OAK FAMILY

The oak family is best known for its large, stately trees. Such species as the live oak (*Quercus virginiana* Mill.), laurel oaks (*Q. hemisphaerica* Bartr. ex. Willd., *Q. laurifolia* Michx.), and southern red oak (*Q. falcata* Michx.) are well known and much revered in many parts of Florida. In addition to the trees, the family also contains several species that commonly remain shrublike or only occasionally reach treelike stature. Like their tree-sized cousins, the shrub-sized members of the family can be distinguished from other shrubs by having acorns for fruit, and by having five-ranked leaves, meaning that the leaves are borne in five rows along the branchlets.

Chinquapin

Photos 108, 109

Castanea pumila (L.) Mill.

Form: Deciduous shrub or small tree to about 20 m tall.

Leaves: Alternate, simple, two ranked, typically elliptic to lance elliptic but variable on a given plant, 4 - 18 cm long, 1 - 8 cm wide, margins dentate with the tip of each tooth being the terminating point for a single lateral vein.

Flowers: Male flowers white, borne in spikes 10 - 18 cm long and arising in spring from the leaf axils.

Fruit: Enclosed in a round, densely spined, sharp-pointed burr, 3 - 4 cm in diameter.

Distinguishing Marks: Most easily recognized by relatively long leaves with dentate margins in conjunction with the small, spiny burr that encloses the fruit.

Distribution: Throughout the Panhandle, eastward to north-central Florida and southward to about Lake County.

Landscape Use: Though not used much for landscaping, this species' attractive foliage, relatively long spikes of white flowers, and interesting fruit make it a good background plant, particularly in sandy areas.

Comment: This is the only shrubby member of Florida's Fagaceae that is not classified in the oak genus. It is closely related to the American chestnut (*C. dentata* [Marshall] Borkh.), but has not succumbed to the same disease that has all but eliminated its more stately cousin.

Chapman Oak

Quercus chapmanii Sarg.

Form: Small, essentially evergreen shrub, sometimes reaching treelike proportions to about 8 m tall.

Leaves: Alternate, simple, elliptic to sometimes obovate or spatulate, 2 - 10 cm long, 1 - 8 cm wide, upper surfaces dark green, shiny, and without pubescence, lower surfaces lightly pubescent, even if only on the veins, margins of at least some leaves entire, margins of others wavy to very shallowly lobed.

Flowers: Male flowers borne in drooping catkins, female flowers very inconspicuous and borne singly or in pairs; both appearing in spring.

Fruit: Acorn 1.5 - 2.5 cm long, borne in a bowl-shaped cup 6 - 8 mm deep and enclosing about half the nut.

Distinguishing Marks: Distinguished from the myrtle and scrub oaks (*Q. myrtifolia* and *Q. inopina*), with which it frequently associates, by each of the latter having the lower surfaces of mature leaves without grayish pubescence and at least some leaves with revolute margins.

Distribution: Coastal and inland sand pine–oak scrub; coastal areas of the Panhandle and throughout the interior peninsula, southward to about Palm Beach County.

Sand Live Oak

Quercus geminata Small

Form: Shrub or small- to medium-sized, semievergreen tree with thick, roughly ridged, and furrowed bark.

Leaves: Alternate, simple, entire, thick, leathery, coarsely veined, 2 - 12 cm long, .5 - 4 cm wide, dark green above, dull gray beneath, margins extremely revolute, making an upside-down leaf take on the appearance of an elongated bowl; petioles densely pubescent.

Fruit: Acorn 1 - 2 cm long, borne in a tapering cup 7 - 10 mm deep.

Distinguishing Marks: Recognized as the only shrub-sized Florida oak with such conspicuously revolute leaves.

Distribution: Deep inland sands, dunes, sand pine–oak scrub, coastal hammocks; throughout northern Florida and southward to Dade and Collier Counties.

Bluejack Oak

Quercus incana Bartr.

Form: Shrub or, more commonly, a small, fast-growing, deciduous tree with dark gray to black, deeply furrowed bark; to about 12 m tall.

Leaves: Alternate, simple, elliptic to lanceolate, entire, 3 - 12 cm long, 1 - 3 cm wide, margins flat as opposed to revolute, upper surfaces bluish or ashy green when mature, lower surfaces silvery tomentose, apices tipped with a short bristle; occasionally a few leaves persist along or near the trunk through the winter and develop a reddish midrib.

Flowers: Male flowers borne in slender, hanging catkins, 5 - 7.5 cm long; appearing in spring.

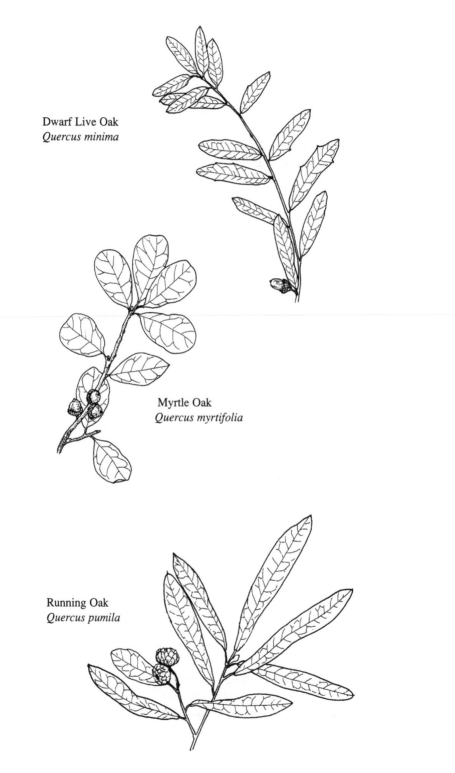

Dwarf Live Oak
Quercus minima

Myrtle Oak
Quercus myrtifolia

Running Oak
Quercus pumila

Fruit: Acorn 1 - 1.5 cm long, rounded, borne in a shallow, reddish-brown cup.

Distinguishing Marks: Most easily distinguished from other shrubby oaks by leaves having ashy-green or bluish upper surfaces and dull-silvery undersurfaces; particularly low specimens of this species might be confused with *Q. pumila*.

Distribution: Sand hills and ridges throughout northern Florida, southward to Lee County.

Scrub Oak

Photo 110

Quercus inopina Ashe

Form: Typically a single-stemmed evergreen shrub not exceeding about 2 m tall, previously reported to reach the stature of a small tree, but seldom found as such today.

Leaves: Alternate, simple, elliptical, 2 - 12 cm long, 1 - 7.5 cm wide, held erect on the branch, margins entire but strongly revolute, lower surfaces with a noticeable, powdery-yellow fuzz.

Flowers: Male flowers borne in hanging catkins, female borne singly or in pairs; appearing April and May, typically later than the quite similar myrtle oak (*Q. myrtifolia*).

Fruit: An acorn, typical of the oak family.

Distinguishing Marks: Very similar to the myrtle oak but distinguished from it by having typically elliptic rather than obovate leaves.

Distribution: Sand pine scrub and scrubby flatwoods in association with sand live oak (*Q. geminata*) and Chapman oak (*Q. chapmanii*); found primarily in a restricted range from southernmost Orange to Highlands Counties; also from a few locations in Hillsborough, Manatee, and Hardee Counties.

Comment: *Q. inopina* was first recognized by W. W. Ashe in 1929. However, it was not included as a distinct species by later authors, including Small (1933) and Wunderlin and Lakela (1980), and was presumably considered to be conspecific with *Q. myrtifolia*. It was again asserted as a distinct species by Ann Johnson and Warren Abrahamson in 1982.

Dwarf Live Oak

Page 136

Quercus minima (Sarg.) Small

Form: A colonial shrub spreading by underground runners; main stem to about 2 m tall, but usually shorter; deciduous at the time of new leaf growth in spring.

Leaves: Alternate, simple, oblong to oblanceolate, stiff, leathery, 3 - 8 cm long, 1 - 4 cm wide; margins entire to irregularly toothed, the latter more commonly toward the tip; lower surface grayish and densely pubescent.

Flowers: Male flowers borne in catkins; appearing in spring.

Fruit: Acorn, 2 - 2.5 cm long.

Distinguishing Marks: The low stature, sandy habitat, and grayish cast to the lower surfaces of leaves, owing to the dense pubescence, is usually enough to distinguish this species from most other shrubby oaks; distinguished from the similar *Q. pumila*, with which it often associates, by having larger acorns with light brown outer surfaces, overwintering leaves, and at least some leaves with sharply tipped lobes.

Distribution: Sandy pinelands and scrub; throughout northern Florida, southward to the southern peninsula.

Comment: Also often seen listed as *Q. virginiana* var. *minima*.

Myrtle Oak

Page 136

Quercus myrtifolia Willd.

Form: Densely vegetated, evergreen shrub or small tree to about 8 m tall.

Leaves: Alternate, simple, variously elliptic, oblong, or oval, 2 - 8 cm long, 1 - 5 cm wide, margins entire or lobed, and revolute, upper surfaces dark green, lower surfaces dull to yellowish green, lower surfaces of at least the mature leaves without pubescence.

Flowers: Male flowers borne in hanging catkins; appearing in spring.

Fruit: Acorn, typical of the oak family.

Distinguishing Marks: Distinguished from Chapman oak (*Q. chapmanii*) by revolute leaf margins and glabrous lower leaf surfaces, from *Q. inopina* by the latter's leaves being generally elliptic rather than obovate and being held erect on the branch.

Distribution: Coastal regions of the Panhandle, eastward to sand scrub regions of the central peninsula, southward to Dade County on the east coast and Collier County on the west coast.

Governor's Plum
Flacourtia indica

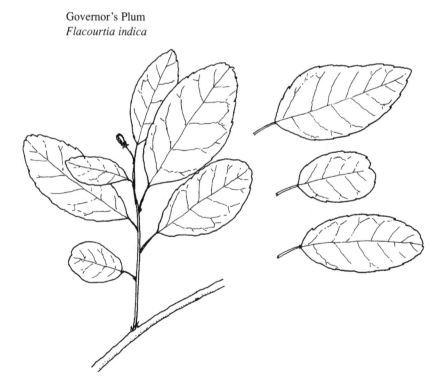

Running Oak

Page 136

Quercus pumila Walt.

Form: A colonial, mostly deciduous shrub (a few leaves overwintering) spreading by underground stems; main stems to about 2 m tall, usually much shorter.
Leaves: Alternate, simple, entire, oblong to narrowly elliptic or spatulate, 3 - 10 cm long, 0.7 - 3 cm wide; lower surface densely covered with grayish pubescence.
Flowers: Male flowers borne in catkins; appearing in spring.
Fruit: Acorn, 8 - 12 mm long.
Distinguishing Marks: Distinguished from similar *Q. minima*, with which it often associates, by having smaller acorns with their exposed outer surfaces mostly black or dark brown, all (or nearly all) leaves unlobed and without sharp-pointed bristles, and by being deciduous in fall, with only a few leaves overwintering; potentially confused with *Q. incana*, which has leaves with bluish-gray, rather than green, upper surfaces.
Distribution: Pine flatwoods and sandy pinelands; throughout north Florida and southward to the southern peninsula.

FLACOURTIACEAE — FLACOURTIA FAMILY

The Flacourtiaceae is a large tropical and neotropical family represented in the New World by a wide-ranging collection of genera. The single woody species found in Florida is a spiny, nonnative shrub of Asian origin.

Governor's Plum

Page 138, Photo 111

Flacourtia indica (Burm. f.) Merrill

Form: Shrub or small tree to about 7 m tall, often with spines in the leaf axils.
Leaves: Alternate, simple, leathery, ovate to elliptic, 5 - 8 cm long; margins crenate-dentate; apices pinched to a point.
Flowers: Yellowish, borne in clusters at the leaf axils, appearing primarily in summer.
Fruit: A purplish, rounded, edible berry, 1 - 2 cm in diameter.
Distinguishing Marks: The spines in the leaf axils in conjunction with the leathery, crenate-dentate leaves set this species apart.
Distribution: Native to Asia; well-established in southern Florida.
Landscape Use: This species has been widely planted in southern Florida for its flowers and edible fruit. It is now listed as a Category II pest plant by the Florida Exotic Pest Plant Council and should no longer be planted.

GOODENIACEAE — GOODENIA FAMILY

The Goodeniaceae include 14 genera of shrubs and herbs, at least half of which are restricted to Australia. Members of the family are noted for being confined almost exclusively to dry areas with open vegetation. The single genus present in the southeastern United States is found only in southern Florida, and only on dunes and arid, near-coastal habitats.

Scaevola, Ink-Berry, Beach-Berry   Photo 112
Scaevola plumieri (L.) Vahl

Form: Many branched, erect to trailing, essentially herbaceous evergreen shrub with drooping branches; to about 1.2 m tall.

Leaves: Alternate but clustered near the tips of the branches, simple, entire, shiny green, thick, fleshy, 2.5 - 7 cm long.

Flowers: White to pinkish white, unique and conspicuous, fan shaped, with 5 - 6 lobes, all of which are only one side; appearing year-round.

Fruit: Smooth, shiny black, juicy drupe, 1 - 2.5 cm long.

Distinguishing Marks: Distinguished from all but half-flower (*S. sericea* Vahl) by the distinctive flower. The latter is a troublesome exotic woody shrub that was introduced from Hawaii and has taken hold on many south Florida dunes, along saline shores, and in coastal hammocks. It is similar in many respects to ink-berry but has leaves that are usually longer than 7.5 cm, white fruit, and a generally more robust habit. *S. sericea* is listed as a Category I pest plant by the Florida Exotic Pest Plant Council and is fast becoming one of south Florida's more common coastal shrubs.

Distribution: Dunes and near coastal areas; tropical and semi-tropical portions of the state, including the Keys.

Landscape Use: Often used in coastal areas as an attractive ground cover and to prevent erosion. The introduced species mentioned above is also used in this way, but should be avoided due to its opportunistic and weedy nature.

GUTTIFERAE (CLUSIACEAE; HYPERICACEAE) — ST. JOHN'S-WORT FAMILY

The Guttiferae are characterized by having secretory cavities and/or canals throughout most of the plant body. Though not obvious to the average observer, it is this characteristic from which the family's Latin name is derived. Worldwide, the family contains about 50 genera and 900 species, mostly restricted to the tropics and sub-tropics. Only the genera *Clusia* and *Hypericum* are found in Florida. The former is represented in the Keys by the autograph tree (*C. rosea*), a stiff-leaved tree (though some observers also consider it a shrub) that is an often-used ornamental and only questionably native. The latter genus includes a number of difficult-to-distinguish species, many of which are woody shrubs.

Average observers generally have little difficulty recognizing that a particular plant is a member of the *Hypericum* genus. Distinguishing between the various species of *Hypericum*,

Hypericum apocynifolium

however, is a much more demanding task. Even though the following descriptions attempt to highlight the most obvious differences between species, making accurate identifications in the field will likely continue to constitute a challenge, especially for very similar species. The first thing to note when examining a St. John's-wort is whether its flowers have four or five petals and sepals, and whether the flowers are borne singly or in many-flowered clusters. The second thing to note is the length of the leaves and whether the leaves are linear and needle-like, or more elliptic, lanceolate, or oblong. Equipped with this basic knowledge and paying particular attention to the measurements in the descriptions below should lead to an accurate identification in most cases. (**Note:** Leaf sizes vary considerably on individual species of St. John's-wort. The length measurements in the following descriptions generally refer to each species' larger leaves.)

Though few *Hypericum* species are recommended for ornamental or landscape use, many are attractive shrubs which bloom profusely. A garden which includes a variety of *Hypericum* species would assure bright yellow flowers during at least three seasons.

Autograph Tree, Pitch Apple, Balsam Apple   Photo 113
Clusia rosea Jacq.

Form: Medium-sized evergreen tree or treelike shrub, commonly not exceeding about 10 m tall.

Leaves: Opposite, obovate, simple, very stiff, 7 - 18 cm long, 5 - 13 cm wide, upper surfaces dull green, lower surfaces yellow-green, margins entire but slightly turned under, apices notched; petiole distinctly grooved at the base.

Flowers: Lustrous, attractive, appearing mostly in the summer, petals white with tinges of pink, center of flower yellow.

Fruit: Large, globose, 5 - 6 cm in diameter, brown at maturity, splitting to expose large red seeds and orange arils.

Distinguishing Marks: Similar in some respects to seven-year apple (*Casasia clusiifolia*), but having much stiffer leaves that are dull, rather than shiny, green.

Distribution: Sometimes considered native; however, its wide use in landscaping but lack of frequent naturalization makes this latter assumption quite questionable.

Landscape Use: This is a heavily used ornamental. It is most common along roadways and in highway medians in south Florida, especially along U. S. 1 in parts of the Keys. Its stiff leaves, attractive flowers, and distinctive fruit all contribute to its popularity.

Hypericum apocynifolium Small   **Page 141**

Form: Erect, slender, loosely branched, evergreen shrub to about 2 m tall.
Leaves: Opposite, simple, entire, lanceolate to elliptic, 3 - 6 cm long, 1 - 2.5 cm wide.
Flowers: Yellow, borne in loose, many-flowered clusters at the end of the main stem; petals five in number, to about 1 cm long; stamens numerous.
Fruit: An egg-shaped capsule to about 1 cm long, 5 - 7 mm wide.
Distinguishing Marks: Most similar to *H. nudiflorum* and *H. frondosum*, the other two species of St.Johns-wort with comparatively large elliptic leaves; distinguished from the former by having many-flowered clusters rather than having flowers borne in three- to eight-flowered clusters, and by flower petals being generally longer than 8 mm, from the latter by having smaller flowers and leaves that do not separate easily and cleanly from the stem.
Distribution: Wooded ravines, slopes, and bluffs; central Panhandle.

Hypericum brachyphyllum (Spach.) Steud. ─────────────────────────── **Page 143**

Form: Erect, single-stemmed, evergreen shrub; potentially to about 1.5 m tall, often shorter.
Leaves: Opposite, simple, needlelike, larger leaves 6 - 10 mm long; margins strongly turned under and bearing conspicuous black dots (when seen with 20x magnification).
Flowers: Yellow, with five petals, typically borne individually in the leaf axils; sepals five in number, needlelike, to about 3.5 mm long; stamens many; blooming summer through fall; just before opening, the flower buds are often bright red and offer an attractive contrast to the deep green foliage.
Fruit: A narrow, nearly cylindrical capsule, main body usually not exceeding about 5 mm long.
Distinguishing Marks: Distinguished from other *Hypericum* with five-petaled flowers and linear leaves, by larger leaves being less than 11 mm long, from the very similar *H. reductum*, a plant more often of dry, sandy sites, by the current species' more erect habit and by the size of its fruit capsules typically being shorter than 5 mm.
Distribution: Pond edges, wet flatwoods, ditches; throughout northern Florida, southward to the southernmost peninsula.

Sponge-Bark Hypericum or St. John's-Wort   Photo 114
Hypericum chapmanii P. Adams

Form: Typically a shrub with soft, spongy bark, sometimes takes on the appearance of a small tree to about 4 m tall.
Leaves: Small, needlelike, 8 - 25 mm long, crowded at nodes of branches and branchlets.
Flowers: Yellow, with five petals and five sepals, characterized by a mass of conspicuous stamens at the center; usually borne solitary in the leaf axils, sometimes in three-flowered clusters; blooming in summer.

Hypericum brachyphyllum

St. Peter's-Wort
Hypericum crux-andreae

Fruit: An ovate capsule that contains a tiny seed; capsule to about 6 mm long.

Distinguishing Marks: Distinguished from most other *Hypericum* by combination of five-petaled flowers, main stem leaves being needlelike and generally longer than 13 mm, and young stems and leaves lacking a whitish cast; from the very similar *H. fasciculatum*, by having thick, very spongy bark, and flowers and fruit that are more commonly (though not always) borne solitary in the leaf axils.

Distribution: Cypress ponds, wetter portions of flatwoods, flatwoods depressions, sometimes in conjunction with cypress (*Taxodium* spp.), blackgum (*Nyssa biflora* Walt), and sweet bay (*Magnolia virginiana* L.), other times in relatively monospecific stands; often in standing water; endemic to the central Panhandle from about Santa Rosa County to the Ochlockonee River.

Hypericum cistifolium Lam.   **Photo 115**

Form: Single-stemmed (sometimes with a few branches), evergreen shrub to about 1 m tall.
Leaves: Opposite, simple, predominantly lanceolate, varying to more linear-lanceolate, 1.5 - 3 cm long, about 7 mm wide, with a single vein; without a petiole; both surfaces dotted, the lower surface more conspicuously so.
Flowers: Yellow, with five petals and sepals, 10 - 12 mm wide; stamens many; blooming summer and fall.
Fruit: A dark, elliptic capsule, about 5 mm long.
Distinguishing Marks: Distinguished from other species of *Hypericum* with five-petaled flowers and nonlinear leaves by having comparatively smaller flowers that are only to about 12 mm wide; from most wetland *Hypericum* by having flowers borne in branched terminal clusters that often extend well beyond the uppermost leaves.
Distribution: Swales on barrier islands and back beaches, flatwoods, wet pinelands and roadsides, edges of wet savannas; throughout northern Florida, southward to the southern peninsula.

St. Peter's-Wort   Page 143
Hypericum crux-andreae (L.) Crantz

Form: Evergreen shrub to about 1 m tall, with reddish, flaking bark.
Leaves: Opposite, simple, entire, lanceolate to oblong or oblanceolate, 2 - 3 cm long.
Flowers: Yellow, 2 - 3 cm wide at maturity; petals four in number, 1 - 1.8 cm long; sepals four in number, the inner two narrowly lanceolate, the outer two more rotund to nearly rounded, 1 - 1.5 cm long, about as wide at the base as long, both surfaces of all four sepals covered with dots; appearing in summer.
Fruit: An egg-shaped capsule, varying to about 1 cm long.
Distinguishing Marks: The combination of comparatively large (for *Hypericum*), generally non-clasping leaves, four-petaled flowers, and distinctly two-sized sepals help distinguish this species.
Distribution: Ranging from moist flatwoods, and pond and marsh edges to sandy pine–oak ridges; throughout northern Florida, southward to the central peninsula.

Edison's St. John's-Wort, St. Peter's-Wort, St. Andrew's-Crosses

Photo 116

Hypericum edisonianum (Small) Adams & Robeson

Form: Erect shrub to about 1.5 m tall with mostly unbranched, pale brown stems that are essentially leafless below the branches.

Leaves: Opposite, without stalks, elliptic to oblong, entire, leathery, 1 - 2 cm long, upper surfaces whitish green, lower surfaces paler green; bases of leaves with conspicuous, reddish-brown glands.

Flowers: Yellow, spreading, with four petals and a tuft of yellow stamens; blooming throughout the year.

Fruit: Small capsule typical of the genus.

Distinguishing Marks: Distinguished from the very similar *H. crux-andreae* by having narrower leaves and a more bushy habit.

Distribution: Bottoms of seasonal ponds, low spots in flatwoods, low prairies; endemic to Highlands, Glades, and DeSoto Counties.

Comment: Listed as threatened by the Florida Department of Agriculture and as a candidate for federal listing by the U. S. Fish and Wildlife Service.

Hypericum exile P. Adams

Page 146, Photo 117

Form: Evergreen shrub with a slender, flexible main stem to about 1 m tall; branches typically few, strongly ascending and arising from about midstem upwards, thus giving the plant a somewhat cylindrical appearance.

Leaves: Opposite, simple, needlelike, 1 - 2.5 cm long; margins conspicuously and strongly rolled under and bearing tiny dots (requires magnification to see clearly).

Flowers: Yellow; petals five, curving, about 7 mm long, stamens many; sepals also five in number and about 7 mm long; blooming late spring.

Fruit: A cylindrical, reddish-brown capsule, the main body about 7 mm long.

Distinguishing Marks: Distinguished from other *Hypericum* with five-petaled flowers by the leaves being linear and the stem leaves being generally longer than 13 mm, in combination with the slender, flexible, relatively unbranched main stem that usually does not exceed about 8 mm in diameter.

Distribution: Flatwoods and savannas; central Panhandle, endemic to Bay, Franklin, Gulf, Liberty, and Washington Counties.

Sandweed

Photo 118

Hypericum fasciculatum Lam.

Form: An erect, evergreen, single-stemmed shrub with many branches at the top, sometimes with prop roots at the base of the stem; 1.5 - 2 m tall, or a little more; bark buff, burnt orange, or cinnamon colored.

Leaves: Opposite, simple, linear, entire, 1.3 - 2.6 cm long (larger leaves); margins rolled under and dotted; upper surface dotted; axils of main leaves having short branchlets which also contain leaves.

Hypericum exile

Flowers: Yellow, with five sepals and five petals, petals 6 - 9 mm long; stamens many; blooming spring through fall.

Fruit: A narrowly egg-shaped, reddish-brown capsule, main body 3 - 5 mm long.

Distinguishing Marks: Distinguished from most other *Hypericum* by combination of five-petaled flowers, main stem leaves being needlelike and generally longer than 13 mm, and stems lacking a whitish cast; from the very similar *H. chapmanii*, by having flowers and fruit more commonly (though not always) borne in threes in the leaf axils, and by the main stems being firm to the grasp with thin bark rather than thick and spongy.

Distribution: Most often in standing water on the edges of ponds, ditches, and depressions; throughout north Florida, southward to the southern peninsula.

Hypericum frondosum Michx.

Form: A branched shrub to about 3 m tall.

Leaves: Opposite, simple, elliptic to oblong, 3 - 6 cm long, 1 - 2 cm wide; margins entire to very inconspicuously crenate-dentate and somewhat revolute.

Flowers: Yellow, 2.5 - 4 cm across the open petals, with five petals and five sepals; stamens many; blooming in early summer.

Fruit: Capsule to about 1.2 cm long.

Distinguishing Marks: Distinguished from other *Hypericum* by combination of compara-tively large, five-petaled flowers, relatively long and wide-elliptic to oblong (not needlelike)

Hypericum galioides

leaves, smooth bark, and leaves that separate easily from the stem; similar to *H. apocynifoli-um*, but having much larger flowers and fruiting capsules usually longer than 1 cm.

Distribution: Only one station is known for this species in Florida, north of the city of Chattahoochee near Neal Landing in Jackson County.

Hypericum galioides Lam.   **Page 147**

Form: A bushy, spreading, evergreen shrub to about 1.5 m tall.

Leaves: Opposite, simple, narrowly oblanceolate, 2 - 3 cm long, to about 7 mm wide.

Flowers: Yellow, to about 1.5 cm wide when open, with five sepals and petals; borne in short-stalked clusters in the leaf axils; stamens many; appearing in summer and fall.

Fruit: A small, more or less egg-shaped capsule, 4 - 5 mm long.

Distinguishing Marks: Of the five-petaled *Hypericum* with nonneedlelike leaves, the present species and *H. cistifolium* have the most narrow leaves; the latter species differs from the present by having smaller flowers that are borne in terminal clusters rather than in short axillary clusters.

Distribution: Swamps, cypress wetlands, flatwoods and wet pinelands, river and stream banks; throughout northern Florida. This is one of the more common species of *Hypericum* in wet woodlands.

St. Andrew's-Cross   **Page 148**
Hypericum hypericoides (L.) Crantz

Form: An erect, evergreen, freely branched shrub with one to several main stems, numerous main and axillary branches, and reddish-brown bark that sheds in thin strips; to about 1.5 m tall.

Leaves: Linear to oblong, entire, mostly 0.8 - 2.5 cm long and less than 0.6 cm wide, both surfaces punctate dotted (but more distinctly so on lower surface).

Flowers: Yellow with a mass of stamens; four petals, each to about 1 cm long; four green sepals, two of which are large, ovate, and easily seen, the other two minute, inconspicuous, and lanceolate; flowers typically borne solitary above the last pair of leaves on a branchlet; blooming summer and fall.

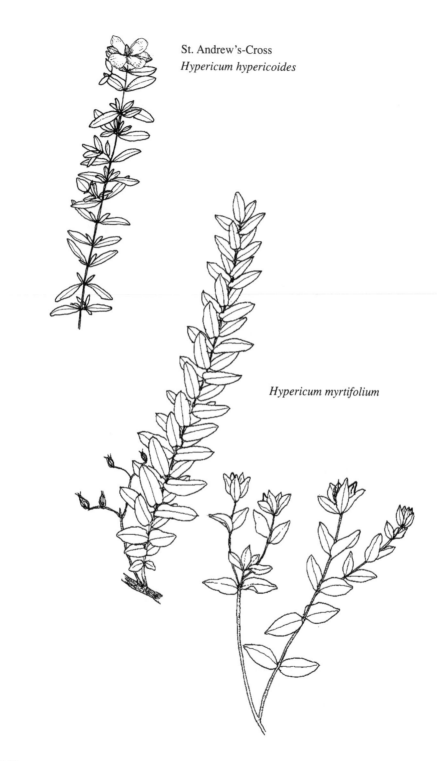

St. Andrew's-Cross
Hypericum hypericoides

Hypericum myrtifolium

Fruit: Ovate capsules, to about 1 cm long and containing tiny black seeds.

Distinguishing Marks: Very similar in appearance to *H. suffruticosum*, distinguished by combination of taller growth habit, flower stalks being less than 6 mm long, flower stalks becoming reflexed after anthesis, and the pair of bracts subtending the flower being located at the base of the flower stalk rather than at the base of the flower, itself.

Distribution: Found in a variety of habitats from sandhills, floodplain woodlands, and hammocks to pine flatwoods and upland woods; throughout northern Florida and southward to at least Collier and Dade Counties; not found in the Keys.

Landscape Use: Probably not used much ornamentally; however, its hardiness and tolerance of a wide variety of circumstances make it a good candidate for cultivation.

Hypericum lissophloeus P. Adams   **Photo 119**

Form: Flexible, evergreen shrub to about 4 m tall with smooth, silvery-gray outer bark that exfoliates in curly plates, and brown inner bark; often with conspicuous adventitious prop roots extending from the lower stem.

Leaves: Opposite, simple, needlelike, 1.2 - 1.7 cm long, with a bluish-green cast; margins rolled under.

Flowers: Yellow, with five petals and sepals, usually borne singly in the leaf axils, sometimes borne in threes; stamens many and nearly obscuring the petals; blooming summer and fall.

Fruit: A reddish-brown capsule, main body to about 7 mm long.

Distinguishing Marks: Most easily distinguished by combination of five-petaled flowers, smooth, almost slick-to-the-touch, silvery-gray bark of the upper stem, and conspicuous prop roots at the base of the stem.

Distribution: Banks of sinkhole ponds and lake shores; endemic to Bay and Washington counties.

Comment: Listed as endangered by the Florida Department of Agriculture and as a candidate for listing by the U. S. Fish and Wildlife Service; despite its status, the plant is locally common within its range and habitat requirements.

Hypericum microsepalum (T. & G.) Gray ex S. Wats.   **Photo 120**

Form: A low, bushy-branched shrub not exceeding about 1 m tall.

Leaves: Opposite, simple, narrowly elliptic to oblanceolate, not exceeding about 1.5 cm long, commonly not longer than about 1 cm; margins rolled under.

Flowers: Yellow, very showy in early spring, 1.5 - 2 cm wide, with four petals and sepals; sepals narrow, all four small and nearly the same size, inconspicuous from above; stamens many; blooming in early spring.

Distinguishing Marks: Distinguished by combination of four-petaled flowers and uniformly narrow sepals.

Fruit: A cylindrical capsule, narrowing toward the apex, less than 4 mm long.

Distribution: One of the most common St. John's-worts in wet pine flatwoods; from Madison and Taylor Counties westward to Walton County.

Hypericum reductum

Hypericum myrtifolium Lam. **Page 148**

Form: Erect, loosely branched, slender shrub to about 1 m tall.

Leaves: Opposite, simple, triangular in outline, 1 - 3 cm long.

Flowers: Yellow, with five petals and sepals, 2 - 2.5 cm across when open; sepals elliptic, to about 1 cm long and conspicuous, reminiscent of small leaves, with a whitish bloom on the undersurfaces; appearing in spring and summer.

Fruit: A dark brown to nearly black egg-shaped capsule to about 8 mm long.

Distinguishing Marks: Similar in leaf shape only to *H. tetrapetalum*, distinguished most easily by flowers having five, rather than four, petals and sepals.

Distribution: Flatwoods, pond edges, depressions in pine woods, sometimes standing in shallow water; throughout northern Florida, southward to the southern peninsula.

Hypericum nitidum Lam.

Form: Bushy-branched evergreen shrub with thin, tight, grayish to brownish bark that exfoliates only in small flakes; to about 3 m tall.

Leaves: Opposite, simple, needlelike, spreading, 1.5 - 2.5 cm long; margins rolled under.

Flowers: Yellow, typically borne singly or in small clusters, with five sepals and petals; sepals very narrow to needlelike; stamens many; appearing late spring and throughout the summer.

Fruit: A narrow, tapering capsule, 4 mm or less in length.

Distinguishing Marks: Difficult to distinguish from both *H. exile* and *H. fasciculatum*; usually bearing many more flowers at anthesis than either of the other two, and by bark being darker, grayish, tight, and exfoliating in only small flakes rather than larger strips.

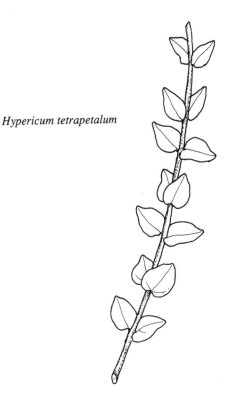

Hypericum tetrapetalum

Distribution: Banks of blackwater streams, wet pine flatwoods, edges of ponds; infrequent throughout northern Florida.

Hypericum nudiflorum Michx. ex. Willd.

Form: Erect, slender, sparsely branched, evergreen shrub to about 2 m tall.
Leaves: Opposite, simple, entire, lanceolate to elliptic, 3 - 6 cm long, 1 - 2.5 cm wide, both surfaces finely dotted.
Flowers: Yellow, to about 1.5 cm wide at maturity, with five petals, borne in three- to eight-flowered clusters at the ends of the main stem; petals 6 - 8 cm long; appearing early to midsummer.
Fruit: A rounded capsule, 4 - 5 mm long.
Distinguishing Marks: Most similar to *H. apocynifolium* (pictured on p. 141) and *H. frondosum*, the other two species of St.John's-wort with comparatively large elliptic leaves; distinguished from the former by having three- to eight- rather than many-flowered clusters, and by the flower petals being generally longer than 8 mm, from the latter by having leaves that do not separate easily from the stem.
Distribution: Bottomlands, river banks, wet hammocks; Panhandle.

Broombrush
Hypericum prolificum L.

Form: Evergreen shrub 3 - 12 dm tall with two-winged branches.
Leaves: Opposite, simple, narrowly lanceolate to narrowly elliptic, 2 - 8 cm long.
Flowers: Deep yellow, 2 - 2.5 cm across, with five petals and sepals; appearing in summer.
Fruit: Narrow capsule, 8 - 10 mm long.
Distinguishing Marks: The comparatively long leaves and restricted range distinguish this species.
Distribution: Rocky slopes and sandy woods; Volusia County.

Hypericum reductum P. Adams   **Page 150**

Form: Typically a reclining, bushy-branched, evergreen shrub, to about 5 cm tall and as much as 1 m across; sometimes with an erect growth habit.
Leaves: Opposite, simple, needlelike, conspicuously short, usually not longer than about 5 mm.
Flowers: Yellow, with five petals and sepals, petals about 8 mm long, stamens many; appearing in spring and summer.
Fruit: A nearly cylindric capsule, main body 4 - 9 mm long, usually exceeding 5 mm in length.
Distinguishing Marks: Distinguished from most other species of *Hypericum* with five-petaled flowers and linear leaves by main stem leaves being shorter than 11 mm; from the very similar *H. brachyphyllum* by the present species' typically reclining habit and its fruit capsules typically exceeding 5 mm in length.
Distribution: Sandy soils of pine–oak scrub ridges and inland dunes; throughout northern Florida, southward to the central peninsula.

Hypericum suffruticosum Adams & Robson   **Photo 121**

Form: Very low-growing shrub typically less than 15 cm tall with a slender, reddish-brown stem; some plants erect in form, others decumbent.
Leaves: Elliptic to oblong, entire, less than 1 cm long, 2 - 3 mm wide, conspicuously punctate dotted on upper surfaces (requires magnification), less so, if at all, on lower surfaces.
Flowers: Yellow, with stalks 6 - 12 mm long and a mass of stamens; four petals, each 5 - 7 mm long; four green sepals, two ovate in shape and quite obvious, the other two small and barely, if at all, evident; appearing mostly in the spring.
Fruit: Ovate to elliptic capsule to about 4 mm long.
Distinguishing Marks: Similar in several respects to *H. hypericoides*, distinguished from it by combination of low growth habit, flower stalks being longer than 6 mm, flower stalks being erect rather than reflexed, and by bracts subtending the flower being located at the base of the flower, rather than at the base of the flower stalk.
Distribution: Dry pinelands; throughout northern Florida southward to about Polk County.

Hypericum tetrapetalum Lam.

Page 151, Photo 122

Form: Slender, evergreen shrub to about 1 m tall.

Leaves: Opposite, simple, oblong to ovate, heart shaped at the base, 1 - 2 cm long.

Flowers: Yellow, 2.5 - 3 cm across when open, with four petals and sepals; two sepals narrow, two wide, heart shaped at the base, but almost rounded in outline; stamens many; appearing spring through fall.

Fruit: An elliptic capsule to about 6 mm long.

Distinguishing Marks: The four-petaled flowers in conjunction with the heart-shaped bases of the leaves are diagnostic; most similar to *H. myrtifolium* but having flowers with four rather than five petals.

Distribution: Flatwoods and pond edges; much of northern Florida from about Okaloosa County eastward and southward to the southern peninsula.

HAMAMELIDACEAE — WITCH HAZEL FAMILY

The witch hazel family is composed of about 23 genera and 100 species worldwide, most of which are concentrated in China. Three woody members of the family are present in Florida. The well-known sweetgum (*Liquidambar styraciflua* L.), a stately tree with star-shaped leaves, is probably the most often seen and widely recognized member of the family, while the witch hazel (*Hamamelis virginiana*) has the best reputation, primarily for its supposed medicinal qualities. *Fothergilla*, the other genus, contains two species in the southeastern U. S., only one of which is found in Florida. All members of the family are characterized by distinctive leaves, though those of the latter two genera can be easily confused.

Witch-Alder

Photo 123

Fothergilla gardeni Murray

Form: A low, slender, deciduous shrub with two-ranked leaves; seldom exceeding about 1 m tall.

Leaves: Alternate, simple, obovate to nearly round, 2 - 6 (occasionally 8) cm long, 1.5 - 3

Witch-Hazel
Hamamelis virginiana

(occasionally 5) cm wide; margins crenate, especially toward the apices, rarely entire; surfaces with star-shaped pubescence.

Flowers: Small, white, tipped with pink, borne in dense, conspicuous clusters at the ends of branches; appearing in early spring prior to the new leaves.

Fruit: A capsule.

Distinguishing Marks: The two-ranked, crenate-edged, obovate leaves are reminiscent of witch hazel (*Hamamelis virginiana*); the smaller leaves (predominantly less than, rather than more than, 6 cm long) and conspicuous flowers distinguish it from this latter species.

Distribution: Uncommon near swamps and savannas; Panhandle.

Landscape Use: This is a very good specimen plant for native gardens or as an understory shrub. It is relatively low growing and produces very attractive flowers that are sure to invite comment.

Witch Hazel

Page 153

Hamamelis virginiana L.

Form: Deciduous shrub or small tree to about 8 m tall with a short, low-branching trunk and zigzag twigs.

Leaves: Alternate, simple, two ranked, oval to obovate, 6 - 15 cm long, to 10 cm wide, margins undulate or scalloped, dull green in summer, turning pale yellow in autumn; bases typically asymmetrical on either side of the midvein.

Flowers: Yellow and very distinctive with four, small, ribbonlike petals, each 1 - 1.5 cm long, appearing in late fall and winter.

Fruit: A short, pubescent, four-pointed, two-valved capsule, 1 - 1.6 cm long.

Distinguishing Marks: The distinctive leaves, flowers, and fruit make it difficult to confuse this species with any other north Florida shrub save the witch alder (*Fothergilla gardeni*); the latter has leaves predominantly less than 6 cm long and is very rare in Florida.

Distribution: Slopes, ravines, low woods, moist hillsides, mesic woods; throughout the Panhandle and northern Florida, southward to about Lake County.

Landscape Use: Since this species flowers late in the year, and the leaves turn a beautiful yellow before dropping, it is particularly good for fall color in a natural landscape; tolerates shade. Its tiny ribbonlike flower petals are a conversation piece in the garden.

Comment: Witch hazel is a widely distributed species that ranges across much of the eastern United States as well as into the Canadian provinces of Ontario and Nova Scotia. The common name for the plant originated in colonial America and likely resulted from the use of the tree's forked twigs as divining rods, reminiscent of the way hazel was used in England. However, it is for the purported medicinal value of its bark, leaves, and twigs that the plant is probably best known. Home-remedy experts extol the witch hazel for its astringent, hemostatic, and anti-inflammatory properties, and cosmetic manufacturers sometimes incorporate its alcoholic extract in the formulation of women's makeup. The plant has been used in the treatment of dysentery, diarrhea, hemorrhages, bruises, and abrasions; and mixtures of witch hazel, bayberry bark, cayenne pepper, and the bark of prickly ash (*Zanthoxylum* spp.) have been used to relieve the discomfort of varicose veins.

HIPPOCASTANACEAE — BUCKEYE FAMILY

The buckeye or horse chestnut family is composed of two closely related genera, one of which is found in the north temperate zone, the other only from southern Mexico to northwestern South America. The best known member of the family is probably the Ohio buckeye (*Aesculus glabra* Willd.) which ranges from the northern portions of Alabama, Mississippi, and Texas to Iowa, Missouri, southern Michigan, and eastern Pennsylvania. However, several additional tree-sized buckeye species are native to the continental United States and another, the horse chestnut (*A. hippocastanum* L.), was introduced in colonial times and has become an often-used and now naturalized ornamental.

Florida's only member of the genus is the red buckeye (*A. pavia*), a delicate and attractive shrub or small tree confined in Florida almost entirely to the northern part of the state. Like all members of the genus, the red buckeye is distinguishable by its palmately compound leaves with five leaflets. It is the only shrub or tree in the state with such foliage.

Red Buckeye

Photos 124, 125

Aesculus pavia L.

Form: Deciduous shrub or small tree to about 12 m tall.

Leaves: Opposite, palmately compound with long petioles, overall leaf length 18 - 32 cm; leaflets five (occasionally seven) in number, elliptic, 5 - 15 cm long, margins finely toothed.

Flowers: Bright red, showy, borne in spreading clusters at the tips of the branches, each cluster 10 - 25 cm long; appearing early to midspring.

Fruit: A light brown capsule 3 - 6 cm in diameter, splitting to expose several hard, reddish-brown, poisonous seeds.

Doctor Vine
Hippocratea volubilis

155

Distinguishing Marks: Distinguished as the only north Florida shrub or tree with palmately compound leaves with five leaflets.

Distribution: Slopes, bottoms, ravines, bluffs, hammocks, rich mesic woods; throughout the Panhandle and northern Florida, southward to Seminole County.

Landscape Use: The bright red flowers and distinctive leaves give this plant a special charm. It does well in shade, but flowers best in full sun and is preferred for shrubby borders or along the edges of woodlands. As might be expected due to its natural habitat, it prefers well-drained, rich soils.

Comment: The red buckeye takes its common name from the combination of its striking inflorescence and hard, reddish-brown seeds. In the first throes of spring, sometimes even as early as mid-February, the plant produces a showy panicle of scarlet red, tubular flowers that are especially conspicuous in the dim light of a mature forest understory. The complete flowering appendage is held upright at the tip of the developing central stem. Later in the season the flowers give way to a large brownish capsule that eventually splits to expose the several kernellike seeds.

HIPPOCRATEACEAE — HIPPOCRATEA FAMILY

The Hippocratea family is composed almost entirely of climbing vines with simple, opposite, crenate to serrate leaves, and small flowers. Only a single member of the family is found in Florida. However, the family is closely related to the Celastraceae, or staff tree family, which is well represented among the state's woody flora. The genus *Hippocratea* contains about 120 species worldwide, most of which are tropical. The stems of some of the African species are so tough that they have been used to build suspended, netlike walkways through the jungle.

Doctor Vine

Page 155

Hippocratea volubilis L.

Form: Large, woody, much-branched climbing vine to about 20 m long.

Leaves: Opposite, elliptic to ovate, margins crenate-serrate to undulate, somewhat leathery, 5 - 15 cm long, typically V-shaped upward from the central vein.

Flowers: Borne in branched clusters 4 - 12 cm long; individual flowers white, small, 4 - 8 mm wide; appearing in spring and summer.

Fruit: Capsule, 4 - 8 cm long, egg shaped to narrowly oblong.

Distinguishing Marks: The relatively large, deeply reflexed leaves, regular branching, and clusters of tiny white flowers help identify this plant; the branches wrap around its host.

Distribution: Hammocks, mangrove swamps, hardwood swamps (such as Fakahatchee Strand); south Florida and the Keys.

Comment: This plant is often seen in dense networks in mangrove swamps and hammock edges.

ILLICIACEAE — STAR-ANISE FAMILY

The *Illiciaceae*, or star anise family, is composed of a single genus with 35 to 40 species worldwide, most of which are native to southeastern Asia. Only two species occur in the United States; both are found in Florida. The family takes its common name from the star-shaped fruits that appear after flowering. Ethereal oil cells in the plant's tissues account for the pungent odor that arises from bruised leaves of members of this family.

Florida Anise

Photo 126

Illicium floridanum Ellis

Form: Evergreen shrub or small tree to about 8 m tall.

Leaves: Alternate, simple, entire, elliptical with sharp-pointed tips, 6.5 to 15 cm long, 2 - 6 cm wide, usually clustered near the tips of the branches; the crushed foliage has a distinctive, pungent odor of anise.

Flowers: Ornate, crimson red (but see comment below), 2.5 - 6 cm wide, with as many as 30 petals, 15 pistils, and 30 stamens; appearing early to midspring.

Fruit: Remains of the star-shaped fruit can be found on at least a few plants almost any time of year.

Distinguishing Marks: The showy flowers and pungent odor of its crushed leaves set this plant apart.

Distribution: Moist ravines and steepheads; inland throughout the Panhandle, eastward to the Ochlockonee River.

Landscape Use: Florida anise is a cold-tolerant evergreen that serves well as a background or specimen shrub. It prefers rich, moist, acidic soil and does equally well in shade or full sun. Its flowers are unique and interesting, and its shiny green foliage quite attractive.

Comment: The somewhat odd structure of its rather complicated flowers is one of the star anise's most interesting features. Its multiparted flowers are unlike many so-called perfect flowers, which generally contain numerous stamens, a single pistil, and 3 - 6 petals. A rare, white-flowered (and sometimes intermediate pinkish-flowered) form of this species is also known from the bluffs and ravines region on the east side of the Apalachicola River in Liberty County, as well as from stations in Mississippi. This latter form is more correctly identified as *I. floridanum* Ellis f. *album* F.G. Mey. & Mazzeo.

Yellow Anise

Photo 127

Illicium parviflorum Michx. ex Vent.

Form: Shrub or small tree.

Leaves: Similar to Florida anise, except lacking the sharp-pointed tip, exhibiting a strong aroma when crushed.

Flowers: Yellow, small, less than 2 cm wide, having 12 - 15 tepals, 6 - 7 stamens; appearing in spring.

Distinguishing Marks: Distinguished from Florida anise (*I. floridanum*) in naturally occurring populations by smaller flowers which are yellow and have fewer petals, and by not overlapping in distribution.

Distribution: Hammocks and wetlands along spring-fed streams; endemic to several north-central counties, including Marion, Lake, and Volusia; more often seen as a landscape plant.

Landscape Use: This plant is probably more often used ornamentally than the Florida anise (*I. floridanum*). It serves equally well to soften the corners of homes, as a shrub set off in the yard, or as a hedge or background plant. Cultivated specimens usually have an overall healthier look than do those found in the plant's natural habitat.

LABIATAE (LAMIACEAE) — MINT FAMILY

The mints compose a large, mostly herbaceous family that is distributed worldwide. Members of the family are best known for their opposite leaves, which typically exhibit a strong, minty aroma when crushed, in conjunction with their usually colorful, irregular flowers. The family's herbaceous species are often distinguished by having square stems, a character that does not always hold up with the family's woody species.

The genera *Conradina* and *Calamintha* are sometimes difficult to distinguish from each other by beginning plant enthusiasts due to the similarity of their leaves and irregular flowers. The two are most easily separated by examining the lower surfaces of leaves with a hand lens. Those of the *Conradina* species will be gray-pubescent with appressed or matted hairs. Those of *Calamintha* will have erect or spreading hairs.

Only a few of the accounts that follow include comments about landscape value. It is likely that most mint species would do well planted in ornamental gardens. However, it should be noted that many of these species, especially those of the genus *Dicerandra*, hybridize readily and may be difficult to maintain in their pure form under cultivation.

Lavender Basil or Ashe's Savory   **Photo 128**

Calamintha ashei (Weatherby) Shinners

Form: Bushy, strongly aromatic shrub to about 5 dm tall, with youngest shoots stiff, slender, erect or ascending, greenish brown, with a covering of fine hairs.

Leaves: Opposite, simple, mostly linear, to about 1.2 cm long, 2 - 4 mm wide; surfaces gray-green and hairy; margins revolute.

Flowers: White to pale rose pink or pale pinkish purple, tubular, two lipped, lower lip with darker spots near the base; overall length to about 1.5 cm; appearing in spring.

Fruit: Tiny, nearly round, pale brown, smooth nutlet to about 1.5 mm long.

Distinguishing Marks: Distinguished from *C. coccinea* by flowers being less than 2 cm long rather than over 2.5 cm long and pale pinkish-purple rather than scarlet red.

Distribution: Central Florida scrub and dry pinelands; primarily Highlands County with a disjunct population in the southwestern corner of the Ocala National Forest, Marion County.

Comment: Listed as threatened by the Florida Department of Agriculture and as a Category 2 candidate for listing by the U. S. Fish and Wildlife Service.

Red Basil or Scarlet Basil

Photo 129

Calamintha coccinea (Nutt.) Benth.

Form: Low, multibranched, tardily deciduous shrub to about 1 m tall; very young stems often somewhat squarish.

Leaves: Opposite, simple, entire, oblanceolate, 0.5 - 2 cm long, to about 1 cm wide; minty aromatic when crushed; margins often rolled under; lateral veins on both surfaces obscure, midveins evident, both surfaces with dots (requires magnification).

Flowers: Bright red, tubular, with a drooping, speckled lower lip, 3 - 5 cm long; blooming from late spring to midfall.

Fruit: A small, brown nutlet.

Distinguishing Marks: The red tubular flowers and small, opposite, aromatic leaves distinguish this species.

Distribution: Sandy pine ridges; throughout the Panhandle and north Florida, southward to the central peninsula; very conspicuous along highways in the western Panhandle during late summer and fall.

Landscape Use: A good plant for dry, sandy areas, especially in the western Panhandle.

Toothed Basil

Photo 130

Calamintha dentata Chapm.

Form: Strongly aromatic, partially evergreen shrub to about 5 dm tall with slender, erect, gray-brown bark that cracks and peels off in thin strips.

Leaves: Opposite, simple, without petioles; lower leaves about 1 cm long, upper leaves somewhat shorter; margins of lower leaves with small teeth toward the apices (may require magnification to see clearly), margins of upper leaves often without teeth; both surfaces covered with small dots and fine hairs.

Flowers: Tubular, two lipped, borne in the axils of middle to upper leaves; flower tubes white, petals pinkish with darker maroon to purplish spots, sepals suffused with purple; appearing spring to fall.

Fruit: Rounded, light brown nutlet, about 0.5 - 1.5 mm in diameter.

Distinguishing Marks: The sessile, slightly dentate leaves set this species apart from the Panhandle's other two members of the genus.

Distribution: Sandy, pine–oak ridges; central Panhandle from about Walton to Gadsden, Liberty, and Wakulla Counties.

Comment: Recognized as a candidate for listing by the U. S. Fish and Wildlife Service.

Calamintha georgiana (Harper) Shinners

Photo 131

Form: Low, multibranched, deciduous shrub to about 8 dm tall.

Leaves: Opposite, simple, elliptic to ovate, varying considerably in size along the stem, main stem leaves 1 - 3.5 cm long; margins entire to more often with blunt teeth.

Flowers: Whitish, suffused with pale lavender, tubular with a distinct, speckled lower lip; to about 1.5 cm long; appearing in early fall.

Fruit: A tiny, light brown nutlet.

Distinguishing Marks: The two-lipped whitish to pale lavender flowers and comparatively large, aromatic leaves with conspicuous petioles help distinguish this species from other members of the genus.

Distribution: Dry, sandy sites; sporadic and uncommon in the Panhandle, reported from Holmes and Gadsden Counties; more common in Georgia.

Short-Leaved Rosemary   Photo 132

Conradina brevifolia Shinners

Form: Slender, loosely branched shrub, to about 1 m tall.

Leaves: Opposite, simple, linear, entire, pale green, fleshy, predominantly 4 - 8.2 mm long; both surfaces with grayish pubescence.

Flowers: Irregular, pale lavender with pink to purple markings and pubescent on the outside, yellowish white with spots of deep purple on the inside of the lower lip, borne in clusters of one to six from the uppermost leaf axils; appearing in spring.

Fruit: A tiny nutlet.

Distinguishing Marks: Most similar to (and considered by some authorities to be conspecific with) *C. canescens*. The plants are, indeed, almost identical to field observation. The two are most easily distinguished from each other by geographic range; no other *Conradina* is likely to be found within the extremely restricted range of *C. brevifolia*.

Distribution: White sand scrub; Highlands and Polk Counties.

Comment: Listed as endangered by the U. S. Fish and Wildlife Service. If valid, this is one of the rarest species of *Conradina* in Florida. It was first described in 1962 and is only known from a limited number of sites. As implied above, some authorities do not accept this plant as a valid species. Wunderlin (1982), for example, lists *C. canescens* in the region generally assumed to be the geographic range of *C. brevifolia*, but does not mention the latter species.

Minty Rosemary or Wild Rosemary   Photo 133

Conradina canescens (T. & G.) Gray

Form: Bushy, evergreen shrub commonly to about 5 dm tall; young twigs squarish.

Leaves: Opposite, simple, linear, entire, to about 1 cm long; both surfaces with a dense covering of grayish pubescence; minty aromatic when crushed.

Flowers: Whitish to pale lavender, conspicuously two lipped, lower lip dotted with darker purple spots; flowering much of the year, from spring into late fall.

Fruit: A tiny nutlet.

Distinguishing Marks: This is the only near-coastal plant with linear, aromatic leaves and conspicuously two-lipped, pale lavender flowers; distinguished from the Apalachicola rosemary (*C. glabra*) by leaves being densely pubescent on both surfaces.

Distribution: Mature dunes, sandy areas, sandy pine ridges; Panhandle from about Liberty and Franklin Counties westward (but see the comment for *C. brevifolia*, above).

Etonia Rosemary

Photo 134

Conradina etonia Kral & McCartney

Form: Slender, wandlike, evergreen shrub (deciduous in 2 - 3 years) to 1.5 m tall with many, often arching branches; new shoots only about 1 mm in diameter and hairy.
Leaves: Opposite, narrowly to broadly oblanceolate to spatulate, 1.5 - 3 cm long, 2 - 9 mm wide; margins tightly rolled under; upper surfaces hairy, dull green, with many small dots; lower surfaces densely hairy and with a conspicuously raised midrib.
Flowers: Borne in clusters of 1 - 12, lavender rose to lavender blue in color; individual flowers hairy, tubular, two lipped (bilabiate), characteristic of other members of the genus.
Fruit: Small, rounded nutlets.
Distinguishing Marks: Most similar and geographically closest to *C. grandiflora*; the present species may be distinguished from the latter and all other members of the genus by having very evident lateral veins on the lower surfaces of leaves, and by its very restricted geographic range.
Distribution: Uncommon and restricted to a few scrub locations, Putnam County.
Comment: Listed as endangered by the U. S. Fish and Wildlife Service.

Apalachicola Rosemary

Photo 135

Conradina glabra Shinners

Form: Bushy, evergreen shrub potentially to about 8 dm tall; young twigs squarish.
Leaves: Opposite, simple, linear, 1 - 1.5 cm long; lower surfaces with a dense covering of grayish pubescence, upper surfaces without pubescent or with only inconspicuous pubescence; minty aromatic.
Flowers: White to lavender, two lipped, lower lip dotted with reddish spots, 12 - 18 mm long, typically borne in abundance in spring and early summer.
Fruit: A tiny nutlet.
Distinguishing Marks: Similar to the minty rosemary (*C. canescens*) but distinguished from it by the upper surfaces of leaves being only lightly or not at all pubescent; distinguished from other plants with which it associates by its two-lipped flowers and the minty aroma of its leaves.
Distribution: Longleaf pine–turkey oak woods; along the east side of the Apalachicola River in Franklin and Liberty Counties.
Comment: Listed as threatened by the Florida Department of Agriculture and as endangered by the U. S. Fish and Wildlife Service.

Large-Flowered Rosemary

Photo 136

Conradina grandiflora Small

Form: Essentially evergreen, aromatic shrub with slender, curving branches, usually 1 - 1.5 m tall; bark grayish and peeling.

Leaves: Opposite, linear to needlelike, entire, typically 1 - 1.5 cm long; margins revolute; apices blunt; upper surfaces shiny, dark green with small black dots, lower surfaces grayish white with a dense covering of fine hairs.

Flowers: Blue, two lipped, upper lip to about 2 cm long; appearing year-round.

Fruit: Rounded, smooth, blackish nutlets.

Distinguishing Marks: Distinguished from other members of the genus by larger flowers borne on evident stalks.

Distribution: Sandhills and sand pine scrub; endemic to Florida's Atlantic Coastal Ridge from about Volusia to Broward Counties.

Landscape Use: The dependence of this species on its specialized habitat makes it difficult to cultivate.

Comment: Listed as endangered by the Florida Department of Agriculture and as a Category II candidate for listing by the U. S. Fish and Wildlife Service.

Garrett's Mint or Christman's Dicerandra   Photo 137
Dicerandra christmanii Huck & Judd

Form: A much-branched perennial shrub to about 5 dm tall; growing from a woody base.

Leaves: Opposite, oblong to narrowly ovate, entire, 2 - 15 mm long, 1 - 2.5 mm wide, both surfaces with glandular dots, margins entire, apices rounded; borne essentially without petioles.

Flowers: Tubular with flaring petals, white with purple dots, to about 1 cm long; anthers bright yellow; appearing July to November and borne in clusters of one to three.

Fruit: A fused collection of four brown nutlets.

Distinguishing Marks: Very similar to *D. frutescens*, distinguished from it in flower by having bright yellow rather than lavender anthers.

Distribution: Rare and known from only five locations in yellow-sand scrub southeast of Sebring in Highlands County.

Comment: All four of Florida's named woody *Dicerandra* species are rare plants that are endemic to Florida and display highly restricted ranges. In addition, there are two other species, at least one of which has yet to be described and named, that are quite rare. One of these taxa is found on the Atlantic Coastal Ridge near Titusville, the other in Polk County (McCormick, et. al., 1993). The present species was first described in 1989 after being recognized as distinctive by Steven P. Christman, for whom it is named. It was first collected by Ray Garrett in 1948 (hence the common name) but was thought for many years to be a specimen of the very similar *D. frutescens*. It is listed as endangered by the U. S. Fish and Wildlife Service.

Long-Spurred Balm or Robin's Mint
Dicerandra cornutissima R. Huck

Form: Low, aromatic shrub with thin, brown to gray-brown bark that peels off in plates; often matlike.

Leaves: Opposite, linear, entire, 1.5 - 2.5 cm long, 0.8 - 1.5 mm wide, stiff; margins wavy; apices notched.

Flowers: White suffused with pink to rose purple, two lipped, to about 1.3 cm long; appearing summer through fall.

Fruit: Brown, rounded nutlets, about 1 mm long.

Distinguishing Marks: The only woody *Dicerandra* found within its range.

Distribution: Sand pine scrub; Marion and Sumter Counties.

Comment: Listed as endangered by both the Florida Department of Agriculture and U. S. Fish and Wildlife Service. Its common name is for Robin Huck, who described it.

Scrub Balm or Lloyd's Mint

Dicerandra frutescens Shinners

Form: Low, densely branched to scraggly shrub, to about 5 dm tall with numerous ascending branches.

Leaves: Opposite, linear, linear elliptic, or linear oblanceolate, entire, numerous, 1.5 - 2.5 cm long, 2 - 3 cm wide; apices rounded; upper surfaces dark green with a depressed midrib, lower surfaces paler with a raised midrib.

Flowers: White, two lipped, about 2 cm long, borne in pairs in the axils of larger leaves; appearing summer through fall.

Fruit: Rounded, brownish nutlet about 1 mm long.

Distinguishing Marks: Very similar to *D. christmanii*; distinguished from other mints by its white flowers with purple spots, from the latter species by its lavender anthers.

Distribution: Oak scrub; Highlands County, endemic to Lake Wales Ridge; Christman and Judd (1990) report that this species is limited to yellow sand scrub on the flanks of the Lake Wales Ridge and not in the sandhills or white sand scrub as often reported.

Comment: Listed as endangered by both the Florida Department of Agriculture and the U. S. Fish and Wildlife Service. One of its common names is after Lloyd Shinners, who described it. A recent study (Eisner, et. al., 1990) isolated a new natural product in the tissues of this species. The product, *trans*-pulegol, is held in glandular capsules in the leaf blade and is released when the leaf is injured, presumably to deter the attacks of insects. The authors of the study suggest that the "discovery of a new natural product from an endangered species raises questions about the chemical implications of species extinction."

Spotless-Petaled Balm, Lakela's Mint, Olga's Mint   Photo 138

Dicerandra immaculata Lakela

Form: Low, aromatic shrub to about 5 dm tall; older specimens much branched.

Leaves: Opposite (but often appearing whorled), entire, linear to narrowly oblong, 1.5 - 3 cm long, about 3.5 mm wide, essentially stalkless; apices callused; both surfaces covered with many small dots.

Flowers: Tubular, two lipped, petals pink (a white-flowered population has been reported), 1.5 - 2 cm long, without spots; anthers white; appearing summer through fall.

Fruit: Rounded, pale brown nutlet, about 1 mm long.

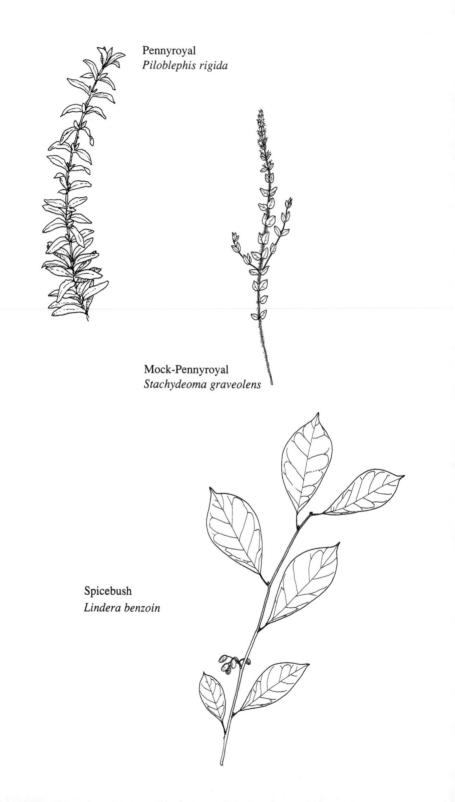

Pennyroyal
Piloblephis rigida

Mock-Pennyroyal
Stachydeoma graveolens

Spicebush
Lindera benzoin

Distinguishing Marks: Distinguished by lacking spots on the flower petals.

Distribution: Sand pine scrub; endemic to St. Lucie and Indian River Counties, reportedly introduced into Martin County.

Comment: Rare, first reported by Florida botanist Olga Lakela in 1963 (hence two of the common names); listed as endangered by both the Florida Department of Agriculture and the U. S. Fish and Wildlife Service.

Pennyroyal

Piloblephis rigida (Batr. ex Benth.) Raf.

Page 164

Form: A diffusely branched, somewhat woody, aromatic shrub or subshrub; erect to strongly reclining, or lying flat; branches to about 7 dm long and hairy.

Leaves: Opposite, entire, lanceolate, numerous, to about 1 cm long.

Flowers: Pale purple, two lipped, the lower lip with dark purple spots, a little less than 1 cm long; borne in dense, conspicuous clusters at the ends of the branches; appearing year-round.

Fruit: Tiny nutlets, about 1 mm long.

Distinguishing Marks: The dense clusters of pale purple flowers, sandy habitat, strongly aromatic properties, and relatively small leaves help distinguish this common species.

Distribution: Common in dry, sandy sites, pinelands; throughout southern, central, and northeastern Florida; endemic.

Mock-Pennyroyal

Stachydeoma graveolens (Chapm. ex Gray) Small

Page 164

Form: A low, aromatic, bushy, evergreen shrub; leaves on lower stems widely spaced, those toward the tip of the branches numerous, closely spaced, and with a purplish hue; only the older stems woody.

Leaves: Opposite, simple, oblong, small, to about 1 cm long, 5 - 6 mm wide; without petioles; margins of mature leaves varying from entire to indistinctly toothed, often rolled under; upper surface with long hairs.

Flowers: Whitish with rose-purple coloring, tubular and two lipped, borne singly in the leaf axils, to about 1 cm long; appearing primarily in summer.

Fruit: A tiny nutlet.

Distinguishing Marks: The aromatic, purplish-tinted leaves in conjunction with the whitish and purplish flowers are helpful field marks.

Distribution: Sand ridges in pinelands and flatwoods; from Leon and Wakulla Counties westward to Bay County.

Comment: Listed as endangered by the Florida Department of Agriculture and as a candidate for federal listing by the U. S. Fish and Wildlife Service. This plant is often seen listed under the scientific synonym *Hedeoma graveolens* Chapmn.

LAURACEAE — LAUREL OR BAY FAMILY

The laurels compose a large family of nearly 2,500 species in over 35 genera, most of which are found in the tropical or warm-temperate zones of both hemispheres, with centers in both America and Southeast Asia. The family is said to be represented by as many as 40 genera with up to 2,500 species, depending upon the authority referenced. Most temperate members of the family have small, inconspicuous, six-parted flowers. The family is best known for the aromatic oils that are contained with the leaves of most of its members. The leaves of many of the Lauraceae exhibit a distinctive, pungent, often baylike odor when crushed, which helps in identifying members of the family. The bay leaf of commerce is from a member of this family.

Spicebush
Lindera benzoin (L.) Blume

Page 164

Form: Deciduous shrub, with spicy, aromatic leaves and twigs.

Leaves: Alternate, simple, entire, ovate to elliptic, 6 - 12 cm long, 3 - 5 cm wide, upper surfaces medium-dark green, lower surfaces grayish and pubescent at least along the central vein, but often pubescent throughout; apices often tapering to a point; margins entire but fringed with hairs; larger leaves borne near the tips of branches, often with conspicuously smaller leaves below.

Flowers: Yellow, small, clustered along the branches, often at the point at which the leafy branchlets arise from the main branch, appearing in February, typically before the leaves.

Fruit: An oblong, bright red, aromatic drupe, 8 - 10 mm long, often remaining on the plant into winter after all leaves have fallen.

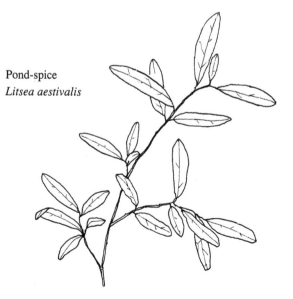

Pond-spice
Litsea aestivalis

Distinguishing Marks: Most readily recognized by the spicy aroma of crushed leaves (especially new ones) in conjunction with the tiny hairs that form a fringe along the leaf margin.

Distribution: Bluffs, slopes, hammocks, and floodplains; northeastern Florida as well as Jackson, Calhoun, Gadsden, and Liberty Counties in the eastern Panhandle, which are the southernmost locations of its range.

Landscape Use: This plant is sometimes available through native plant nurseries. It is an excellent specimen plant for calcium-rich soils and will tolerate shade. Its bright red fruit, which appears in the fall, is much more noticeable than its small flowers and provides food for wildlife. The plant is dioecious, hence both male and female plants are needed to produce fruit.

Comment: Two other members of this genus have also been reported from Florida. The first, Jove's-fruit or pondberry (*L. melissaefolia* [Walt.] Blume), was previously reported from the Panhandle but, according to Godfrey (1988), has not been collected in the state for well over a century. It has narrower leaves than spicebush and reportedly inhabits pond and swamp margins in parts of Alabama, Georgia, Missouri, and both North and South Carolina. The second species, *L. subcoriacea* Wofford, was first known from wet, evergreen shrub bogs of southern Mississippi and Louisiana but was later also found in Alabama, Georgia, and North and South Carolina. It has recently been reported in Florida from Putnam County and from Eglin Air Force Base in the Panhandle. According to Wofford (1983), it may be separated from *L. benzoin* by its smaller leaves (4 - 7.5 cm long, 2 - 3.5 cm wide) which are more leathery than membranaceous, and more elliptic than obovate. Wofford also reports that its leaves are faintly lemon scented when crushed, rather than strongly spicy, as in *L. benzoin*, and that it occurs mostly in boggy habitats in association with black titi (*Cliftonia monophylla*), sweetbay (*Magnolia virginiana*), and swamp bay (*Persea palustris*), rather than in more upland, mesic habitats.

Pond-Spice

Page 166, Photo 139

Litsea aestivalis (L.) Fern.

Form: Deciduous, multibranched shrub with zigzag branchlets; 2 - 5 m tall.

Leaves: Alternate, simple, entire, lanceolate to narrowly oblong, 1 - 3 cm long, 0.5 - 1 cm wide.

Flowers: Small, yellow, borne in clusters of two to four near the ends of branches or in the axils of newly forming leaves; appearing in February, prior to new leaf growth.

Fruit: A rounded, bright-red drupe, 4 - 6 mm in diameter.

Distinguishing Marks: The small leaves, rounded red drupes, and clusters of tiny yellow flowers that appear before the new leaves help distinguish this species.

Distribution: Edges of pineland ponds and swamps; sporadic and local in north Florida.

Landscape Use: Pond-spice is not readily available but can be found at some native plant nurseries. Regardless of its name, it does well in rich soil in shaded areas and is prized for its bright red fruit.

Comment: Listed as threatened by the Florida Department of Agriculture and as a candidate for federal listing by the U. S. Fish and Wildlife Service.

Lancewood

Ocotea coriacea (Sw.) Britt.

Photo 140

Form: Small, evergreen understory shrub or tree, potentially to about 15 m tall.

Leaves: Alternate, simple, entire, lanceolate, 7 - 15 cm long, 2.5 - 5 cm wide, usually tapering to a long-pointed tip, sharply fragrant when crushed.

Flowers: Creamy white, borne in clusters, each flower 5 - 7 mm in diameter; appearing primarily in spring.

Fruit: A dark blue, rounded drupe.

Distinguishing Marks: Distinguished from the similar red bay (*Persea borbonia*) by undersurfaces of leaves being green rather than grayish white.

Distribution: Most common in hammocks and pinewoods of southernmost Florida and the Keys but also found as far north as Cape Canaveral on the east coast.

Comment: Sometimes seen listed as *Nectandra coriacea* (Sw.) Griseb.

Red Bay

Persea borbonia (L.) Spreng.

Photo 141

Form: Evergreen shrub or tree to about 18 m tall.

Leaves: Alternate, simple, entire, lanceolate, 2 - 15 cm long, 1.5 - 6 cm wide, aromatic when crushed; flowering when of low stature.

Flowers: Small, greenish, borne in loose clusters in the leaf axils; appearing spring through fall in various parts of the state.

Fruit: A rounded, dark blue drupe, to about 1.2 cm in diameter.

Distinguishing Marks: Distinguished from other *Persea* and *Ocotea* by lower leaf surfaces being grayish white below, resulting from very short, appressed pubescence which cannot be seen without magnification and which appears like minute golden flecks; the regular occurrence of leaf galls also provides a helpful identification clue.

Distribution: Hammocks, bluffs, and scrub; common throughout the state, including the Keys.

Comment: There has been some disagreement among taxonomic botanists about whether the red bay, swamp bay (*P. palustris*), and silk bay (*P. humilis*) actually constitute separate species. Some believe that eventually all will be considered conspecific. They are treated as distinct species here, and all can be readily separated in the field. All three of these plants share the same genus with the closely related avocado (*P. americana* Mill.), a well-known fruit tree that was probably first imported by the Spaniards during the early explorations of the new world.

Silk Bay

Persea humilis Nash

Form: Evergreen shrub or small tree with characteristically blackish trunk, branches, and twigs.

Swamp Bay
Persea palustris

Sassafras
Sassafras albidum

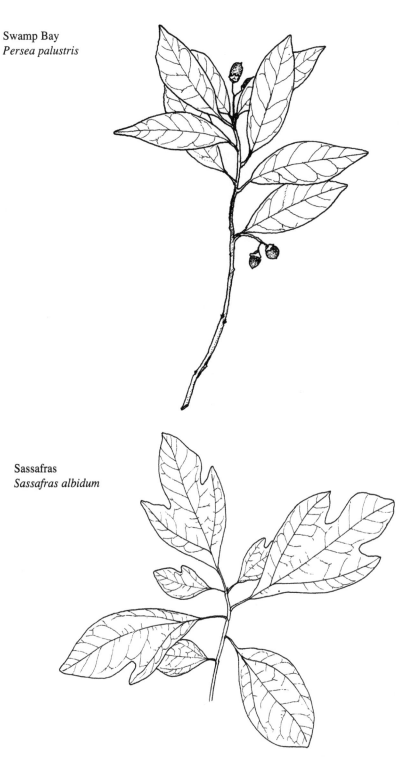

Leaves: Alternate, simple, entire, lanceolate, 3 - 10 cm long, 1 - 3 cm wide; lower surfaces with dense, bronze-colored pubescence that turns grayish with age.

Fruit: A rounded drupe to about 1.5 cm in diameter.

Distinguishing Marks: Distinguished from other species of *Persea* by blackish branches in conjunction with undersurfaces of leaves being covered with dense pubescence that is smooth and silky to the touch.

Distribution: Common component of the white sand scrub of central Florida, also rarely in southeastern and southwestern Florida.

Comment: See note above for *P. borbonia*.

Swamp Bay
Page 169

Persea palustris (Raf.) Sarg.

Form: Evergreen shrub or small tree to about 12 m tall.

Leaves: Alternate, simple, entire, lanceolate or long-elliptic, 5 - 20 cm long; appearing in spring.

Fruit: An oblong drupe to about 1 cm in length.

Distinguishing Marks: Similar in appearance to the red bay (*P. borbonia*) and lancewood (*Ocotea coriacea*), distinguished from both as well as spicebush (*Lindera benzoin*) by undersurfaces of leaves having dense, brownish, shaggy pubescence that is especially copious along the midrib (may require magnification); leaves also often contain galls, similar to red bay.

Distribution: Swamps, coastal swales, and spring margins; common throughout northern Florida and southward to the southern peninsula.

Comment: See note above for *P. borbonia*.

Sassafras
Page 169, Photo 142

Sassafras albidum (Nutt.) Nees

Form: Small, attractive, deciduous tree typically to about 15 m tall, bark with odor of root beer when crushed.

Leaves: Alternate, simple, 5 - 15 cm long, typically characterized by having two or three terminal lobes which often give the leaves the appearance of mittens or three-fingered gloves, but some leaves on some plants unlobed.

Flowers: Small, greenish yellow, 5 - 8 mm across at maturity, appearing in spring near the ends of naked branches.

Fruit: A fleshy, ovoid, dark-blue drupe, 8 - 15 mm long.

Distinguishing Marks: Distinguished from all other plants by the characteristic leaf shape.

Distribution: Dry bluffs, secondary woods, and disturbed sites; throughout the Panhandle and northern part of the state, south to about Orange, Lake, Sumter, and Citrus Counties.

Landscape Use: The mittenlike, soft-green leaves, small but interesting early spring flowers, ease of cultivation, and unique history of this plant make it an excellent understory plant; will reach tree stature.

LEGUMINOSAE (FABACEAE) — BEAN FAMILY

The bean family constitutes one of North America's largest and most diverse plant families. There are many woody and herbaceous species found in Florida, many of which are native. A large number have also been introduced, are used as ornamentals, particularly in southern Florida, and are prized for their showy flowers and attractive pods. In addition to the nearly 40 species described below, there are many more that are likely to become naturalized and may eventually become established components of Florida's flora.

The family Leguminosae (also sometimes referred to as the Fabaceae) is so large that some botanists have divided it into a number of subfamilies. Future botanical revisions may elevate these subfamilies to family status. Regardless of whether this happens, members of the family seem to form a natural group.

Because of its size and complexity, nomenclatural changes to the bean family have been many and varied. The latest and most comprehensive revision was completed by Duane Isely in 1989 and published in 1990. The treatment below follows this revision. Synonyms (previous names) are given where appropriate to help the reader make cross-references with older, perhaps more familiar, names.

In addition to those species described below, two species of *Albizia* are also found in Florida: woman's tongue (*A. lebbeck* [L.] Benth.) of southern Florida, and mimosa (*A. julibrissin* Durazz.) of northern Florida. Both are typically spreading, low-branched trees that sometimes flower when of low stature. They are mentioned here for completeness. Their large, bipinnately compound leaves with many leaflets are very conspicuous.

Tamarindillo

Page 172

Acacia choriophylla Benth.

Form: Large shrub or small, bushy tree with only short, inconspicuous pairs of spines on either side of the base of the leafstalk.

Leaves: Alternate, bipinnately compound, 10 - 20 cm in overall length, pinnae in one to three opposing pairs; leaflets elliptic, numbering 6 - 16 per pinna, 1 - 3 cm long, margins entire and revolute, apices rounded to notched.

Flowers: Bright yellow, globular, headlike cluster, about 1 cm in diameter, appearing in spring and early summer.

Fruit: A flat pod about 5 cm long.

Distinguishing Marks: Distinguished from other species of *Acacia* by inconspicuous spines and by having longer, broader leaflets.

Distribution: Rare and restricted to the border separating high hammocks from the mangrove zone; known predominantly from a small population of only a few plants on North Key Largo; otherwise rarely encountered in natural settings in the Lower Keys and in cultivation or rarely escaped from cultivation.

Landscape Use: As a group the several acacias make good landscape plants. Their small leaflets, thorny branches, and brightly colored flower heads make them suitable for hedge, background, or accent. Most species are extremely drought tolerant, easy to care for, and fast growing.

Tamarindillo
Acacia choriophylla

Sweet Acacia
Acacia farnesiana

Comment: This species is listed as endangered by the Florida Department of Agriculture, but is considered by some to be a tropical waif that arrived via storms or birds and not a species in need of protection.

Sweet Acacia   Page 172
Acacia farnesiana (L.) Willd.

Form: Evergreen shrub or small, much-branched tree to about 5 m tall, with slightly zigzag branches that are armed with paired, whitish spines.

Leaves: Alternate, often crowded on short spur twigs, bipinnately compound, pinnae in two to six opposing pairs, overall leaf 2 - 10 cm long; leaflets linear, 3 - 6 mm long, numbering 10 - 25 pairs per pinna.

Flowers: Borne in rounded, bright-yellow, headlike clusters, 1 - 1.3 cm in diameter, each held on stalks 1.5 - 2 cm long; appearing in spring.

Fruit: A blunt-tipped, cylindric, purplish-red pod, 4 - 8 cm long.

Distinguishing Marks: Distinguished from Small's acacia (*A. smallii*) by the latter species being found chiefly in the extreme western Panhandle, from pineland acacia (*A. pinetorum*) by larger leaflets; from *A. macracantha* by pinnae usually not exceeding about ten in number.

Distribution: Shell middens, coastal hammocks, and pinelands; generally from about Citrus County southward but also rarely reported in northeastern Florida and at one station on St. Vincent Island in the Panhandle.

Landscape Use: See *A. choriophylla*, above.

Comment: The name *A. farnesiana* commemorates Cardinal Odoardo Farnese, who first cultivated the plant in Italy in the early 1600s. There are about 1,200 species of *Acacia*, many of which have thorny branches. Some have ball-like flowers, like those described here, others have spikes. Most are found in the tropics and subtropics and are important for timber, fuel wood, perfumes, and tannin. Acacias also have a long history of ceremonial, ritual, and ornamental uses. The Shittah tree of the Israelites was an *Acacia*, and a branch of *Acacia* is placed in the coffin at Masonic funerals. The Tabernacle and the Arc of the Covenant of Biblical fame were reportedly built from the wood of *Acacia*, and some have proposed that Jesus's crown-of-thorns was fashioned from an acacia branch. Acacia trees are called wattles in some parts of the world and thorn trees in other parts, and the scientific name for the genus derives from the Greek word for thorny. In the late 1600s the current species was widely planted in Europe.

Long Spine Acacia or Steel Acacia   Photo 143
Acacia macracantha Humb. & Bonpl. ex Willd.

Form: Large, spreading shrub or small, spreading tree to about 7 m tall, with conspicuous paired spines along its branches, spines to about 4 cm in length.

Leaves: Alternate, bipinnately compound, pinnae in 10 - 17 opposing pairs, overall leaf to about 10 cm long; leaflets linear in shape, about 3 mm long and very narrow, 23 - 30 pairs on each pinna.

Flowers: Yellow, borne in globular heads that are typically less than 1 cm in diameter; appearing in spring.

Fruit: A cylindrical pod to about 8 cm long.

Distinguishing Marks: Distinguished from other species of *Acacia* by having pinnae in 10 to 17 pairs and typically longer spines.

Distribution: Reportedly native to southern Florida and the Keys but very rare; known from one sandy ridge on Ramrod Key, from northeast Dade County, also reported as escaped from cultivation in Manatee County.

Landscape Use: See comment above for *A. choriophylla*.

Pine or Pineland Acacia   Photo 144
Acacia pinetorum Hermann

Form: Sprawling, wiry, much-branched shrub with characteristically zigzag, spine-studded branches; spines in pairs, usually about 1 cm long.

Leaves: Alternate, bipinnately compound, barely exceeding 1 cm in length, pinnae in three to four opposing pairs; leaflets linear, narrow, less than 3 mm long, 9 - 15 pairs per pinna.

Flowers: Yellow, borne in headlike clusters, less than 1 cm in diameter; appearing in spring.

Fruit: A pointed, cylindric pod.

Distinguishing Marks: Very similar to the sweet acacia (*A. farnesiana*), but distinguished from it by having shorter leaves with leaflets less than 3 mm in length, and pointed fruit; distinguished from twisted acacia (*A. tortuosa*) by having smaller leaves and spines; distinguished from other species of *Acacia* by having zigzag branches and being typically found in pine rockland habitat.

Distribution: Pinelands and pine rockland, scrub, clearings in hammocks; locally common from about Lee County southward, including the Keys.

Landscape Use: See comment above for *A. choriophylla*.

Small's Acacia
Acacia smallii Isely

Form: Deciduous shrub or small, broad-crowned tree to about 5 m tall, armed with pairs of very sharp spines.

Leaves: Alternate, bipinnately compound, pinnae in three to four pairs, overall leaf 3 - 5 cm long, 3 - 4 cm wide; leaflets linear, 2.5 - 5 mm long, commonly about 30 per pinna in 9 - 17 pairs.

Flowers: Golden yellowish to orange, borne in ball-like heads, 8 - 10 mm in diameter, on stalks to about 1 cm in length; appearing in late spring.

Fruit: A linear pod, 3 - 10 cm long.

Distinguishing Marks: Similar in appearance to *A. farnesiana*, distinguished from it by having pinnae mostly in four pairs rather than having some with more than four pairs, by flower stalks generally being 1 cm or less in length, and by occurring in Florida only in the western Panhandle.

Distribution: Sandy places near the edges of saltwater bays; found in Florida primarily in the extreme western Panhandle near Pensacola but perhaps also in other places along the Panhandle coast.

Landscape Use: See comment above for *A. choriophylla.*

Comment: Whether this plant is native to Florida is conjectural. During the nineteenth century Pensacola was noted as an active port that received ships from all over the world. Many ships visiting the port arrived empty of cargo in preparation for loading west Florida's famous longleaf pine timber. Prior to loading, most ships discarded large quantities of ballast, which included a variety of waste materials. It was not uncommon for these materials to contain seeds from foreign plants. As a result, many nonnatives became established along the shores of Pensacola Bay. It is not clearly known whether Small's acacia became established in this way, or whether its appearance is a natural extension of its range (it is common in parts of Texas). The plant was considered lost to the state from the early 1900s until 1977 when botanists Daniel Ward and James Burkhalter published their rediscovery of the plant. Their report, from which much of the above is paraphrased, suggests that there is strong evidence that the plant is native rather than introduced.

Twisted Acacia

Photo 145

Acacia tortuosa (L.) Willd.

Form: Shrub to small, spiny, wide-crowned tree with zigzag branches.

Leaves: Alternate but mostly clustered from spurs, bipinnately compound, less than 10 cm in overall length, pinnae in four to eight opposing pairs, each pinna containing 15 - 20 pairs of leaflets; leaflets linear, narrow, 3 - 4 mm long.

Flowers: Borne in fragrant, globular, yellow heads, about 1 cm in diameter; appearing in spring.

Fruit: A cylindric pod, 8 - 10 cm long.

Distinguishing Marks: Distinguished from other species of *Acacia* with conspicuously zigzag branches by having longer spines and longer leaflets, from sweet acacia (*A. farnesiana*) by leaves mostly with more than ten, rather than less than ten, pinnae.

Distribution: Uncommon on shell mounds and along roadsides in southern Florida.

Landscape Use: See comment above for *A. choriophylla.*

False Indigo or Bastard Indigo

Page 177, Photo 146

Amorpha fruticosa L.

Form: Typically a bushy deciduous shrub to about 4 m tall, rarely treelike.

Leaves: Alternate, odd-pinnately compound, 1 - 3 dm long; leaflets numbering 9 - 35 per leaf, elliptic to oblong or lanceolate, 1 - 5 cm long, 0.5 - 3 cm wide, more or less glandular punctate, often densely pubescent.

Flowers: Borne in dense, elongated racemes to about 2 dm long, with conspicuous golden-yellow anthers set against deep blue or purple petals; appearing mid- to late spring.

Fruit: A small, curved, one-seeded pod to about 8 mm long.

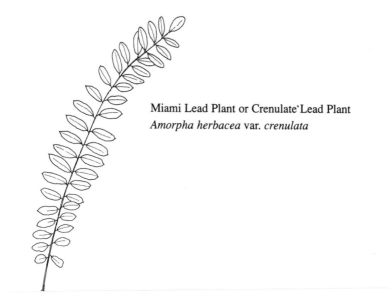

Miami Lead Plant or Crenulate Lead Plant
Amorpha herbacea var. *crenulata*

Distinguishing Marks: The showy, purple and yellow flowers which appear in spring and early summer are distinctive.

Distribution: Wet woods, banks of river and streams, floodplain woods; throughout northern Florida, southward to about Lake Okeechobee and north Palm Beach County.

Comment: There are also several species of *Baptisia*, which are also called indigo, that occur in Florida. Though all are herbaceous, many are perennial and take on a shrublike appearance. They typically have showy racemes that are quite conspicuous when in flower.

Miami Lead Plant or Crenulate Lead Plant   Page 176

Amorpha herbacea Walt. var. *crenulata* (Rydberg) Isely

Form: A shrub with slender, purplish branches; 1 - 1.5 m (perhaps to 3 m) tall.

Leaves: Alternate, pinnately compound, to about 17 cm in overall length; leaflets 11 - 29 in number, oblong, green above, paler below, 1 - 3 cm long, apices often bearing a tiny point, margins crenulate.

Flowers: White to pale lavender, showy, borne in racemes 15 - 20 cm long; appearing in spring; similar in general appearance to those of *A. fruticosa* (pictured in photo 146).

Fruit: A small pod, 6 - 11 mm long.

Distinguishing Marks: The long racemes of white flowers with green to purple receptacles and compound leaves with crenulate leaflets help distinguish this species.

Distribution: Rock pinelands; endemic to Dade County in areas underlain by Miami limestone.

Comment: Listed as endangered by both the Florida Department of Agriculture and the U. S. Fish and Wildlife Service. Some authorities report this species as *A. crenulata* Rydberg.

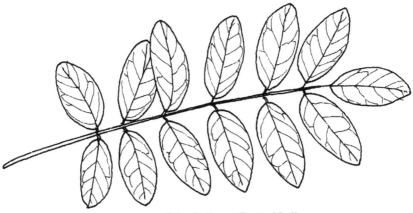

False Indigo or Bastard Indigo
Amorpha fruticosa

Leadplant or Indigo Bush

Amorpha herbacea Walt. var. *herbacea*

Form: Colonial shrubs with reddish-brown, finely-grooved stems; to about 1.5 m tall.

Leaves: Alternate, pinnately compound, 7 - 15 cm long; leaflets numbering 13 - 49, each 1 - 3 cm long, to about 1 cm wide, elliptic to ovate, densely pubescent below, central vein extending beyond the tip of the leaflet into a blunt, swollen tip.

Flowers: Varying from white to pale bluish-purple, borne in groups of densely flowered, showy racemes at the tips of the branches, each raceme 1 - 3 dm long; appearing late spring and summer.

Fruit: A small, hairy, resinous pod, 4 - 5 mm long.

Distinguishing Marks: The numerous terminal racemes of white to bluish-purple flowers in conjunction with the pinnately compound leaves help distinguish this species; similar in general appearance to the photograph of *A. fruticosa* (photo 146), but distinguished by paler flowers and overall smaller and more numerous leaflets.

Distribution: Low, moist areas, flatwoods, scrub; throughout the state, considered woody only in south Florida.

Gray Nicker Bean, Sea Bean, Fever Nut, Hold-Back

Caesalpinia bonduc (L.) Roxb. **Photo 147**

Form: Erect to arching, sometimes vinelike, shrub; branches covered with sharp, curving spines and typically scrambling over other vegetation for distances of up to 6 m.

Leaves: Opposite, bipinnately compound with 4 - 5 pairs of pinnae, overall leaf length reaching about 40 cm or more; leaflets ovate to elliptic, typically 2 - 5 cm long, shiny green.

Flowers: Yellow, with five petals, borne in long, conspicuous clusters in the leaf axils; individual flowers 1 - 2 cm wide when fully open; appearing year-round.

Fruit: A reddish-brown, flat, elliptic, very spiny pod, 4 - 9 cm in diameter; splitting at maturity to expose 1 - 3 gray seeds to about 2 cm in diameter.

Distinguishing Marks: The densely spiny stems and fruit distinguish this species from most other plants; the gray, rather than yellow, seeds help distinguish it from *C. major*, the other common nicker bean.

Distribution: Coastal areas, mangroves; southernmost Florida and the Keys.

Landscape Use: This plant is sometimes used as a natural barrier in locations where it is desirable to prevent disturbance, hence the last of its common names listed above.

Yellow Nicker Bean or Yellow Nicker   Photo 148
Caesalpinia major (Medic.) Dandy & Exell

Form: A sprawling, scrambling, sometimes vinelike shrub very similar in general form to *C. bonduc*.

Leaves: In general form like those of *C. bonduc* (above), except that the leaflets are perhaps, on average, slightly larger.

Flowers: Similar to *C. bonduc*; appearing year-round.

Fruit: Pods like those of *C. bonduc*; seeds yellow.

Distinguishing Marks: Distinguished from *C. bonduc* by having yellow, as opposed to gray, seeds.

Distribution: Coastal areas, mangroves; southernmost Florida and the Keys.

Landscape Use: See *C. bonduc*.

Caesalpinia
Caesalpinia pauciflora (Griseb.) C. Wright ex Sauvella

Form: An erect, bushy shrub to about 2 m tall, with paired spines at the base of the leafstalks.

Leaves: Opposite, bipinnately compound, usually four or more pairs of pinnae; leaflets oblong, notched at the apices, typically 1 - 2 cm long.

Flowers: Yellow, with conspicuous stamens, similar to the other two members of the genus; appearing year-round.

Fruit: An oblong, tapered pod to about 4 cm long.

Distinguishing Marks: The comparatively smaller leaflets and more narrow, tapered pod distinguish this species from the other two members of the genus.

Distribution: South Florida and the Keys; most conspicuous in pinelands of Big Pine Key.

Bay Bean or Seaside Bean

Page 179, Photo 149

Canavalia rosea (Sw.) DC.

Form: Prostrate, evergreen vine to several or more meters in length; base and lower portions of main stem rigid and appearing woody, to about 3 cm in diameter.

Leaves: Alternate, compound with three entire, obovate to oval or nearly rounded leaflets; apices of leaflets notched or rounded, each leaflet 7 - 9 cm long.

Flowers: Irregular, showy, purple to violet, to about 3 cm long; appearing year-round.

Fruit: Prominently ribbed pod, to about 15 cm long, becoming woody.

Distinguishing Marks: The showy, purple flowers, trifoliolate leaves, and coastal habitat help distinguish this species.

Distribution: Coastal strand; most common from about central Florida southward, but also reported from Shired Island in Dixie County. It is interesting to note that A. W. Chapman (1860) reported this plant from St. Vincent Island on the Panhandle coast, but it is not known to exist there today.

Landscape Use: This is an attractively flowering vine that is very good for dry, salty areas.

Comment: Bay bean is extremely salt tolerant, and its seeds are dispersed by ocean currents. It is one of south Florida's most important beach-loving vines. It is also sometimes seen listed by the synonym *C. maritima* Thouars.

Eastern Redbud

Page 180

Cercis canadensis L.

Form: Typically a small, attractive, deciduous, relatively short-lived tree (not usually exceeding about 20 years in age) to about 8 m tall, with a short, grayish trunk; sometimes flowering and fruiting when of low stature.

Leaves: Alternate, simple, two ranked, entire, typically heart shaped in overall form with cordate bases, 5 - 12.5 cm long.

Flowers: Appearing (often in great profusion) in spring before leaf growth, borne in clusters of four to eight separate flowers, dark magenta to purplish in color.

Fruit: A flattened pod, 4 - 10 cm long and shaped somewhat like the blade of a dinner knife.

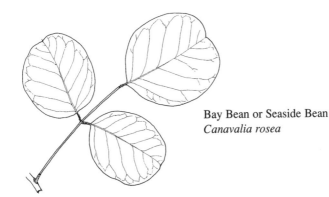

Bay Bean or Seaside Bean
Canavalia rosea

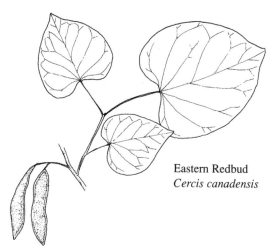

Eastern Redbud
Cercis canadensis

Distinguishing Marks: The arresting flowers and heart-shaped leaves help in identifying this plant.

Distribution: Understory of rich woods, roadsides, and yards from the central Panhandle southward down the western peninsula to about Citrus County.

Landscape Use: The eastern redbud is one of north Florida's best-loved trees. Its exquisitely colored flowers range from light pink to magenta and normally appear in early spring, before the tree puts out new leaves. Its blooms are so beautiful and appear in such profusion along the naked branches that the tree is often considered to produce one of the most spectacular splashes of early spring color. This factor alone explains why the tree is often found planted in yards and gardens, as well as alongside city streets.

Comment: Eastern redbud is sometimes called Judas tree after the betrayer of Christ who hanged himself on one of the plant's close relatives. Legend holds that the flowers were once white, but turned pink in disgrace.

Big Pine Partridge Pea or Key Cassia   Photo 150

Chamaecrista lineata (Swartz) Greene var. *keyensis* (Pennell) Irwin & Barn.

Form: Prostrate to erect woody shrub or perennial herb, 3 - 8 dm tall.

Leaves: Alternate, compound, to about 3 cm long; leaflets pale green, oblong, 0.5 to 1.5 cm long, numbering to about 16 per leaf and borne in pairs.

Flowers: Irregular, predominantly yellow with orange splotches near the base of the petals, to about 2.5 cm wide when mature; typically borne singly in the leaf axils; appearing in spring and summer.

Fruit: A slender pea, 2.5 - 5 cm long, 4 - 5 mm in diameter.

Distinguishing Marks: Most easily recognized by the pale green leaflets, woody stem, and yellow and orange flowers.

Distribution: Endemic to pinelands and hammock edges of the Florida Keys; most common on Big Pine, No Name, and Cudjoe Keys.

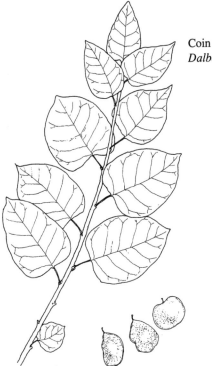

Coin Vine
Dalbergia brownei

Comment: Listed as threatened by the Florida Department of Agriculture and as a candidate for listing by the U. S. Fish and Wildlife Service. This plant is often seen listed as *Cassia keyensis* (Pennell) Macbride.

Coin Vine
Dalbergia brownei (Jacq.) Urb.

Page 181

Form: Sprawling, scandent, or trailing woody shrub to at least 5 m long; sometimes forming dense tangles by scrambling and climbing vinelike over adjacent plants; older branches somewhat ropelike and with lateral spines.

Leaves: Alternate, compound but leaves on mature plants usually with a single leaflet, making the leaf appear simple, leaves on young plants or prostrate branches typically with three leaflets; leaflets leathery, distinctly reticulately veined, dark green with a slightly yellowish midrib, elliptic to ovate, 2 - 10 cm long.

Flowers: Small, white to pinkish, 8 - 10 mm long, borne in the leaf axils; appearing in spring and summer.

Fruit: Flat, oval, or oblong pod to a little more than 1 cm in diameter; becoming copper colored at maturity and resembling a coin, hence the common name.

Distinguishing Marks: The sometimes compound leaves, hairless upper surfaces of leaves, and spines on older branches distinguish this species from *D. ecastophyllum*; the coinlike

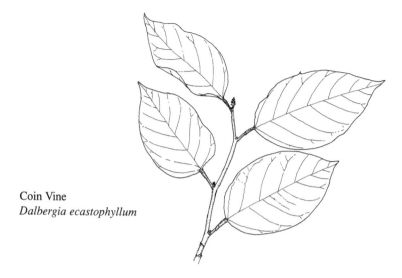

Coin Vine
Dalbergia ecastophyllum

fruit helps distinguish it from other species.

Distribution: Edges of hammocks and mangroves in the Keys.

Landscape Use: Appropriate for trellises, but see comment below for *D. ecastophyllum*.

Comment: The seeds of this plant are known to float and remain viable even in saltwater, which has helped the distribution of this plant in the tropics. Also see comment below for *D. ecastophyllum*. Florida's species of *Dalbergia* are two of about 120 species of tropical plants in this genus, most of which are trees.

Coin Vine

Page 182

Dalbergia ecastophyllum (L.) Taubert

Form: A scandent or sprawling shrub to trailing vine with reclining branches; stems to about 8 m in length; older branches without spines.

Leaves: Alternate, unifoliolate, leathery, glossy green, ovate to elliptic, 5 - 15 cm long; apices usually pinched to a sharp point, sometimes rounded.

Flowers: White to suffused with pink, to about 1 cm long, borne in clusters in the leaf axils.

Fruit: A flat, coppery, single-seeded, rounded, coinlike pod, 2 - 3 cm wide.

Distinguishing Marks: The combination of coppery-colored, coinlike pod, compound but unifoliolate leaves, and leaflet with sparse pubescence on both sides distinguish this species.

Distribution: Edges of mangroves or on shell mounds within mangroves, coastal hammocks, dunes; south Florida.

Landscape Use: A fast-growing plant that is useful in near-coastal situations, especially near mangroves; tolerant of salty soils.

Comment: The generic name of this plant and the one above is derived from the name of 18th century botanists, Nil and Carl Dalberg, colleagues of Carl von Linne. The crushed roots and bark of the plant contain toxins that have been used to stun or stupefy fish, thus allowing them to be easily caught by hand.

Coral Bean, Cardinal Spear, Cherokee Bean   Photos 151, 152

Erythrina herbacea L.

Form: Deciduous, erect, commonly prickly, often herbaceous, multistemmed shrub from a woody base; definitely shrublike or even treelike in south Florida where it grows to about 5 m tall.

Leaves: Alternate, compound, trifoliolate, overall leaf to about 15 - 20 cm long, up to about 6 cm wide; leaflets shaped like arrowheads or spearheads in overall outline, widest near the bases and tapering to pointed apices, each leaflet 2 - 10 cm long, dull green in color.

Flowers: Bright red, long, and tubular, 3 - 6.5 cm long, borne in showy, vertical racemes, appearing in late spring and summer, often when the plant is leafless.

Fruit: Pod narrow, 5 - 20 cm long, constricted between the obvious seed pouches, splitting to expose hard, red seeds.

Distinguishing Marks: Distinguished from all other Florida trees and shrubs by its uniquely shaped trifoliolate leaf.

Distribution: Found in a variety of habitats; nearly throughout the state.

Landscape Use: The bright red flowers make this a good accent plant, especially for sunny locations. The splitting seed pods are also attractive, but the bright red seeds are poisonous.

Comment: Some authors have treated the south Florida form of this plant as *E. arborea* (Chapman) Small because it more often becomes woody and arborescent than does its counterpart in the northern part of the state. Isely considers this difference to be only a "manifestation of climatic adaptation" (Isely, 1990, p. 65) and follows Krukoff and Barneby (1974) in treating the two as forms of a single species.

Indigo   Page 184

Indigofera suffruticosa Mill.

Form: Deciduous shrub or perennial herb to about 2 m tall, with angled stems clothed with grayish hairs; often clump forming.

Leaves: Alternate, pinnately compound with 7 - 15 leaflets; leaflets mostly elliptic, entire, 2 - 3 cm long, 1 - 1.5 cm wide; surfaces of leaflets varyingly covered (depending upon age) by blond hairs that divide into two branches (requires magnification).

Flowers: Reddish to purplish, small, borne in spikelike clusters in the leaf axils; appearing summer to fall.

Fruit: A cylindrical pod, 1 - 2 cm long.

Distinguishing Marks: Distinguished by the combination of compound leaves, obvious leguminous fruit, and pubescence of all parts being branched; most similar to *Amorpha fruticosa* but the latter has punctate leaves which lack branched hairs.

Distribution: Nonnative, naturalized in pinelands, open woods, vacant lots; nearly throughout Florida southward to the southernmost peninsula.

Comment: A second member of this genus, hairy indigo (*I. hirsuta* L.) is similar in appearance by being erect (to about 1.5 m tall) and shrubby but is an annual or biennial herb. It is found in many parts of Florida and is distinguished by the conspicuous covering of brownish pubescence on its stem.

Indigo
Indigofera suffruticosa

Bush Clover
Lespedeza thunbergii

Bush Clover
Lespedeza bicolor Turcz.

Form: A few- to many-stemmed shrub to about 3 m tall; woody portions usually confined to the lower stem.

Leaves: Alternate, compound with three leaflets; leaflets entire, elliptic to oval, mostly averaging 2 - 5 cm long (sometimes longer), 1 - 2 cm wide (sometimes wider); upper surfaces of mature leaves only slightly, if at all, pubescent, lower surfaces varying in the amount of pubescence.

Flowers: Purple, tubular, to about 1.5 cm long, borne in racemes from the leaf axils; appearing late summer and fall.

Fruit: A small, flat pod, 5 - 8 mm long; seeds green or splotched with purple.

Distinguishing Marks: The trifoliolate leaves in combination with the purple flowers and small, flat fruit pods help distinguish the species; distinguished from *L. bicolor* by the seeds being green or only splotched with purple, by the leaflets being oval rather than narrowly elliptic, and by the lobes of the calyx being shorter than the tube.

Distribution: Native to Japan, planted for game food; naturalized primarily in northern Florida but sparingly southward to about Hernando County.

Comment: About a dozen species of *Lespedeza* occur in Florida, most of which are native and herbaceous. All are noted for their trifoliolate leaves. Members of this genus are sometimes confused with one of the several beggar lice (*Desmodium* sp.), which have similar flowers and leaves. The two genera can be most easily distinguished by the lateral veins of the leaflets. Those of *Lespedeza* diverge at nearly right angles to the midvein and are distinctly parallel with each other; those of *Desmodium* diverge at angles approaching 45 degrees. The two nonnative species described here are the state's only woody members of the genus.

Bush Clover
Page 184

Lespedeza thunbergii (DC.) Nakai

Form: A few- to many-stemmed shrub to about 3 m tall; woody portions usually confined to the lower stem.

Leaves: Alternate, compound with three leaflets; leaflets entire, elliptic to ovate or lanceolate, mostly averaging 3 - 6 cm long, 2 - 4 cm wide; surfaces of mature leaves with a uniform covering of short pubescence.

Flowers: Purple, tubular, borne in racemes from the leaf axils; appearing in early summer.

Fruit: A small, flat pod, 5 - 8 mm long; seeds purple.

Distinguishing Marks: The trifoliolate leaves in combination with the purple flowers and small, flat fruit pods help distinguish the species; distinguished from *L. bicolor* by the seeds being purple, by the leaves being narrowly elliptic rather than oval, and by the calyx lobes being longer than the tube.

Distribution: Planted for game food; naturalized primarily in northern Florida.

Comment: See *L. bicolor*, above.

Lead Tree or Jumbie Bean

Photo 1553

Leucaena leucocephala (Lam.) de Wit

Form: Shrub or small, spineless tree to about 10 m tall.

Leaves: Alternate, bipinnately compound, overall leaf 10 - 30 cm long; pinnae in four to eight pairs, each with 10 - 20 pairs of opposite, oblong leaflets, 8 - 14 mm long.

Flowers: Borne in yellowish-white to whitish globose heads to about 2 cm in diameter; appearing year-round.

Fruit: A flat, reddish-brown to brown pod, 8 - 20 cm long, 1 - 2 cm wide, often borne in dense, hanging clusters.

Distinguishing Marks: The whitish flowering heads and flattened pod set this species apart from most other south Florida trees and shrubs.

Distribution: Exotic species established in hammocks and waste places of the coastal strand; Hillsborough County southward and throughout the Keys.

Landscape Use: This species is listed as a Category II pest plant by the Florida Exotic Pest Plant Council. It should not be used in landscaping.

Small's Lupine or Gulfcoast Lupine

Photo 154

Lupinus westianus Small

Form: Low, compact shrub to about 1.5 m tall and 1 m in diameter; mostly herbaceous, woody only on lower portions of the stem; young stems (and most other parts of the plant) copiously covered with a soft, woolly pubescence.

Leaves: Alternate, simple, entire, elliptic, 3 - 8 cm long, 2 - 5 cm wide; petioles conspicuous, 1 - 4 cm long; both surfaces covered with a dense covering of soft, woolly hairs.

Flowers: Showy, borne in an erect raceme to about 3 dm tall, blue to purplish blue with a dark purplish-red spot; appearing in April and May.

Fruit: A shaggy, elliptic to oblong pod, 1.5 - 2.5 cm long.

Distinguishing Marks: The only Panhandle plants that are likely to be confused with the current species are *L. diffusus* Nutt. and *L. villosus* Willd., both of which are somewhat more common, also quite woolly pubescent, generally smaller in stature, and usually described as herbs. The former can be distinguished by having a cream-colored rather than purplish-red central spot on the flower, the latter by flowers that are more reddish-purple or pink than blue. Neither of the other species has short (as opposed to long) pubescence, that is evenly distributed from the stem, petiole, and leaf surfaces. *L. westianus* also differs vegetatively from these latter plants by lacking stipules.

Distribution: Dune areas, open sands, sandy disturbed areas; Franklin to Santa Rosa Counties in the Panhandle. A variety of gulf coast lupine, *L. westianus* var. *aridorum* (McFarlin ex Beckner) Isely, also described as a woody-stemmed or woody-branched herb, is a plant of the Lake Wales Ridge and the southern peninsula's white sand scrub, chiefly in Orange and Polk Counties. It was, until recently, listed under the specific name, *L. aridorum* McFarlin ex Beckner.

Comment: Listed as threatened by the Florida Department of Agriculture, and as a candidate for federal listing by the U. S. Fish and Wildlife Service.

Blackbead or Ram's Horn
Pithecellobium keyense

Blackbead or Ram's Horn

Page 187

Pithecellobium keyense Britton ex Britton & Rose

Form: Commonly a small, wide-spreading, rarely spiny evergreen shrub, reaching the stature of a small tree to about 6 m tall.

Leaves: Alternate, bipinnately compound; pinnae numbering two, each typically with only two leaflets (thus four leaflets per leaf); leaflets obovate, oval to elliptic, commonly 2.5 - 5 cm long, 1.2 - 4 cm wide, apices often notched.

Flowers: Borne in whitish-yellow or pink heads, 1.5 - 2.5 cm in diameter, on stalks 2 - 3.5 cm long, appearing from February throughout the spring.

Fruit: A narrow, flattened, curving pod, 5 - 20 cm long, 7 - 10 mm wide.

Distinguishing Marks: Distinguished from the catclaw (*P. unguis-cati*) by having overall larger leaves and leaflets, and by less commonly exhibiting spines at the leaf bases.

Distribution: Sandy soils adjacent to beaches and hammocks; Lee, Palm Beach, and Broward Counties southward and throughout the Keys.

Comment: Also commonly seen listed as *P. guadalupense* (Pers.) Champ. In addition to this and the next species, both of which are native, at least one cultivated species of *Pithecellobium* has also escaped and become established in southern Florida. *P. dulce* (Roxb.) Benth. is a shrub or small tree, also with four-foliate leaves. It differs from the other two species by having flowers that typically do not exceed 2.5 mm in length and are borne on a densely pubescent stalk; the flowers of the other two are generally longer than 3 mm and are borne on hairless stalks.

Catclaw or Catclaw Blackbead

Page 188

Pithecellobium unguis-cati (L.) Benth.

Form: Spiny evergreen shrub or small, multitrunked tree to about 7 m tall; stems slightly zigzag, often containing sharp spines to about 5 mm long.

Leaves: Alternate, bipinnately compound, overall leaf 2.5 - 8 cm long; pinnae numbering two, each with only two leaflets; leaflets bright green, obovate to elliptic, 1.5 - 6 cm long, 1 - 3.5 cm wide.

Flowers: Borne in whitish to yellow-green heads, 1 - 2 cm in diameter, borne from the leaf axils on stalks 1.5 - 2.5 cm long; appearing at any time of year.

Fruit: An oblong, reddish, curving pod, 5 - 15 cm long.

Distinguishing Marks: Distinguished from *P. keyense* by having generally smaller leaves and leaflets, and by more commonly having spiny branches and spines at the leaf bases.

Distribution: Shell mounds, roadsides, hammocks, sand ridges; from about Manatee County southward on the west coast, Dade County southward on the east coast, throughout the Keys.

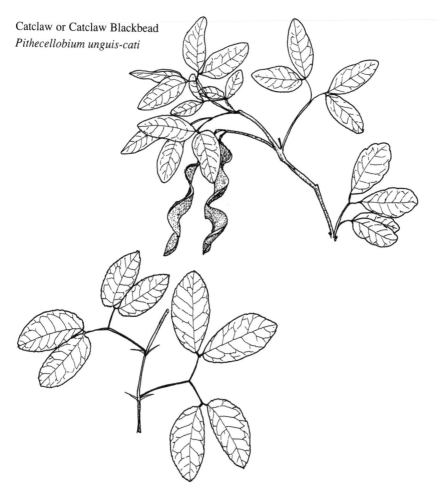

Catclaw or Catclaw Blackbead
Pithecellobium unguis-cati

Kudzu Vine

Pueraria lobata (Willd.) Ohwi.

Form: Deciduous, hairy, twining vine spreading rapidly and typically forming dense tangles that strangle native vegetation; older stems woody, leathery, brown.

Leaves: Alternate, compound with three leaflets; base of terminal leaflet usually flared into two lobes, bases of lateral leaflets more often flared into only one lobe; leaflets to 20 cm long, 12 cm wide at their widest point; petioles quite variable in length and ranging from 3 to 30 cm, those of mature leaves are the longest.

Flowers: Purple, fragrant, borne in showy racemes; appearing summer through fall.

Fruit: A woolly, flattened, brownish pod, 4 - 10 cm long.

Distinguishing Marks: The distinctive leaves and typically invasive growth habit distinguish the species.

Distribution: Native to Asia, introduced for erosion control; most likely seen along roadways; throughout northern Florida, generally southward to Hillsborough and Polk Counties, but also reported from Broward County and as becoming established in Dade County.

Landscape Use: This is an extremely aggressive weed that is hazardous to native flora and is very difficult to eradicate or control once started. It is listed as a Category I pest plant by the Florida Exotic Pest Plant Council and is definitely not recommended for landscape use.

Comment: This plant was once estimated to cover nearly three million acres of southern landscape. It was introduced into the United States in 1876 at the Philadelphia Centennial Exposition. Later it was introduced to the New Orleans area at another exposition. It is from this latter introduction that it escaped and became established in the southeast.

Kudzu Vine
Pueraria lobata

Bristly Locust

Robinia hispida L.

Form: A many-branched deciduous shrub to about 3 m tall; young parts of the plant covered with relatively long, stiff, purplish hairs.

Leaves: Alternate, pinnately compound, to about 3 dm in overall length; leaflets ranging 7 - 19 in number, broadly elliptic to ovate or oblong, 1 - 5 cm long, 1 - 3.5 cm wide, well-spaced on the central leaf stem.

Flowers: Reddish purple or purple to pinkish, appearing in spring and borne in showy, drooping racemes, each flower 1.5 - 3 cm long and very conspicuous.

Fruit: A densely hairy, essentially cylindrical pod, 3 - 8 cm long.

Distinguishing Marks: The pinnate leaves, purple to pink flowers, and very hairy stems and central leaf stalk distinguish the species; in many respects similar to *R. pseudoacacia*.

Distribution: Occasionally naturalized from cultivation in north Florida.

Landscape Use: The attractive flowers and easy maintenance have made this an attractive landscape plant along roadsides and in gardens; especially good for erosion control.

Black Locust   Page 190

Robinia pseudoacacia L.

Form: Typically a deciduous tree to about 25 m tall, with paired spines at the leaf bases; sometimes flowering and fruiting when of shrub stature.

Leaves: Alternate, odd-pinnately compound, 20 - 36 cm long; leaflets 7 to 19 in number, elliptic, 2 - 6 cm long, 1 - 2.5 cm wide; leaflets often "closing" at night, hence sometimes described as "sleeping".

Flowers: Fragrant, irregular, showy, creamy white with a yellow spot on the upper petal, appearing in February and early spring and borne from the leaf axils in drooping racemes that resemble the inflorescences of the American wisteria (*Wisteria frutescens*).

Fruit: A flattened pod, 5 - 10 cm long, about 1 cm wide.

Distribution: Disturbed sites, secondary woods, sometimes planted as an ornamental; native to the southern Appalachians and generally restricted in Florida to the vicinity of Leon, Gadsden, and Madison Counties but also reported from Marion County.

Black Locust
Robinia pseudoacacia

Landscape Use: Used along roadsides, dry landscapes, and woodland edges; prefers full sun to only partial shade but is tolerant of most soils. In parts of its range the plant has found value in stabilizing eroding slopes; perhaps more troublesome than beneficial in the suburban landscape due to its thorns, its messy nature, and the tendency of its roots to crack concrete drives and patios.

Comment: The wood of the black locust is quite durable and has been used in shipbuilding, for fence posts, and in the fabrication of furniture. The leaves are eaten by livestock, and the flowers are reported to be both edible and the source of a delectable honey. However, some parts of the plant are said to have poisonous properties.

Privet Senna

Page 191, Photo 155

Senna ligustrina (L.) Irwin & Barneby

Form: Herbaceous to partly woody shrub with smooth stems; to about 2 m tall.

Leaves: Alternate, pinnately compound, 13 - 27 cm long, with 12 - 22 paired leaflets; leaflets lanceolate, 2 - 6 cm long, 1 - 2 cm wide, hairy below when young, becoming glabrous with age; petiole with a pointed gland near the base.

Flowers: Yellow with brownish dots, petals 1 - 1.5 cm long; appearing year-round.

Fruit: A flattened pod, to about 13 cm long.

Distinguishing Marks: The combination of comparatively large leaflets and long, flattened pods helps set this species apart from many members of the genus *Cassia*, of which it was long considered a species.

Distribution: Common along hammock margins and on disturbed sites; central and southern Florida, especially the coastal counties.

Privet Senna
Senna ligustrina

Bahama Senna

Page 192, Photo 156

Senna mexicana (Jacq.) Irwin & Barn. var. *chapmanii* (Isely) Irwin & Barn.

Form: Spreading or erect shrub to about 2 m tall.

Leaves: Alternate, pinnately compound with up to ten, paired, light green, elliptic leaflets; leaflets 2 - 6 cm long; apices of leaflets often bearing a sharp point.

Flowers: Bright, golden yellow, often borne profusely in the axils of the uppermost leaves, each flower to nearly 3 cm wide at maturity; likely to flower year-round, but most prolifically in fall and winter.

Fruit: Flat, brown pod to about 10 cm long.

Distinguishing Marks: Differs from most species of *Cassia* and *Senna*, with which it is most easily confused, by having larger leaflets in conjunction with a woody stem.

Distribution: Roadsides, pinelands; southern mainland and the Keys.

Landscape Use: Easily propagated from seed and extremely salt-tolerant.

Comment: This plant is often seen listed as *Cassia chapmanii* Isley.

Senna pendula (Willd.) Irwin & Barn. var. *glabrata* (Vogel) Irwin & Barn.

Form: Large, evergreen shrub to about 4 m tall, with somewhat zigzag stems.

Leaves: Alternate, pinnately compound, with 3 - 5 pairs of leaflets; leaflets rounded and increasing in size toward the end of the leaf; middle leaflets 1.5 - 3.5 cm long.

Flowers: Bright yellow, bilaterally symmetrical, borne in long-stalked clusters from the leaf axils; 3 - 5 cm in width when fully open; appearing fall and winter.

Fruit: A dry, segmented pod, mostly 7 - 15 cm long, 1 - 1.5 cm in diameter.

Distinguishing Marks: The rounded leaves that increase in size toward the apices and irregular, bright yellow flowers help distinguish the species.

Distribution: Native to South America and cultivated statewide; escaped in south Florida.

Landscape Use: Hardy and easy to grow once established; does better near the coast (due to sensitivity to cold) in the northern part of the state.

Comment: Also known by the scientific synonym, *Cassia coluteoides* Coll.

Bahama Senna
Senna mexicana var. *chapmanii*

Rattlebush or Rattlebox

Sesbania drummondii (Rydb.) Cory

Form: Erect, deciduous, widely branched shrub; commonly 1 - 3 m tall; sometimes dying to the ground in winter.

Leaves: Alternate, pinnately compound, 2 - 3 dm in overall length; leaflets in 10 - 20 pairs, each leaflet 1 - 3 cm long, to about 1 cm wide, those in the center of the leaf larger than those on either end, margins entire.

Flowers: Yellow to sometimes orange yellow (latter color perhaps due to hybridization with *S. punicea*), irregular, borne from the leaf axils in racemes to about 1 dm long; appearing in late summer.

Fruit: An oblong, four-winged, light brown pod, 2 - 8 cm long, 1 - 1.5 cm wide; wings thin and separated by a deep, narrow trough.

Distinguishing Marks: The yellow to orange-yellow flowers distinguish this species from *S. punicea*; distinguished from *S. virgata* by having thin, rather than thick, wings on the pod, and by the wings being separated by a deep, narrow trough rather than a shallow, wide one.

Distribution: Mainly in coastal areas including near brackish marshes, also disturbed sites; western Panhandle, especially near Pensacola.

Comment: This species is sometimes seen listed as *Daubentonia drummondii* Rydb. There are at least two annual species of *Sesbania* (*S. marginata* DC., *S. macrocarpa* Muhl. ex Raf.). These two, as well as the annual bladderpod (*Glottidium vesicarium* [Jacq.] Mohr), which was until recently known as *Sesbania vesicaria* (Jacq.) Ell., are quite similar to the yellow-flowered sesbans described here.

Bequilla

Sesbania emerus (Aubl.) Urban

Form: A short-lived, irregularly branched shrub with glabrous stems.

Leaves: Alternate, pinnately compound, 1 - 2 dm in overall length; leaflets borne in 15 - 25 pairs, each leaflet oblong, 1 - 2.5 cm long.

Flowers: Yellow, sometimes tinged with red, borne in three- to six-flowered racemes; appearing summer through fall.

Fruit: An angled, linear, unwinged pod, 1.5 - 2 dm long with many seeds.

Distinguishing Marks: The yellow flowers which are less than 3 cm long, glabrous stems, and many-seeded pods help distinguish this species from others within its range.

Distribution: Native to Mexico and Central America, introduced, or perhaps native, to southern Florida and Key West; primarily found in disturbed sites.

Comment: Isely (1990) limits distribution of *S. emerus* to subtropical Florida and considers reports of this species farther north to be *S. exaltata* (Rafinesque) Cory, an erect, annual herb.

Sesban, Daubentonia, Spanish Gold, Purple Sesban

Sesbania punicea (Cav.) Benth.   **Photos 157, 158**

Form: Erect, deciduous, widely branched shrub; commonly 1 - 3 m tall.

Leaves: Alternate, pinnately compound, 1 - 3 dm in overall length; leaflets in 10 - 17 pairs, each leaflet 1 - 3 cm long, to about 1 cm wide, those in the center of the leaf at least some-what larger than those on either end, margins entire.

Flowers: Red to orange red, irregular, borne from the leaf axils in racemes of 5 - 30 flowers; raceme to about 12 cm long; appearing late spring to fall.

Fruit: An oblong, four-winged, dark brown pod, 2 - 8 cm long, 1 - 1.5 cm wide; wings wavy or notched.

Distinguishing Marks: The red flowers distinguish this species from the other sesbans.

Distribution: Native to South America but naturalized in many locations across north Florida and southward to the south-central peninsula.

Landscape Use: Fast growing and useful along wooded borders and other sunny locations; easily established and readily self seeds to form small colonies; the bright reddish-orange flowers are especially showy and attractive.

Silky Sesban

Sesbania sericea (Willd.) DC.

Form: Short-lived, unarmed to only slightly-prickly branching shrub to about 2 m tall.

Leaves: Alternate, pinnately compound, 1 - 2 dm in overall length, with 10 - 20 pairs of leaflets; leaflets narrowly oblong, 1 - 4 cm long, with a tiny point at the apices; lower sur-faces of leaflets silky pubescent (hence the common name).

Flowers: Orange, orange yellow, or greenish yellow, borne in a few-flowered raceme that is 2 - 6 cm long; appearing spring through fall.

Fruit: A linear pod, to about 15 cm long, 2 - 5 mm wide, with 20 - 30 seeds.

Distinguishing Marks: The combination of bipinnate leaves, irregular orange flowers, and silky pubescence on the lower surfaces of leaflets distinguish this species from other sesbans.

Distribution: Key West; rare in Broward County.

Sesbania virgata (Cav.) Pers.

Form: Erect, deciduous, widely branched shrub; commonly 1 - 3 m tall.

Leaves: Alternate, pinnately compound, 1 - 3 dm in overall length; leaflets in 13 to 16 pairs, each leaflet 1 - 3 cm long, to about 1 cm wide, those in the center of the leaf larger than those on either end, margins entire.

Flowers: Yellow, irregular, borne from the leaf axils in racemes to about 1 dm long.

Fruit: An oblong, four-winged, dark brown pod, 3 - 6 cm long, to about 1 cm wide; wings thick and separated by a wide, shallow trough.

Distinguishing Marks: The yellow flowers distinguish this species from *S. punicea*; distin-guished from *S. drummondii* by having thick, rather than thin, wings on the pod, and by the wings being separated by a wide, shallow trough rather than a deep, narrow one.

Necklace Pod
Sophora tomentosa

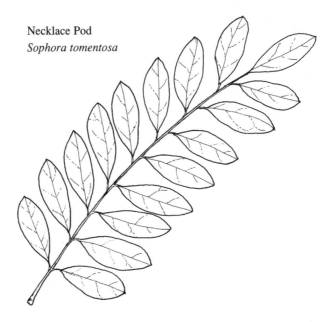

Distribution: Native to Mexico, naturalized in Florida mainly in coastal areas and waste places of the western Panhandle.

Necklace Pod

Page 195, Photos 159, 160

Sophora tomentosa L.

Form: Shrub but sometimes reaching the stature of a small tree to about 6 m tall; the entire plant covered with white to grayish hairs.

Leaves: Alternate, odd-pinnate, overall leaf to about 30 cm long; leaflets irregularly opposite, 11 to 21 in number, thick, bright green, obovate to elliptic, 2 - 5 cm long, 1 - 3 cm wide.

Flowers: Yellow, irregularly shaped, borne in long, terminal racemes, 10 - 33 cm long; appearing year-round.

Fruit: A pod, 5 to 20 cm long, 5 - 10 mm in diameter, conspicuously constricted between the seed cavities.

Distinguishing Marks: The leaves of this plant are superficially similar to those of Mexican alvaradoa (*Alvaradoa amorphoides*) of the family Simaroubaceae. However, the two plants never grow in the same habitat nor display the same growth form. The latter is usually upright in form and occurs inside hammocks, whereas *S. tomentosa* is mainly shrubby, occurs on the edges of coastal hammocks, and has yellow flowers.

Distribution: Scrub and hammock margins of the coastal strand of southern Florida, more common in the Keys.

Comment: Isely assigns Florida's plants to *S. tomentosa* var. *truncata* T. & G.

American Wisteria

Page 197, Photo 161

Wisteria frutescens (L.) Poir. in Lam.

Form: High climbing, deciduous twining vine often climbing on shrubs and trees; 2 - 15 m long.

Leaves: Alternate, odd-pinnately compound, 1 - 3 dm in overall length, with long petioles, 2 - 6 cm long; leaflets 9 - 15 in number, entire, lanceolate, 2 - 8 cm long, 1 - 2.5 cm wide.

Flowers: Purplish blue to blue; borne in many-flowered racemes 4 - 25 cm long; appearing April to August after the new leaves have matured.

Fruit: A narrowly oblong pod 4 - 12 cm long.

Distinguishing Marks: The bluish flowers, sprawling vinelike habit, and compound leaves help distinguish this species from most other plants; distinguished from *W. sinensis* by flowering after new leaf growth, by lacking dense pubescence on the pod, by shorter leaves, and by the somewhat shorter flowering racemes.

Distribution: Wet areas around streams, lakes, ponds, and swamps; throughout northern Florida, southward to the north-central peninsula.

Landscape Use: This is a good, native landscape plant, especially for trellises and patio coverings. It is not as often used as the exotic Chinese wisteria, described below.

Chinese Wisteria

Page 197, Photo 162

Wisteria sinensis (Sims) Sweet

Form: Aggressive, high climbing vine that often grows into the tops of trees; to about 20 m long.

Leaves: Alternate, odd-pinnately compound, 1 - 4 dm in overall length; leaflets numbering 7 - 13, broadly lanceolate to elliptic, entire, 4 - 10 cm long, 2 - 6 cm wide.

Flowers: Blue, borne in long racemes 1 - 4 dm long, appearing in spring before or at the very early stages of new leaf growth.

Fruit: A densely pubescent, narrowly linear pod to about 15 cm long.

Distinguishing Marks: The pubescent pod, earlier flowering period, and longer flowering racemes distinguish this species from *W. frutescens*.

Distribution: Native to China but widely planted in yards and gardens; naturalized and weedy mostly near plantings, throughout northern Florida.

Landscape Use: Though this plant is listed as a Category II pest plant by the Florida Exotic Pest Plant Council and should no longer be planted, it is still an often-used ornamental and one of the first flowers of spring. It is vigorous and tolerant of many soils but does not do well in salt air. It is often seen freestanding and trained as a shrub or very small tree. In the latter form it is most often used as an open shrub in yards, or intermixed with other non-native flowering plants, such as azaleas.

American Wisteria
Wisteria frutescens

Chinese Wisteria
Wisteria sinensis

LEITNERIACEAE — CORKWOOD FAMILY

The Leitneriaceae is thought to be the only family of the order Leitneriales. The primitive corkwood, described below, is the family's only species.

Corkwood   Photo 163

Leitneria floridana Chapm.

Form: Single-stemmed deciduous shrub or small tree potentially to about 8 m tall (but typically much shorter), with a narrow, upright shape, few, if any, branches, and reddish-brown bark; central stem with small, but conspicuous, buff-colored spots of cork.

Leaves: Alternate, simple, elliptic, 5 - 20 cm long, 2 - 5 cm wide, upper surfaces of mature blades glabrous and shiny, lower softly pubescent.

Flowers: Tiny, borne from the central stem in cylindrical catkins to about 5 cm long (male catkins 2 - 5 cm long, female catkins 1 - 2 cm); typically appearing February to March.

Fruit: A smooth, brown, leathery, elliptic drupe, 1.5 - 2.5 cm long, flattened on one side, rounded on the other.

Distinguishing Marks: The upright, generally unbranched shape and corky bark are distinctive.

Distribution: Rare and scattered, known in Florida from only four general locations: in the vicinity of the tributaries, estuaries, and barrier islands of the lower Apalachicola River, in the St. Marks National Wildlife Refuge, in the Big Bend Wildlife Management Area, and along the Waccasassa River in Levy County.

Landscape Use: Though not commonly used in Florida landscaping nor readily available from native plant nurseries, corkwood has been used effectively farther north, especially in Illinois. According to Sternberg and Wilson (1995), it requires full sun but tolerates a wide array of soils with reasonable moisture, and is resistant to insects.

Comment: This plant produces Florida's lightest wood. Its stems seem brittle to the touch, almost as if they are dead. Corkwood is a very primitive plant with a quite disjunctive range and is one of Florida's more unique and interesting species. It is the only existing member of the family Leitneriaceae which is considered by most taxonomists to be the only existing family of the order Leitneriales. Fossil evidence indicates that the species may have once been found in Siberia and western Russia. Today, however, it is confined entirely to several widely separated sites in the eastern and southeastern United States, including locations in southeastern Missouri, eastern Arkansas, southeastern Texas, southern Georgia, and northern Florida. It is listed as threatened by the Florida Department of Agriculture.

LOGANIACEAE — LOGANIA FAMILY

The Logania family is a heterogeneous family consisting mostly of herbaceous species in Florida. In the tropics it also includes a number of shrubs, trees, and high climbing vines. All members of the family have opposite, simple leaves and tubular flowers. Only two woody species are found in Florida, both of which are vines. The butterfly bush (*Buddleja lindleyana* Fortune ex Lindley), a popular ornamental that is used in north Florida gardens to attract skippers, butterflies, and buckeyes, is also a member of this family.

Yellow Jessamine or Swamp Jessamine

Gelsemium rankinii Small

Form: An evergreen, twining, trailing vine; often growing high into trees.
Leaves: Opposite, simple, entire, ovate to broadly lanceolate, 3 - 7 cm long, 1 - 2.5 cm wide.
Flowers: Yellow, not fragrant, tubular with flared petals; appearing February to April; sepals with acuminate apices.
Fruit: An ellipsoid capsule, 1 - 1.6 cm long, 6 - 8 mm wide.
Distinguishing Marks: The climbing nature, tubular yellow flowers, and opposite leaves distinguishes this from all but *G. sempervirens* (pictured in photo 164); distinguished from the latter by having non-fragrant flowers, by leaves being more commonly ovate than lanceolate, and by the tips of the sepals being acuminate rather than blunt or rounded.
Distribution: Swamps, wetlands, bogs; throughout the Panhandle from about Leon and Wakulla Counties westward.
Landscape Use: This plant is as attractive as its close relative *G. sempervirens*, described below. Its preference for wetlands makes it less often used and perhaps less suited for ornamental purposes.

Carolina Jessamine, Yellow Jessamine, Poor Man's Rope

Gelsemium sempervirens (L.) Jaume St. Hil.   **Page 200, Photo 164**

Form: High climbing or twining, evergreen vine; often climbs high into trees.
Leaves: Opposite, simple, entire, lanceolate, 6 - 9 cm long, to about 1.5 cm wide, with a long-tapering tip.
Flowers: Bright yellow, fragrant, tubular with flared petals; appearing December to March, depending on location (earlier dates apply to the southern parts of its range); sepals with blunt or rounded apices.
Fruit: An oblong capsule, 1.4 - 2.5 cm long, 0.8 - 1.2 cm wide.
Distinguishing Marks: The yellow, fragrant flowers, more commonly lanceolate leaves, and apices of the sepals with blunt to rounded tips distinguish this species from *G. rankinii*.
Distribution: Well-drained woodlands, disturbed sites, suburban yards; throughout northern Florida, southward to the south-central peninsula.
Landscape Use: A very good plant for winter color. It is easy to start and easy to maintain and does well on trellises or other upright structures.
Comment: All parts of this plant are poisonous to eat due to the presence of several alkaloids.

Carolina Jessasmine, Yellow Jessamine, Poor Man's Rope
Gelsemium sempervirens

LORANTHACEAE — MISTLETOE FAMILY

The Loranthaceae constitute a collection of parasitic plants that lack normal roots. They are best known in Florida from the upper branches of an assortment of forest and hammock trees. They are most easily seen in north Florida during winter when deciduous trees lose their leaves, leaving the conspicuous green patches of mistletoe easily visible among the naked branches. Both species described below are quite distinctive and readily recognized in the field as members of the mistletoe genus.

It should be noted that the mistletoes with inconspicuous flowers (such as those described below and others in the genus *Phoradendron*) have been treated as belonging to the family Viscaceae by some authors (Kuijt, 1982). Those that divide the mistletoes into two families do so on the basis of differences within the flowers and fruits, and based upon the supposition that the two groups evolved from different ancestors.

Mistletoe   Page 201

Phoradendron leucarpum (Raf.) Rev. & M. C. Johnston

Form: A parasitic, bushy-branched, evergreen shrub forming conspicuous clumps in the tops of trees; clumps to about 1 m in diameter.

Leaves: Opposite, simple, entire, leathery, elliptic to oval or nearly rounded, 1.5 - 6 cm long, 1 - 4 cm wide.

Flowers: Inconspicuous, appearing in fall and borne in spikes in the leaf axils.

Fruit: A rounded, white to slightly yellowish drupe, 4 - 6 mm in diameter.

Distinguishing Marks: This is the only common, clump-forming, aerial plant in Florida; most easily seen in deciduous trees during winter.

Distribution: Common in a variety of situations throughout Florida.

Comment: Until 1989, when this plant's name was reassigned based on the rules of botanical nomenclature, its scientific name was *Phoradendron serotinum* (Raf.) M. C. Johnston, by which it is still commonly seen listed.

Mistletoe
Phoradendron leucarpum

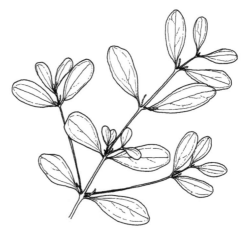

Mahogany Mistletoe
Phoradendron rubrum (L.) Griseb.

Form: Parasitic, evergreen shrub with flatish twigs, typically growing high in large mahogany trees; forming clumps to about 1.2 m in diameter.
Leaves: Opposite, simple, entire, elliptic, to about 4 cm long.
Flowers: Small, inconspicuous, borne in spikes in the leaf axils.
Fruit: A rounded, yellow to orange drupe, about 4 mm in diameter.
Distinguishing Marks: One of only two clump-forming, aerial shrubs found in Florida; distinguished from *P. leucarpum* by orange rather than white (or only slightly yellowish) fruits.
Distribution: Mahogany trees; North Key Largo.
Comment: Listed as endangered by the Florida Department of Agriculture and not reported in naturally occurring populations for about 20 years. The survival of this species, if it is still extant, is likely to be dependent upon the survival of Florida's mahogany populations. According to Campbell (1995), a few plants have been, until recently, cultivated in yards in the southern parts of the state, but even these plants may no longer exist due to storms, pruning, or too much shade.

LYTHRACEAE — LOOSESTRIFE FAMILY
The Lythraceae or loosestrife family is a collection of approximately 26 genera and nearly 600 species. Members of the family typically have opposite or whorled leaves and regular flowers. Most members of the family are herbs or shrubs. Florida's two woody species include the native swamp loosestrife, a predominantly aquatic plant, and the nonnative crape myrtle. The latter is counted among the state's naturalized flora and is an often-used ornamental.

Swamp Loosestrife, Water-Willow, Willow-Herb, Tie-Down
Decodon verticillatus (L.) Ell.   **Page 203, Photo 165**

Form: An aquatic, emergent shrub; lower stems woody and peeling in thin strips at the water level.
Leaves: Opposite to whorled, simple, entire, nearly elliptic to more commonly lanceolate, to about 20 cm long and 5 cm wide.
Flowers: Showy, lavender to purplish pink, bell shaped, with 4 - 7 crinkled petals, each to about 1.5 cm long; borne in conspicuous clusters in the leaf axils and appearing in summer, chiefly July to September.
Fruit: A rounded capsule, 4 - 7 mm in diameter.
Distinguishing Marks: The relatively long, predominantly lanceolate leaves, aquatic habit, and frilly flowers distinguish the species.
Distribution: Swamps, edges of ponds, marshes, and lakes; throughout northern Florida.
Landscape Use: This is an excellent plant for adorning the edges of pools and ponds; requires standing water.

1.   Florida Yew   page 2
       Taxus floridana

2.   Torreya   page 2
       Torreya taxifolia

3.   Coontie   page 4
       Zamia pumila

4.   Century Plant   page 6
       Agave sisalana

5.   Spanish Daggar   page 6
       Yucca aloifolia

6.   Beargrass   page 7
       Yucca flaccida

7. Silver Palm   page 10
    Coccothrinax argentata

11. Catbrier   page 14
    Smilax auriculata

8. Needle Palm   page 10
    Rhapidophyllum hystrix

12. Wild Sarsaparilla   page 16
    Smilax glauca

9. Dwarf Palmetto   page 12
    Sabal minor

10 Saw Palmetto   page 13
    Serenoa repens

13. Bamboo-Vine   page 16
    Smilax laurifolia

17. Brazilian Pepper page 24
Schinus terebinthifolius

14. Coral Greenbrier page 20
Smilax walteri

18. Poison Ivy page 25
Toxicodendron radicans

15. Winged Sumac page 22
Rhus copallina

19. Poison Sumac page 26
Toxicodendron vernix

16. Smooth Sumac page 22
Rhus glabra

20. Pond Apple page 27
Annona glabra

21. Flag Pawpaw page 28
Asimina incarna

23. Flag Pawpaw page 30
Asimina obovata

22. Pawpaw page 30
Asimina longifolia

24. Small-Fruited Pawpaw page 31
Asimina parviflora

25. Pawpaw   page 33
     Asimina reticulata

26. Dog Banana   page 34
     Asimina triloba

27. White Squirrel-Banana   page 35
     Deeringothamnus pulchellus

28. Yellow Squirrel-Banana   page 36
     Deeringothamnus rugelii

29. Pineland Allamanda   page 36
     Angadenia berterii

30. Devil's Potato   page 38
Echites umbellata

31. Mangrove Rubber Vine   page 38
Rhabdadenia biflora

32. Wild Allamanda   page 40
Urechites lutea

33. Pearl Berry   page 40
Vallesia antillana

34. Pearl Berry   page 40
Vallesia antillana

35. Dahoon   page 43
Ilex cassine

36. Possum-Haw   page 45
Ilex decidua

37. Myrtle-Leaved Holly   page 46
    Ilex myrtifolia

41. Saltwort   page 53
    Batis maritima

38. Yaupon   page 47
    Ilex vomitoria

42. Nandina   page 54
    Nandina domestica

39. Devil's Walking Stick   page 48
    Aralia spinosa

43. Cross-Vine   page 56
    Bignonia capreolata

40. Black Mangrove   page 52
    Avicennia germinans

47. **Smooth Strongbark** page 60
Bourreria cassinifolia

44. **Trumpet-Creeper** page 57
Campsis radicans

48. **Bahama Strongbark** page 61
Bourreria ovata

45. **Catalpa** page 58
Catalpa bignonioides

49. **Geiger Tree** page 63
Cordia sebestena

46. **Yellow Elder** page 59
Tecoma stans

50. **Sea Lavender** page 60
Argusia gnaphalodes

51.   Sweet Shrub   page 65
Calycanthus floridus

52.   Cinnamon Bark   page 65
Canella winterana

53.   Jamaica Caper   page 66
Capparis cynophallophora

54.   Limber Caper   page 67
Capparis flexuosa

55.   Coral Honeysuckle   page 69
Lonicera sempervirens

56.   Elderberry   page 69
Sambucus canadensis

57   Arrow-Wood   page 71
     Viburnum dentatum

58. Possum-Haw   page 72
     Viburnum nudum

59. Walter Viburnum   page 72
     Viburnum obovatum

60. Walter Viburnum   page 72
     Viburnum obovatum

61. Rhacoma   page 74
     Crossopetalum rhacoma

62. Hearts-A-Bustin'-With-Love   page 75
     Euonymus americanus

63. Hearts-A-Bustin'-With-Love   page 75
     Euonymus americanus

64. Eastern Wahoo   page 76
     Euonymus atropurpureus

65.   False Boxwood   page 77
      Gyminda latifolia

66.   Florida Mayten   page 77
      Maytenus phyllanthoides

67.   Coco-Plum   page 79
      Chrysobalanus icaco

68.   Gopher Apple   page 80
      Licania michauxii

69.   Sweet Pepperbush   page 81
      Clethra alnifolia

70.   Buttonwood   page 82
      Conocarpus erecta

71.   Climbing Aster   page 84
      Aster carolinianus

72.   Groundsel Tree   page 86
       Baccharis glomeruliflora

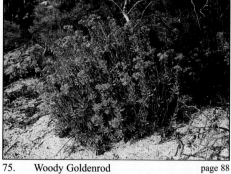

75.   Woody Goldenrod   page 88
       Chrysoma pauciflosculosa

73.   Sea-Oxeye   page 87
       Borrichia arborescens

76.   *Garberia heterophylla*   page 90

74.   Sea-Oxeye   page 87
       Borrichia frutescens

77.   *Jacquemontia havanensis*   page 92

80.   Black Titi   page 98
      Ciftonia monophylla

78.   Jacquemontia   page 94
      Jacquemontia pentantha

81.   Common Persimmon   page 100
      Diospyros virginiana

79.   Swamp Dogwood   page 95
      Cornus amomum

82.   Rosemary   page 102
Ceratiola ericoides

84.   Tar-Flower   page 103
Befaria racemosa

83.   Agarista   page 103
Agarista populifolia

85.   Spotted Wintergreen   page 104
Chimaphila maculata

86. Trailing-Arbutus page 104
Epigaea repens

87. Dangleberry page 107
Gaylussacia tomentosa

88. Mosier's Huckleberry page 106
Gaylussacia mosieri

89. Hairy Wicky page 107
Kalmia hirsuta

90. Mountain Laurel page 108
Kalmia latifolia

91. Stagger Bush page 111
Lyonia ferruginea

92. Fetterbush page 113
Lyonia lucida

93.   **Climbing Heath**   page 115
    Pieris phillyreifolius

94.   **Alabama Azalea**   page 116
    Rhododendron alabamense

95.   **Florida Flame Azalea**   page 116
    Rhododendron austrinum

96.   **Pinxter Bloom**   page 117
    Rhododendron canescens

97.   **Chapman's Rhododendron**   page 117
    Rhododendron minus var. *chapmanii*

98.   **Swamp Azalea**   page 118
    Rhododendron viscosum

99.   **Sparkleberry**   page 118
    Vaccinium arboreum

100. Highbush Blueberry page 119
Vaccinium corymbosum

104. Pineland Croton page 125
Croton linearis

101. Mayberry page 121
Vaccinium elliottii

105. Manchineel page 128
Hippomane mancinella

102. Shiny Blueberry page 121
Vaccinium myrsinites

106. Sebastian-Bush page 132
Sebastiania fruticosa

103. Deer Berry page 121
Vaccinium stamineum

107. Corkwood page 132
Stillingia aquatica

108. Chinquapin page 134
Castanea pumila

112. Scaevola page 140
Scaevola plumieri

109. Chinquapin page 134
Castanea pumila

113. Autograph Tree page 141
Clusia rosea

110. Scrub Oak page 137
Quercus inopina

111. Governor's Plum page 139
Flacourtia indica

114. Sponge-bark Hypericum page 142
Hypericum chapmanii

115. *Hypericum cistifolium*   page 144

117. *Hypericum exile*   page 145

116. Edison's St. John's-Wort   page 145
Hypericum edisonianum

118. Sandweed   page 145
Hypericum fasciculatum

119. *Hypericum lissophloeus*   page 149

121. *Hypericum suffruticosum*   page 152

122. *Hypericum tetrapetalum*   page 153

120. *Hypericum microsepalum*   page 149

123. Witch-Alder   page 153
       Fothergilla gardeni

124. **Red Buckeye**   page 155
      Aesculus pavia

128. **Lavender Basil**   page 158
      Calamintha ashei

125. **Red Buckeye**   page 155
      Aesculus pavia

129. **Red Basil**   page 159
      Calamintha coccinea

126. **Florida Anise**   page 157
      Illicium floridanum

127. **Yellow Anise**   page 157
      Illicium parviflorum

130. **Toothed Basil**   page 159
      Calamintha dentata

131.   *Calamintha georgiana*   page 159

132.   Short-Leaved Rosemary   page 160
       Conradina brevifolia

133.   Minty Rosemary   page 160
       Conradina canescens

134.   Etonia Rosemary   page 161
       Conradina etonia

135.   Apalachicola Rosemary   page 161
       Conradina glabra

136. Large-Flowered Rosemary   page 161
      Conradina grandiflora

138. Spotless-Petaled Balm   page 163
      Dicerandra immaculata

137. Garrett's Mint   page 162
      Dicerandra christmanii

139.   Pond-Spice   page 167
       Litsea aestivalis

140.   Lancewood   page 168
       Ocotea coriacea

141.   Red Bay   page 168
       Persea borbonia

142.   Sassafras   page 170
       Sassafras albidum

143. Long Spine Acacia   page 173
      Acacia macracantha

144. Pine Acacia   page 174
      Acacia pinetorum

145. Twisted Acacia   page 175
      Acacia tortuosa

146. False Indigo   page 175
      Amorpha fruticosa

147. Gray Nicker Bean   page 177
      Caesalpinia bonduc

148. Yellow Nicker Bean   page 178
      Caesalpinia major

149. Bay Bean   page 179
      Canavalia rosea

150. Big Pine Partridge   page 180
      Chamaecrista lineata var. *keyensis*

151.   Coral Bean   page 183
     Erythrina herbacea

155.   Privet Senna   page 191
     Senna ligustrina

152.   Coral Bean   page 183
     Erythrina herbacea

156.   Bahama Senna   page 192
     Senna mexicana var. *chapmanii*

153.   Lead Tree   page 186
     Leucaena leucocephala

157.   Sesban   page 194
     Sesbania punicea

154.   Small's Lupine   page 186
     Lupinus westianus

158.   Sesban   page 194
     Sesbania punicea

159. Necklace Pod   page 195
Sophora tomentosa

160. Necklace Pod   page 195
Sophora tomentosa

162. Chinese Wisteria   page 196
Wisteria sinensis

163. Corkwood   page 198
Leitneria floridana

161 American Wisteria   page 196
Wisteria frutescens

164.　Carolina Jessamine　　　　page 199
Gelsemium sempervirens

165.　Swamp Loosestrife　　　　page 202
Decodon verticillatus

166.　Crape Myrtle　　　　page 203
Lagerstroemia indica

167.　Ashe Magnolia　　　　page 204
Magnolia ashei

168.　Locust Berry　　　　page 205
Byrsonima lucida

169.　Upland Cotton　　　　page 207
Gossypium hirsutum

170.　*Hibiscus coccineus*　　　　page 208

171. Sea Hibiscus page 208
Hibiscus tiliaceus

172. Mangrove Mallow page 210
Pavonia spicata

173. Southern Sida page 210
Sida acuta

174. Tetrazygia page 212
Tetrazygia bicolor

175. Carolina Moonseed page 216
Cocculus carolinus

176. Osage-Orange page 220
Maclura pomifera

177.   Odorless Bayberry   page 226
Myrica inodora

179.   Marlberry   page 228
Ardisia escallonioides

178.   Coral Ardisia   page 226
Ardisia crenata

180.   Marlberry   page 228
Ardisia escallonioides

181.   Surinam Cherry   page 233
Eugenia uniflora

182.   Long-Stalked Stopper   page 234
      Mosiera longipes

183.   Twinberry   page 235
      Myrcianthes fragrans

184.   Blolly   page 237
      Guapira discolor

185.   Pisonia   page 239
      Pisonia rotundata

186.   Ogeechee Tupelo   page 240
      Nyssa ogeche

187.   Gulf Graytwig   page 242
      Schoepfia chrysophylloides

188.   Hog Plum   page 242
      Ximenia americana

189.   Pygmy Fringe Tree   page 243
      Chionanthus pygmaeus

190.   Fringe Tree   page 243
        Chionanthus virginicus

191.   Fringe Tree   page 243
        Chionanthus virginicus

194.   Long-Fruited Primrose Willow   page 252
        Ludwigia octovalvis

192.   Gold Coast Jasmine   page 247
        Jasminum dichotomum

195.   Primrose-Willow   page 252
        Ludwigia peruviana

193.   Wax-leaf Ligustrum   page 249
        Ligustrum lucidum

196.   Corky-stemmed Passion-flower   page 254
        Passiflora suberosa

197.   Bloodberry   page 254
Rivina humilis

198.   Coral Vine   page 256
Antigonon leptopus

200.   Large-leaved Jointweed   page 258
Polygonella macrophylla

199.   Sea Grape   page 257
Coccoloba uvifera

201.   Jointweed   page 259
Polygonella polygama

202.　Virgin's-Bower　　　　　　page 263
　　　Clematis virginiana

203.　Leatherflower　　　　　　page 261
　　　Clematis glaucophylla

204.　New Jersey Tea　　　　　page 265
　　　Ceanothus americanus

205.　Little Leaf Red Root　　　page 266
　　　Ceanothus microphyllus

206.　Wild Coffee　　　　　　page 266
　　　Colubrina arborescens

207.　Colubrina　　　　　　　page 266
　　　Colubrina asiatica

208.   Cuban Colubrina   page 267
Colubrina cubensis

212.   Red Chokeberry   page 274
Aronia arbutifolia

209.   Carolina Buckthorn   page 271
Rhamnus caroliniana

213.   Yellow Haw   page 277
Crataegus flava

210.   Florida Ziziphus   page 272
Ziziphus celata

214.   Yellow Haw   page 277
Crataegus flava

211.   Red Mangrove   page 273
Rhizophora mangle

215.   Parsley Haw   page 278
Crataegus marshallii

216.　Littlehip Hawthorn　　　page 281
Crataegus spathulata

217.　Southern Crabapple　　　page 284
Malus angustifolia

218.　Southern Crabapple　　　page 284
Malus angustifolia

219.　Ninebark　　　page 284
Physocarpus opulifolius

220.　Chickasaw Plum　　　page 286
Prunus angustifolia

221.　Carolina Laurel Cherry　　　page 286
Prunus caroliniana

222. **Hog Plum**   page 287
     Prunus umbellata

225. **Cherokee Rose**   page 289
     Rosa laevigata

223. **Firethorn**   page 288
     Pyracantha sp.

226. **Swamp Rose**   page 290
     Rosa palustris

224. **McCartney Rose**   page 288
     Rosa bracteata

227. **Mysore Raspberry**   page 294
     Rubus niveus

228.   Seven-Year Apple   page 295
       Casasia clusiifolia

229.   Lily Thorn   page 296
        Catesbaea parviflora

230.   Buttonbush   page 296
        Cephalanthus occidentalis

231.   Snowberry   page 297
        Chiococca alba

232.   Snowberry   page 297
        Chiococca parvifolia

233.   Black Torch   page 298
        Erithalis fruticosa

234.   Beach Creeper   page 298
        Ernodea littoralis

235.   Velvetseed   page 299
       Guettarda elliptica

239.   *Morinda citrifolia*   page 301

236.   Rough Velvetseed   page 300
       Guettarda scabra

240.   Indian Mulberry   page 301
       Morinda royoc

237.   Scarlet Bush   page 300
       Hamelia patens

241.   Indian Mulberry   page 301
       Morinda royoc

238.   Partridge Berry   page 300
       Mitchella repens

242.   Pinckneya   page 303
       Pinckneya bracteata

243. Wild Coffee page 304
Psychotria ligustrifolia

246. Pride of Big Pine page 306
Strumpfia maritima

244. Wild Coffee page 304
Psychotria nervosa

247. Pride of Big Pine page 306
Strumpfia maritima

248. Key Lime page 308
Citrus aurantifolia

245. Randia page 306
Randia aculeata

249. Orange Jessamine   page 309
Murraya paniculata

253. Heart-leaved Willow   page 314
Salix eriocephala

250. Trifoliate Orange   page 310
Poncirus trifoliata

254. Florida Willow   page 315
Salix floridana

251. Biscayne Prickly Ash   page 312
Zanthoxylum coriaceum

252. Coastal Plain Willow   page 314
Salix caroliniana

255. Small Pussy Willow   page 316
Salix humilis

256. Florida Cupania   page 317
    Cupania glabra

257. Varnish Leaf   page 317
    Dodonaea viscosa

258. Inkwood   page 318
    Exothea paniculata

259. Gum Bumelia   page 322
    Bumelia lanuginosa

260. Tough Bumelia   page 326
    Bumelia tenax

261.   *Bumelia thornei*   page 327

262. Satin Leaf   page 327
Chrysophyllum oliviforme

266. Miccosukee Gooseberry   page 332
Ribes echinellum

263. Wild Dilly   page 328
Manilkara bahamensis

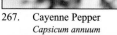

267. Cayenne Pepper   page 336
Capsicum annuum

264. Oak-Leaf Hydrangea   page 330
Hydrangea quercifolia

265. Summer Dogwood   page 331
Philadelphus inodorus

268. Day Jessamine   page 336
Cestrum diurnum

269.　Christmas Berry　　　　　page 337
　　　Lycium carolinianum

271.　Nightshade　　　　　page 338
　　　Solanum diphyllum

272.　Blodgett's Nightshade　　　　　page 338
　　　Solanum donianum

273.　Potato Tree　　　　　page 338
　　　Solanum erianthum

270.　Bahama Nightshade　　　　　page 337
　　　Solanum bahamense

274. Waltheria   page 341
     Waltheria indica

277. Big Leaf Snowbell   page 344
     Styrax grandifolia

275. Two-winged Silverbell   page 343
     Halesia diptera

278. Bay Cedar   page 345
     Suriana maritima

276. American Snowbell   page 343
     Styrax americanum

279. Horse Sugar   page 346
     Symplocos tinctoria

280. Silky-Camellia   page 347
     Stewartia malacodendron

281. Leatherwood   page 350
      Dirca palustris

284. Fiddlewood   page 356
      Citharexylum fruticosum

282. Yellow Alder   page 351
      Turnera ulmifolia

285. Java Glorybower   page 357
      Clerodendrum speciosissimum

283. Beautyberry   page 356
      Callicarpa americana

286. Bleeding Heart   page 358
      Clerodendrum thomsoniae

287. Golden Dewdrop   page 358
      Duranta repens

290. Wild Lantana   page 359
      Lantana involucrata

288. Golden Dewdrop   page 358
      Duranta repens

291. Trailing Lantana   page 360
      Lantana montevidensis

292. Porterweed   page 361
      Stachytarpheta urticifolia

289. Lantana   page 358
      Lantana camara

293. Summer Grape   page 367
Vitis aestivalis

295. Muscadine   page 368
Vitis rotundifolia

296. Muscadine   page 368
Vitis rotundifolia

294. Sweet Winter Grape   page 367
Vitis cinerea

297. Lignum Vitae   page 371
Guaiacum sanctum

Swamp Loosestrife, Water-Willow,
Willow-Herb, Tie-Down
Decodon verticillatus

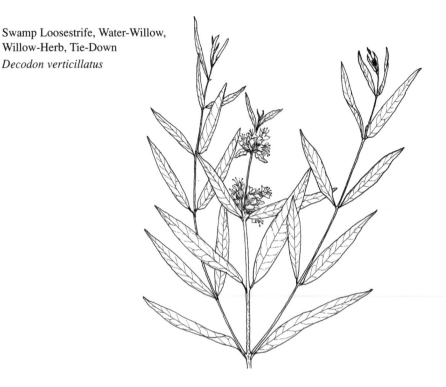

Crape Myrtle

Photo 166

Lagerstroemia indica L.

Form: Deciduous shrub or small tree to about 7 m tall with twisted branches and smooth, brownish-orange bark that sometimes flakes off in large patches.

Leaves: Both opposite and alternate, simple, entire, predominately elliptic, 2 - 7 cm long, 1 - 4 cm wide.

Flowers: Inflorescence a large, showy panicle up to 30 cm long and nearly as wide, individual flowers white, pink, red, or purple; petals stalked, frilly, crinkled, generally numbering six per flower, each with a long, slender claw; appearing from early spring throughout the summer.

Fruit: A brown, woody, egg-shaped capsule that splits from the top.

Distinguishing Marks: The showy flowers that appear throughout the summer are distinctive.

Distribution: Widely planted throughout the state; naturalized in areas near dwellings or in fields.

Landscape Use: The crape myrtle is a popular landscape plant that has found wide use in gardens and lawns across much of Florida and the southeastern United States. It is particularly well known as a roadside plant, and its beautiful white, pink, red, or purple flowers are often used to add an attractive border to southern yards. When in bloom it is one of the state's most conspicuous plants.

MAGNOLIACEAE — MAGNOLIA FAMILY

The large, showy flowers of the Magnoliaceae are this family's link with a long history and a remote origin. Members of the family are closely related to members of the Annonaceae, which includes the pawpaws and pond apple. The original magnolias, of which only a few species are left, were among the first trees to develop flowers and at one point ranged nearly worldwide. Fossil evidence indicates that they, along with ancient gymnosperms, were once distributed widely throughout Europe, western North America, Canada, and even Greenland before being pushed southward by the advancing glaciers of the ice ages. Today's members of this family are the descendants of what may be the world's most ancient family of dicotyledonous trees and are well represented today in both the southeastern United States and eastern Asia. The Ashe magnolia is Florida's only shrubby member of the genus.

Ashe Magnolia
Magnolia ashei Weatherby

Photo 167

Form: Deciduous shrub or small understory tree to about 6 m tall, recognized immediately by the huge leaves and flowers.

Leaves: Alternate, simple, entire, up to about 60 cm long and 30 cm wide, green above, whitish beneath, bases eared or lobed.

Flowers: Huge, with purple suffused at the base of the creamy white petals, up to 30 cm wide when fully opened; appearing in March and April.

Distinguishing Marks: Distinguished from all other Florida shrubs or trees by huge leaves with eared, or cordate, bases.

Distribution: Rich hardwood forests of bluffs and ravines; from the western Panhandle, eastward to about Leon County.

Landscape Use: This is an interesting species that produces particularly large and distinctive flowers; it is often planted in north Florida as an ornamental and is readily available from most native plant nurseries.

Comment: Listed as endangered by the Florida Department of Agriculture. Commonly seen listed as *Magnolia macrophylla* Michx. subsp. *ashei* (Weatherby) Spongberg. The ranges of the current species and *M. macrophylla* are well-separated geographically (the latter occurs well north of Florida) and their differences are easily perceived.

MALPIGHIACEAE — MALPIGHIA FAMILY

The Malpighiaceae is a large, primarily tropical, family that consists of as many as 65 genera and between 700 and 1300 species. Although several members of the malpighia family have been introduced into Florida and are commonly used for ornamental purposes, the locust berry, or Key byrsonima, is the only member of the family that is considered native to the state. It is part of a small genus that contains about 100 other trees and shrubs.

Locust Berry or Key Byrsonima

Photo 168

Byrsonima lucida (Mill.) DC.

Form: Multitrunked evergreen shrub or occasionally a small tree to about 6 m tall, with smooth, light brown bark, spreading branches, and jointed twigs.
Leaves: Opposite, simple, entire, leathery, dark, shiny green above, dull yellow green below, mostly oblanceolate to spatulate, 2 - 6 cm long, 0.5 - 2 cm wide, some leaves with acuminate apices, others rounded; base of petiole thickish and clasping the stem.
Flowers: White or pink at first but turning yellow or rose red, borne in long, upright clusters of 5 - 12 individual flowers, each flower held on its own long stalk; appearing most profusely in spring, but may be present during other times of the year as well.
Fruit: Reddish brown, berrylike, round, 5 - 8 mm in diameter.
Distinguishing Marks: Most easily recognized by the combination of jointed twigs (although sometimes obscurely so), opposite leaves, clasping petioles, and showy flowers.
Distribution: Primarily associated with the pinelands where it is normally a shrub, sometimes approaching tree stature in hammocks (especially on Big Pine Key and No Name Key); found in the U. S. only in southern Florida and the Keys; frequent and common in Dade County's pine rocklands and on Big Pine Key.
Landscape Use: Not often seen in cultivation but probably suited for use; when in bloom it is many flowered and very attractive.

MALVACEAE — MALLOW FAMILY

Members of the Malvaceae, or mallow family, are well known for their prominent, colorful, showy blossoms. Perhaps no other family has so many species with such ornate flowers. The family is represented in Florida by a large number of native and ornamental plants, many of which are herbaceous or woody shrubs. Probably the best known members of the family are found in the *Hibiscus* genus, though some of the family's other genera are equally beautiful when in bloom.

Abutilon permolle (Willd.) Sweet

Page 206

Form: Low, evergreen shrub with slender branches, to about 2 m tall.
Leaves: Alternate, simple, heart shaped with crenate margins, 5 - 13 cm long; bases deeply cordate; surfaces pale green, with star-shaped hairs (requires magnification), and soft and velvety to the touch.
Flowers: Bright yellow with five, spreading petals; to about 4 cm wide when fully opened and borne on conspicuous stalks in the leaf axils; petals to about 1 - 1.5 cm long; appearing year-round.
Fruit: A multilocular, cuplike structure, each locule (carpel) with numerous seeds.
Distinguishing Marks: The heart-shaped leaves and bright yellow flowers are distinctive.
Distribution: South Florida and the Keys.

Abutilon permolle

Upland Cotton or Wild Cotton
Gossypium hirsutum

Cienfuegosia yucataniensis Millsp.

Form: A low shrub with erect branches; to about 1 m tall.
Leaves: Alternate, simple, lanceolate, 2.5 - 7 cm long, larger leaves nearer the bottom of the stem; margins entire to lobed.
Flowers: Bright yellow, with five petals; about 2.5 cm wide when fully opened.
Fruit: A three- to five-valved capsule.
Distinguishing Marks: The yellow flowers, erect stems, low stature, and lanceolate leaves combine to help distinguish this species.
Distribution: Coastal hammocks; Keys.

Upland Cotton or Wild Cotton
Page 206, Photo 169
Gossypium hirsutum L.

Form: Short, low-branched shrub or small, bushy tree to about 4 m tall.
Leaves: Alternate, usually three lobed, cordate at the base, 5 - 15 cm long, with long petioles.
Flowers: Showy, creamy white to pale yellow with a reddish spot at the base of each petal; appearing intermittently throughout the year.
Fruit: A triangular capsule that exposes a cottony seed covering when opened.
Distinguishing Marks: Distinguished from both the portia tree (*Thespesia populnea*) and sea hibiscus (*Hibiscus tiliaceus*) by having black dots on the leaves.
Distribution: Tropical thickets and disturbed sites along the extreme southwestern coast and the Keys.
Landscape Use: Wild cotton forms a bushy shrub when given room to grow. The showy flowers and cottony fruit make it an attractive ornamental for use in yards.
Comment: Upland cotton is listed as endangered by the Florida Department of Agriculture and is one of the state's rarest plants. It was once widespread along the hammock–mangrove ecotone of southern Florida and is an ancestor of the southern United State's commercially-grown cotton crop. Its demise has resulted from fear of the pink bole worm, an invertebrate that is known to attack and destroy the plant. The insect was found on south Florida's wild cotton in the early 1930s, which led to a U. S. Department of Agriculture initiative designed to eradicate the plant and prevent the worm from spreading northward. However, there is little evidence that this eradication program has had any appreciable impact on anything but the continued existence of the plant itself.

Wild Hibiscus
Page 208
Hibiscus poeppigii (K. Spreng.) Garcke

Form: A slender shrub to about 2 m tall.
Leaves: Alternate, simple, triangular in overall shape but with three lobes, 2.5 - 8 cm long; margins crenate to dentate; lower surfaces covered with fine hairs.
Flowers: Bright red, borne singly in the axils of the uppermost leaves, nodding; petals 2 - 2.6 cm long.

Wild Hibiscus
Hibiscus poeppigii

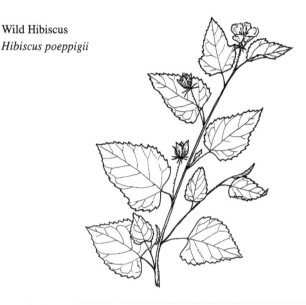

Fruit: A pubescent capsule with star-shaped hairs, to about 1 cm long.

Distinguishing Marks: The bright red flowers and crenate-dentate, triangular leaves are diagnostic.

Distribution: Hammocks; south Florida and the Keys.

Landscape Use: Members of this genus are sought after landscape plants due to their typically large, showy flowers.

Comment: There are a number of large, showy *Hibiscus* species in Florida, many of which are nonnative and herbaceous. At least two develop into large, shrubby plants, especially in southern Florida, and bear mention here. Both have been described by Long and Lakela (1971) as woody herbs. *H. coccineus* Walt. is found in wet areas in several parts of the state, including sporadic occurrences in the Panhandle. It has showy red flowers (see photo 170), and coarsely dentate, deeply five-lobed leaves and grows to about 2 m tall. It is only rarely used ornamentally. *H. grandiflorus* Michx. is another native, large-flowered species of swamps and marshes that is also to 2 m tall. It has ovate to deltoid, serrate leaves that are only shallowly three-lobed (if lobed at all).

Sea Hibiscus or Mahoe

Page 209, Photo 171

Hibiscus tiliaceus L.

Form: Evergreen shrub or small, spreading, sometimes crooked tree to about 9 m tall.

Leaves: Alternate, heart shaped, 10 - 30 cm long, apices pinching to a cuspidate point, margins entire to toothed.

Sea Hibiscus or Mahoe
Hibiscus tiliaceus

Flowers: Large and showy, typical of hibiscus genus, yellow early in the day, turning red by evening (the photo shows a flower in transition); appearing year-round.

Distinguishing Marks: Distinguished from the portia tree (*Thespesia populnea*) by leaves having mainly 9 to 11 veins rather than predominately 7 veins, by lower surfaces of leaves being copiously covered with whitish, stellate hairs, by leaves being generally more rounded, and by tips of leaves being cuspidate rather than tapering; from upland cotton (*Gossypium hirsutum*) by leaves lacking black spots.

Distribution: Although there has been some disagreement about whether the sea hibiscus is a native species, it is generally agreed today that the plant originated in Asia and is only a naturalized addition to the state's flora.

Landscape Use: This plant is listed as a Category II pest plant by the Florida Exotic Pest Plant Council. It is cultivated widely in disturbed coastal sites of the southern peninsula and the Keys and valued for its nearly circular, dark green leaves and attractive flowers. It is very tolerant of dune front locations. It is easy to maintain but has the potential to invade and disrupt native plant communities.

Comment: At Ding Darling National Wildlife Refuge there is a population of *Hibiscus* (shown to me by Dick Workman) that is in most respects similar to *H. tiliaceus* but with flowers that have yellow rather than red centers. The plants with yellow-centered flowers generally have smaller leaves overall than neighboring plants with red-centered flowers. Some suggest that those with yellow-centered flowers constitute a different species that might be native to the state. The final resolution of this taxonomic problem will certainly prove interesting.

Mangrove Mallow

Photo 172

Pavonia spicata Cav.

Form: Large shrub to about 3 m tall; stems with short, spreading, inconspicuous hairs.

Leaves: Alternate, lanceolate or elliptic to ovate, or somewhat heart shaped, mostly entire, 6 - 15 cm long.

Flowers: Green to greenish yellow, 2 - 3 cm long; appearing at any time of year.

Fruit: To about 1 cm long.

Distinguishing Marks: The large, heart-shaped leaves in conjunction with the interesting greenish-yellow flowers are good field marks.

Distribution: Generally confined to the shores of bays and near mangrove borders; southern Florida.

Landscape Use: An attractive shrub for use in south Florida lawns.

Comment: Two other members of this genus that are native to South America are reported as escaped from cultivation and sometimes established in Florida. *P. spinifex* (L.) Cav. has ovate leaves, 5 - 10 cm long and is mostly confined to coastal areas; *P. hastata* Cav. has leaves that are 2 - 5 cm long and shaped like an arrowhead, with the basal lobes at right angles to the central leaf axis (or hastate, hence the specific name).

Southern Sida

Page 211, Photo 173

Sida acuta Burm.

Form: An erect, primarily herbaceous shrub with a woody base, 0.3 - 1 m tall.

Leaves: Alternate, simple, two ranked, lanceolate to ovate, 2 - 10 cm long, slightly asymmetrical on either side of the central vein, margins coarsely serrate, stipules conspicuous, 1 - 1.5 cm long, prominently three veined.

Flowers: Yellow, white or rarely yellowish white, appearing year-round and borne singly on short stalks in the leaf axils.

Fruit: Capsule, mature carpels 7 - 12 in number, 3 - 4 mm long at maturity, each containing one seed.

Distinguishing Marks: The conspicuous, leaflike stipules, yellow flowers, and coarsely dentate, slightly asymmetric leaves are characteristic.

Distribution: Disturbed sites, pinelands, thin woods behind dunes; throughout the southeast, southward to the Keys.

Comment: At least four other members of this genus are found in Florida, two of which are perennial, two annual. The perennial species, which also sometimes appear somewhat shrublike, include heartleaf sida (*S. cordifolia* L.), a frequent species that has heart-shaped leaves which are covered with velvety hairs, and narrowleaf sida (*S. elliottii* Torr. & Gray), a less frequent species with linear leaves. The two annuals are arrowleaf sida (*S. rhombifolia* L.) and prickly sida (*S. spinosa* L.).

Southern Sida
Sida acuta

Seaside Mahoe or Portia Tree

Page 212

Thespesia populnea (L.) Soland. ex Correa

Form: Large shrub or small, bushy, evergreen tree to about 9 m tall.

Leaves: Alternate, simple, entire, heart shaped in overall form, 5 - 20 cm long, to about 12 cm wide, bases cordate.

Flowers: To about 8 cm in diameter, showy, characteristic of the hibiscus genus, yellow with a red center that turns darker near the end of the day; appearing year-round.

Fruit: A leathery, nearly round capsule to about 4 cm in diameter, yellow at first but turning black at maturity and persisting on the tree as a dry husk.

Distinguishing Marks: Distinguished from sea hibiscus (*Hibiscus tiliaceus*) by leaves with usually 7 main veins rather than 9 to 11 as in the latter species, and by leaf blades lacking stellate hairs.

Distribution: Exotic species of coastal hammocks and beaches from about Lee County southward and throughout the Keys.

Landscape Use: The portia tree is another of Florida's introduced ornamentals and has been frequently used as a street tree because of its attractive foliage and large, showy flowers, and because it is very salt tolerant. It is listed as a Category I pest plant by Florida's Exotic Pest Plant Council and is not recommended for landscape use.

Comment: The portia tree originates from India but is pantropical in distribution and is now found widely in southern Florida. Its generic name, *Thespesia*, derives from the Greek word for divine, and the tree is considered sacred in Tahiti and throughout much of the Pacific; its specific name refers to its poplarlike leaves. In its native range the portia tree has been used for cordage, coffee bags, and paper and rope making. Its wood, which is resistant to attack from termites, has been used for fashioning cabinets, wheels, gun stocks, boats, houses, and musical instruments. The flowers are reported to be eaten, and the fruit has been used medicinally to treat skin sores. A string fiber is made from its bark.

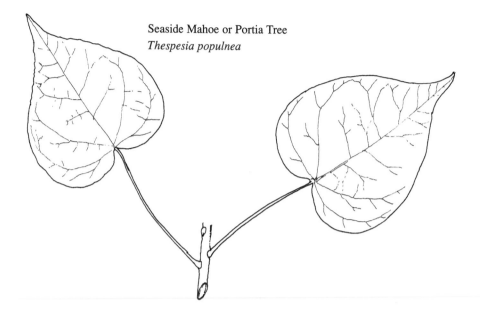

Seaside Mahoe or Portia Tree
Thespesia populnea

MELASTOMATACEAE — MEADOW BEAUTY FAMILY

The meadow beauty family is a rather large collection of about 200 genera and 4500 species of mostly tropical plants, many of which are native to South America. Only two of the family's genera occur naturally in the United States, both of which are represented in Florida. In addition to the state's single species of *Tetrazygia*, which is described below, the family is also represented in Florida by several species that are commonly referred to as meadow beauties. The latter plants are members of the genus *Rhexia* and are herbaceous species that are most often found in seasonally wet, acidic soils such as Florida's extensive pine flatwoods community.

Tetrazygia or Florida Tetrazygia   Photo 174

Tetrazygia bicolor (Mill.) Cogn.

Form: Generally an evergreen shrub in the pinelands, barely reaching the dimensions of a small, spindly tree inside hammocks.

Leaves: Opposite, lanceolate, curving, simple, 7.5 - 20 cm long, 2.5 - 4 cm wide, with three distinctive, lengthwise veins; upper surface conspicuously raised between depressed lateral veins; margins entire but rolled under.

Flowers: Inflorescence a showy, terminal cluster, 1 - 2 dm long; flowers with five white petals encircling a mass of ten yellow stamens; appearing late spring into summer.

Fruit: Berrylike, black, rounded, 8 - 10 mm long.

Distinguishing Marks: This plant's distinctive leaf and venation pattern make it unlikely to be confused with any other south Florida shrub or tree, except, perhaps, for the several members of the genus *Psychotria* (see the family Rubiaceae, below). However, the flowers of the two genera are quite different.

Distribution: Locally common and generally restricted to pinelands of the Miami Rock Ridge of Dade County, but also found in and along the margins of nearby hammocks.

Landscape Use: Probably not much used ornamentally, but probably should be. It is not difficult to maintain, has distinctive leaves, and is very attractive during its rather extended flowering period.

MELIACEAE — MAHOGANY FAMILY

The mahogany family is composed of about 500 species in 50 genera, most of which are found in the tropical regions of Africa, Asia, Australia, and South America. Only one species in each of two genera occur in the United States. The true mahoganies of the genus *Swietenia*, of which Florida's mahogany is only one of two species, constitute one of the family's smallest sub-divisions. The chinaberry (*Melia azedarach*), Florida's only other member of the family, is a nonnative species that is found most abundantly in the northern parts of the state. However, it also often escapes from cultivation in peninsular Florida and the Keys.

Chinaberry or Pride of India   Page 214
Melia azedarach L.

Form: Commonly a small- to medium-sized, spreading, deciduous tree to about 15 m tall, with smooth, purplish bark; often flowering and fruiting when of low, shrublike stature.

Leaves: Alternate, long petioled, primarily bipinnately compound but sometimes tripinnately compound, overall leaf up to about 50 cm long; leaflets dark green above, paler below, 2 - 7 cm long, 1 - 2 cm wide, pointed at the tip, margins sharply toothed, some leaflets with one or two deeply incised lobes at the base, some with stalks 1 - 2 cm long, others sessile.

Flowers: With five (sometimes six) narrow, purplish, slightly recurved petals, appearing in spring and borne in conspicuous branched clusters.

Fruit: A rounded, fleshy, yellow or yellowish drupe, 1 - 1.5 cm in diameter.

Distinguishing Marks: The five-petaled, blue flowers, bipinnately compound leaves, and distinctive hanging clusters of fruit, particularly throughout the winter, help distinguish this species.

Distribution: Fence rows, woodlands, disturbed places near dwellings; introduced and escaped throughout the state and reported sparingly from the Keys, more common in northern Florida and southward to the south-central peninsula.

Landscape Use: The chinaberry is a fast-growing Asian species that has been widely planted as a tree in the southern United States. It has been most prized for its attractive clusters of purplish-blue flowers that appear in early summer and for its rounded, yellowish berries that appear in the fall. The berries are poisonous to humans and some other mammals but are relished by a variety of songbirds who sometimes gorge themselves so heavily that they become temporarily intoxicated from the bitter juice. However, it is now considered a weed in Florida and is listed as Category I pest plant by the Exotic Pest Plant Council. It should not be used as a landscape plant.

Chinaberry or Pride of India
Melia azedarach

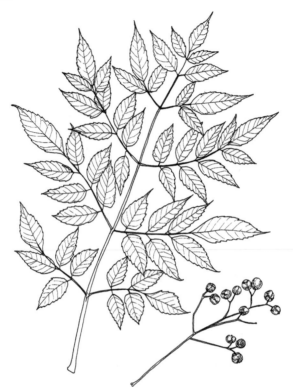

Cupseed
Calycocarpum lyonii

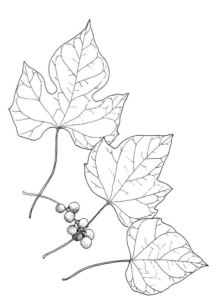

Comment: The leaves of the Chinaberry have insecticidal properties and have been used as flea powder or to protect stored clothing from insects, and the oil from the seeds has been used in oil lamps. A chinaberry leaf (or leaves) pressed between the pages of a book will purportedly keep insects from attacking its paper or binding. The wood has been used as fuel as well as for cabinet making and the fabrication of tool handles. Various parts of the plant have been employed medicinally in warmer regions of the world, including uses as a diuretic and lice deterrent, as well as in the treatment of headaches and skin diseases such as leprosy. The specific name for the Chinaberry derives from Arabic and means free, or noble. Though a weed tree and considered a pest in some countries, it is regarded as sacred in parts of India and garlands of its delicate blue flowers are placed on temple altars in Ceylon.

MENISPERMACEAE — MOONSEED FAMILY

This is a family of approximately 65 genera and 350 species ranging in warm regions throughout the world. Though the four species described below are all climbing vines, the family also includes shrubs and trees.

Cupseed

Page 214

Calycocarpum lyonii (Pursh) A. Gray

Form: A scrambling, deciduous vine; often herbaceous, sometimes with woody stems to about 1 cm in diameter.

Leaves: Alternate, simple, variable in size, deeply palmately lobed to heart shaped, lobes numbering 3 - 5 (rarely 7), larger leaves to about 25 cm long; margins entire to sparsely dentate; upper surfaces often with distinctive, though scattered, stiff, sharp-pointed hairs (requires magnification).

Flowers: Small, greenish to cream colored with 6 sepals, borne in elongated clusters opposite or nearly opposite the leaves; appearing from spring to early summer.

Fruit: A rounded drupe to about 2.5 cm long, green at first but black at maturity; borne in hanging, grapelike clusters.

Distinguishing Marks: The large, variously lobed leaves are distinctive in this plant's common habitat. The creeping cucumber (*Melothria pendula* L., family Cucurbitaceae) is a common, perennial, herbaceous vine that is also found on floodplains and at the edges of alluvial swamps as well as other sites. This latter species has superficially similar, though generally smaller leaves (2 - 8 cm wide), small, yellow flowers, and fruits that look like tiny cucumbers.

Distribution: Alluvial swamps, rich river bottoms, associated slopes, banks, and ravines; Panhandle from about Jefferson County westward.

Cissampelos pareira L.

Form: High climbing to shrubby woody vine.

Leaves: Alternate, simple, entire, bright green, orbicular, 6 - 12 cm long, 4 - 10 cm wide,

THE SHRUBS AND WOODY VINES OF FLORIDA

palmately veined with 3 - 7 veins; petioles commonly much longer than the leaf blades.

Flowers: Small, borne in elongated clusters from the leaf axils.

Fruit: A hairy, rounded drupe, 4 - 10 mm in diameter.

Distinguishing Marks: The nearly round leaves set this species apart from most other hammock species.

Distribution: Hammocks, very rare if still extant in south Florida; last reported at Matheson Hammock in Dade County (Roger Hammer, personal communication).

Carolina Moonseed, Redberry Moonseed, Snailseed, Coralbeads

Cocculus carolinus (L.) DC   **Page 217, Photo 175**

Form: Twining, high-climbing deciduous vine, woody at the base, older stems distinctly roughened.

Leaves: Alternate, simple, entire, shallowly lobed to heart shaped, 4 - 14 cm long; petioles about as long as the leaf blades.

Flowers: Small, greenish, with 6 sepals and 6 petals, borne in clusters to about 13 cm long; appearing in summer.

Fruit: Mature fruit a rounded, bright red drupe, 6 - 8 mm in diameter and borne in conspicuous clusters.

Distinguishing Marks: The shallowly lobed, heart-shaped leaves and bright red fruiting clusters are distinctive.

Distribution: Mixed woods, fields, thickets, fences; throughout northern Florida.

Landscape Use: The bright red fruits that appear in late summer and early fall are very attractive as well as good wildlife food; though not readily available nor often used, this species is easy to grow, easy to control, and has potential as a cultivated vine.

Moonseed
Page 217

Menispermum canadense L.

Form: A slender, twining vine with a ribbed stem.

Leaves: Alternate, simple, entire, variable in size, mostly 10 - 15 cm long and wide, with 3 - 7 blunt to sharp-pointed lobes; petioles as long as the leaf blades, conspicuously slender, joining the undersurface of the leaf blade slightly inside of, rather than at, the margin (peltate).

Flowers: Small, greenish yellow to greenish white, borne in long-stalked clusters at the leaf axils.

Fruit: A bluish-black drupe about 6 - 15 mm in diameter; borne in hanging clusters.

Distinguishing Marks: The peltate leaves in conjunction with the blue-black fruit are diagnostic.

Distribution: Rich woods; chiefly Gadsden County.

Carolina Moonseed, Redberry
Monseed, Snailseed, Coralbeads
Cocculus carolinus

Moonseed
Menispermum canadense

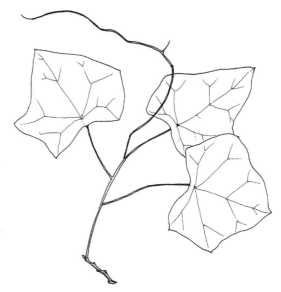

MORACEAE — MULBERRY FAMILY

The mulberry family consists mostly of trees or shrubs with milky sap, mainly of the tropics and subtropics. The family includes six genera, four of which are represented in Florida, and nearly 1,100 species.

Paper Mulberry

Page 218

Broussonetia papyrifera (L.) Vent.

Form: Small, thicket-forming, fast-growing shrub or small deciduous tree with milky sap, to about 15 m tall.

Leaves: Alternate, opposite, or whorled on the same plant, simple, very hairy, 6 - 20 cm long, 5 - 15 cm wide; margins toothed and sometimes lobed; upper surfaces of mature blades rough to the touch; petioles 4 - 15 cm long.

Flowers: Female flowers borne in round, hanging clusters; male flowers appearing in spring and borne in drooping, elongated clusters.

Fruit: Orange to red and aggregated into globular clusters that are 2 - 3 cm in diameter.

Distinguishing Marks: Distinguished from other mulberries of genus *Morus* by leaf arrangement, from most other north Florida shrubs and trees by leaf shape.

Distribution: Frequent in disturbed sites and near human habitations; northern half of the state south to the Tampa area; occasionally found as an escape in south Florida.

Landscape Use: The fast-growing nature, dense shade provided by mature specimens, and tolerance of poor conditions once made this imported plant an oft-planted ornamental. The fruit is very attractive to birds. However, the plant is now listed as Category II by the Florida Exotic Pest Plant Council and should not be used in landscaping.

Comment: The inner bark of this plant was used in China and Japan in the making of paper, hence the common name. It has no commercial value in the United States and was imported primarily as an ornamental tree.

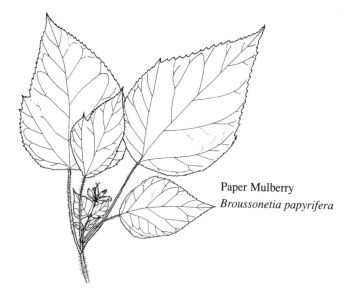

Paper Mulberry
Broussonetia papyrifera

Common Fig

Ficus carica L.

Form: Multitrunked deciduous shrub or tree to about 10 m tall.

Leaves: Alternate, large, broad, deeply incised into 3 - 5 lobes, each lobe with its own apparent central vein, upper surface rough to the touch due to the presence of stiff hairs.

Flowers: Produced in a receptacle near the ends of branches; appearing in spring and summer.

Fruit: Pear shaped, edible, tasty, recognized as those available at supermarkets and produce stands.

Distinguishing Marks: Most easily recognized by its deeply incised leaves.

Distribution: Planted for its fruit throughout the state, perhaps more common in the southern counties where it is sometimes seen in disturbed sites or along roadsides.

Landscape Use: The common fig is one of the world's most widely cultivated plants; at least 700 varieties have been described. It is often seen near old homesteads in Florida and the southeastern U. S. generally, and is planted primarily for its fruit and dense foliage, and for its attractiveness to wildlife.

Comment: This is the ancient fig mentioned often in the early books of The Bible. Its specific name refers to Caria, an ancient country in Asia Minor, from where it is thought to originate. Its fruits are seedless, very tasty, and probably served as a staple food for much of the ancient civilized world.

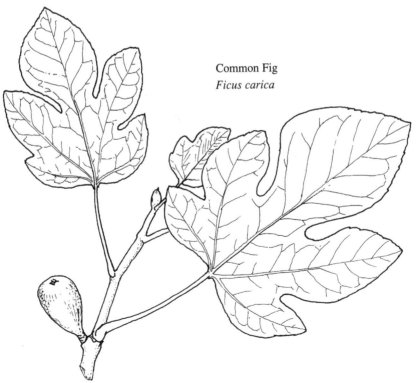

Common Fig
Ficus carica

Osage-Orange, Hedge-Apple, Bow-Wood

Photo 176

Maclura pomifera (Raf.) Schneid.

Form: Large shrub or small to medium-sized deciduous tree to about 15 m tall; twigs often (but not always) having conspicuous, sharp spines that are borne in the leaf axils.

Leaves: Alternate, simple, entire, ovate, 7 - 15 cm long, 5 - 8 cm wide, bases often rounded and appearing slightly heart shaped, surfaces dark green above, paler beneath, apices often tapering to a long point.

Flowers: Small, borne in rounded receptacles near the ends of branches; appearing in spring.

Fruit: Distinctively collected into a large, compact conglomeration, 10 - 14 cm in diameter, superficially taking on the appearance of an orange, except green in color and somewhat more knobby.

Distinguishing Marks: The large, round, knobby fruit is an easy field mark in summer and early fall.

Distribution: Sporadic and uncommon across northern Florida and southward to about Marion County, probably most common in the central Panhandle.

Comment: The scientific name for osage orange is in honor of American geologist William Maclure as well as for its orangelike pome. It is the only member of its genus and has been widely used for a variety of purposes. Two of its common names derive from the Osage Indians of Arkansas and Missouri who found the wood quite strong and used it in the fabrication of bows. In addition, long before barbed wire and fence posts separated midwestern cattle territory or bordered eastern America's private lands, the osage-orange was touted as an outstanding hedgerow plant, hence the name hedge apple. It is fast growing and sun tolerant, and its tightly compact, orange-sized collection of fruits were once shipped widely for use in planting living fences that helped to control the movement of cattle. Government agriculturists and foresters also encouraged the planting of osage-orange as a protection against the destructive forces of the wind-induced erosion caused by the excessive droughts of the early 1900s. According to Loran Anderson, professor of botany at Florida State University, the fruit has also been used in Kansas basements as a "bug repellent" and would presumably work in Florida as a deterrent to cockroaches and spiders.

White Mulberry

Page 221

Morus alba L.

Form: Large shrub or small- to medium-sized deciduous tree with glabrous, lustrous twigs, to about 25 m tall; often flowering and fruiting when of shrublike stature.

Leaves: Alternate, simple, very variable in size from about 6 to as much as 20 cm in length, some plants with most leaves tending toward one extreme or the other; margins toothed and variously lobed or unlobed, lobes more characteristic of small leaves and those leaves found on shrubby saplings than those on mature trees, lobes sometimes reaching nine in number but characteristically fewer; upper surfaces of leaves shiny green and smooth to the touch.

Flowers: Male flowers borne in elongated clusters; female flowers borne in rounded clusters; appearing in spring and summer.

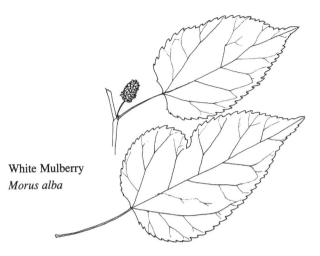

White Mulberry
Morus alba

Fruit: Usually white to pinkish but sometimes almost black, arising from the leaf axils, and held in globular clusters, 1 - 2 cm long.

Distinguishing Marks: Distinguished from red mulberry (*M. rubra*) by having smooth upper leaf surfaces.

Distribution: Native to Asia but widespread nearly throughout Florida except the southern-most counties, often in disturbed sites but also naturalized along stream banks and in bot-tomland woodlands.

Landscape Use: This and the native red mulberry (*M. rubra*), below, have both been used ornamentally for their fruit, shade, and attractive leaves, but some people avoid both species due to the mess that the fruit makes when it falls. Both are easy to grow. The white mulber-ry, in particular, has been cultivated for thousands of years as the food plant of the silk worm and was introduced into the United States, particularly the southeast, in an attempt to start a silk industry in this country.

Comment: This plant has a long history of medicinal uses. Teas made from various parts of the plant have been used to ease coughs, treat headaches, reduce joint pain, and cure respi-ratory problems.

Red Mulberry Page 222

Morus rubra L.

Form: Large shrub or small deciduous tree to about 20 m tall; flowering and fruiting when of shrublike stature.

Leaves: Alternate, simple, generally appearing large and heart shaped, 10 - 18 cm long, 6 - 13 cm wide, bases cordate, margins toothed and sometimes divided into lobes (lobing more common on shrubby plants), similar in shape to leaves of the white mulberry (*M. alba*) but usually less shiny and usually not having more than three lobes per leaf.

Flowers: Greenish, borne in hanging clusters; appearing in spring and summer.

Red Mulberry
Morus rubra

Fruit: Similar to white mulberry but more elongated, averaging more than 2 cm in length.

Distinguishing Marks: Distinguished from white mulberry (*M. alba*) by leaves with upper surfaces being dull green and scabrid, from most other trees and shrubs with a similar leaf shape by broken leaf stems exuding a milky sap (see also *Broussonetia papyrifera*).

Distribution: Hammocks, floodplain and bottomland woods, pinelands, uplands; native understory tree found throughout the state except for the two southernmost counties and the Keys.

Landscape Use: See *M. alba*, above.

Comment: The black mulberry (*Morus nigra* L.), which has been cultivated for so long that its original range is difficult to discern, is also cultivated in southern Florida and is probably escaped into disturbed sites. It may be distinguished from red mulberry by its black fruit, and by the lack of hairs on the undersurfaces of its leaves.

MYOPORACEAE — MYOPORUM FAMILY

This is a small, Old World family of five genera and about 100 species. Most members of the family occur in Australia. The single species described below is the New World's only representative of the family.

White-Alling

Page 223

Bontia daphnoides L
.

Form: Shrub or small, mostly evergreen tree to about 8 m tall, with an erect, slender, pale-brown trunk.

Leaves: Alternate, simple, lanceolate, to about 12 cm long, similar in appearance to the bays of the genus *Persea*.

Flowers: Tube shaped with a purplish, hairy, downturned lower lip, otherwise yellow, borne singly; to about 2 cm long; appearing any month of the year.

Fruit: Yellow, fleshy, olivelike, with the remains of the pistil extending well beyond the tip; borne on long stalks.

Distinguishing Marks: The yellow fruit with long stalks and distinctive remains of the pistil are characteristic.

Distribution: Found mostly near shorelines, salt flats, and mangroves; perhaps native to southern Florida, more likely introduced.

Landscape Use: Used throughout the tropics as a street and yard tree; especially recommended for seaside gardens.

White-Alling
Bontia daphnoides

MYRICACEAE — BAYBERRY FAMILY

The bayberry family is a small, ancient family of only three genera and about 50, usually aromatic, species. Fossil records date the family to at least the Late Cretaceous period, or about 100 million years ago. Members of the family were apparently more numerous then and their distribution more widespread. Today, the family is composed primarily of trees and shrubs of midtemperate to subtropical distribution. Two genera are represented in the southeastern United States; only one genus with three species is found in Florida.

Wax Myrtle or Southern Bayberry

Myrica cerifera L.

Page 225

Form: Evergreen shrub or small tree to 12 m tall, often with several trunks and dense foliage.
Leaves: Alternate, simple, narrowly oblanceolate, 3 - 15 cm long, 1 - 2 cm wide, typically toothed toward the apices, aromatic when crushed, upper and lower surfaces covered with amber-colored dots that require magnification to see clearly.
Flowers: Borne in catkins at the leaf axils, catkins to about 2 cm long and appearing in early spring, often in great profusion; male and female flowers borne on separate plants.
Fruit: A small but conspicuous, rounded, waxy, bluish drupe, 2 - 4 mm in diameter.
Distinguishing Marks: Likely to be confused in north Florida only with the swamp candleberry (*M. heterophylla*), but distinguished from it by the latter having larger leaves with amber dots only on the lower surface; leaves superficially similar to the crabwood (*Ateramnus lucidus*) of southern Florida but distinguished from it by the latter's distinctive, shouldered leaf base, and lack of odor when crushed.
Distribution: Found in a wide variety of habitats throughout Florida including the Keys; one of the state's most widespread plants.
Landscape Use: Often used in hedges and as a background plant, particularly where a naturalistic landscape is desired; easy to establish, grow, and care for; tolerant of a wide range of soils and conditions, including salt spray. Wax myrtle will become a large plant in good conditions; pruning every year or two will keep it in check.
Comment: The wax myrtles are well-known species with long histories of popular and practical uses. Early colonists gathered the berries and melted down the waxy coatings to produce delicately fragrant candles. They also used the plant for a variety of medicinal purposes, including as a treatment for stomach aches, ulcers, dry skin, and the common cold.

Swamp Candleberry or Evergreen Bayberry

Myrica heterophylla Raf.

Page 225

Form: Evergreen shrub to about 3 m tall, or small tree to about 5 m tall and at least 10 cm in diameter.
Leaves: Alternate, simple, oblanceolate, 6 - 12 cm long, to about 5 cm wide, upper surface glabrous, lower dotted with amber-colored scales; margins often toothed toward the apices; aromatic when crushed.

Wax Myrtle or Southern Bayberry
Myrica cerifera

Swamp Candleberry or Evergreen Bayberry
Myrica heterophylla

Flowers: Individual flowers small, borne in catkins; appearing in spring; male and female flowers borne on separate plants.

Fruit: A rounded, knobby drupe, 2 - 4.5 mm in diameter.

Distinguishing Marks: Distinguished from the southern wax myrtle (*M. cerifera*) by generally larger, thicker leaves with only the lower surfaces of leaves being covered with amber-colored dots.

Distribution: Bogs, swamps, flatwoods depressions, and similar wet areas; throughout the Panhandle and northern Florida.

Odorless Bayberry   Photo 177

Myrica inodora Bartr.

Form: Evergreen shrub or small tree with smooth, glabrous twigs, to about 7 m tall.

Leaves: Alternate, simple, entire, slightly revolute, elliptic, leathery or somewhat rubbery to the touch, dark green above, 4 - 8 cm long, 2 - 3 cm wide, upper and lower surfaces copiously punctate, apices narrowed to a blunt point, bases tapered and appearing to extend a little ways down the petioles.

Flowers: Individually inconspicuous; appearing in spring.

Fruit: A black, rounded drupe with a conspicuously roughened surface, 6 - 7 mm in diameter.

Distinguishing Marks: Most easily recognized in its habitat by roughened fruit typical of *Myrica* species in conjunction with entire, nonaromatic leaves.

Distribution: Bogs, swamps, flatwoods, and similar places; restricted in Florida to the Panhandle from about Leon and Wakulla Counties westward.

MYRSINACEAE — MYRSINE FAMILY

The Myrsinaceae are composed of more than 1,000 species in over 30 genera worldwide. Only members of the genera *Ardisia* and *Myrsine* occur in Florida's shrub flora. Both are confined predominately to the southern parts of the state and are common components of tropical hammocks and the edges of the pinelands, though at least one nonnative species is an often-used ornamental in the northern parts of the state.

Coral Ardisia   Photo 178

Ardisia crenata Sims.

Form: Low-growing, evergreen shrub to about 2 m tall.

Leaves: Alternate, simple, leathery, very dark green, lanceolate, to about 14 cm long; margins wavy to undulate and conspicuously crenate.

Flowers: Small, white or pink, to about 1 cm wide or a little more; appearing in spring and borne at the ends of special lateral branches.

Fruit: A red (occasionally white) drupe, one seeded, to about 1 cm in diameter; borne in showy, drooping clusters below the leaves, hence the name coral ardisia; long lasting, mostly persisting from fall to spring.

Distinguishing Marks: The wavy-edged leaves and attractive, bright red fruit are distinctive.

Distribution: Occasionally escaped in central Florida, more commonly so in northern Florida; usually near plantings.

Landscape Use: Though this is an easy-to-grow, attractive, and often-used landscape plant, it is listed as a Category I pest plant by the Florida Exotic Pest Plant Council. It is becoming a very troublesome weed and a threat to native species in many places, particularly in the more northern parts of the state. It should not be planted.

Comment: This is one of several species of *Ardisia* that is used as an ornamental.

Shoebutton Ardisia Page 227

Ardisia elliptica Thunb.

Form: Shrub or small tree with smooth stems.

Leaves: Alternate, simple, entire, elliptic to oblong or obovate, 10 - 15 cm long; lower surfaces dotted; petioles 4 - 8 mm long.

Flowers: White, borne in clusters at the leaf axils.

Fruit: A one-seeded drupe, red at first but black at maturity, about 5 mm in diameter.

Distinguishing Marks: Separated from other members of the genus by flowers being borne in axillary, rather than terminal, clusters.

Distribution: Hammocks, disturbed sites; nonnative and naturalized in southern Florida.

Landscape Use: This plant is used in landscape plantings for its attractive foliage and fruit but is very invasive in hammocks, easily spread by birds, and is not recommended for landscape or ornamental use. It is listed as a Category I pest plant by the Florida Exotic Pest Plant Council.

Comment: See comment for *A. crenata*, above.

Shoebutton Ardisia
Ardisia elliptica

Marlberry

Photos 179, 180

Ardisia escallonioides Schlecht. & Cham.

Form: Most often an evergreen shrub, sometimes a small tree to about 7 m tall.

Leaves: Alternate, simple, lanceolate, leathery, entire, often reflexed upward from the central axis, 10 - 15 cm long, 3 - 5 cm wide, arranged spirally along the branch, blades often curving downward lengthwise, upper surfaces shiny green.

Flowers: White, fragrant, arising in dense clusters at the ends of branches and very conspicuous, appearing almost any time of year.

Fruit: A shiny, black drupe, 7 - 9 mm in diameter.

Distinguishing Marks: Potentially confused with myrsine (*Myrsine floridana*) but distinguished from it by young stem tips being brown rather than green, and by the terminal flower clusters.

Distribution: Native component of hammocks and pinelands; from about Volusia and Hillsborough Counties southward along the coast; from about Highlands and Okeechobee Counties southward inland; throughout the Keys.

Landscape Use: This is an excellent evergreen with dark foliage; its white flowers and shiny fruit are quite attractive.

Myrsine or Rapanea

Page 229

Myrsine floridana A. DC.

Form: Evergreen shrub or small tree with light gray bark, to about 6 m tall.

Leaves: Alternate but close together, simple, leathery, entire but margins often rolled under, crowded near the ends of the branches, 6 - 12 cm long, 1 - 4 cm wide, upper surfaces shiny green, apices often notched; flowering and fruiting generally along leafless portions of the branches.

Flowers: Small, white, borne along the stem and appearing mainly in the winter.

Fruit: Rounded, dark blue to black at maturity, green when young, 4 - 7 mm in diameter, evident at almost any time of year.

Distinguishing Marks: Potentially confused with marlberry (*Ardisia escallonioides*) but distinguished from it by young stem tips being green rather than brown, and by the flowers being borne along the stem; the saying "myrsine is green" helps in remembering the former character.

Distribution: Coastal hammocks and pinelands from about Manatee and Volusia Counties southward, including the Keys; small populations also found in Levy and Citrus Counties.

MYRTACEAE — MYRTLE FAMILY

The myrtle family is a complex and confusing-to-identify collection of plants represented by at least seven genera in Florida, only some of which are native to the state. The family has undergone a rather long history of dramatic changes in taxonomic classification. Exacting

Pale Lidflower
Calyptranthes pallens

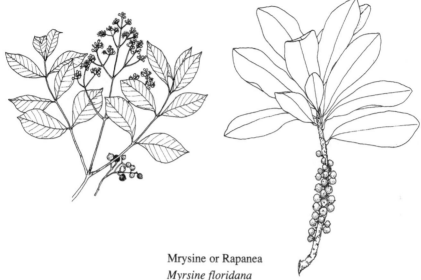

Mrysine or Rapanea
Myrsine floridana

distinctions have been difficult to define for many of the family's genera and species, resulting in a wide range of synonymous scientific names. The family contains about 80 genera that include about 3,000 species. Most members of the family (in Florida) have opposite, leathery, simple leaves.

Pale Lidflower   Page 229

Calyptranthes pallens Griseb.

Form: Evergreen shrub or sometimes a small tree to about 8 m tall; with smooth, gray to scaly bark and distinctive branching, branchlets produced in pairs at each leaf node, each branchlet then terminating at the next pair of leaves.

Leaves: Opposite, entire, aromatic, elliptic, 3 - 8 cm long, 1.2 - 2.2 cm wide, apices and bases tapering to long, blunt points.

Flowers: Small, greenish to white, borne in many-flowered clusters near the ends of twigs; generally appearing in early summer.

Fruit: A round, juicy berry, 0.5 - 1.2 cm in diameter, reddish at first, turning purplish black at maturity.

Distinguishing Marks: Very similar to myrtle-of-the-river (*C. zuzygium*), distinguished from it by undersurfaces of leaves being finely hairy and by the central leaf veins on the upper surfaces of leaves not being ridged, from white stopper (*Eugenia axillaris*) by distinctive branching pattern of the branchlets.

Distribution: Hammocks of Dade and Monroe Counties, including the Keys.

Myrtle-of-the-River

Page 230

Calyptranthes zuzygium (L.) Sw.

Form: Evergreen shrub or small tree to about 7 m tall in Florida with smooth, light gray bark and distinctive branching; branchlets produced in pairs at each leaf node, each branchlet then terminating at the next pair of leaves.

Leaves: Opposite, simple, entire, elliptic to ovate with long, tapering apices, 3.5 - 6 cm long, 1.8 - 3.8 cm wide, central vein ridged and raised above the upper leaf surface.

Flowers: Borne in small clusters at the leaf axils with many stamens but no petals; generally appearing in early summer.

Fruit: A rounded berry, to about 1 cm in diameter.

Distinguishing Marks: Distinguished from pale lidflower (*C. pallens*) by having lower leaf surface glabrous rather than finely hairy at maturity and by the midvein being noticeably ridged and raised above the upper leaf surface, especially toward the base; from white stopper (*Eugenia axillaris*) by distinctive branching pattern of the branchlets.

Distribution: Hammocks of Dade and Monroe Counties, including the Keys.

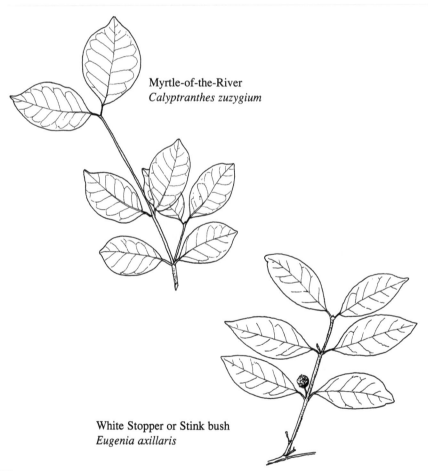

Myrtle-of-the-River
Calyptranthes zuzygium

White Stopper or Stink bush
Eugenia axillaris

White Stopper or Stink Bush

Eugenia axillaris (Sw.) Willd.

Form: Evergreen shrub or small tree to about 8 m tall, with smooth, grayish-white, scaly bark.

Leaves: Opposite, simple, leathery, entire, ovate, 3 - 7 cm long, 1.5 - 4 cm wide, upper surfaces dark green, lower surfaces paler with tiny black dots, petioles generally reddish in color, apices tapering to a blunt point; emitting an offensive, skunklike odor when crushed or bruised.

Flowers: White, small, fragrant, borne in summer in axillary clusters; appearing year-round.

Fruit: A juicy, reddish to black berry, 1 - 1.2 cm in diameter.

Distinguishing Marks: Similar to the rare spiceberry eugenia (*E. rhombea*) but distinguished from it by having flower stalks usually shorter than the flowers and by the bark of the trunk being whitish rather than brownish gray or clay colored.

Distribution: Common in coastal hammocks from the central peninsula southward and throughout the Keys.

Comment: The stoppers of the genus *Eugenia* exhibit great inconsistency in their historical names. Currently, it is generally agreed that four *Eugenia* species inhabit southern Florida. Two of these, the white stopper (*E. axillaris*) and Spanish stopper (*E. foetida*), are common and widespread. The red-berry stopper (*E. confusa*), with characteristically long-pointed leaves, is only an occasional resident of hammocks and is not common. The red stopper (*E. rhombea*), which is most similar in appearance to the white stopper, is a rare species found very sparingly in the Keys. All are noted for their opposite, evergreen, aromatic, punctate leaves, a characteristic which helps immensely in separating them from all but a handful of south Florida trees and shrubs.

Red-Berry Stopper

Eugenia confusa DC.

Form: Evergreen shrub or small tree to about 6 m tall with light gray, scaly bark and a straight trunk.

Leaves: Opposite, simple, entire, stiff, elliptic to ovate, 3 - 7 cm long, 2 - 4 cm wide; apices long tapered and curving downward; upper surfaces shiny, lower surfaces duller and with small black dots.

Flowers: White, small, approximately 6 mm wide; appearing year-round.

Fruit: A bright red berry, 5 - 8 mm in diameter.

Distinguishing Marks: Most easily recognized by opposite, stiff, very shiny, long-pointed leaves with drooping apices.

Distribution: Hammocks of southernmost Florida and the upper Keys; not common.

Comment: Listed as threatened by the Florida Department of Agriculture.

Red-Berry Stopper
Eugenia confusa

Spanish Stopper or Box Leaf Eugenia
Eugenia foetida

Spiceberry Eugenia or Red Stopper
Eugenia rhombea

Spanish Stopper or Box Leaf Eugenia

Page 232

Eugenia foetida Pers.

Form: Small evergreen shrub or tree to about 6 m tall with smooth, gray, sometimes mottled, bark.

Leaves: Opposite, simple, entire, leathery, aromatic, elliptic to obovate, upper surfaces dark green, lower surfaces yellow green and bearing tiny black dots, 2 - 6 cm long, 1.4 - 4 cm wide.

Flowers: White, small, borne in axillary racemes, mildly fragrant, with many white, thread-like stamens; appearing year-round.

Fruit: A rounded berry, turning from reddish orange to black or brown at maturity, to about 8 mm in diameter.

Distinguishing Marks: Recognized as the state's only *Eugenia* with a rounded, rather than tapered, leaf apex; distinguished from long-stalked stopper (*Mosiera longipes*) by the latter having leaves mostly shorter than 2 cm and conspicuously long-stalked flowers.

Distribution: Hammocks of southern Florida, primarily from Collier and Palm Beach Counties southward and throughout the Keys, but extending northward along the east coast at least to Brevard County; also found in pinelands of the Lower Keys.

Spiceberry Eugenia or Red Stopper

Page 232

Eugenia rhombea (Berg) Krug & Urban

Form: Shrub or small, upright evergreen tree with smooth, brownish-gray or clay-colored bark, to about 8 m tall in much of its range, to about 3 m in Florida.

Leaves: Opposite, simple, leathery, dark green above, yellow green below, ovate, 3 - 6 cm long, 1.5 - 4 cm wide, apices tapering to a long, blunt point, margins entire and appearing to be outlined in yellow.

Flowers: Small, white, a little more than 1 cm wide, borne in few-flowered clusters; appearing year-round.

Fruit: A rounded berry, orange red at first but turning black at maturity, 7 - 9 mm in diameter.

Distinguishing Marks: Similar in appearance to the white stopper (*E. axillaris*), distinguished from it by having flower stalks usually longer than the flowers, and brownish-gray bark.

Distribution: Rare species found in its natural habitat in only a few locations in the upper and lower Keys, including a substantial and well-protected population on North Key Largo; also reported as rare in coastal hammocks of Lee County (Wunderlin, 1982).

Comment: Listed as endangered by the Florida Department of Agriculture.

Surinam Cherry

Photo 181

Eugenia uniflora L.

Form: Evergreen shrub or small tree to about 5 m tall; young stems often with at least a few reddish hairs.

Leaves: Opposite, simple, entire, egg shaped, 3 - 7 cm long; upper surfaces dark green and shiny, paler below; young leaves are distinctively wine colored and often contain at least a few reddish hairs.

Flowers: White, fragrant, with many stamens, borne either in short, few-flowered racemes at the leaf axils, or borne singly at the axils of the lower leaves (hence the specific name); petals less than 1 cm long; appearing year-round.

Fruit: A ribbed, rounded, orange-red to nearly black, juicy berry, 2 - 3 cm in diameter.

Distinguishing Marks: The comparatively large fruit (for a *Eugenia*) and at least some flowers borne singly in the leaf axils are diagnostic among the stoppers as well as among most other South Florida opposite-leaved shrubs or trees.

Distribution: Native to Brazil but well established in southern Florida.

Landscape Use: Surinam cherry is an often-used hedge plant that responds well to pruning, tolerates a variety of soils, and does best in full sun. However, it is listed as a Category I pest plant by the Florida Exotic Pest Plant Council and is not recommended for landscape use.

Comment: This plant was probably imported for its edible, cherrylike fruit which can be eaten raw or made into preserves or jelly.

Long-Stalked Stopper

Page 234, Photo 182

Mosiera longipes (Berg) Small

Form: Typically an evergreen shrub in south Florida pinelands, sometimes forming a small tree to perhaps 4 m tall in hammocks of the Keys.

Leaves: Opposite, simple, entire, ovate to oval, usually less than 3 cm long, upper surfaces shiny green, lower surfaces paler, veins reddish.

Flowers: White to pink with four petals, to nearly 1.5 cm wide at maturity, produced singly on conspicuously long stalks; appearing most profusely in late spring and early summer.

Fruit: A round, black berry, 6 - 10 mm in diameter.

Distinguishing Marks: The small, oval leaves and long-stalked fruit are diagnostic.

Distribution: Hammocks and pinelands; Dade and Monroe Counties, including the Keys.

Comment: This species is often seen listed under the scientific synonym *Psidium longipes* (Berg.) McVaugh, which is only one of many of the plant's synonyms.

Long-Stalked Stopper
Mosiera longipes

Twinberry, Twinberry Stopper, or Simpson Stopper

Myrcianthes fragrans (Sw.) McVaugh   **Page 235, Photo 183**

Form: Evergreen shrub or small tree to about 8 m tall with distinctive reddish, smooth, flaking bark similar to that of the guava.

Leaves: Opposite, simple, entire, aromatic, leathery, elliptic to ovate, 1 - 8 cm long, 1 - 4 cm wide, both surfaces covered with tiny, often blackish, dots.

Flowers: White, borne in long-stalked clusters, each flower with many spreading stamens; appearing year-round.

Fruit: Rounded, 6 - 10 mm in diameter, red, red brown, or orange.

Distinguishing Marks: Most easily distinguished by reddish flaking bark in combination with opposite leaves.

Distribution: Hammocks from about Volusia County southward, excluding the Keys.

Comment: Recognized as a candidate for federal listing by the U. S. Fish and Wildlife Service.

Twinberry, Twinberry
Stopper, or Simpson Stopper
Myrcianthes fragrans

Guava   Page 236

Psidium guajava L.

Form: Evergreen shrub or low, spreading tree to about 10 m tall with angled twigs and scaly stems.

Leaves: Opposite, simple, coarse, entire, elliptic to oblong, dark green above, paler below, 4 - 15 cm long, with prominent, pinnately arranged veins that are impressed on the upper surface and raised on the lower.

Flowers: Fragrant, to about 4 cm wide at maturity, with white petals and a mass of white and yellow stamens, borne singly in the leaf axils; appearing year-round.

Fruit: A large, yellow berry, 3 - 6 cm in diameter.

Distinguishing Marks: Easily distinguished by the combination of coarse, opposite leaves with prominent venation, scaly bark, and angled twigs.

Distribution: Hammocks and disturbed sites where escaped from cultivation; from Brevard and Pinellas Counties southward.

Landscape Use: The guava is native from the West Indies to Peru but has been widely cultivated in the tropics and southern Florida as a fruit tree. It and the strawberry guava (mentioned below) are listed as Category I pest plants by the Florida Exotic Pest Plant Council. Guava fruit, which is rich in vitamin C (perhaps 2 to 5 times that of a fresh orange), has been made into jelly, and its juice has been canned and sold as a beverage.

Comment: The strawberry guava (*P. cattleianum* Sabine), a South American native, has also escaped from cultivation and rarely becomes established in the south-central and southern peninsula. It differs from *P. guajava* by having smaller leaves that lack the latter's conspicuous venation.

Guava
Psidium guajava

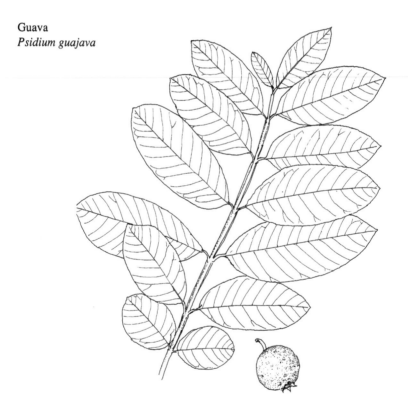

Downy Myrtle
Rhodomyrtus tomentosus (Ait.) Hassk

Form: An attractive, bushy, evergreen ornamental shrub to about 3 m tall; stems bearing a soft pubescence.

Leaves: Opposite, simple, ovate to elliptic, entire, green above, grayish and woolly below, 5 - 7 cm long.

Flowers: Showy, pink, to about 2 cm wide, borne in the leaf axils; appearing late spring into very early summer.

Fruit: Purple, ovoid berry, 1 - 1.5 cm in diameter.

Distinguishing Marks: The woolly leaves, showy, pink flowers with many conspicuous stamens, and purple berries help to distinguish the species.

Distribution: Native to Australia and Asia; escaped from cultivation in frost-free areas of the state, northward to about Lee and Martin Counties.

Landscape Use: Though this is a popular landscape plant in the southern regions of the state, it is listed as a Category I pest plant by the Florida Exotic Pest Plant Council. It is extremely invasive, difficult to control, and its use in the landscape is strongly discouraged. It has found popularity as a landscape plant because it is attractive, easy to grow, tolerates salt air, and does well in full sun or partial shade.

Comment: The fruit of downy myrtle is used in pies and preserves as well as eaten raw.

NYCTAGINACEAE — FOUR-O'CLOCK FAMILY

The Nyctaginaceae, or four-o'clock family, consists of about 30 genera and 300 species worldwide. Most North American members of the family are herbaceous rather than woody, and the family may be best known in Florida for the bougainvillea (*Bougainvillea* spp.), a collection of colorful tropical vines that are used ornamentally in the southern part of the state. The family takes its common name from the four-o'clock, or marvel of Peru (*Mirabilis jalapa* L.), a temperate species that is cultivated for its bright red, tubular flowers. This latter species is quite showy and occurs as a frequent and weedy escape in the southwestern U. S. as well as in scattered localities throughout the southeastern coastal plain. With these two exceptions, however, the family is otherwise of little economic importance.

Blolly or Beefwood   Photo 184
Guapira discolor (K. Spreng.) Little

Form: Evergreen shrub or small, bushy tree to about 13 m tall, with smooth, gray bark.

Leaves: Opposite (sometimes subopposite to alternate), elliptic to obovate, light green in color, leathery, simple, 1 - 7 cm long, to about 2.5 cm wide, margins entire but thickened, veins obscure except for the central vein which is yellowish green and translucent when held up to the light; petioles grooved; apices rounded.

Flowers: Tiny, greenish, tubular, without petals, borne in clusters, male and female flowers borne on separate plants and appearing mostly in spring and summer.

Fruit: Bright red, juicy, berrylike, oval, to about 1.3 cm in diameter, usually appearing in summer and fall.

Distinguishing Marks: Most easily recognized by opposite leaves with yellowish-green, translucent midveins, grooved petioles, and bright red, juicy berries.

Distribution: Hammocks and coastal scrub; Atlantic coast from about Cape Canaveral southward, including the Keys.

Comment: In 1933, J. K. Small listed another blolly (*Torrubia floridana* Britton) from Rock Key, Florida. (It is instructive to note that Small used the scientific name *T. longifolia* [Heimerl] Britton instead of *G. discolor* for what is now called blolly.) In a note to his description, Small mentioned that the plant had been collected nearly a century earlier but had not been found since. On December 29, 1994, south Florida naturalists Keith Bradley and Roger Hammer discovered a population of plants on Long Key that closely resembles *G. discolor*, except that their leaves and twigs are copiously pubescent rather than glabrous, the key difference Small used to distinguish the two blolly species. Later, Bradley discovered another population on Boca Grande. Hammer suggests that since the newly discovered populations were found growing in conjunction with *G. discolor*, and that since there are no apparent intermediate forms, the newly found plants might be representatives of the lost species. The name blolly derives from the English word loblolly, which refers to thickets growing in moist depressions. Blolly, then, actually means thicket, an apt appellation for this thicket-forming species.

Cockspur, Devil's Claws, or Pull-And-Hold-Back   Page 239
Pisonia aculeata L.

Form: Sprawling, shrubby, or sometimes treelike, vine with distinctive opposite branching, and paired, very sharp, curved spines at the leaf axils; young stems covered with tawny hairs; older stems with dark bark.

Leaves: Opposite or subopposite, simple, entire, ovate to elliptic, 2 - 8 cm long, 1 - 5 cm wide; dull green.

Flowers: Yellow green, without petals, tiny and inconspicuous, borne in clusters at the leaf axils; appearing spring through summer.

Fruit: Dry, rounded to oblong, ribbed, softly hairy, sticky, 7 - 9 mm long.

Distinguishing Marks: The combination of opposite branching, opposite leaves, and curving spines is diagnostic.

Distribution: Hammocks and pinelands; south Florida and the Keys.

Comment: Although currently limited to an essentially tropical distribution, members of this genus once ranged much farther north. Fossil evidence indicates that at least one, now extinct, species probably flourished in the area of what has become north Florida's Apalachicola River drainage basin. This latter plant appears to have existed near the end of the Oligocene Epoch, or about 25 million years ago, and offers convincing evidence of the radically different environmental circumstances that likely defined Florida's landscape in prehistoric times.

Cockspur, Devil's Claws, or
Pull-And-Hold-Back
Pisonia aculeata

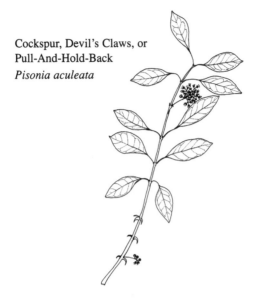

Pisonia or Cockspur

Photo 185

Pisonia rotundata Griseb.

Form: Evergreen shrub or small, spreading tree with gray bark; potentially to about 5 m tall.
Leaves: Opposite, simple, stiff, elliptic to obovate, averaging 2.5 - 10 cm long, margins entire but somewhat revolute, dull green above with conspicuously depressed and light-colored veins.
Flowers: Tiny, green and white, without petals, borne in compact clusters; appearing March through May.
Fruit: Rounded, 5 - 6 mm in diameter, quite sticky.
Distinguishing Marks: Most easily recognized by its opposite, elliptical leaves with conspicuously depressed veins.
Distribution: Native to, but rare in hammocks and scrub of the lower Keys, especially Big Pine Key.

NYSSACEAE — TUPELO FAMILY

The sour gum or tupelo family (Nyssaceae) is a small collection of only three genera and less than ten species. In prehistoric times the family was probably widely distributed worldwide, but today it is restricted almost solely to eastern North America and China. That the present-day members of the Nyssaceae are of ancient lineage is evident from a remarkable fossil record that places representatives of the family on most of the earth's major continents and in all major geologic time periods from the Eocene through the Pliocene (Eyde, 1966). Only two of Florida's four members of the genus *Nyssa* are described below. The other two consistently reach tree stature.

Some authors have concluded that the genus *Nyssa* would be more correctly placed in the family Cornaceae (Burckhalter, 1992) than Nyssaceae. Indeed, the genera *Nyssa* and *Cornus* have long been assumed to be closely related. However, with a single exception, members of the two genera can be easily distinguished from each other in the field solely on the basis of leaf arrangement. Species of *Cornus* have opposite leaves (except *C. alternifolia*), those of *Nyssa*, alternate.

Ogeechee Tupelo or Ogeechee Lime
Nyssa ogeche Bartr. ex Marsh.

Photo 186

Form: Typically a small deciduous tree or very large shrub with several leaning trunks, potentially to about 20 m tall, often forming very dense stands.

Leaves: Alternate, simple, entire, elliptic, 8 - 15 cm long, 5 - 8 cm wide.

Flowers: Male flowers borne in rounded, compact clusters; appearing primarily in April and May.

Fruit: A reddish, fleshy drupe, 2 - 4 cm long.

Distinguishing Marks: Distinguished from water tupelo (*N. aquatica* L., a tree not described here) with which it is most nearly similar by having petioles less than 3 cm long and by the length of the fruit stalk equaling or exceeding the length of the fruit.

Distribution: River swamps, backwaters, bay heads, bottomland woods; from Walton to Hamilton Counties.

Comment: Ogeechee tupelo has several uses. In April and May the plant bears clusters of small white flowers that produce an abundance of sweet nectar that makes them attractive to bees and other insects. The trees are famous in north Florida for the smooth-tasting "tupelo honey" that bees derive from this nectar. The fruits of all the tupelos are eaten by wildlife, but the acidic juice of ogeechee fruit has sometimes even been used by humans as a substitute for limes, hence one of its common names.

Nyssa ursina Small

Page 241

Form: Low, single- to multi-stemmed shrub often not exceeding about 1.5 m tall, often shorter; sometimes arborescent with a relatively thick trunk to about 10 cm in diameter; stems medium brown in color.

Leaves: Alternate, simple, entire, numerous, narrowly elliptic, 2.5 - 7 cm long, 1 - 2 cm wide, dark, shiny green above and often purplish spotted, especially as the season progresses; fall leaves, in particular, reddish to purplish in color nearly throughout; in almost every respect like the leaves of blackgum (*N. biflora* Walt., a tree not described here, but see comment below).

Flowers: Male flowers small, borne in small clusters at the leaf axils.

Fruit: Green at first, turning dark blue, more rounded than oblong (as in *N. biflora*), 8 - 13 mm long, typically borne in pairs on the fruit stalk.

Distinguishing Marks: Distinguished from other shrubs of savannas by purplish-spotted leaves and by fruit borne two to the stalk.

Nyssa ursina

Distribution: Restricted to fire-prone savannas, open herb bogs, wet edges of pineland swamps in Calhoun, Gulf, and Liberty Counties; seemingly associated only with the region of the lower Apalachicola River.

Comment: This plant was originally described by Small (1927), who gave it its specific epithet because its fruit is a favorite of bears. It is listed as a distinct species by some authorities (Clewell, 1985) and as a synonym for *N. biflora* by others (Godfrey, 1988). *N. biflora* is a medium-sized to large deciduous tree to about 35 m tall that is often found in bay swamps and pond margins throughout the northern two-thirds of the state. Whether *N. ursina* is distinct from or an ecoform of the latter species is somewhat conjectural; the only difference between the two seems to be one of form, which may be the result of frequent fire or poor soil nutrients. In either case, the plant described here definitely flowers and fruits when of low stature and is, therefore, included as a shrub.

OLACACEAE — XIMENIA OR OLAX FAMILY

Members of the Olacaceae make up a small family of less than 30 genera and not more than 200 species worldwide. The family is primarily tropical to subtropical in distribution and includes representatives in Africa, Asia, Australia, and India as well as the Americas. One species in each of two genera are found in the United States. Both are restricted to southern Florida. Many members of this family (as are the two described below) are known to be parasitic on the roots of other plants (see comment below for *Ximenia americana*).

Gulf Graytwig or Whitewood

Photo 187

Schoepfia chrysophylloides (A. Rich.) Planch.

Form: Evergreen shrub or small, erect tree to about 10 m tall, with crooked branches, and brittle, zigzag branchlets, and whitish twigs.

Leaves: Alternate, simple, ovate to elliptic, entire, 3 - 7.5 cm long, 2 - 5 cm wide, with wavy edges, exhibiting a strong odor when crushed.

Flowers: Red to orange tinted, small, and sweet scented, appearing throughout the winter from about October to March.

Fruit: A red, ovoid drupe, 10 - 12 mm long.

Distinguishing Marks: Most easily recognized by the smooth, almost white, brittle, zigzag branchlets, and conspicuously reddish-purple new growth; the shape of some leaves is somewhat similar to those of the white stopper (*Eugenia axillaris*) but the leaves are alternate rather than opposite.

Distribution: Uncommon in hammocks of southern Florida, mainly on the Keys.

Hog Plum or Tallowwood

Photo 188

Ximenia americana L.

Form: Evergreen shrub or small tree to about 9 m tall with irregular, sometimes sprawling branches, and sharp spines in the leaf axils.

Leaves: Alternate, simple, entire, elliptic to ovate, 2.5 - 7 cm long, 1.2 - 4 cm wide, upper surfaces shiny green, lower surfaces paler.

Flowers: Yellowish white, fragrant, with four hairy petals, to about 12 mm wide; appearing spring through fall.

Fruit: A rounded drupe, 2 - 3 cm long; green at first, bright yellow at maturity, candylike to the taste and very palatable.

Distinguishing Marks: Distinguished from species of *Bumelia* by each leaf having a tiny tooth at its apex and a grooved petiole, both of which require magnification to see clearly.

Distribution: Hammocks and scrub from central Florida southward and throughout the Keys; also known from swamps in Fakahatchee Strand State Preserve.

Comment: The hog plum is known to be semiparasitic on the roots of other species, a feature common to a number of members of the olax family. Laboratory research indicates that this parasitism is neither host specific nor a mandatory part of the plant's life cycle. The plant's haustoria (roots that have been modified for parasitism) have been found on several associated species, and healthy plants without haustoria have also been observed. The attachment of *Ximenia* haustoria to other plants seems to cause no visible loss to the host, nor any particular increase in vigor to the parasite.

OLEACEAE — OLIVE FAMILY

The olive family is composed of about 30 genera and more than 500 species worldwide. Six genera containing about 20 species are found in Florida, 13 of which are included among our vines and shrubs. Members of the family are characterized by opposite leaves that may be either simple or compound. In the temperate portions of the state, where the majority of these plants are found, the opposite leaf arrangement alone is enough to quickly narrow the field of possible choices about a particular plant's identity. A number of Florida's members of this family were introduced as ornamentals and have now become naturalized, sometimes to the detriment of native plants.

Pygmy Fringe Tree

Photo 189

Chionanthus pygmaeus Small

Form: Small shrub seldom exceeding about 2 m tall (but sometimes reported to be as much as 4 m, which probably stems from its confusion with the more northern-ranging fringe tree [*C. virginicus*]).
Leaves: Opposite, simple, elliptic, entire, leathery, 3 - 10 cm long.
Flowers: Appearing in spring and borne in loosely branching clusters from the leaf axils; petals four, white, linear, to about 1 cm long.
Fruit: Purple drupes, to 2 cm long.
Distinguishing Marks: The small form, restricted habitat, and smaller flower petals help distinguish this species from *C. virginicus*.
Distribution: Deep, coarse, white sands of the central Florida scrub; endemic from Polk to Highlands Counties.
Landscape Use: A showy shrub or small tree for dry, sandy sites, such as those sites in the lower peninsula where this species is found.
Comment: Listed as endangered by both the Florida Department of Agriculture and the U. S. Fish and Wildlife Service.

Fringe Tree, Grandsie-Gray-Beard, Old Man's Beard

Chionanthus virginicus L. **Photos 190, 191**

Form: Deciduous shrub or small tree to about 10 m tall.
Leaves: Opposite, simple, entire, lanceolate to oval, variable in size, 10 - 20 cm long, 1.8 - 10 cm wide, upper surfaces dark green and glabrous, lower surfaces paler; petioles narrowly winged and often suffused with purplish-red coloration.
Flowers: Unique, appearing in March, borne in showy pendent clusters, each with four conspicuous, linear, creamy-white petals that generally exceed 1 cm in length.
Fruit: An egg-shaped, olivelike drupe, 1 - 2.5 cm long, dark blue to nearly black, fruiting clusters subtended by up to several pairs of leaflike bracts.
Distinguishing Marks: No other Florida shrub or tree (except *C. pygmaeus*) has flowers that resemble this species; distinguished from this latter species by large form and larger flower petals.

Distribution: Found in a wide variety of habitats and often planted as an ornamental across the Panhandle and northern Florida, southward to about Sarasota County.

Landscape Use: Often used in yards, mostly for the showy white flowers that appear in spring. Does well in full sun but prefers slightly acid soil with medium moisture. Fringe tree is relatively slow growing and typically doesn't flower until five to seven years old.

Swamp Privet   Page 244

Forestiera acuminata (Michx.) Poir. in Lam.

Form: Deciduous shrub or small tree to 13 m tall; often with arching branches.

Leaves: Opposite, simple, lanceolate, 4 - 12 cm long, 2 - 3.5 cm wide, many leaves conspicuously tapering to long-pointed apices and bases; margins serrate; petioles 5 - 20 mm long.

Flowers: Yellow, appearing in early spring and borne in small, axillary clusters.

Fruit: An ovoid to ellipsoid drupe, 10 - 15 mm long, 7 - 10 mm wide.

Distinguishing Marks: Distinguished from other opposite-leaved trees by long-tapering and distinctly sharp-pointed leaf tip in conjunction with serrated leaf margins.

Distribution: Primarily found in river swamps and floodplains across the Panhandle, eastward to the Suwannee River.

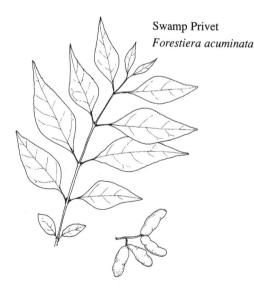

Swamp Privet
Forestiera acuminata

Godfrey's Privet
Forestiera godfreyi

Godfrey's Privet

Forestiera godfreyi L. C. Anderson

Form: Deciduous shrub or small tree to about 5 m tall with rigid branches and a leaning trunk.

Leaves: Opposite, simple, ovate to elliptic, 5 - 8 cm long, 2.3 - 4 cm wide, margins finely serrate from about their middles to their apices; petioles 2 - 10 mm long and at least moderately pubescent.

Flowers: Yellowish green and tiny, borne in tight clusters in the leaf axils; appearing mid-January to mid-February.

Fruit: A dark blue drupe, 10 - 12 mm long, 6 - 9 mm wide.

Distinguishing Marks: Leaves similar in appearance to *F. ligustrina*, distinguished by being larger and by having a uniform covering of pubescence on both the petioles and stems between the leaf nodes, rather than pubescence of the stems typically being in two longitudinal bands; from the leaves of Florida privet (*F. segregata*) by the latter's generally smaller size and the abundant punctations on their lower surfaces.

Distribution: Moist, calcareous woods; sporadically from about Liberty to Marion Counties.

Comment: This plant was described by Florida State University (FSU) botanist Loran Anderson who named the plant for Robert Godfrey, another FSU botanist whose work is well known in both Florida and the southeast.

Forestiera ligustrina (Michx.) Poir. in Lam.

Form: Most often described as a shrub with a leaning trunk, sometimes superficially appearing treelike to about 4 m tall.

Leaves: Opposite, simple, 2 - 5 cm long, less than 2 cm wide, lower surfaces sparsely to densely pubescent, margins inconspicuously toothed from their bases to their apices, apices blunt or rounded.

Forestiera ligustrina

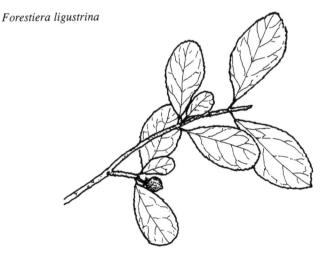

Flowers: Tiny, borne in clusters at the leaf axils, appearing mid- to late summer or very early fall.

Fruit: A blue to black drupe, 7 - 8 mm long.

Distinguishing Marks: Similar to and easily confused with specimens of Walter viburnum (*Viburnum obovatum*) but distinguished by lacking punctations on the lower surfaces of leaves, distinguished from Godfrey's privet (*F. godfreyi*) by smaller leaves that are toothed throughout their margins rather than predominantly above the middle, by petioles being only sparsely pubescent, and by having pubescence of the stems in two longitudinal bands between the leaf nodes.

Distribution: Upland mixed woods and in soils underlain closely by limestone; throughout the Panhandle and eastward to the northwestern peninsula.

Florida Privet

Page 246

Forestiera segregata (Jacq.) Krug & Urban

Form: Evergreen to tardily deciduous shrub or small tree seldom exceeding 3 m tall.

Leaves: Opposite to subopposite, simple, elliptic to oblanceolate, entire, 1.5 - 5 cm long, 1.2 - 2 cm wide, lower and upper surfaces of blades glabrous.

Flowers: Small, greenish yellow, borne in clusters from the leaf axils; appearing in spring.

Fruit: A black, rounded drupe, 5 - 7 mm in diameter.

Distinguishing Marks: Distinguished from other treelike species of *Forestiera* with blunt-tipped leaves by leaves with entire margins and by lower surfaces of leaves being finely punctate.

Distribution: Most common in coastal hammocks, scrub, and thickets, southward from Dixie County on the west coast, from Nassau County on the east coast; the only *Forestiera* species found in the Keys.

Florida Privet
Forestiera segregata

Gold Coast Jasmine

Photo 192

Jasminum dichotomum Vahl

Form: Scrambling and climbing, evergreen woody vine with smooth stems.

Leaves: Opposite, unifoliolate and appearing simple, ovate to nearly rounded, 5 - 7 cm long; upper surfaces shiny green; apices pinched to a point.

Flowers: Pink in the bud, white at maturity, tubular, about 3 cm long, fragrant, borne abundantly but opening at night; appearing any time of year.

Fruit: A black, two-lobed berry.

Distinguishing Marks: The conspicuous, abundant, tubular flowers, and shiny unifoliolate leaves help distinguish this species; without flowers or fruit this species can be mistaken for *Chiococca alba.*

Distribution: Exotic, originating in Ghana and the west coast of Africa, probably introduced into Florida by Dr. David Fairchild; now naturalized and permanently established in hammocks of southern Florida.

Landscape Use: Popular but very weedy ornamental planted for its shiny leaves and profuse flowering; invasive, difficult to control, and not recommended for landscape use. It is listed as a Category I pest plant by the Florida Exotic Pest Plant Council.

Comment: There are more than 200 members of this genus found in tropical and sub-tropical countries around the world, many of which are found in Florida. All of Florida's species have been imported for ornamental use; some have escaped from cultivation and become established. In addition to the present species and the next, the southern and south-central peninsula contain scattered, locally established populations of Arabian jasmine (*J. sambac* Ait.), which is listed as a Category II pest plant for Florida, pinwheel jasmine (*J. nitidum* Skan), star jasmine (*J. multiflorum* [Burm. f.] Andr.), and poet's jasmine (*J. officinale* L.). The yellow-flowered Japanese jasmine (*J. mesnyi* Hance) is common in the north-central peninsula and throughout northern Florida and has been said to be one of the state's most overused nonnative shrubs.

Brazilian Jasmine

Page 248

Jasminum fluminense Vellozo

Form: Climbing, evergreen woody vine; stems densely hairy when young, without hairs at maturity.

Leaves: Opposite, trifoliolate; leaflets ovate, 5 - 7 cm long; terminal leaflet borne on a long stalk.

Flowers: White, fragrant, tubular, with narrow, spreading petals, borne in clusters; appearing abundantly during spring.

Fruit: A black, two-lobed berry.

Distinguishing Marks: Distinguished from *J. dichotomum* by having trifoliolate leaves.

Distribution: Southernmost peninsula.

Landscape Use: Popular ornamental for its abundant, fragrant, slightly curved flowers. However, its aggressive nature makes it a troublesome and difficult-to-control weed. It is

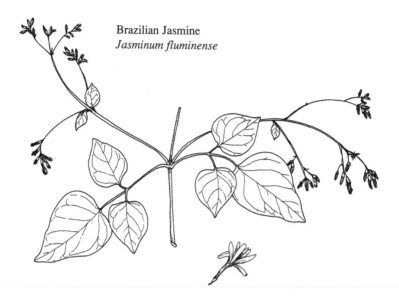

Brazilian Jasmine
Jasminum fluminense

listed as a Category I pest plant by the Florida Exotic Pest Plant Council and should not be used in landscaping.

Comment: The botanical history of this plant suggests the widespread transporting and ornamental use of members of its genus. Though it is native to Africa, the present species was first described from Brazil where it had been introduced by the Portuguese. Also see comment for *J. dichotomum*, above.

Japanese Ligustrum

Page 249

Ligustrum japonicum Thunb.

Form: Evergreen shrub to about 3 m tall; twigs roughened when older.

Leaves: Opposite, simple, entire, leathery, ovate to elliptic, 3 - 8 cm long, 2.5 - 4 cm wide; both surfaces covered with fine dots (requires magnification).

Flowers: Numerous, small, white, fragrant, borne in large, conspicuous clusters at the ends of the branches; appearing in spring.

Fruit: A black to blue-black, oblong drupe, 8 - 12 mm long.

Distinguishing Marks: Most similar to and often confused with *L. lucidum*; distinguished by having leaves that typically do not exceed 8 cm in length, that are flat rather than V-shaped, and that have blunt, rather than pointed, apices; distinguished from *L. sinense* by the latter's overall smaller leaves.

Distribution: A nonnative species often seen in cultivation; rarely naturalized in moist, mixed woodlands of northern Florida, very invasive and well-established in hammocks of southeastern Florida, especially in Dade County.

Japanese Ligustrum
Ligustrum japonicum

Landscape Use: A popular landscape plant, especially as a barrier or border along driveways, roadsides, or suburban lot lines. Though it is hardy and easy to grow in full sun or partial shade, it is listed as a Category II pest plant by the Florida Exotic Pest Plant Council because escaped plants can become troublesome weeds, hence landscape use of the plant should be avoided.

Wax-leaf Ligustrum, Glossy Privet, Tree Privet, Wax-Leaf Privet

Photo 193

Ligustrum lucidum Ait.

Form: Evergreen shrub or small tree to about 5 m tall.

Leaves: Opposite, simple, entire, coarse, dark green in color, 6 - 15 cm long, to about 5 cm wide, apices narrowing to sharp points; blades typically V-shaped from the central vein.

Flowers: Small, white, fragrant, appearing in the spring, borne in terminal clusters.

Fruit: A black drupe, 4 - 8 mm long, evident on the plant for much of the year.

Distinguishing Marks: Distinguished from Chinese privet (*L. sinense*) by larger leaves and glabrous twigs, from Japanese ligustrum (*L. japonicum*) by the larger leaves being generally longer than 8 cm, and by the leaves being V-shaped from the central vein.

Distribution: Asian species used as an ornamental throughout the state; rarely escaped and naturalized, mainly in upland woods.

Landscape Use: See *L. japonicum*, above. Listed as a Category II pest plant by the Florida Exotic Pest Plant Council.

Chinese Privet
Ligustrum sinense

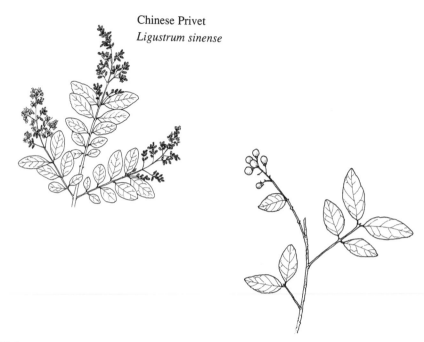

Chinese Privet

Page 250

Ligustrum sinense Lour.

Form: Tardily deciduous shrub or slender tree to about 10 m tall; with pubescent twigs.

Leaves: Opposite, simple (but borne on long branchlets so as to superficially appear compound), entire, oval to elliptic, 1.5 - 6 cm long, 1 - 2 cm wide; petioles pubescent.

Flowers: Small, four petaled, bright white, fragrant, appearing in April and May, borne in showy, spreading, multiflowered clusters at the tips of branchlets.

Fruit: A rounded drupe, 4 - 5 mm in diameter.

Distinguishing Marks: Distinguished from glossy privet (*L. lucidum*) and Japanese ligustrum (*L. japonicum*) by smaller leaves and densely pubescent rather than glabrous twigs; distinguished from the several species of *Forestiera* by leaf margins being entire rather than at least partially serrate.

Distribution: Nonnative, naturalized and pestiferous along streams, in floodplains, and in disturbed sites, often near plantings; Santa Rosa to Jefferson Counties.

Landscape Use: An often-used landscape plant. Cultivated plants often have variegated, creamy white and green leaves, and are often sold by the name variegated ligustrum. Escaped plants generally have green leaves. This plant is very aggressive and has been listed as a Category I pest plant by the Florida Exotic Pest Plant Council. It should not be used in landscaping.

Comment: *L. sinense* readily escapes from cultivation and becomes naturalized. It is listed as a troublesome exotic for much of the southeast and is difficult to control where it invades natural woodlands or streambanks.

Wild Olive or Devilwood

Osmanthus americanus (L.) Benth. & Hook. f. ex A. Gray

Form: Evergreen shrub or tree to about 15 m tall with a short trunk that typically branches close to the ground.

Leaves: Opposite, simple, entire, elliptic to obovate, 5 - 15 cm long, 1.8 - 5.5 cm wide, margins revolute.

Flowers: Small, creamy white, appearing February through April, borne in short, spreading clusters in the leaf axils, petals numbering four and fused together so as to form a tube 3 - 5 mm long.

Fruit: A distinctive, oval, dark blue to purple drupe, 1 - 1.5 cm long.

Distinguishing Marks: Distinguished from similarly leaved species of the Lauraceae, particularly those of the genus *Persea*, and from the superficially similar horse sugar (*Symplocos tinctoria*) by having opposite, rather than alternate, leaves.

Distribution: Found in a wide variety of habitats, including flatwoods, bay swamps, scrub, maritime hammocks, floodplains, and wooded bluffs; throughout northern Florida, southward to Highlands County.

Landscape Use: This species and the next are the only two native species of *Osmanthus* in the United States. The present species is not widely used for landscaping, but should be. It is closely related to the two popular, widely planted nonnative olives, tea olive (*O.* x *Fortunei* Carriere) and sweet olive (*O. fragrans* [Thunb.] Lour.).

Osmanthus megacarpa (Small) Small ex Little

Form: Shrub or tree that is generally similar to the wild olive described above.

Distinguishing Marks: Distinguished as a separate species by some authors, as a variety of the wild olive (*O. americanus*) by others; distinguished from the latter by larger fruit that measures 2 - 2.5 cm in diameter.

Distribution: Sand pine scrub from about Marion County southward to Highlands and Desoto Counties.

Wild Olive or Devilwood
Osmanthus americanus

ONAGRACEAE — EVENING-PRIMROSE FAMILY

The evening-primrose family consists mostly of herbaceous perennials with only a few shrubs or trees. Only one or two members of the genus *Ludwigia* are considered shrublike in Florida, and even these are not always so. Several genera of the family have horticultural utility, including the shrubby genus *Fuchsia* and the herbaceous genus *Oenothera*. Several members of the latter genus are found in Florida and usually bear the common name of the family.

Primrose-Willow

Photo 195

Ludwigia peruviana (L.) Hara

Form: Multistemmed shrub, 1 - 4 m tall; lower portions of stems woody, upper portions herbaceous and copiously pubescent.

Leaves: Alternate, simple, lanceolate to narrowly elliptic, 5 - 15 cm long, to about 3 cm wide; both surfaces pubescent, the lower often densely so; venation on lower surface very obvious.

Flowers: Yellow, conspicuous, with four, obovate to nearly rounded, petals, 1 - 3 cm long; petals subtended by four, large, conspicuous, green sepals; appearing year-round in more southern parts of the state, but most abundantly in fall in northern Florida.

Fruit: A four-angled capsule, 1 - 3 cm long.

Distinguishing Marks: The bright yellow, four-petaled flowers and shaggy-pubescent stems help identify this species.

Distribution: Most often in shallow water of ditches, canals, and marshy areas; throughout the state but much more common in central and southern Florida from about Gainesville southward.

Comment: Several other members of this genus, most notably the hairy primrose-willow (*L. leptocarpa* [Nutt.] Hara) and the long-fruited primrose-willow (*L. octovalvis* [Jacq.] Raven), are perennial and take on a somewhat shrublike appearance. The former is similar in appearance to the latter (see photo 194), in having alternate leaves and lacking a winged stem, but is hairy and has flower parts that are in fives rather than fours. It should be noted that there are many herbaceous members of this genus in Florida, many of which have flowers very similar to the two species described here. Distinguishing among these species in the field may prove challenging.

PASSIFLORACEAE — PASSION FLOWER FAMILY

The passion flower family consists mostly of climbing herbs with alternate leaves and tendrils growing from the leaf axils. Several species of the family are cultivated for their fruit in the tropics, others in warm parts of the world for their showy flowers. The family takes its common name from myths and stories that have been told about its complicated and intricate blossoms, which are said to include many symbols of the crucifixion of Christ. The Christian symbolism of their flowers probably began with the conquistadors who reportedly saw the symbolism as divine inspiration for their missionary work (Menninger, 1970).

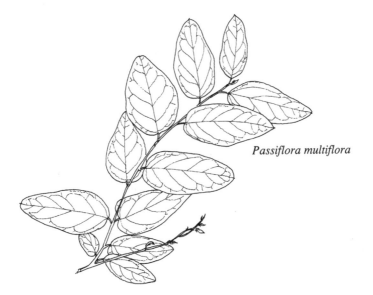

Passiflora multiflora

Passiflora multiflora L.   **Page 253**

Form: A perennial, semi-woody vine; stem copiously pubescent with white, velvety hairs.

Leaves: Alternate, simple, entire, ovate to elliptic, 5 - 12 cm long; with raised veins on the lower surfaces.

Flowers: White with yellowish-green sepals; appearing year-round.

Fruit: A rounded, purplish-black berry, 6 - 8 mm in diameter.

Distinguishing Marks: The whitish, copiously pubescent stems help distinguish the species.

Distribution: Hammocks; Elliot Key, Key Largo and other sites in the Keys.

Comment: There are nearly 400 species of *Passiflora* native to the New World, many of which are herbaceous vines. Several species are found in Florida, some of which are native, some exotic. The common passion flower, apricot vine, or maypop (*P. incarnata* L.) with blue to lavender flowers, three-lobed leaves, and large, green fruit is a trailing, mostly herbaceous vine found throughout the state. *P. pallens* Poepp. ex Mast., also known as passion flower, is a south Florida species with three-lobed leaves and large, distinctive stipules. *P. sexflora* Juss. is a mostly herbaceous to sometimes woody vine of south Florida hammocks and Everglades keys which has stems covered with long, shaggy hairs. *P. lutea* L. is a mostly north Florida species with relatively wide, shallowly three-lobed leaves and yellowish flowers. In addition to the above natives, *P. edulis* Sims, *P. foetida* L. (love-in-a-mist), and *P. biflora* have escaped and become locally established in various parts of southern Florida. Of these latter plants, *P. edulis* (the widely cultivated passion fruit of the tropics) is a semi-woody to woody vine that has become well-established in Dade and other counties south of Lake Okeechobee, and is reported to be spreading. It may be distinguished from other members of the genus by the large, leaflike bracts that subtend the flowers.

Corky-stemmed Passion-flower

Photo 196

Passiflora suberosa L.

Form: Glabrous to slightly pubescent, climbing or trailing vine; older stems with corky wings.

Leaves: Alternate, quite variable, entire to three lobed, simple, 4 - 10 cm long, with conspicuous glands on the leaf stalk, just below its attachment to the leaf.

Flowers: Greenish, without petals, to about 9 mm long, typical of passion flowers; appearing year-round.

Fruit: Berry, 5 - 10 mm in diameter, globose, green at first, turning purple to black, borne on a conspicuous stalk.

Distinguishing Marks: The corky stems and petiolar glands help distinguish this species.

Distribution: Hammocks and pinelands; from about Dixie County southward to the Keys.

Comment: See comment for *P. multiflora*, above.

PHYTOLACCACEAE — POKEWEED FAMILY

The Phytolaccaceae encompass a collection of mostly herbs, shrubs, and vines of tropical and subtropical distribution. The pokeweed (*Phytolacca americana* L.), a large, herbaceous, common weed across Florida and the southern United States is probably the best known member of the genus. Only one member of the family (described below) is considered woody in Florida, and even its status as such is somewhat questionable.

Bloodberry or Rouge Plant

Photo 197

Rivina humilis L.

Form: Vine or erect, mostly herbaceous shrub with a woody base; to about 2 m tall.

Leaves: Alternate, simple, lanceolate with a long-tapering point, 3 - 15 cm long; margins entire but wavy.

Flowers: Small, white to pink, with four sepals but no petals, borne in spiked clusters at the ends of branches; spikes to about 8 cm long; appearing year-round.

Fruit: Rounded, bright red berry, 2 - 4 mm long; arguably the most conspicuous feature of the plant.

Distinguishing Marks: The bright red berries in terminal clusters and wavy-edged leaves set this species apart.

Distribution: Common in hammocks and disturbed sites; central and southern peninsula and the Keys.

Landscape Use: Easy to grow and maintain; the red fruits are attractive.

PIPERACEAE — PEPPER FAMILY

The pepper family includes a collection of mostly climbing herbs and shrubs as well as a few trees. The genus *Piper*, of which one species is described below, is the family's only genus with economic importance and is best known for the species *P. nigrum* L. The dried fruits of this latter plant are known as black pepper when left whole, and as white pepper when their outer layer is removed. The family also includes the genus *Peperomia*, a collection of often-used ornamental plants.

Bamboo Piper

Piper aduncum L.

Page 255

Form: Evergreen multistemmed, woody shrub (or small tree outside of Florida) with finely hairy, yellow-green, slightly zigzag stems.

Leaves: Alternate, broadly lanceolate to narrowly elliptic with long-tapering tips, 13 - 25 cm long, 3.5 - 8 cm wide; bases asymmetrical on either side of the central vein; leaf tissue with small dots when backlighted and seen with magnification; aromatic with a pepper odor when crushed; lateral veins long and curving back toward the midvein near the leaf tip.

Flowers: Yellowish, tiny, borne in conspicuous, curving spikes opposite the leaves.

Fruit: A tiny, pale green drupe.

Distinguishing Marks: The finely hairy yellowish stems, distinctive curving raceme, and peppery aroma of crushed leaves distinguish this species.

Distribution: Native to the West Indies, and from Mexico to Peru and Brazil; escaped and established in several hammocks in Dade County.

Comment: *P. auritum* Kunth, another of the pipers, is also present in Dade County, according to Roger Hammer, but is apparently not as widespread as the bamboo piper.

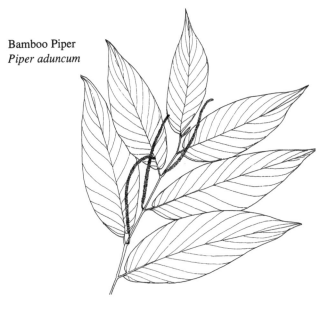

Bamboo Piper
Piper aduncum

POLYGONACEAE — BUCKWHEAT, SMARTWEED, OR KNOTWEED FAMILY

The Polygonaceae compose a predominantly North American family of about 30 genera and 700 species, including seven genera in the southeast and five in Florida. Though the family is generally considered to be of little importance economically, at least one of its members has been used widely for ornamentation. The sea grape (*Coccoloba uvifera*), one of two *Coccoloba* species found in Florida [the other is the tree pigeon plum (*C. diversifolia* Jacq.)], has been distributed widely and is highly valued for its utility as a landscape plant.

Coral Vine or Rose of Montana   Photo 198
Antigonon leptopus Hook. & Arn.

Form: Perennial, mostly herbaceous climbing vine with a woody base.

Leaves: Alternate, simple, bright green, ovate to nearly triangular (like an arrowhead) or heart shaped, 3 - 15 cm long; margins wavy.

Flowers: Rose to purplish, to about 2 cm long; showy, borne in long racemes, appearing spring through fall in Florida, nearly year-round in other parts of the tropics.

Fruit: Dry, winged, to nearly 1 cm long; inconspicuous.

Distinguishing Marks: The triangular to heart-shaped leaves and long, distinctive flowering racemes help distinguish this vine.

Distribution: Native to Mexico but found in Florida in disturbed sites, along roadsides, and in hammocks, where escaped from cultivation; mostly central and southern peninsula but also introduced and perhaps escaping in northern Florida in the vicinity of Tallahassee.

Landscape Use: An invasive exotic that should be discouraged as a landscape plant; listed as a Category II pest plant by the Florida Exotic Pest Plant Council. Coral vine is typically used as an arbor or fence vine, or on porches where quick shade is desired. It does well in full sun, does not tolerate frost, and is planted throughout the southeast but naturalized only in Florida. The flowers become larger with age and are attractive to bees.

Comment: This plant may have been one of the first species taken from Mexico to Europe by the Spaniards. It has been under cultivation for many years in many parts of the tropical world and a number of color varieties are known. Nearly 30 common names in various languages are known.

Eardrop Vine or Ladies' Eardrops   Page 257
Brunnichia ovata (Walt.) Shinners

Form: High-climbing herbaceous to woody vine with evident tendrils and ridged stems.

Leaves: Alternate, deciduous, simple, ovate in overall shape with truncate to nearly heart-shaped bases, 5 - 15 cm long, 3 - 5 cm wide; margins entire but wavy.

Flowers: Greenish, borne in spikes from the leaf axils; appearing in summer.

Fruit: Brown, dry, winged, about 8 mm long, developing with the elongation and hardening of the floral tube.

Eardrop Vine or Ladies' Eardrops
Brunnichia ovata

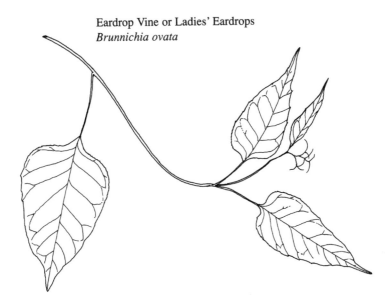

Distinguishing Marks: Distinguished from other high-climbing vines in north Florida by combination of alternate leaves, leaf blades definitely longer than broad, and climbing by tendrils.

Distribution: Uncommon along riverbanks, near swamps, and in floodplain woods; from about the Ochlockonee River westward in the Panhandle.

Sea Grape
Coccoloba uvifera (L.) L.

Photo 199

Form: Varying widely in habit from a low, spreading evergreen shrub to a small tree about 6 m tall.

Leaves: Alternate, orbicular, to 27 cm long and wide, green above with reddish veins, bases typically cordate.

Flowers: Very small and borne in racemes and appearing nearly year-round.

Fruit: Egg shaped, fleshy, 1.8 - 2.5 cm long, hanging in long, grapelike clusters, turning from greenish to red to purple with maturity.

Distinguishing Marks: The large, orbicular leaves of the sea grape make this species unlikely to be confused with any other south Florida shrub or tree.

Distribution: Coastal hammocks and dunes, often used as a landscape plant; from about Hillsborough and Brevard Counties southward along the coasts and throughout the Keys.

Landscape Use: The sea grape has been planted along seashores in many of the world's warmer regions and is prized for its hardiness, orbicular evergreen leaves, and attractive, grapelike pendants of green to reddish fruits. The first use of *Coccoloba* in cultivation dates back to 1690 when two separate species, one of which was our sea grape, were brought to England by New World explorers. Through the years, a variety of specimens of several species have shown up in greenhouses, arboreta, and botanical gardens around the world. Within the last several decades, *C. uvifera* has even found use as a low-maintenance potted plant. Probably nowhere is this genus used more extensively for ornamentation than in southern Florida. Throughout the lower peninsula and the Keys, sea grape is often seen gracing lawns as well as decorating shopping centers, roadside medians, and driveway entrances.

Comment: In their extensive treatment of the trees of Puerto Rico and the Virgin Islands, Little and Wadsworth (1964) report that Nathaniel Britton considered it probable that the sea grape was the first American land plant seen by Christopher Columbus. The sea grape takes its name from its grapelike fruit. The reddish to purplish berries are eaten raw as well as fashioned into jellies and wines, and are best gathered by spreading a cloth under a fruit-laden tree, then shaking the trunk vigorously.

Large-Leaved Jointweed   Photo 200
Polygonella macrophylla Small

Form: Essentially deciduous, perennial, few- to unbranched, subshrub or shrub with a brittle stem; woody portions of the stem to about 1 m tall, entire stem to about 2 m; sometimes a few leaves persisting for more than one season.

Leaves: Alternate, simple, entire, somewhat fleshy or rubbery to the touch, obovate and tapering toward the base, 2 - 6 cm long, 1 - 2 cm wide; apices rounded.

Flowers: Pinkish to bright red, borne in racemes in a loosely branched panicle; individual flowers very small but racemes very showy during the fall blooming season.

Fruit: Small, brown, single-seeded.

Distinguishing Marks: The jointed flowering branchlets, small red flowers, relatively large (in comparison with other members of the genus), rubbery leaves, and sandy habitat set this plant apart.

Distribution: Sand scrub, often in association with Florida rosemary (*Ceratiola ericoides*) and minty rosemary (*Conradina* sp.); scattered along the Panhandle coast from about Franklin County westward; particularly large populations of this plant can be found at Henderson Beach and Grayton Beach State Recreation Areas.

Comment: Listed as threatened by the Florida Department of Agriculture and decreasing in numbers due to the loss of scrub habitat within its historical range. Florida's flora also includes several additional species of *Polygonella* not described here. While some of these grow from a woody taproot, most are annual and typically do not take on a shrubby aspect. These additional species include two relatively widespread plants commonly referred to as wireweed (*P. ciliata* Meisn. and *P. gracilis* [Nutt.] Meisn.), as well as the sandhill wireweed (*P. fimbriata* [Elliott] Horton), and the rare scrub endemic hairy wireweed (*P. basiramia* [Small] Nesom & Bates, also listed as *P. ciliata* Meisn. var. *basiramia* [Small] Horton).

Woody Wireweed or Small's Jointweed
Polygonella myriophylla (Small) Horton

Form: A mat-forming, sprawling shrub with slender, reddish brown, flaking, zigzag stems.

Leaves: Alternate, fleshy, margins entire but wavy, linear to spatulate in shape, 3 - 10 mm long.

Flowers: Tiny, with five white sepals less than 4 mm long, the three largest sepals with a green stripe down the center; borne on short stalk less than 3 mm long; flowering branchlets with distinctive joints when seen with magnification; appearing summer through fall.

Fruit: A dry, reddish-brown, thin-walled, single-seeded nutlet, about 3 mm long.

Distinguishing Marks: Most easily recognized by its small leaves, matlike appearance, restrictive habitat, and jointed flowering branchlets.

Distribution: Sand scrub; endemic to the Lake Wales Ridge in the lower central peninsula, especially Orange, Osceola, Polk, Highlands, and DeSoto Counties.

Comment: Listed as endangered by the U. S. Fish and Wildlife Service; a rare plant due to the increase of real estate development and to the proliferation of orange groves across its previous range.

Jointweed

Page 260, Photo 201

Polygonella polygama (Vent.) Engelm. & Gray

Form: Low deciduous shrub branching close to the ground, often appearing somewhat compact and globular in general shape; woody portions of main stems usually less than 2 dm tall, flowering stems extending well beyond the woody branches, contributing to an overall height of as much as 7 dm tall.

Leaves: Alternate, simple, entire, spatulate to oblanceolate, 0.5 - 2 cm long, 2 - 4 mm wide, veins obscure; apices rounded.

Flowers: Individually small, but borne in conspicuous racemes at the ends of leafy branches; flowering branchlets with distinctively jointed appearance when viewed with magnification; appearing summer through fall.

Fruit: Dry, brown, single seeded.

Distinguishing Marks: Distinguished from most woody plants by jointed flowering branchlets; from *P. myriophylla* by the erect, bushy stature; from *P. macrophylla* by much smaller leaves.

Distribution: Scrub, pinelands, longleaf pine–scrub oak ridges, well-drained woods; throughout most of north Florida, southward to DeSoto County, with disjunct populations in both Palm Beach and Broward Counties.

Sandhill Wireweed

Page 260

Polygonella robusta (Small) Nesom & Bates

Form: Perennial, woody shrub to about 1 m tall.

Leaves: Alternate, simple, linear, 2 - 6 cm long.

Flowers: White to pink, individually tiny, with fringed inner sepals, borne in conspicuous racemes 2 - 5 cm long; appearing summer through fall.

Fruit: A tiny, dry nutlet to about 2 mm long.

Distinguishing Marks: Most easily distinguished from other members of the genus by the

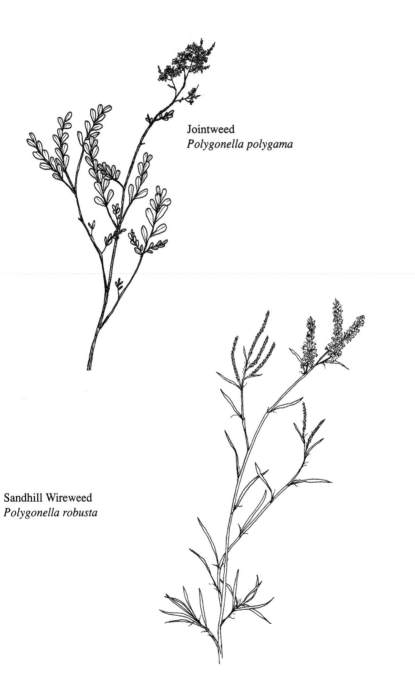

Jointweed
Polygonella polygama

Sandhill Wireweed
Polygonella robusta

long bristles that fringe the tubular sheaths at the bases of the leaves, in conjunction with the fringed inner sepals (requires magnification to see clearly).

Distribution: Common in pinelands, scrub, and sandhills of the central ridge.

Comment: Some authorities list this species as *P. fimbriata* (Ell.) Horton var. *robusta* (Small) Horton. However, the present species and *P. fimbriata*, an herbaceous species of northern Florida and the Panhandle, are distinguishable by distribution.

RANUNCULACEAE — CROWFOOT FAMILY

The Ranunculaceae is a family of mostly herbaceous perennials with a few woody to semi-woody climbing vines. Most members of the family contain alkaloids and are poisonous to eat. Some members of the genera *Delphinium* and *Clematis* (several native species of the latter are described below) are well-known garden ornamentals that come in a variety of colors. The common name for the family derives from the crowfoot-shaped leaves or leaflets of many of its members.

Virgin's-Bower or Woodbine   Page 262
Clematis catesbyana Pursh

Form: Herbaceous vine with older, lower stems woody and shedding in long strips; commonly scrambling over vegetation and into trees.

Leaves: Opposite, pinnately compound with five leaflets, the leaflets also sometimes divided again into three parts; leaflets ovate, ranging in size to about 6 cm long, 4.5 cm wide; margins of leaflets toothed to three lobed; the drawing on p. 262 shows a single compound leaf.

Flowers: Small, white, with four petallike sepals, borne in very showy clusters from the leaf axils; appearing in July and August.

Fruit: Very showy, with many plumelike structures forming a cluster to 5 cm wide.

Distinguishing Marks: The compound leaves with five-toothed leaflets, in conjunction with the showy clusters of plumelike fruit help distinguish this species from other members of its genus.

Distribution: River banks, fences, lowland and upland woods; Panhandle, eastward to about Dixie County.

Comment: At least three herbaceous *Clematis* species are also found in Florida but are not described here. The common pine-hyacinth (*C. baldwinii* Torr. & Gray) is an erect herb of pinelands throughout much of the state. The two leatherflowers or vase vines (*C. crispa* L. and *C. reticulata* Walt.) have attractive, blue, bell-shaped flowers that appear in spring and summer.

Leatherflower   Page 263, Photo 203
Clematis glaucophylla Small

Form: Generally herbaceous vine with lower and older stems woody; herbaceous stems reddish to purplish brown.

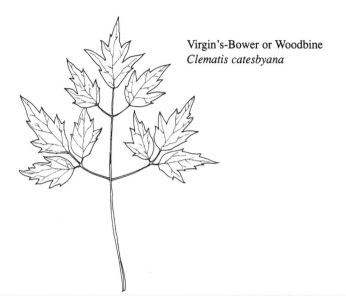

Virgin's-Bower or Woodbine
Clematis catesbyana

Leaves: Opposite, pinnately compound, with 2 - 5 leaflets; leaflets 8 - 10 cm long, 6 - 8 cm wide, ovate; bases of leaflets usually heart shaped; margins of leaflets entire; lower surfaces grayish white when young (hence the specific name), but becoming green with age.

Flowers: Rose purple outside, whitish inside; appearing in summer.

Fruit: Dry, rounded, individually small and inconspicuous but borne in a very conspicuous, rounded mass of plumes.

Distinguishing Marks: The combination of entire margins and grayish-white undersurfaces of young leaflets, and rose-purple flowers set this species apart from other members of its genus.

Distribution: Rich slopes, floodplain woods, river banks; western and central Panhandle.

Comment: See comment for *C. catesbyana*, above.

Clematis terniflora DC

Form: Vine with older portions of the stems woody, herbaceous stems light green; climbing over shrubs and into small trees.

Leaves: Opposite, pinnately compound with (mostly) five leaflets varying to simple; leaflets ovate, 2 - 10 cm long, 1.5 - 6 cm wide; margins entire and not lobed.

Flowers: Whitish, star shaped, densely pubescent, with spreading sepals; appearing mid- to late summer.

Fruit: Small, dry, dull brown, 5 - 8 mm long.

Distinguishing Marks: The whitish flowers set this species apart from *C. glaucophylla*, to which it is most similar.

Distribution: Native to Asia; escaped and sparsely naturalized near plantings, along lake margins, and in disturbed sites in north Florida, south to about Marion County.

Landscape Use: Popular and common southern landscape plant; requires full sun.

Comment: See comment for *C. catesbyana*, above.

Leatherflower
Clematis glaucophylla

Virgin's-Bower or Woodbine

Photo 202

Clematis virginiana L.

Form: Climbing or sprawling, mostly herbaceous vine with an angled stem; stem woody and to a little more than 1 cm in diameter at the base.

Leaves: Opposite, pinnately compound with three leaflets, petioles to about 10 cm long; leaflets ovate, 2 - 10 cm long, 1 - 6 cm wide; leaflet margins serrate to occasionally lobed, sometimes entire; bases truncate to heart shaped.

Flowers: Whitish, star shaped, borne profusely in very showy clusters from the leaf axils; appearing summer through fall.

Fruit: Dry, rounded, less than 5 mm long, dark brown to greenish brown; borne in a conspicuous, rounded mass of plumes.

Distinguishing Marks: Very similar to *C. catesbyana* but having three, rather than five, leaflets.

Distribution: Wet woods, disturbed sites, stream banks; from the easternmost Panhandle across northern Florida and southward to the central peninsula.

Landscape Use: A popular landscape plant; hardy, easy to grow, with no major insect pests or diseases; ideal for porches, arbors, and fences.

Comment: See comment for *C. catesbyana*, above. Some authorities list *C. catesbyana* as a synonym for this species, thus indicating that the two are the same species.

Yellow-Root or Brook-Feather

Xanthorhiza simplicissima Marsh.

Form: Low, deciduous shrub to about 8 dm tall, with brittle stems; wood of stems and roots yellow.

Leaves: Alternate (but closely set), compound, typically with five leaflets but sometimes fewer; leaflets 10 - 12 cm long; margins of leaflets conspicuously toothed (from about the middle outward), the teeth of different sizes; petiole and rachis pubescent, typically with curving hairs (requires magnification).

Flowers: Maroon to greenish brown, borne from the leaf axils in conspicuous, drooping racemes, each raceme 5 - 15 cm long; appearing mostly in March.

Fruit: Dry, yellowish, shiny, splitting open at maturity to expose a single, rounded, reddish seed.

Distinguishing Marks: This plant's low shrubby stature and compound leaves with five, strongly toothed leaflets and yellow wood set it apart.

Distribution: Uncommon in shady places near springs or along river banks; from the central Panhandle westward.

Comment: Listed as endangered by the Florida Department of Agriculture.

RHAMNACEAE — BUCKTHORN FAMILY

The buckthorn family consists mostly of tress, shrubs, and woody vines, many of which have conspicuous thorns. A number of the family's genera have economic or horticultural value. Several members of the genus *Rhamnus*, of which one species appears in Florida, are the source of green and yellow dyes as well medicinal substances, and members of the genus *Ceanothus*, of which two species are described below, have been hybridized to produce a variety of showy and highly prized cultivars. The family consists of nearly 60 genera and about 900 species of both tropical and temperate distribution. The northernmost species in the family extend to about 55 degrees north latitude, a line that runs through northern Canada near the southern shores of Hudson Bay. Less than 20 percent of the species found in North America are trees. The most distinguishable characteristic for distinguishing most members of this family in the field is the presence of conspicuously parallel veins on the leaf surfaces.

Rattan Vine or Supple-Jack   Page 265

Berchemia scandens (Hill) K. Koch

Form: Deciduous, unarmed, tough but pliable woody vine; potentially climbing high into trees; particularly mature specimens have large, corkscrewlike, twining stems.

Leaves: Alternate, simple, oval to elliptic, 3 - 8 cm long, to about 4 cm wide; margins entire, sometimes wavy; upper surfaces shiny green; veins on both surfaces quite conspicuous and parallel, in this respect similar to those of the American beech (*Fagus grandifolia* Ehrh.), or the present species' close relative Carolina buckthorn (*Rhamnus caroliniana*), described below.

Rattan Vine or Supple-Jack
Berchemia scandens

Flowers: Small, greenish to greenish white, borne on branchlets from the leaf axils; appearing in spring.

Fruit: A blue-black, oblong drupe, 5 - 7 mm long; with a whitish cast when mature.

Distinguishing Marks: The viney habit in combination with the distinctive parallel veins is diagnostic.

Distribution: Wet woods, swamps, bottomlands; throughout north Florida, southward to the northern Big Cypress Preserve in Collier County and Everglades National Park in Dade County.

Landscape Use: This is a pest-free vine and an excellent wildlife food. It is not often used in landscaping, perhaps because its strong stems will eventually girdle and kill trees, but its dark green, parallel-veined leaves and conspicuous clusters of fall fruit make it deserving of more consideration.

New Jersey Tea Photo 204
Ceanothus americanus L.

Form: Low, deciduous, often many-branched shrub to about 1 m tall; with a woody root; young stems with long, shaggy, and short, curly hairs.

Leaves: Alternate, simple, broadly lanceolate and long tapering toward the apices, 2 - 9 cm long, 1 - 4 cm wide; bases slightly heart shaped; margins finely toothed; with two lateral veins beginning at the midvein and ascending the length of the blade.

Flowers: White, small but borne in conspicuous clusters near the ends of the stem or in the axils of the uppermost leaves; appearing late spring and into summer.

Fruit: Dark brown drupe, 3 - 5 mm in diameter.

Distinguishing Marks: The showy flower clusters and broadly lanceolate leaves with three main ascending veins help distinguish the species.

Distribution: Mixed pine–oak–hickory woods, well-drained pinelands, prairies, sandhills; common but somewhat local throughout northern Florida and southward to about Lake Okeechobee.

Landscape Use: This is a good species to plant in front of larger shrubs, in large patches, or along woodland borders; it is easy to grow. It is not often used but does well in dry soils, in full sun or light shade, and is particularly showy in massed plantings.

Comment: The flower clusters, leaves, and roots were once dried and used as tea, hence one of its common names. It is also reported that a lotion made from the leaves was once believed to be useful in removing freckles.

Little Leaf Red Root   Photo 205
Ceanothus microphyllus Michx.

Form: Low, evergreen, bushy shrub to about 8 dm tall; with slender, yellow branches.

Leaves: Alternate, simple, elliptic, minute in size, usually less than 6 mm long, perhaps as long as 8 mm; margins entire or with a total of only two to four teeth; veins on upper surfaces obscure, evidently three-veined on lower surfaces.

Flowers: Tiny but borne in conspicuous clusters, mostly at the ends of the branches; appearing in spring.

Fruit: A smooth, black drupe; about 5 mm wide.

Distinguishing Marks: The tiny leaves and yellow branches set this species apart.

Distribution: Sandhills, dry woods, flatwoods, well-drained pinelands; throughout northern Florida, southward to about Highlands County.

Wild Coffee, Coffee Colubrina, Snakebark   Photo 206
Colubrina arborescens (Mill.) Sarg.

Form: Evergreen shrub or small tree to about 8 m tall.

Leaves: Alternate, simple, entire, leathery, ovate, 5 - 14 cm long, 2.8 - 6.5 cm wide, upper surfaces dark green and glabrous, lower surfaces with reddish hairs and small, black dots.

Flowers: Greenish to yellowish, fragrant, tiny, borne in clusters in the leaf axils, the entire cluster usually not exceeding about 12 mm in width; appearing year-round.

Fruit: A capsule, rounded, purple to black, 6 - 10 mm in diameter, splitting at maturity to expose three seeds.

Distinguishing Marks: Most easily recognized, in conjunction with other characters, by rusty red pubescence on the younger stems and twigs.

Distribution: Hammocks of the Florida Keys and southern Everglades.

Colubrina or Latherleaf   Photo 207
Colubrina asiatica (L.) Brongn.

Form: Bushy shrub, often trailing, or scrambling; spreading and producing thickets to about 1 m tall; individual plants potentially to about 3 m tall; stems smooth.

Leaves: Alternate, simple, dark shiny green above, ovate to elliptic, to about 10 cm long; margins serrate and somewhat wavy; apices pointed.

Flowers: Small, greenish, with five petals; borne at the leaf axils; petals only about 2 mm long; appearing year-round.

Fruit: A drupe 6 - 10 mm in diameter.

Distinguishing Marks: The bright green, ovate leaves with finely toothed and wavy margins help identify this species.

Distribution: Nonnative but naturalized in the Florida Keys and southern peninsula; a very aggressive colonizer along roadsides, on dunes and beaches, and in disturbed sites and the edges of hammocks.

Landscape Use: This plant is listed as a Category I pest plant by the Florida Exotic Pest Plant Council and is not recommended for landscape use due to its tendency to overcome and crowd out native species.

Cuban Colubrina or Cuban Snakebark   Page 267, Photo 208
Colubrina cubensis (Jacq.) Brongn.

Form: Evergreen shrub or small tree to about 9 m tall.

Leaves: Alternate, simple, leathery, long elliptic to oblong, 5 - 10 cm long, 1.5 - 4 cm wide, both upper and lower surfaces pubescent but lower more so, veins on upper surfaces conspicuously depressed, margins shallowly and irregularly crenate.

Flowers: Tiny, borne in small clusters in the leaf axils; appearing year-round.

Fruit: A rounded capsule, 6 - 9 mm in diameter.

Distinguishing Marks: The conspicuously depressed veins on the upper surfaces of leaves help separate this species from the other two species of *Colubrina*.

Distribution: Uncommon in hammocks of the Miami Rock Ridge and Everglades keys; also present in Cuba and the Bahamas.

Comment: Florida's plant is generally referred to *C. cubensis* var. *floridana* M. C. Johnston.

Cuban Colubrina or Cuban Snakebark
Colubrina cubensis

Soldierwood
Colubrina elliptica

Soldierwood

Page 268

Colubrina elliptica (Sw.) Briz. & Stern

Form: Typically an evergreen shrub, sometimes a small tree with orange-brown bark, potentially reaching a height of 15 m.

Leaves: Alternate, simple, ovate to lanceolate, entire, soft to the touch, 4 - 12 cm long, 4 - 6 cm wide, shiny dark green above, pubescent below with rusty hairs, margins with two conspicuous glands near the base of the blade.

Flowers: Greenish-yellow, small, borne in clusters at the leaf axils; appearing year-round.

Fruit: A rounded, reddish-orange capsule, 6 - 9 mm in diameter.

Distinguishing Marks: Distinguished from other *Colubrina* by soft, rather than leathery, leaves and marginal glands, from Cuban colubrina (*C. cubensis*) by leaves lacking crenate margins.

Distribution: Widespread across the Caribbean basin, in Florida only in hammocks of the extreme southern peninsula and the upper Keys.

Chew Stick

Page 269

Gouania lupuloides (L.) Urban

Form: Arching or climbing, deciduous, vinelike shrub with smooth stems.

Leaves: Alternate, simple, ovate to elliptic, 5 - 10 cm long; margins crenate to coarsely serrate; apices pinched to a point.

Flowers: Small, white to yellowish, with five petals, borne in conspicuous racemes at the ends of the branches; racemes 6 - 15 cm long; appearing in spring.

Fruit: A winged drupe, 8 - 12 mm wide.

Distinguishing Marks: The alternate, crenate to dentate leaves, winged fruit, and vinelike habit are usually enough to identify this species.

Distribution: Mangroves and coastal hammocks; Florida Keys and southern Florida, from about Brevard and Manatee Counties southward.

Comment: This species takes its common name from its stems, which are chewed in the West Indies to clean the teeth and medicate the gums.

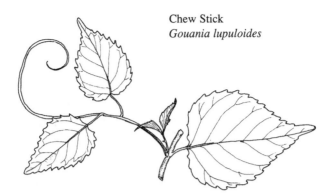

Chew Stick
Gouania lupuloides

Black Ironwood or Leadwood Page 270

Krugiodendron ferreum (Vahl) Urban

Form: Evergreen shrub or small tree to about 9 m tall with densely leafy and spreading branches.

Leaves: Opposite (less often subopposite or slightly alternate), simple, entire, pliable, elliptic to oval, 2.5 - 6 cm long, 2 - 2.6 cm wide, margins wavy, apices rounded but with a conspicuous notch that contains a short, inconspicuous bristle (usually requires magnification to see clearly).

Flowers: Small, yellowish green, borne in few-flowered clusters at the leaf axils; appearing in spring.

Fruit: A rounded to ovoid drupe, black, 5 - 10 mm in diameter, appearing in summer and fall.

Distinguishing Marks: Most easily distinguished from other hammock species by pliable, glossy, opposite leaves with notched apices and short, finely pubescent petioles.

Distribution: Hammocks of the Keys and southern peninsula, northward along the east coast to about Brevard County.

Comment: At a weight of about 89 pounds per cubic foot, black ironwood sinks in sea water and is considered to be the heaviest wood in the United States. It is extremely strong and is sometimes used to fashion fence posts.

Darling Plum or Red Ironwood Page 270

Reynosia septentrionalis Urban

Form: Evergreen shrub or small tree potentially to about 10 m tall but usually shorter.

Leaves: Opposite, simple, entire, oval to obovate, dark green above, stiff, leathery, 1.5 - 3 cm long, to about 1.5 cm wide, apices notched.

Flowers: Tiny, yellowish green, without petals, borne in clusters at the leaf axils; appearing throughout spring and into early summer.

Fruit: An egg-shaped, purple to black, edible drupe, 1 - 2 cm long, with a spiny tip.

Distinguishing Marks: Distinguished from black ironwood (*Krugiodendron ferreum*) by

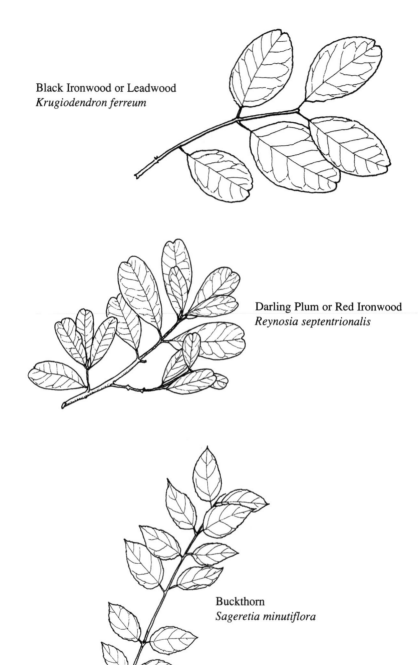

Black Ironwood or Leadwood
Krugiodendron ferreum

Darling Plum or Red Ironwood
Reynosia septentrionalis

Buckthorn
Sageretia minutiflora

having dull, dark green, and stiff, rather than pliable, glossy green leaves, from both species of *Capparis*, which also have leaves with notched apices, by opposite, rather than alternate, leaves.

Distribution: Hammocks of southernmost Florida and the Keys.

Carolina Buckthorn   Photo 209

Rhamnus caroliniana Walt.

Form: Deciduous shrub or small, unarmed tree, 10 - 14 m tall with young twigs that are reddish brown and pubescent.

Leaves: Alternate, simple, elliptic, 5 - 12 cm long, 3 - 5 cm wide, margins irregularly and minutely serrate, sometimes with small, rounded teeth; lateral veins conspicuously parallel.

Flowers: Tiny, campanulate, yellowish to whitish, borne in June in small clusters in the leaf axils.

Fruit: A rounded berry, first red but turning black at maturity, to about 1 cm in diameter.

Distinguishing Marks: Most easily recognized by the parallel lateral leaf veins.

Distribution: Occasionally found in moist, deciduous forests, shell middens, and calcareous woods; north Florida southward to about Orange County.

Landscape Use: The fruit of this species is enjoyed by birds and its distinctively parallel leaf veins are interesting and attractive. It is probably not readily available from native plant nurseries but once established in the garden, new seedlings and young plants under about 1 m tall are easily transplanted. Due to its scattered distribution and lack of abundance, specimens should not be taken from the wild.

Comment: Most members of the genus *Rhamnus* have thorny branches, a characteristic not true of *R. caroliniana*, the only member of the genus occurring naturally in Florida.

Buckthorn   Page 270

Sageretia minutiflora (Michx.) Mohr.

Form: Slender, tardily deciduous shrub to about 3 m tall or vinelike, with a slender, arching main stem; branches of mature, larger specimens often with sharp, leafy or nonleafy thorns.

Leaves: Opposite, simple, leathery, ovate, 0.5 - 6 cm long; apices long tapering; margins finely toothed and wavy, each tooth with a tiny point (requires magnification).

Flowers: Fragrant, white, borne in spikes at the ends of branches; spikes generally 1 - 4 cm long; appearing late summer.

Fruit: A rounded, purplish-red to blackish drupe; 5 - 9 mm in diameter; splitting at maturity to expose three leathery nutlets.

Distinguishing Marks: The combination of leafy thorns (on some, usually more mature plants), finely toothed leaves, and terminal spikes of white flowers separate this species from most other Florida shrubs or vines.

Distribution: Hammocks, sandy sites, shell mounds, calcium-rich areas; throughout northern Florida, southward to about Lee and Brevard Counties.

Florida Ziziphus

Photo 210

Ziziphus celata Judd and Hall

Form: A much-branched, deciduous shrub with kneelike joints that give a zigzag appearance to the stems; secondary branches with thorn-tipped shoots.

Leaves: Alternate to fascicled, simple, elliptic to obovate, entire, small in size, to about 1 cm long and 0.5 cm wide, with a prominent midvein that is raised above the lower surface; petioles short, to about 3 mm long.

Flowers: White, five petaled, with yellow-green sepals (a character that is obvious from a little distance), borne solitary in leaf axils, very small, less than 3 mm long; appearing in winter (primarily December to February).

Fruit: A green (when young), ellipsoid drupe, turning bright yellow at maturity, averaging about 1.6 cm long and 1.1 cm wide.

Distinguishing Marks: The zigzag branches, small, entire leaves, and scrub habitat distinguish the species; probably most similar to scrub plum (*Prunus geniculata*), which has a similar habit but finely toothed leaves.

Distribution: Very rare, restricted to five known locations in Polk and Highlands Counties; prefers the transition zone between sand pine scrub and longleaf pine. A number of specimens are currently under cultivation at Bok Tower Gardens near Lake Wales.

Comment: According to Judd and Hall (1984), this plant was first discovered and collected by botanist Ray Garrett in March, 1948. His specimen (the only known material of the species until its rediscovery in 1987) was forwarded to the University of Florida, where it could not be immediately identified by the staff at the university or by visiting botanists, though most observers assumed it to be a Rhamnaceae. On a visit to the Field Museum of Natural History in Chicago many years later, Dr. Walter Judd noted the plant's similarity to the genus *Ziziphus*. Upon his return to Florida, and after examining many specimens of the genus, Judd and Dr. David Hall described the new species. They awarded the specific name *celata*, which means hidden, in respect to "the frustrating taxonomic history of the plant" (Judd and Hall, 1984). In 1987 Kris Delaney (Delaney, et. al., 1989) discovered a population of this species in Polk County, and in 1988 discovered a second population in Highlands County. This time fruit was found on one specimen and was described for the first time. Today, five populations are known. The plant is very similar to Z. *parryi* Torrey, a species of arid regions of southern California. It is currently listed as an endangered species by the U. S. Fish and Wildlife Service.

Ziziphus celata is currently being cultivated at Bok Tower Gardens for eventual reintroduction into native habitat. Bok Tower Gardens is a Participating Institution of the Center for Plant Conservation and the specimens of *Ziziphus* at the Garden are maintained as part of the National Collection of Endangered Plants. According to Tammera Race (1994 and personal communication), curator of endangered species at the Garden, 80 seedlings are currently under cultivation in the Garden's greenhouse and 300 seeds are currently in seed storage. All of the Garden's living specimens were propagated from root cuttings that were taken from living plants in their natural setting. The success Bok Tower Gardens has had at cultivating this species bodes well for its preservation.

A second member of this genus, the date tree or jujube (Z. *jujube* Mill), has also been reported as naturalized in Bay County (Anderson, 1988). This latter plant is native to Europe and is rarely escaped from cultivation in the southeast (except, perhaps, for southwest Louisiana, where it is rather common). It is typically a small, deciduous tree.

RHIZOPHORACEAE — RED MANGROVE FAMILY

This is one of the three mangrove families represented in Florida. The red mangrove genus *Rhizophora*, is a relatively small, pantropical collection of less than eight evergreen tree species of which *R. mangle* is the sole representative in Florida. It is the most easily recognized of Florida's native mangrove species and is a common constituent of the state's mangrove forests.

Red Mangrove
Photo 211

Rhizophora mangle L.

Form: Evergreen shrub or small tree, usually not exceeding about 8 m tall; often with reddish prop roots.

Leaves: Opposite, entire, leathery, elliptic, 4 - 15 cm long, 2 - 5 cm wide.

Flowers: With four yellowish to white petals, borne in clusters of two or three at the leaf axils; appearing year-round.

Fruit: Brown, egg shaped, 2.4 - 3.6 cm long, germinating while still attached to the tree and sending out a distinctive, cigar-shaped seedling up to 30 cm long.

Distinguishing Marks: Distinguished from white mangrove (*Laguncularia racemosa*) by the present species' dark, shiny green upper surfaces of leaves, from black mangrove (*Avicennia germinans*) by the latter's pale green lower surfaces of leaves, from both by numerous reddish prop roots that arise from the lower trunk and branches, and the long radicles (or germinating seeds) that appear from early summer into the fall.

Distribution: Confined to shallow waters of coastal bays, lagoons, creeks, and rivers; from Levy and Volusia Counties southward and throughout the Keys.

Comment: As a group, the mangroves exhibit a variety of interesting ecological adaptations that have helped insure success in their primarily saline surroundings. The first of these adaptations has to do with salt tolerance, the second with reproduction. Red mangroves, for example, are primarily salt excluders and have developed a remarkable facility for filtering out salt at the surface of the roots, thus insuring that predominately fresh water is taken into their systems.

Red mangroves have also developed a rather extraordinary method for insuring reproductive success. Unlike most plants, which have seeds that typically germinate only after falling from the plant and coming into contact with an appropriate growing medium, the seeds of red mangroves are viviparous. They germinate while still attached to the tree, and the seedlings develop from the still-attached fruit. These odd-looking, cigar-shaped appendages are often referred to as radicles, or propagules, and are intimately connected with the mangroves' mechanism for seed dispersal. After they reach sufficient development, the propagules drop from the tree and are carried by tides and currents to locations that are sometimes far distant from the mother tree. When they come into contact with an exposed muddy substrate in a protected body of quiet, shallow water, they put down roots and attach themselves to the bottom.

ROSACEAE — ROSE FAMILY

The Rosaceae constitute a relatively large and quite well-known family of trees, shrubs, and herbs. The family encompasses more than 100 genera and over 3,000 species worldwide, many of which are of significant economic importance. Aside from the plums, cherries, and blackberries described below, the roses are the source of a number of other foods, including almonds, apricots, loquats, nectarines, peaches, quinces, raspberries, rose hips, and straw-berries. In addition, some rose species have also been used as home remedies for a variety of medical disorders, others in the manufacture of perfumes, and still others as outstanding ornamental and landscape plants. Some genera in the family, especially *Prunus*, *Malus*, and *Rosa*, have been the source of many horticultural cultivars.

Downy Serviceberry, Shadblow, Shadbush, Serviceberry

Amelanchier arborea (Michx. f.) Fern.   **Page 275**

Form: Deciduous shrub or small tree with a smooth, gray trunk, to about 12 m tall.
Leaves: Alternate, simple, oval to ovate, 3 - 9 cm long, 2 - 4 cm wide, margins finely ser-rate, bases typically cordate; petioles conspicuous, averaging about 2 cm long.
Flowers: Star shaped with five white to pinkish, spreading petals, 1.5 - 2 cm long, appear-ing in early spring prior to the emergence of new leaves.
Fruit: Berrylike, reddish to dark purple, 5 - 10 mm in diameter.
Distinguishing Marks: Similar to several species of the genus *Prunus*, but distinguished from them and other shrubs and trees with alternate, simple leaves with serrated margins by having longish petioles in conjunction with the lateral leaf veins being appressed to the cen-tral vein for a short distance before diverging to the leaf edges, the latter seen most easily on the upper surface, particularly near the base, but only with magnification.
Distribution: Stream banks and open woodlands; restricted in Florida to the Panhandle.
Landscape Use: This interesting shrub or small tree is not often used but makes a nice addi-tion to a naturalistic landscape, especially in wet areas along ponds or slow-moving streams; its reddish fruit is aesthetically pleasing to humans and a relished food source for wildlife.
Comment: The derivation of the name service berry is not well known. One story holds that in an earlier era, people in the northern U. S. who died in winter could not be buried due to the frozen ground. Hence, the funeral service had to wait until the ground thawed, a time which coincides with the flowering period of the service berry. Another of its common names is associated with "the time when the shad run"; purportedly the flowering period of this plant also coincides with the spawning season of this delectable fish.

Red Chokeberry   **Photo 212**

Aronia arbutifolia (L.) Ell.

Form: Deciduous shrub, 2 - 3 m tall.
Leaves: Alternate, simple, elliptic to oval or oblanceolate, 4 - 10 cm long, 1.5 - 4 cm wide; margins finely toothed; central vein on upper surface with scattered, reddish-purple glands (requires magnification).

Downy Serviceberry, Shadblow, Shadbush, Serviceberry
Amelanchier arborea

Flowers: Attractive, white at maturity, pinkish when in the bud or just opening, about 1 cm across when fully expanded, borne in showy, many-flowered clusters with new leaf growth; appearing in early spring.

Fruit: Rounded, red, berrylike, 6 - 9 mm long, often seen during winter when the plant is entirely without leaves.

Distinguishing Marks: This plant is easiest to learn in early spring when in flower. At this time the oval to elliptic, finely toothed leaves, in conjunction with the early flowering period is diagnostic. During other times of the year, look for the purplish-red glands along the central vein; fruiting specimens without leaves are sometimes confused with the deciduous hollies.

Distribution: Relatively common in moist flatwoods, bogs, and along the edges of wet savannas and titi swamps; throughout northern Florida, southward to the central peninsula.

Landscape Use: Probably not much used in landscaping but perhaps should be; the combination of early spring flowering, fall color, bright red fruit throughout most of the winter, and tendency to become more densely vegetated with age make it good for use along woodland edges, as an understory shrub, or in groups in isolated beds. In favorable situations chokeberry develops colonies quickly and may require at least some bit of maintenance to control.

May Haw or Apple Haw

Crataegus aestivalis (Walt.) Torr. & Gray

Form: Deciduous shrub or tree to about 8 m tall, often armed with sharp, conspicuous thorns to about 4 cm long and borne at the leaf axils.

Leaves: Alternate, simple, shiny green, stiffish, 2 - 8 cm long, 1 - 3.6 cm wide, margins coarsely toothed to lobed; leaf blades with tufts of hair at least in the proximal vein axils beneath, or if uniformly pubescent then densely so; the pubescence pale grayish on very young leaves, rusty brown on mature leaves.

Flowers: With five white to pinkish petals, borne individually or in clusters of two to four from leaf axils; appearing midspring.

Fruit: Juicy, red, rounded, 8 - 10 mm in diameter, typical of haws with remains of the sepals evident at the distal end.

Distinguishing Marks: Some leaves on any plant superficially similar to Washington thorn (*C. phaenopyrum*), but distinguished from them by having lateral veins terminating only at the tips of marginal teeth; other leaves similar to those of the cockspur haw(*C. crus-galli*), but distinguished from them by having tufts of hairs in the vein axils on the lower leaf surface.

Distribution: Wet areas, in and near standing water; throughout the Panhandle and southward to about the Gainesville area.

Landscape Use: As a group, the several species of haws make attractive additions to naturalistic landscapes; all have attractive flowers and showy fruit, and many have attractive trunks and conspicuously thorny branches.

Comment: The hawthorns constitute one of the most taxonomically confusing groups of trees and shrubs in eastern North America. The many species are so closely related, so nearly similar, and hybridize so easily that botanists are not agreed on the actual number of representatives in the genus. By current count, there are at least nine hawthorns represented in Florida. However, they are part of a large and complex collection of plants that is sometimes said to include up to 150 species in North America. As might be imagined, learning to identify the haws can present a significant challenge to the amateur botanist. Many of us will have to be content with knowing these plants only by genus rather than by species. The current volume describes all nine of these species found in Florida. Some are more treelike than shrublike. Given the difficulty in distinguishing members of the genus, it seems appropriate to include them all.

May Haw or Apple Haw
Crataegus aestivalis

Cockspur Haw or Hog Apple

Crataegus crus-galli L.

Form: Sometimes a shrub, more often a small deciduous tree to about 10 m tall with thorny branches and clusters of thorns along the trunk.

Leaves: Alternate, simple, oblanceolate, 2 - 6 cm long, 0.8 - 3 cm wide, margins serrate to coarsely toothed, not lobed, upper surfaces glabrous, deep green and conspicuously lustrous.

Flowers: Roselike, with five white petals, 0.5 - 1.5 cm wide at full maturity; appearing in midspring.

Fruit: Dull red to reddish orange or copper colored, to about 1 cm or a little more in diameter, borne on a long stem, typical of haws with remains of the sepals evident at the distal end.

Distinguishing Marks: Some leaves similar to the unlobed leaves of the littlehip hawthorn (*C. spathulata*), but differing from it slightly in habitat and by the latter having leaf veins terminating in both the marginal teeth and the sinuses between them, rather than just in the teeth; distinguished from May haw (*C. aestivalis*) by lacking tufts of hairs in the vein axils on the lower surfaces of the leaves.

Distribution: Open woodlands and upland woods; throughout northern Florida and the Panhandle.

Landscape Use: Not often mentioned as a landscape plant, but probably useful. The dark green leaves and attractive flower and fruit clusters make it an interesting addition to a naturalistic landscape.

Yellow Haw

Crataegus flava Ait.

Form: Deciduous shrub or small tree to about 5 m tall with thorny branches, thorns measuring to about 6 cm long, branches sometimes drooping at their extremities; bark of young trees grayish, furrowed, blocky, and oaklike, bark of older trees also furrowed but often much darker.

Cockspur Haw or Hog Apple
Crataegus crus-galli

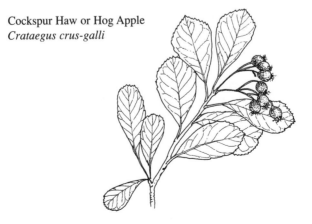

Leaves: Alternate, simple, 2 - 5 cm long, 1 - 3 cm wide, widest above the middle, toothed and shallowly lobed, part of the blade often extending down the petiole in narrow wings; marginal teeth tipped with a tiny red gland (requires magnification).

Flowers: Fragrant, showy, 10 - 16 mm wide when fully open, borne individually or in three- to five-flowered clusters at the leaf axils, petals white at maturity; appearing midspring.

Fruit: Red and berrylike, borne on long stems, variable in color from yellow to reddish to purplish, 0.8 - 1.5 cm in diameter, typical of haws with remains of the sepals evident at the distal end.

Distinguishing Marks: Leaves similar in appearance to those of the dwarf haw (*C. uniflora*) but distinguished by having conspicuous red glands at the tip of each marginal tooth when seen with magnification.

Distribution: Common in mixed woodlands, open woods, sandy pinelands; throughout northern Florida and the Panhandle; perhaps the most easily found of Florida's hawthorns.

Landscape Use: Does well in sandy, well-drained soils; the showy flowers, relatively large fruit, and often compact form make it a good background or edge plant in dry areas.

Comment: At least two authors (Huegel, 1993 and Wunderlin, 1982) have ascribed species status to *C. lepida* Beadle or scrub haw. Though many authorities include this species within the synonymy of *C. flava* (in the series *Flavae*), Huegel suggests that the two are distinct species based on fruit measurements (the fruit of *C. lepida* is said to be about half the size of *C. flava*), and the smaller flowers and later flowering period of *C. lepida* (typically early summer rather than late spring). The scientific name for this species is currently in question. Phipps (1988) reports that herbarium specimens of the true *C. flava*, which were collected in the late 1880s, do not match the plant currently referrred to by this name. In fact, Phipps suggests that the true species might even be extinct in nature, or at least very rare. As a result, some authorities (e.g. Herring and Judd, 1995) have ascribed north and notheast Florida specimens of this plant to *C. floridiana* Sarg. Other authorities (e.g. Lance, 1995) suggest that those in the western Panhandle should be ascribed to *C. lacrimata* Small.

Parsley Haw

Page 279, Photo 215

Crataegus marshallii Egglest.

Form: Shrub or, more commonly, a small deciduous tree to about 8 m tall, usually with thorny branches and scaly, splotchy bark of grays and tans, larger specimens sometimes bear multipronged, often leafy thorns along the trunk, these thorns to about 5 cm long.

Leaves: Alternate, simple, triangular in overall outline, 1 - 5 cm long and wide, usually with several deeply incised lobes (hence its common name), each lobe with conspicuous teeth.

Flowers: White to pinkish with showy red anthers, 1.5 - 2 cm wide at full maturity; appearing midspring.

Fruit: Rounded, bright red, 5 - 7 mm long, typical of haws with remains of the sepals evident at the distal end.

Distinguishing Marks: The small, distinctive, deeply incised, rather frilly leaves with truncated bases make this the easiest of the haws to separate from all other north Florida trees.

Distribution: Wooded slopes, moist woods, floodplains; throughout northern Florida, southward to about Hillsborough County.

Parsley Haw
Crataegus marshallii

Washington Thorn or Maple-Leaf Haw
Crataegus phaenopyrum

Landscape Use: The profuse, showy flowers, frilly foliage, and flaking bark of this species are quite attractive and the fruit ripens in fall but remains on the tree during the winter. It is easy to grow, tolerant of most soils, and does well along edges or as a background. As with the other haws, it is a good wildlife food.

Washington Thorn or Maple-Leaf Haw

Page 279

Crataegus phaenopyrum (L. f.) Medic.

Form: Deciduous shrub or small tree to about 10 m tall with sharp, reddish thorns to about 2 cm long.

Leaves: Alternate, simple, ovate, typically 1.5 - 2.5 cm long but variable and having several (to many) leaves to about 7 cm in length, 2 - 5 cm wide, upper surfaces dark green and smooth, margins lobed and toothed, lobes usually three in number, distal lobe narrowing to a sharp point at the apex.

Flowers: White, tiny, borne in many-flowered clusters; appearing in spring.

Fruit: Bright red, rounded, rather small, 4 - 6 mm in diameter, typical of haws with remains of the sepals evident at the distal end.

Distinguishing Marks: At least some leaves having the appearance of miniature maple leaves with blunt, rather than sharp-pointed, serrations; somewhat similar to *C. aestivalis*, *C. pulcherrima*, and *C. viridis*, but distinguished from them by having lateral leaf veins terminating in both the tips of marginal teeth and the sinuses between them rather than only in the tips of the teeth (requires magnification).

Distribution: Low woods; limited to only a few locations in the central Florida Panhandle and Big Bend; fairly common along the drainage of the Choctawhatchee River in Washington and Walton Counties. Populations are also reported from Wakulla County by Robert Godfrey (1988) and Guy Anglin (personal communication).

Landscape Use: Though rare in the wild in Florida and not often used in planted landscapes in the state, this plant is widely used across the more northern portions of the eastern United States and is the source of a number of horticultural cultivars. It is relatively pest free and its bright white flowers and showy red fruit that persists as the plant drops its leaves add to its beauty and utility. Birds relish the fruit. Its ornamental use dates at least to the late 1600s when it was a popular garden specimen in England.

Comment: Though this plant is known in Florida chiefly from Washington County, its common name derives from its early cultivation and landscape use in the nation's capital and is only coincidental to its range in the Sunshine State.

Crataegus pulcherrima Ashe

Page 281

Form: Typically a small deciduous tree, branches with sharp thorns to about 4 cm long, rarely somewhat shrubby; included here to help distinguish it from other members of the genus.

Leaves: Alternate, simple, variously shaped, lobed, and toothed, 2 - 6 cm long, 1 - 4 cm wide, margins coarsely to finely serrate, with dark-purplish-red glands (magnification required) on most petioles and on the tips of leaf serrations.

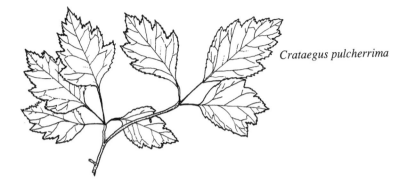

Crataegus pulcherrima

Flowers: White to pinkish, borne in few-flowered clusters, each flower to about 2 cm wide at maturity; appearing in spring.

Fruit: Rounded to a little longer than broad, 7 - 13 mm wide, bright red and usually firm and dry at maturity.

Distinguishing Marks: Similar in appearance to the green haw (*C. viridis*), but distinguished from it by lacking tufted pubescence in the vein axils of the lower surfaces of leaves, and by generally occurring in dry uplands rather than wetlands.

Distribution: Open upland woods; rather spottily distributed in Florida from Walton to Jefferson Counties, and from northeast Florida southward to Alachua County.

Landscape Use: Rarely used in planted landscapes, but probably a good choice for rich, shaded sites.

Littlehip Hawthorn or Small Fruited Hawthorn
Crataegus spathulata Michx.   **Page 282, Photo 216**

Form: Deciduous shrub or small tree to about 8 m tall, often with sharp thorns along slightly zigzag branches; bark brownish and stripping off in thin plates.

Leaves: Alternate, simple, oblanceolate to spatulate in shape and narrowing to a tapered base, 1 - 4 cm long, margins mostly crenate, leaves toward the extremities of the branches may be three lobed and somewhat larger.

Flowers: White to pink, petals triangular, 7 - 10 mm wide when fully mature, borne in dense, showy clusters; appearing in spring.

Fruit: Bright red, rounded, 4 - 7 mm in diameter.

Distinguishing Marks: Most easily distinguished from other haws by the presence of spatulate leaves with strongly tapered bases.

Distribution: Bottomlands, floodplains, and wooded slopes; limited in Florida to the central Panhandle.

Comment: The common names for this species derive from the relatively small size of its fruit in comparison with most other haws.

Landscape Use: The profuse flowering, large shrubby stature, and tolerance of a variety of conditions make this plant a possibility for rich, shady to partly sunny sites.

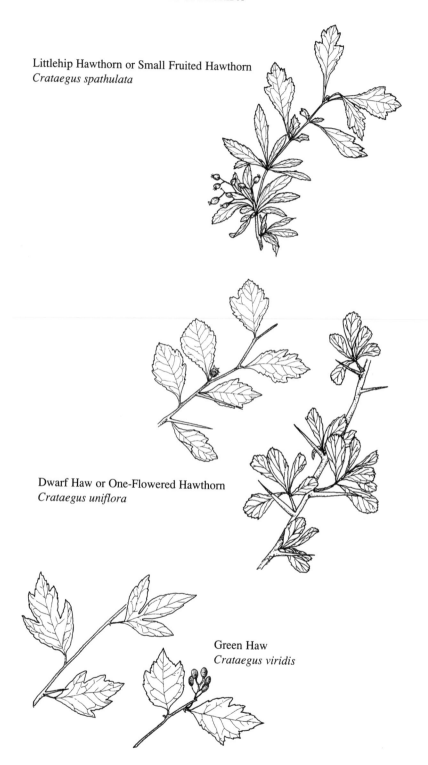

Littlehip Hawthorn or Small Fruited Hawthorn
Crataegus spathulata

Dwarf Haw or One-Flowered Hawthorn
Crataegus uniflora

Green Haw
Crataegus viridis

Dwarf Haw or One-Flowered Hawthorn

Page 282

Crataegus uniflora Muenchh.

Form: Typically a deciduous shrub to about 3 m tall in Florida (treelike north of Florida); branches with thin thorns to about 3 cm long.

Leaves: Alternate, simple, obovate to rounded, 1 - 3 cm long, margins irregularly serrate, upper surfaces shiny.

Flowers: White, usually borne singly, but sometimes in clusters of two or three, to about 1.5 cm wide when open; appearing in spring.

Fruit: Rounded, brownish red, 1 cm in diameter, typical of haws with remains of the sepals evident at the distal end, margins of sepals usually serrate.

Distinguishing Marks: Leaves similar to those of the yellow haw (*C. flava*), may be distinguished from the latter by lacking the conspicuous red glands at the tips of the marginal teeth (requires magnification); also distinguished by smaller fruit, and by flowers and fruits more often being borne singly rather than in clusters.

Distribution: Open woods; Washington County to northeastern Florida, southward to Alachua County.

Green Haw

Page 282

Crataegus viridis L.

Form: Deciduous shrub or small tree, often thornless but sometimes with slender, sharp thorns.

Leaves: Alternate, simple, ovate to elliptic, 3 - 7 cm long, 1.5 - 5 cm wide, margins variously lobed, always toothed, lower surfaces with patches of pubescence at the points where the central and lateral veins intersect; petioles, marginal teeth, and lobes of blades without glands.

Flowers: White to pink, borne in clusters, to about 1.5 cm wide or a little more at maturity; appearing in spring.

Fruit: Red to orange, rounded to slightly elongated, 5 - 8 mm in diameter.

Distinguishing Marks: Similar to *C. pulcherrima*, but differing from it by having tufted pubescence in the vein axils on the lower surfaces of leaves and by occurring primarily in wetland rather than dry upland habitats.

Distribution: Low woods, pond edges, swamps; across northern Florida and throughout the Panhandle.

Landscape Use: As with many haws, this species is showy in both spring and fall with the succession from flower to bright red fruit; does best in somewhat wet areas and is attractive to wildlife; some horticultural cultivars (such as the well-known "Winter King", which may be a hybrid between the present species and *C. phaenopyrum*) are available.

Southern Crabapple

Photos 217, 218

Malus angustifolia (Ait.) Michx.

Form: Deciduous shrub or small tree to about 10 m tall, often with leafy thorns.
Leaves: Alternate but densely clustered on young twigs, simple, variable in shape and size, mostly elliptic to ovate, 2.5 - 5 cm long, 2.5 cm wide, margins serrate and sometimes lobed near the base.
Flowers: Fragrant, showy, five-petaled, typically rich pink in color, borne in clusters of three to five, to about 2.5 cm wide when open; appearing early to midspring.
Fruit: Rounded, yellowish, resembling in shape the crab apple of commerce but smaller, to about 2.5 cm in diameter.
Distinguishing Marks: Similar to and often confused with the haws, distinguished from them by having leafy thorns rather than naked, axillary thorns.
Distribution: Open, upland woods; limited in Florida to the Panhandle.
Landscape Use: This is a beautiful plant with a spreading shape, very showy, fragrant flowers, attractive fruit, and leafy thorns on its branches; the fruit is edible and relished by wildlife; does well in dry to moist sites.

Ninebark

Page 285, Photo 219

Physocarpus opulifolius (L.) Maxim.

Form: Deciduous, several-stemmed shrub with peeling, buff-colored bark; to about 3 m tall.
Leaves: Alternate, simple, ovate in general outline, quite variable even on the same plant, larger ones 4 - 7 cm long, 4 - 5 cm wide, smaller ones averaging 1.5 cm both long and wide; margins finely serrate to crenate, larger ones mostly with two blunt-tipped basal lobes, smaller ones often without lobing; petioles 0.5 - 2 cm long; young leaves typically pubescent with star-shaped hairs; central and lowermost lateral veins arising together.
Flowers: White, sometimes tinged with pink, borne in clusters at the ends of branches, showy; appearing April through June.
Fruit: A two- to four-seeded pod to about 7 mm long.
Distinguishing Marks: The star-shaped pubescence, distinctive leaf shape with central and lower lateral vines arising together, in conjunction with the spraylike flower clusters, are diagnostic among the roses.
Distribution: Wooded stream banks; central Panhandle, the only population currently known in Florida extends across portions of both Jackson and Calhoun Counties.
Landscape Use: An excellent shrub to use as a background or mixed with other shrubs in a naturalistic landscape. Flowering can be extremely showy due to the dense clusters of bright white flowers with red anthers; the later blooming period and prolific blossoms insure color throughout the spring. It does best in rich, moist locations but is tolerant of almost any soil type.
Comment: Listed as endangered by the Florida Department of Agriculture.

Ninebark
Physocarpus opulifolius

Scrub Plum
Prunus geniculata

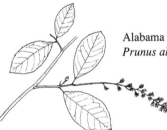

Alabama Cherry or Alabama Chokecherry
Prunus alabamensis

Alabama Cherry or Alabama Chokecherry   Page 285
Prunus alabamensis Mohr

Form: Shrub or small, crooked, deciduous tree.

Leaves: Alternate, simple, oval to obovate, 5 - 8 cm long, 3 - 5 cm wide, margins finely serrate and sometimes wavy, apices blunt; about 1/3 of the midvein on the lower surfaces of several to many leaves with conspicuous, woolly, brownish pubescence; the petioles pubescent.

Flowers: Borne in racemes to about 10 cm long and similar to those of the black cherry (*P. serotina* Ehrh.), a tree not described here; appearing in spring.

Fruit: Rounded, juicy, dark red to black when mature, to about 7 mm in diameter.

Distinguishing Marks: Leaves similar in color and general appearance to those of the black cherry but distinguished from them by having pubescent petioles and branchlets, and by typically being obovate in shape with blunt or rounded apices.

Distribution: Uncommon in sandy, pine–oak woodlands; Panhandle from at least the east side of the Apalachicola River westward.

Comment: This species is sometimes considered a variety of black cherry and may be seen listed as *P. serotina* var. *alabamensis* (Mohr) Little.

Chickasaw Plum

Photo 220

Prunus angustifolia Marsh.

Form: Thicket-forming deciduous shrub or small tree to about 8 m tall.

Leaves: Alternate, simple, lanceolate, typically reflexed upward from the midrib, 3 - 8 cm long, 1 - 2.5 cm wide, margins finely serrate with tips of the teeth bearing tiny red or yellow glands (requires magnification).

Flowers: White, showy, fragrant, less than 1 cm wide when fully open; appearing February through March.

Fruit: Red to yellow, oval, juicy, 1.5 - 2.5 cm long, edible but tart.

Distinguishing Marks: Very similar to, and often difficult to distinguish from, the hog plum (*P. umbellata*), distinguished from it most readily by the gland-tipped leaf serrations (especially on newer leaves), and by slightly larger, red to yellow mature fruit that lacks a whitish coating; also flowering and fruiting earlier than *P. umbellata*.

Distribution: Woodland edges and fence rows; from north Florida southward to DeSoto County.

Landscape Use: This plant blooms profusely in the early spring before new leaf growth and gives the first hint of spring; it does equally well in a solitary location or grouped within naturalistic beds; the fruit is also purported to make excellent jelly; its thicket-forming nature is useful in some situations, but can be controlled if desired.

Comment: In his written account of his travels of Florida, William Bartram (Van Doren, 1955) reports that this plant's common name derives from its popularity as a fruit source with the Chickasaw Indians.

Carolina Laurel Cherry or Cherry-Laurel

Photo 221

Prunus caroliniana (Mill.) Ait.

Form: Evergreen; commonly a tree to about 12 m tall; often seen as a single-stemmed shrub with toothed leaves and then somewhat confusing to identify, also often flowering and fruiting when of shrublike stature.

Leaves: Alternate, simple, leathery, elliptic, 5 - 12 cm long, 1.5 - 4 cm wide, pungently aromatic when crushed; upper surfaces dark green and lustrous, lower surfaces pale green; margins entire or with sharp teeth, some leaves on some plants (particularly young stems) more generously toothed than others; petioles of newer leaves reddish.

Flowers: White, fragrant, borne from the leaf axils in racemes to about 4 cm long, each flower less than 0.5 cm wide when open, appearing in late winter and early spring.

Fruit: A shiny black, oval drupe, 1 - 1.5 cm long.

Distinguishing Marks: Distinguished from other members of the genus by the presence of at least some stiff, mostly entire leaves, in combination with the fruit being borne in short racemes.

Distribution: Found in a variety of habitats due to extensive use as an ornamental and distribution by birds; throughout north Florida, southward to about DeSoto County.

Landscape Use: The glossy foliage, profuse clusters of white flowers, and shiny black fruit make this an excellent choice for a solitary shrub in a large yard; will grow to treelike proportions but may be pruned to produce a large hedge.

Scrub Plum
Prunus geniculata Harper

Page 285

Form: Small, rounded, densely branched, deciduous shrub, usually not exceeding 1.5 m in height, with bent or zigzag branchlets and sharp-pointed twigs; bark of older trees grayish and often covered with lichens.

Leaves: Alternate, elliptic to ovate, 1 - 1.5 cm long; margins finely crenate to serrate (often requires magnification to see clearly); petioles to about 1/3 or 1/2 the length of the blades.

Flowers: White petals, rose-colored sepals, yellow anthers; petals to about 3 mm long; flowers without stalks and essentially sessile; appearing in winter.

Fruit: Small, reddish plums to about 2.5 cm long.

Distinguishing Marks: Distinguished from other, similarly leaved plums by the combination of small stature, sessile flowers, very zigzag branches, and sharp thorns; potentially confused in general form with *Ziziphus celata*, an extremely rare scrub plant, distinguished from it by the finely serrated leaf margins.

Distribution: Sand hills, scrub, and intermediate habitats on the Lake Wales Ridge; from Lake and Polk Counties southward to Highlands County.

Comment: Listed as endangered by the Florida Department of Agriculture and the U. S. Fish and Wildlife Service. The specific name of this plant derives from the word geniculate, which means having kneelike joints or bends, and refers to the plant's zigzag branches.

Hog Plum, Flatwoods Plum, Black Sloe
Prunus umbellata Ell.

Photo 222

Form: Deciduous shrub or small tree to about 6 m tall, often with a crooked trunk.

Leaves: Alternate, simple, oval to elliptic, serrate, 2 - 6 cm long, 1 - 3 cm wide, margins serrate, tips of serrations without glands, apices sharp pointed.

Flowers: White, showy, typically appearing before the leaves, to about 1.5 cm wide when fully open; appearing in spring, usually slightly later in the season than the very similar *P. angustifolia*.

Fruit: A red or yellow drupe when young, typically becoming dark purple to nearly black and glaucous at maturity, 1.5 - 2 cm in diameter.

Distinguishing Marks: Very similar to, and difficult to distinguish from, the chickasaw plum (*P. angustifolia*), distinguished from it most easily by lacking glands at the tips of the leaf serrations (the latter seen only with magnification).

Distribution: Mixed woods, hammocks, pine woods; throughout northern Florida, southward to about Highlands County.

Landscape Use: The attractive profusion of early spring flowers and generally upright stature of this plant make it a good choice for wooded or open yards.

Firethorn or Pyracantha

Photo 223

Pyracantha sp.

Form: Much-branched, evergreen shrub with alternate, spine-tipped branchlets on slightly zigzag branches.

Leaves: Alternate, simple, elliptic to oblong or oblanceolate, dark shiny green, 1 - 4 cm long, to about 1 cm wide; margins entire to very obscurely serrate or crenate; apices rounded or often notched, sometimes pointed.

Flowers: Small, white, with five petals; borne in many-flowered clusters at the ends of new branchlets; appearing in spring.

Fruit: Rounded, orange to bright red, borne in large and very showy clusters that often appear pendent due to the weight of the fruiting branchlet on the branch; typically persisting throughout the winter.

Distinguishing Marks: The dark, shiny green leaves and persistent, bright red fruit are diagnostic.

Distribution: Native to Europe, widely planted, sometimes naturalized; mostly northern Florida.

Landscape Use: This is a widely used nonnative shrub in northern Florida, especially for its evergreen leaves and attractive fruit. It does best as a solitary shrub or as a background plant where it is allowed to achieve its own form; does not tolerate excessive pruning. Its fruit is relished by birds, particularly cedar waxwings.

Comment: There are several species of pyracantha that might be found naturalized in northern Florida; these include *P. coccinea* Roem., *P. fortuneana* (Maxim.) H. L. Li, and *P. koidzumii* (Hayata) Rehd.

McCartney Rose

Photo 224

Rosa bracteata Wendl.

Form: Arching shrub or clambering and vinelike with a combination of grayish and purplish-red, gland-tipped hairs on the stem; with a pair of straight to curved prickles at the leaf nodes; semievergreen.

Leaves: Alternate, pinnately compound with five to nine leaflets; leaflets elliptic to obovate, 1 - 2 cm long, to about 1.2 cm wide; upper surfaces shiny green; margins toothed, each tooth tipped with a purplish gland (requires magnification).

Flowers: Borne in few-flowered clusters, petals white to pinkish; appearing late spring and summer.

Fruit: Hip dark brown and rounded, 1.5 - 2 cm in diameter.

Distinguishing Marks: The combination of grayish and gland-tipped reddish-purple hairs along the stem distinguish this species from other members of the genus.

Distribution: Native to China, escaped from cultivation in oak woods and in the vicinity of plantings; northern Florida.

Landscape Use: See *R. laevigata*.

Carolina Rose

Rosa carolina L.

Form: Deciduous, erect, sparsely branched shrub to about 1.5 m tall; stem armed with few to many thin, straight prickles, prickles commonly to about 1 cm long.
Leaves: Alternate, pinnately compound, with three to nine leaflets; larger leaflets elliptic to oblanceolate, smaller ones more rounded; margins distinctly serrate; rachis pubescent with glandular hairs.
Flowers: Pink, with five, showy petals; petals 2 - 3 cm long; appearing late spring, mainly May; similar in general appearance to those of *R. palustris*, pictured in Photo 226 and on page 290.
Fruit: Hip rounded, red, about 1 cm in diameter.
Distinguishing Marks: The pink flowers in conjunction with the predominantly straight prickles and upland habitat help distinguish this species (but see *R. palustris*).
Distribution: Uncommon in shady, mixed, upland woods; northern Florida.
Landscape Use: Requires dry, well-drained soil; does well in full sun in places where other flowering species are difficult to cultivate.

Cherokee Rose

Photo 225

Rosa laevigata Michx.

Form: Evergreen shrub that sometimes appears vinelike and scrambling over nearby vegetation; stems with stout, curved, reddish-brown prickles.
Leaves: Alternate, pinnately compound with three leaflets; leaflets mostly elliptic and dark green above; margins finely toothed; petioles also commonly bearing prickles.
Flowers: Showy, with five petals and a mass of yellow stamens, borne singly at the leaf axils; petals 3 - 4 cm long; typically appearing during the spring.
Fruit: Hip long, ellipsoid, hairy, reddish, to about 3 cm long, enlarged on the distal end.
Distinguishing Marks: The combination of compound leaves with three leaflets, long, hairy fruit, curved prickles, and showy white flowers set this species apart.
Distribution: Native to China, cultivated and escaped throughout northern Florida and southward to about Sarasota County.
Landscape Use: A historically popular ornamental mostly for its attractive flowers and dark green foliage; weedy and difficult to control, especially if planted adjacent to other vegetation; should be isolated from other plants for best containment.
Comment: Legend alleges that the common name of this plant resulted from the symbolism granted it by a young Cherokee Indian woman. The story holds that the young woman's tribe captured a wounded brave from another tribe during battle and returned with him as a prisoner. While nursing the captive back to health, the Cherokee woman fell in love and decided to return home with him after his recuperation. Knowing that she would never be able to return to her own village, she took a stem of what is now called Cherokee rose with her as a reminder of her home.

Multiflora Rose or Japanese Rose

Rosa multiflora Thunb.

Form: Erect shrub with arching branches armed with pairs of prickles at the leaf nodes and elsewhere along the stem.

Leaves: Alternate, pinnately compound, with distinctive prickly stipules at the base of the leaf stalk; leaflets ranging five to nine in number, usually seven, elliptic to obovate, 1 - 3.5 cm long; margins finely toothed.

Flowers: White to pale pink, borne in midspring in conspicuous, widely branched clusters at the ends of branches; petals 1.5 - 2 cm long.

Fruit: Hip red, rounded, about 7 mm long; borne in conspicuous branched clusters.

Distinguishing Marks: The combination of prickly stipules at the base of the leaf stalk and branched flower clusters is distinctive among the roses.

Distribution: Of Asian origin, cultivated and escaped in northern Florida, chiefly near plantings.

Landscape Use: Used in much of its range as a border or fence plant; potentially weedy and difficult to control, especially so in regions well north of Florida.

Swamp Rose

Page 290, Photo 226

Rosa palustris Marsh.

Form: Erect, deciduous, bushy-branched shrub to about 2 m tall; stems armed with slightly curved prickles that are thickened at the base.

Leaves: Alternate, pinnately compound, with five to nine leaflets; leaflets lanceolate to elliptic, 2 - 6 cm long, 1 - 3 cm wide, finely toothed along the margins.

Flowers: Pink, with five petals, each 2 - 3 cm long; commonly borne singly at the leaf axils; appearing late spring and early summer.

Fruit: Hip red, rounded but somewhat flattened at the ends; about 1 cm in diameter.

Distinguishing Marks: The pink, roselike flowers, curved prickles, and wetland habitat are usually enough to identify this species (but see *R. carolina*).

Distribution: Common along wet edges of streams, ponds, lakes, ditches, swamps, often in standing water; throughout northern Florida, southward to the central peninsula.

Landscape Use: Of use in low wet areas where a showy flowering plant is desired; excellent for the edges of ponds.

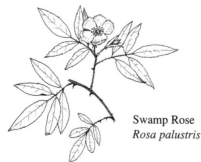

Swamp Rose
Rosa palustris

Memorial Rose
Rosa wichuraiana Crepin.

Form: A trailing, scrambling, or reclining semievergreen vine; stem with prickles.
Leaves: Alternate, pinnately compound with five to nine leaflets; leaflets small, oval to ellip-
tic, not much exceeding 2 cm in length, margins coarsely toothed; petiole, rachis, and mid-
vein of lower surfaces of leaflets often bearing both prickles and purplish-red glands.
Flowers: Pink, 3 - 4 cm wide, borne in clusters at the ends of the branches; appearing in summer.
Fruit: Hip red, egg shaped, 1 - 1.5 cm in diameter.
Distinguishing Marks: The small leaves and leaflets help distinguish this species from most
other native and naturalized roses.
Distribution: Locally escaped from cultivation; northern Florida.
Landscape Use: This is a popular flowering vine, especially for ground cover and in areas
where erosion control is important, such as slopes along highways and railroad beds; it is
very vigorous, will spread quickly, and requires extensive maintenance if planted in restricted locations.

Highbush Blackberry   Page 292
Rubus betulifolius Small

Form: An erect, arching, or clambering, vinelike shrub to about 3 m tall; stem ridged,
grooved, and bearing sharp, commonly curved or hooked prickles.
Leaves: Alternate, palmately compound, those of the main stem mostly with five leaflets
(sometimes only four) and leaf stalk 6 - 10 cm long, leaves of flowering and fruiting branches usually having only three leaflets; leaflets of main stem leaves elliptic to broadly lanceolate with sharply toothed margins, 4 - 10 cm long, the terminal leaflets much the longest;
lower leaflets of main stem with short stalks, terminal ones with longer stalks approaching 4
cm in length.
Flowers: White to suffused with pink (often appearing pink before opening), with five petals,
borne in loose clusters; appearing March and April.
Fruit: A juicy, tasty berry, 1 - 2.5 cm long, 1 - 1.5 cm in diameter.
Distinguishing Marks: The erect stature, ridged stems, and five-foliolate main stem leaves
generally distinguish the species; distinguished from *R. cuneifolius* by lower surfaces of
leaflets not being copiously whitish pubescent.
Distribution: Wet woodlands, stream banks, often near standing water but also in fields and
along fence lines; throughout northern Florida, southward to the central peninsula.
Comment: Some authors list the present species as a synonym for *R. argutus* Link (Clewell,
1985), others list both species without comment about their synonymy (Wunderlin, 1982 and
Foote & Jones, 1989), still others have omitted *R. argutus* without comment (Godfrey, 1988).
The latter author's treatment has been followed here. It should be noted that the several
species of *Rubus* described here constitute what some believe to be only a few of hundreds
of species, varieties, and forms in the eastern United States. There is significant hybridiza-

Highbush Blackberry
Rubus betulifolius

tion between supposed blackberry species, and intergrading forms are often encountered. Though those treated here are generally well-accepted species for Florida, readers should be aware that all plants found in the field may not fit neatly into one of these specific categories.

Sand Blackberry Page 292

Rubus cuneifolius Pursh

Form: An erect or arching shrub to about 1.5 m tall, commonly shorter; stems armed with sharp, stiff, curved prickles.

Leaves: Alternate, palmately compound, main stem leaves commonly with three but sometimes with four or five leaflets, leaves of flowering and fruiting branches typically with three leaflets; petioles and stalks of leaflets also armed with prickles; leaflets mostly obovate, oblanceolate, or spatulate, their lower surfaces with a copious covering of whitish pubescence which is feltlike to the touch.

Flowers: White, with five petals, borne in loose clusters near the ends of branches; appearing March to May.

Sand Blackberry
Rubus cuneifolius

Fruit: A juicy, tasty berry, deep blue to bluish black, 1 - 2.5 cm long.

Distinguishing Marks: The dense, feltlike covering of whitish pubescence on the lower surfaces of the leaflets distinguishes this species from *R. betulifolius*, the other erect blackberry.

Distribution: Common in sandy woods across northern Florida, southward to the southernmost peninsula.

Comment: One of the most popular species of those who enjoy gathering blackberries. See comment for *R. betulifolius*.

Northern Dewberry   Page 293
Rubus flagellaris Willd.

Form: An arching, trailing, or prostrate, vinelike shrub; unarmed or armed with numerous short, sharp, curved prickles; often rooting at the tips of trailing stems; flowering stems reddish purple.

Leaves: Alternate, palmately compound, those of the main stem usually with three leaflets, or occasionally five leaflets, those of flowering and fruiting branches typically with three leaflets; leaflets of main stems ovate, typically with coarsely toothed margins, lower two leaflets commonly lobed only on one side.

Flowers: White, with five petals, appearing April and May.

Fruit: On healthy plants north of Florida the fruit is black at maturity, sweet, and about 2.5 cm long; according to Godfrey (1988), the fruit on Florida specimens is typically much smaller and dryish.

Distinguishing Marks: Distinguished from other blackberries in its range by the combination of trailing habit and main stem leaves often displaying basal lobing.

Distribution: Upland and lowland woods of the Panhandle.

Comment: See comment for *R. betulifolius*.

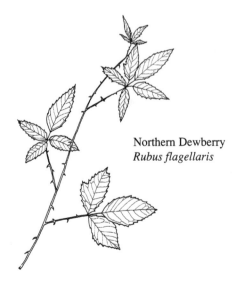

Northern Dewberry
Rubus flagellaris

Mysore Raspberry or Hill Raspberry
Rubus niveus

Mysore Raspberry or Hill Raspberry Page 294, Photo 227
Rubus niveus Thunb.

Form: Shrub to about 2 m tall; stems bearing hooked prickles, 3 - 7 mm long.

Leaves: Alternate, pinnately compound with five to nine leaflets; leaflets elliptic to ovate, 2.5 - 6 cm long, 2 - 3 cm wide the terminal one broadly ovate; margins serrate; undersurfaces of leaflets densely white pubescent; rachis typically bearing curved prickles.

Flowers: Rose purple, densely hairy, borne in branched clusters that bear scattered prickles.

Fruit: A dark red to reddish-black, rounded berry, with whitish hairs; about 1 cm long; maturing January to June with the heaviest concentration in March and April.

Distinguishing Marks: The shrubby form of this species helps separate it from other members of the genus.

Distribution: Native to India, southeastern Asia, the Philippines, and Indonesia; cultivated and escaped in the tropics, including Hawaii and southern Florida.

Landscape Use: An uncommon landscape plant in south Florida for its interesting flowers, edible fruit, and very attractive foliage; does well in full sun.

Comment: This species is also sometimes listed under the scientific synonym *Rubus albescens* Roxb.

Southern Dewberry Page 295
Rubus trivialis Michx.

Form: Trailing, reclining, or prostrate vinelike shrub; stems conspicuously pubescent with reddish hairs (does not require magnification), and armed with straight to curved prickles.

Leaves: Alternate, compound, mostly with five leaflets (sometimes three); leaflets elliptic to lanceolate, 2 - 6 cm long, margins coarsely and doubly toothed.

Flowers: White, sometimes with a pinkish tint, appearing pink before opening, typically borne singly; appearing February to April, earlier than most other blackberries.

Fruit: Juicy, tasty, black at maturity, 1 - 3 cm long.

Distinguishing Marks: Distinguished as the only one of the four species described here with conspicuously purplish-red pubescent stems that exhibit a reclining or prostrate habit.

Distribution: Common in a variety of circumstances from wet to dry woods and woodland

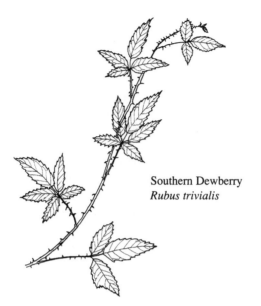

Southern Dewberry
Rubus trivialis

edges, roadsides, suburban yards, fields, fence lines; nearly throughout the state to the southernmost peninsula.

Comment: See comment for *R. betulifolius*.

RUBIACEAE — MADDER FAMILY

The Rubiaceae, or madder family, is one of the largest families of flowering plants. It contains about 500 genera and over 7,000 species worldwide, most of which are herbaceous rather than woody. Twenty-three species are described below. Though the family produces few plants that have economic value, it does include *Coffea arabica* L., which is used to produce coffee. The most popular ornamental member of the genus in Florida is probably *Gardenia jasminoides* Ellis, known by the common name gardenia. This latter species, which is not naturalized and not described below, is highly regarded for its fragrant white flowers that appear in early summer. Most members of the family have showy flowers and opposite, simple leaves which typically display interpetiolar stipules which leave linelike scars between the leaf bases.

Seven-Year Apple   Photo 228
Casasia clusiifolia (Jacq.) Urban

Form: Evergreen shrub or small tree to about 6 m tall.
Leaves: Opposite, simple, obovate, entire, leathery, 5 - 15 cm long, 2.5 - 7.5 cm wide, shiny green above, clustered at the tips of branches.
Flowers: Bright white, star shaped, fragrant; appearing any time of year; male and female

295

flowers appearing on separate plants.

Fruit: Relatively large, green at first, maturing black, hard, egg shaped, 6 - 10 cm long; reportedly edible.

Distinguishing Marks: May be confused only with the balsam apple (*Clusia rosea*) but distinguished from it by having the upper surface of the leaf shiny rather than dull green, and by leaves being less stiff than those of the latter species.

Distribution: Occurs naturally in coastal hammocks and adjacent transition zone of Dade, Monroe, and Broward Counties, including the Keys.

Landscape Use: Though often scrubby in its normal habitat, this plant is quite attractive when cultivated and fertilized; its bright green foliage, showy flowers, and large distinctive fruit add to its charm; regularly used in medians of roads and parking lots.

Comment: Some authorities suggest that the genus *Casasia* be merged into the genus *Genipa*. Hence, this plant might also be seen listed as *Genipa clusiifolia* (Jacq.) Griseb.

Lily Thorn

Photo 229

Catesbaea parviflora Sw.

Form: Small, spiny, evergreen shrub with stiff, elongated, cylindrical, little-branched stems; potentially to about 2 m tall.

Leaves: Opposite, simple, entire, shiny green to yellowish green, obovate, small, 5 - 12 mm long; apices rounded; leaf axils bearing two, sharp, green spines with dark tips that are usually longer than the leaves; often branched at the leaf axil with a short spur containing up to 10 additional leaves.

Flowers: Small, white, funnel-form, with four spreading petals; appearing throughout the year.

Fruit: Small, rounded, white, few-seeded berry.

Distinguishing Marks: The small leaves, sharp spines, stiff branches, and restricted range set this species apart.

Distribution: Open sandy woods, pine rocklands, back dunes; restricted in Florida to Big Pine and Bahia Honda Keys.

Comment: Listed as endangered by the Florida Department of Agriculture.

Buttonbush

Photo 230

Cephalanthus occidentalis L.

Form: Deciduous shrub or small tree, potentially to about 15 m tall but usually much shorter and not exceeding about 3 m.

Leaves: Opposite or in whorls of three to four, simple, entire, lanceolate to elliptic, 6 - 18 cm long, 1.5 - 10 cm wide.

Flowers: Numerous, tiny, white, borne in a hanging, globular, compact, fragrant, pincushionlike head, 2 - 4 cm in diameter; generally appearing late spring and summer in the northern parts of the state, nearly year-round in the southernmost regions.

Fruit: Small, produced in spherical heads.

Distinguishing Marks: Most easily recognized by its simple, elliptic, sometimes whorled leaves and showy, rounded flower heads; vegetatively most similar to the fever tree (*Pinckneya bracteata*) but distinguished from it by having at least some leaves in whorls of three or four.

Distribution: Wet areas and sites with standing water; throughout the state except the Keys.

Landscape Use: Does best in wet areas along the edges of ponds or marshy areas and becomes a large shrub in such locations (it is not tolerant of dry areas). Its flowers are very distinctive and attract bees and butterflies. Buttonbush withstands severe pruning every two or three years, which helps keep its size small and manageable; its deciduous nature can be a limitation in some instances.

Snowberry, Snakeroot, Tears of St. Peter   Photo 231

Chiococca alba (L.) A. Hitchc.

Form: Sprawling, evergreen, multitrunked, often vinelike shrub with yellowish bark, some stems reclining; often climbs on taller vegetation; to about 3 m tall.

Leaves: Opposite, simple, entire, leathery, elliptic to ovate or broadly lanceolate, somewhat V-shaped upward from the central vein, 5 - 11 cm long; apices tapering or pinched to a point.

Flowers: Yellow, bell shaped, five parted; commonly to about 1 cm long; appearing throughout the year.

Fruit: A distinctive and conspicuous, bright white, rounded drupe, 4 - 7 mm in diameter; seeds resemble coffee beans; fruiting mostly in summer and fall.

Distinguishing Marks: The bright white, rounded fruit provide the most distinctive character for this species; distinguished from the similarly fruited *C. parvifolia* by its larger size which is definitely shrubby rather than vinelike, by having yellowish, rather than whitish, flowers, and by having predominantly larger leaves.

Distribution: Common along the edges of hammocks in coastal counties of the central and southern peninsula, northward to about Dixie County on the west coast, farther north on the east coast, throughout the Keys.

Landscape Use: Enjoyed for the bright green, evergreen foliage and bright white fruit; prefers full sun.

Snowberry   Photo 232

Chiococca parvifolia Wullschl. ex Griseb.

Form: Multibranched, evergreen, trailing, vinelike shrub.

Leaves: Opposite, simple, entire, elliptic, dark shiny green above, to about 5 cm long; apices pinched to a point.

Flowers: White to purplish white and bell shaped; appearing year-round.

Fruit: Bright-white drupe, very conspicuous; seeds resemble coffee beans.

Distinguishing Marks: Similar in general aspects to *C. alba*; distinguished from it by having whitish, rather than yellowish, flowers, predominantly smaller leaves, and by its trailing habit.

Distribution: Pinelands and hammock margins; south Florida and the Keys.

Black Torch
Erithalis fruticosa L.

Photo 233

Form: Typically a low, much-branched, evergreen shrub with very dense foliage and a generally rounded shape, sometimes more spindly and treelike where it invades hammocks.
Leaves: Opposite, entire, oval, 2 - 5 cm long, with blunt apices.
Flowers: Small, white, star shaped, with five petals, borne in clusters in the leaf axils; appearing year-round.
Fruit: A rounded drupe to just under 1 cm in diameter, shiny black and conspicuous at maturity.
Distinguishing Marks: Most easily recognized in its typical coastal scrub habitat by its opposite leaves that are closely clustered near the tips of the branches, in conjunction with its shiny black fruit; blolly (*Guapira discolor*) is similar but has leaves more evenly spread along the branch and red fruit; also vegetatively similar to locust berry (*Byrsonima lucida*) but lacks the latter's multicolored flowers and reddish-brown fruit.
Distribution: Coastal scrub and hammocks of the southern peninsula and the Florida Keys.

Beach Creeper or Golden Creeper
Ernodea littoralis Sw.

Photo 234

Form: Prostrate, ascending or reclining, vinelike shrub, potentially to about 1 m tall.
Leaves: Opposite (but numerous and appearing to be borne in clusters), simple, entire, linear to narrowly lanceolate, leathery, shiny green, 1 - 4 cm long.
Flowers: Tubular, whitish, pinkish, to yellowish, with four strongly reflexed and curling petals; borne at the leaf axils; appearing year-round.
Fruit: Small, rounded to oval, yellow, single seeded.
Distinguishing Marks: The tubular flowers, rounded, yellow fruit, and low creeping habit distinguish this species from other dune plants.
Distribution: Common on coastal dunes, generally in full sun; lower central coasts southward and throughout the Keys.

Princewood
Exostema caribaeum (Jacq.) Roem. & Schult.

Page 299

Form: Evergreen shrub or small tree to about 6 m tall with conspicuously jointed twigs.
Leaves: Opposite, simple, leathery, lanceolate to elliptic, entire, 3 - 8 cm long, 1 - 4 cm wide, dark green above, yellowish green below, often reflexed upward from the midrib.
Flowers: White, pinkish, or orange colored, typically appearing from March to May, borne singly in the leaf axils, with a very long, tubelike corolla that spreads into five straplike petals near its apex.

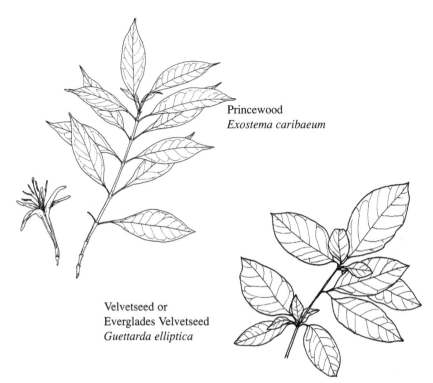

Princewood
Exostema caribaeum

Velvetseed or
Everglades Velvetseed
Guettarda elliptica

Fruit: An upright, woody capsule which splits into two parts at maturity.

Distinguishing Marks: Most easily recognized when not in flower or fruit by the combination of conspicuously jointed twigs and opposite, reflexed leaves.

Distribution: Hammocks and pinelands of the Florida Keys; also sparingly in the southern peninsula.

Velvetseed or Everglades Velvetseed   Page 299, Photo 235
Guettarda elliptica Sw.

Form: Typically a small, spindly, sometimes arching, evergreen shrub or small tree to about 6 m tall.

Leaves: Opposite, simple, entire, oval to obovate, to about 7 cm long and 3 cm wide, dull green and soft to the touch.

Flowers: White to reddish pink, tubular, to about 1 cm long; appearing year-round.

Fruit: A rounded, red to purple berry, 7 - 10 mm in diameter, covered with a velvetlike pubescence.

Distinguishing Marks: Somewhat similar in appearance to the rough velvetseed (*G. scabra*) but distinguished from it by having leaves that are soft to the touch and usually less than 7 cm long.

Distribution: Pinelands and hammocks; extreme south Florida and the Keys, possibly sporadically northward to at least St. Lucie County.

Rough Velvetseed

Photo 236

Guettarda scabra (L.) Vent.

Form: Typically an evergreen shrub to about 1.5 m tall in Everglades pinelands, but reaching the stature of a small, sparsely branched, slender tree to about 5 m tall in the lower Keys or where it invades the hammocks.

Leaves: Opposite, simple, entire, oval, 5 - 15 cm long (though some leaves of hammock specimens may exceed this length), 2 - 8 cm wide, dark green and covered on both surfaces with short, stiff hairs making the leaf very rough to the touch.

Flowers: Tubular, 1 - 3 cm long; appearing year-round.

Fruit: Red, rounded, berrylike, 6 - 12 mm in diameter, covered with a velvetlike pubescence.

Distinguishing Marks: Most easily recognized by its opposite, very rough leaves, which are larger than those of *G. elliptica*.

Distribution: Pinelands and hammocks of south Florida and the Keys; a disjunct population is known from Martin County.

Scarlet Bush or Firebush

Photo 237

Hamelia patens Jacq.

Form: Showy, evergreen shrub or shrubby tree to about 5 m tall.

Leaves: Whorled with three to seven leaves at each node, simple, entire, elliptic, 5 - 15 cm long, 2 - 8 cm wide, blades often reflexed upward from the central vein, petioles and veins reddish.

Flowers: Red to reddish orange, tubular, 1.5 - 4 cm long, borne in axillary or terminal clusters; appearing year-round.

Fruit: A rounded, juicy berry, 5 - 10 mm in diameter, red to purplish black.

Distinguishing Marks: Distinguished from other south Florida and lower peninsula shrubs by whorled leaves with reddish veins and petioles, and by its brightly colored flowers.

Distribution: Hammocks, roadsides, disturbed sites; Highlands County southward and throughout the Keys.

Landscape Use: A very popular landscape plant both for its foliage and its showy, brightly colored, tubular flowers; often used as a hedge along fences, patios, decks, and sidewalks, or as a free-standing shrub; does well in shade and full sun.

Partridge Berry, Twin-Flower, Two-Eyed-Berry

Photo 238

Mitchella repens L.

Form: Very low, evergreen, prostrate, mat-forming, woody shrub with slender stems; leaves not more than a few centimeters above the ground.

Leaves: Opposite, simple, entire, ovate to nearly round in outline, dark green, 0.5 - 2 cm long.

Flowers: Generally white, sometimes with tinges of pink; tubular, to about 1.5 cm long;

borne in pairs on a single stalk; appearing in spring.

Fruit: A rounded, bright-red drupe, 7 - 10 mm in diameter; generally appearing in fall and early winter, at least some fruit in evidence throughout the winter; conspicuous in the ground cover.

Distinguishing Marks: The low growth habit, nearly rounded leaves, and bright-red drupes are diagnostic.

Distribution: Common in moist and rich upland woods; throughout northern Florida, southward to the lower-central peninsula.

Landscape Use: An excellent, easy to grow, native ground cover that often volunteers from surrounding woodlands; the bright red fruit makes an attractive display among fallen leaves during autumn and winter. Partridge berry is also reportedly used in rock gardens.

Morinda citrifolia L.   **Photo 239**

Form: Shrub or small tree with angled stems.

Leaves: Opposite, simple, entire, elliptic, pointed at the apices, shiny green, 12 - 45 cm long, 7 - 25 cm wide.

Flowers: White, borne in a head at the leaf axils, to about 1 cm long.

Fruit: Rounded, fleshy, white to greenish, relatively large, to about 10 cm long and 4 cm in diameter.

Distinguishing Marks: Distinguished from the native *M. royoc* by having much larger leaves.

Distribution: Native to India, naturalized and well established in portions of south Florida, especially along the Atlantic shoreline and at Turkey Point in southern Dade County, in Broward County, and in the Keys where it sometimes sprouts along the edges of the mangroves.

Landscape Use: The large, dark green foliage and interesting fruit are attractive and the plant is easily grown in relatively thin soil and poor situations.

Comment: There are about 60 species of *Morinda* worldwide, most native to the Old and New World tropics. They have orange-colored dye in their root and are characterized by their fleshy fruits which are actually composed of several flowers that are joined together by their ovaries.

Indian Mulberry, Morinda, Yellow Root, Cheese Shrub, Mouse's Pineapple   Page 302, Photos 240, 241

Morinda royoc L.

Form: Evergreen, vinelike shrub to about 3 m tall; stems slender and reclining.

Leaves: Opposite, simple, entire, obovate to oblanceolate, 5 - 10 cm long, pointed at the apices.

Flowers: Small, white to reddish, 6 - 8 mm long, with six spreading petals; appearing year-round.

Fruit: Rounded, yellowish, fleshy, roughened, 2 - 3 cm in diameter; exhibiting a cheeselike aroma when bruised.

Indian Mulberry, Morinda, Yellow Root,
Cheese Shrub, Mouse's Pineapple
Morinda royoc

Distinguishing Marks: The oblanceolate leaves and rounded fleshy fruit are diagnostic; most quickly distinguished from the nonnative, *M. citrifolia*, by the overall shorter leaves.

Distribution: Occasional in coastal hammocks along the edges of the peninsula, more common in tropical hammocks in the south; from about Brevard and Hillsborough Counties southward along the coast and throughout the Keys.

Landscape Use: This plant is probably not much used in landscaping but likely should be; its flowers and foliage are attractive and it tolerates poor conditions.

Sewer Vine or Skunk Vine Page 303
Paederia foetida L.

Form: Perennial, semiwoody, twining vine or climbing shrub.

Leaves: Opposite, simple, entire, broadly lanceolate to elliptic, 3 - 14 cm long; petioles relatively long and slender; bases rounded, truncate, or sometimes slightly heart shaped.

Flowers: Pale lilac, tubular, with four or five lobes, 7 - 11 mm long; appearing in both spring and fall.

Fruit: A dry, rounded, orange to yellow, brittle berry to about 1 cm long.

Distinguishing Marks: The pale lilac flowers and opposite, broadly lanceolate leaves with somewhat heart-shaped bases offer a clue to this plant's identify.

Distribution: Disturbed sites, fence rows, escaped from cultivation; native to Asia, found in Florida mostly in the southern and south-central parts of the state, though also reported from some locations in north Florida.

Comment: This nonnative plant has been reported as present in Florida since at least the early parts of the 1900s (Small, 1913). Its common name refers to the offensive odor given off when the plant is bruised. Another, similar but more recent introduction with the same common name (*P. cruddasiana* Prain), is now also present in southern Florida and is reported by Roger Hammer to be an aggressive, spreading, and a well-established component of Dade County's flora, see Photo # xxx. There are about 20 species of *Paederia*. Most are native to tropical and temperate Asia, but a few are known from the American tropics. Both of the species found in Florida are listed as pest plants by the Florida Exotic Pest Plant Council and should not be used in landscaping.

Pinckneya, Fever Tree, or Fever Bark   Photo 242
Pinckneya bracteata (Bartr.) Raf.

Form: Deciduous shrub or small tree to about 8 m tall.

Leaves: Opposite, simple, oval to elliptic, 4 - 20 cm long, 2.5 - 12 cm wide, often clustered toward the ends of branches, margins entire but sometimes slightly wavy.

Flowers: Corolla tubular, greenish yellow, surrounded by four typically pinkish, yellowish, or rarely whitish sepals, one of which is much enlarged, very showy, and much more petal-like (or even leaflike) than the petals themselves, appearing in late spring and early summer.

Fruit: A rounded capsule, 1 - 3 cm long.

Distinguishing Marks: Most easily recognized by rather large opposite, elliptic leaves and distinctive flowers; distinguished from the similarly-leaved buttonbush (*Cephalanthus occidentalis*) by lacking whorled leaves, and by having pink flowers.

Distribution: Wet areas of bogs, bay swamps, and low pinelands; from about Bay and Washington Counties eastward across northern Florida.

Sewer Vine or Skunk Vine
Paederia foetida

Landscape Use: This is an attractive plant but not easy to grow. However, for the hard-working gardener with patience, its unique flowers can be a conversation piece in a moist urban landscape. It flowers best in locations that are sunny for at least part of the day but is known to bloom profusely in a few roadside locations with no shade. When in full bloom there is no plant more splendid.

Comment: This plant was discovered in the 1750s by John Bartram, one of the New World's most famous and most prolific plant hunters. He and his son William are well known for their travels in Florida. The plant's common name stems from its use as a medicinal herb in colonial America and during the Civil War. Decoctions made from its bark were used as a source of quinine to treat the high fever of malaria victims.

Wild Coffee or Bahaman Wild Coffee
Photo 243

Psychotria ligustrifolia (Northrop) Millsp.

Form: An erect, evergreen, multistemmed shrub to about 2 m tall; stems smooth and without hairs.

Leaves: Opposite, simple, entire, broadly lanceolate to oblanceolate, 5 - 12 cm long; apices pinched to a point; veins on upper surfaces conspicuously depressed; stipules at the bases of the leaf stalks usually conspicuous.

Flowers: White, five-lobed, borne in clusters in the axils of the upper leaves; flower clusters with a distinct and conspicuous stalk; typically appearing in spring and summer.

Fruit: A reddish, ellipsoid drupe, about 5 mm long.

Distinguishing Marks: Distinguished from other members of the genus by the combination of long-stalked flower clusters and lacking dots on the undersurfaces of leaves, as described for *P. punctata*, below; but see comment that follows.

Distribution: Hammocks and pinelands; south Florida and the Keys.

Landscape Use: All of Florida's *Psychotria* species have attractive flowers and interesting foliage and do well as landscape plants.

Comment: The several species of *Psychotria* that are found in Florida are quite similar and are easily separated from most other south Florida plants, except perhaps for Florida tetrazygia (*Tetrazygia bicolor*), by the combination of their shrublike stature and the depressed veins on the upper surfaces of their leaves. However, separating the individual species from each other can be more confusing, especially when first learning them. The notes within the descriptions here highlight the key differences between Florida's four species. They are easiest to distinguish when in flower. The 500 to 800 species of *Psychotria* make it the largest worldwide genus in the madder family.

Wild Coffee
Photo 244

Psychotria nervosa Sw.

Form: An erect, evergreen, branching shrub to about 3 m tall, with smooth to sometimes hairy stems.

Leaves: Opposite, simple, entire, shiny green above, elliptic to obovate, 6 - 15 cm long, to about 5 cm wide; veins conspicuously depressed on the upper surfaces; apices pinched to a point.

Flowers: White, to about 4 mm long, tubular, with four or five lobes, borne in sessile clusters at the axils of the uppermost leaves; typically appearing spring and summer.

Fruit: A red, ellipsoid drupe, 5 - 8 mm long.

Distinguishing Marks: One of two members of the genus with sessile flower clusters; the other, *P. sulzneri*, has greenish-white flowers, and the upper surfaces of its leaves are dull green, rather than shiny green.

Distribution: Common in hammocks and pinelands; central and southern Florida and the Keys.

Landscape Use: See *P. ligustrifolia*.

Comment: See comment above for *P. ligustrifolia*; the present species is sometimes seen listed under the scientific synonym, *P. undata* Jacq.

Wild Coffee **Page 305**

Psychotria punctata Vatke

Form: An erect, branching, evergreen shrub to about 3 m tall; stems without hairs.

Leaves: Opposite, simple, entire, dark shiny green above, elliptic to obovate, 4 - 8 cm long; veins on upper surfaces conspicuously depressed; apices typically rounded or sometimes bluntly pointed; lower surfaces vested with conspicuous dots or spots.

Flowers: White, small, tubular, 4 - 5 mm long; borne in dense, stalked clusters at the axils of the uppermost leaves; appearing year-round.

Fruit: A rounded, red drupe, 5 - 6 mm in diameter.

Distinguishing Marks: Distinguished from *P. ligustrifolia*, the other species with stalked flower clusters, by the conspicuous dots on the lower surfaces of the leaves.

Distribution: Native to Africa; naturalized in southern Florida and the lower Keys.

Landscape Use: See *P. ligustrifolia*.

Comment: See comment above for *P. ligustrifolia*.

Wild Coffee
Psychotria punctata

Wild Coffee
Psychotria sulzneri Small

Form: Erect, branching, evergreen shrub to about 2 m tall; stems pubescent.
Leaves: Opposite, simple, entire, elliptic to lanceolate, 8 - 15 cm long; veins conspicuously depressed on upper surfaces; upper surfaces of leaves dull green.
Flowers: Greenish white, small, tubular, 2 - 3 mm long, borne in sessile clusters in the upper leaf axils; typically appearing in spring and summer.
Fruit: Red, orange, or yellow drupe to about 5 mm long.
Distinguishing Marks: One of two species of wild coffee with sessile flowers; the other, *P. nervosa*, has white flowers and shiny leaves; the present species also always has hairy stems, *P. nervosa* only occasionally does.
Distribution: Common in hammocks and woods; throughout central Florida and southward to the southern peninsula, not the Keys.
Landscape Use: See *P. ligustrifolia*.
Comment: See comment above for *P. ligustrifolia*; the present species is often seen listed under the scientific synonym, *P. tenuifolia* Griseb.

Randia, Indigo Berry, White Indigo Berry
Randia aculeata L.

Photo 245

Form: Typically a small evergreen shrub but very occasionally a short tree with opposite branches; to about 3.5 m tall.
Leaves: Opposite, simple, elliptic to obovate, light green in color, 1 - 5 cm long, blunt toward the apices but having a small, sharp point at the leaf tips; often exhibiting a pair of sharp spines just above the point of leaf attachment.
Flowers: Fragrant, white with five petals, borne along the branch or clustered at the leaf axils and a little more than 1 cm across; appearing year-round.
Fruit: An oval, white to greenish-white berry.
Distinguishing Marks: Most easily recognized by its distinctive opposite branching, by the leaves clustered at the terminus of the branchlets, and by the frequent pairs of wide-angled thorns along the stem.
Distribution: Found in a variety of habitats in southern Florida and the Keys, especially in unburned pinelands and along the margins of coastal hammocks.

Pride of Big Pine, Strumpfia, Snowbank
Strumpfia maritima Jacq.

Photos 246, 247

Form: Low, profusely branched shrub, usually less than 1 m tall; branches pubescent.
Leaves: Whorled, simple, entire, linear, leathery, 1 - 2.5 cm long, usually borne crowded near the ends of branches; margins strongly and conspicuously revolute, so much so that the lower surface is almost concealed from view.

Flowers: White to pink with five spreading petals, small, only about 6 mm across when fully opened; borne in clusters at the leaf axils; appearing year-round.

Fruit: A small, fleshy, usually white drupe, 4 - 6 mm long.

Distinguishing Marks: Most easily confused with bay cedar (*Suriana maritima*), distinguished from it by having darker leaves with revolute margins.

Distribution: Coastal strand, usually in salty soils; restricted primarily to the lower Keys, especially Big Pine Key.

Comment: Listed as endangered by the Florida Department of Agriculture.

RUTACEAE — RUE FAMILY

The Rutaceae, or rue family, is a rather large family of about 150 genera and perhaps as many as 1600 species, most of which are trees and shrubs. Sometimes referred to as the citrus family, it is widely distributed in the tropical and temperate regions of the world but is most abundant in tropical America, South Africa, and Australia. Members of the family are distinguished by secretory cavities in their stems, leaves, flowers, and fruits. The punctate dots caused by these cavities are often visible to the naked eye from the underside of the leaves when they are held up to the light. The cavities contain volatile, aromatic oils and help in differentiating the Rutaceae from such closely related families as the Simaroubaceae, Meliaceae, Zygophyllaceae, and Burseraceae. As might be expected, members of the genus *Citrus* are among the family's more economically important species.

Torchwood

Page 308

Amyris elemifera L.

Form: Evergreen shrub or tree with light brown bark, to about 5 m tall.

Leaves: Opposite, compound; leaflets three (rarely five) in number, quite limber and drooping, 2.5 - 7.5 cm long, light green, ovate to ovate-lanceolate, with entire margins, long-pointed tips, and glandular dots on the upper surfaces.

Flowers: Tiny, white, borne in clusters up to 5 cm long; appearing year-round.

Fruit: A purple to black, ovoid drupe with obvious glandular dots, about 0.5 - 1 cm long.

Distinguishing Marks: Most easily recognized by drooping, light green, opposite, and relatively small compound leaves.

Distribution: Primarily found in wet coastal hammocks; from about the center part of the state southward along the east coast and throughout the Keys.

Comment: Two species of torchwood are often listed as part of Florida's flora. Both are extremely similar in appearance. The balsam torchwood (*A. balsamifera* L.) is generally considered to be the more restricted of the two species and was purportedly found in hammocks of Dade County and perhaps other locations in the lower peninsula, whereas *A. elemifera* is more widespread and extends from the Keys up the eastern coast to about the center of the state. *A. balsamifera* is said to more commonly have five, rather than three, leaflets, and to have leaflets predominantly more than, rather than predominantly less than, 5 cm long. According to Dan Austin, professor of biology at Florida Atlantic University, some claim that

Torchwood
Amyris elemifera

the presence of balsam torchwood in Florida is questionable and might actually be attributed to a misidentification of *A. elemifera*. The present species takes its specific name from Mexican elemi, a fragrant resin used in the production of both medicine and varnish.

Key Lime

Photo 248

Citrus aurantifolia (Christm.) Swingle

Form: Small, shrubby evergreen to about 5 m tall with thorny branches; sometimes treelike.
Leaves: Alternate, simple, ovate-elliptic, shiny, dark green, aromatic, 5 - 8 cm long, margins crenate, petioles often conspicuously but narrowly winged (a character that is common to many members of the *Citrus* genus).
Flowers: White, with four or five petals and up to 25 stamens but only one pistil; appearing in late spring.
Fruit: Rounded, 2.5 - 5 cm in diameter, turning from green to yellow as it ripens; maturing from late fall to spring.
Distinguishing Marks: Leaves similar to those of *C. aurantium*, distinguished from it by geographic range.
Distribution: Naturalized in coastal hammocks of southern Florida and the Keys.
Landscape Use: The key lime is sometimes grown in suburban lawns, primarily for its fruit.
Comment: The Key lime actually comes from southeastern Asia and is not native to any part of Florida. However, it is naturalized in the Keys and has been made famous by the tart-tasting Key lime pie in which it is the main ingredient. A large number of other nonnative members of the *Citrus* genus are also present in Florida and are often cultivated and sometimes escaped. These include the citron (*C. medica* L.), grapefruit (*C. paradisi* Macf.), lemon (*C.*

limon [L.] Burm.), sweet orange (*C. sinensis* [L.] Osbeck), pummello (*C. grandis* [L.] Osbeck), and tangerine (*C. reticulata* Blanco).

Sour Orange or Seville Orange
Citrus aurantium L.

Form: Evergreen shrub or small tree to about 6 m tall, sometimes bearing sharp spines along the twigs.

Leaves: Alternate, simple, entire, elliptic to ovate, 5.5 - 12 cm long, 3 - 10 cm wide, often bearing a conspicuous wing on either side of the petiole (a character that is common to many members of the *Citrus* genus).

Flowers: White, radially symmetrical, fragrant, borne in small, axillary clusters, petals numbering four to eight; appearing in spring.

Fruit: Like an orange, orange to reddish orange in color, 6 - 9 cm in diameter, rough on the surface and with a bitter taste.

Distinguishing Marks: Most easily recognized by the combination of conspicuously winged petiole and large, orangelike fruit; leaves similar to those of *C. aurantifolia* pictured in Photo 248.

Distribution: Cultivated but naturalized in many parts of the state; found growing wild in coastal shell middens of the more northern parts of the state, and hammocks of the southern peninsula.

Landscape Use: Commonly cultivated.

Comment: Though the seville orange is widespread across much of central and southern Florida and is not difficult to find, it is not native. Its fruit is acidic and bitter to the taste and has a thick rind and hollow core. Also see comment for *C. aurantifolia*, above.

Orange Jessamine or Orange Jasmine   Page 310, Photo 249
Murraya paniculata (L.) Jackson

Form: Evergreen shrub or small tree to about 6 m tall; stems with scattered hairs.

Leaves: Alternate, pinnately compound with three to nine leaflets; leaflets ovate to obovate, predominantly 2 - 5 cm long; aromatic when bruised.

Flowers: White, fragrant, 1 - 2.5 cm long, with pointed petals.

Fruit: An attractive, rounded, bright red berry, 1 - 1.5 cm long.

Distinguishing Marks: The pinnately compound, alternate leaves with three to nine smallish leaflets and fragrant flowers offer the best clue to this plant's identity.

Distribution: Native to Southeast Asia, now escaped from cultivation and very occasional in a few hammocks of Dade County.

Landscape Use: Used primarily as a hedge plant or background tree in south Florida gardens; tolerates full sun or moderate shade. Listed as a Category II pest plant by the Florida Exotic Pest Plant Council and not recommended for further landscape use.

Trifoliate Orange or Mock Orange
Poncirus trifoliata

Orange Jessamine or Orange Jasmine
Murraya paniculata

Trifoliate Orange or Mock Orange

Page 310, Photo 250

Poncirus trifoliata (L.) Raf.

Form: Deciduous shrub or small tree to about 7 m tall with conspicuous, typically green, sharp-pointed thorns along the twigs.

Leaves: Alternate, compound, with three leaflets and conspicuously winged petioles; leaflets obovate with minutely crenate margins, to about 8.5 cm long.

Flowers: White, rotate, conspicuous, 3 - 6 cm wide, with five to seven petals; appearing in spring.

Fruit: Yellow and appearing orangelike, 4 - 5 cm in diameter.

Distinguishing Marks: Distinguished from all other species by the combination of trifoliolate leaves with winged petioles, bright green stems, and sharp axillary thorns.

Distribution: Cultivated and occasionally escaped along woodland borders, and fence- and hedgerows in northern Florida; sometimes found in woodlands.

Wafer Ash, Hop Tree, Stinking Ash, Skunk Bush

Page 311

Ptelea trifoliata L.

Form: Small, spreading, deciduous shrub or small tree to about 7.5 m tall with light brown to reddish-brown, strongly scented bark.

Leaves: Alternate, compound, with long petioles; leaflets typically three in number but sometimes five, varying considerably in size and shape, exhibiting a musky odor when crushed; terminal leaflet elliptic to oval, margins entire to sometimes crenate or serrate; lateral leaflets ovate to lanceolate, typically inequilateral on either side of the central vein.

Flowers: Greenish white, borne in a widely branched panicle near the end of the branchlets;

Wafer Ash, Hop Tree, Stinking Ash, Skunk Bush
Ptelea trifoliata

appearing in spring.

Fruit: A flattened, winged samara; samaras borne at the ends of branches in rounded clusters; each samara to about 2 cm wide.

Distinguishing Marks: Most easily recognized by alternate, trifoliolate leaves with long petioles, and the waferlike fruit which gives the plant its common name; leaves superficially similar to those of bladdernut (*Staphylea trifolia*) but being borne alternate rather than opposite, and by the terminal leaflet being short- or unstalked.

Distribution: Bluffs and rich woodlands across northern Florida, southward to about Orange County.

Landscape Use: Does best in well-drained soil with a limestone subsurface but will also tolerate rich soil. The fruiting clusters make the plant an important center of garden conversation during the late spring fruiting period.

Comment: The fruit of this tree was once used as a substitute for hops in brewing beer, hence one of its common names. It was also used medicinally in the treatment of fevers and digestive irregularities.

Prickly Ash or Toothache Tree

Zanthoxylum americanum Mill.

Form: Generally a deciduous shrub, rarely a small, slender tree to a maximum height of about 10 m; branches with sharp thorns.

Leaves: Alternate, pinnately compound, 15 - 20 cm in overall length, rachis bearing sharp prickles; leaflets numbering 5 - 11, pubescent on their lower surfaces, ovate to oval, 1.5 - 6 cm long, 1.5 - 2 cm wide, margins entire to crenate.

Flowers: Borne in small, axillary clusters, petals green with red tips; male and female flowers borne on separate plants.

Distinguishing Marks: The leaves and thorns are similar to those of *Z. clava-herculis*; the present species may be distinguished from the latter plant by having thorns primarily in pairs at nodes along the stem rather than scattered between the stem nodes.

Distribution: Mostly a tree of more northern climes; known in Florida only from limited locations in Gadsden and Jackson Counties, and one station in Levy County.

Comment: Listed as endangered by the Florida Department of Agriculture. The scientific name *Zanthoxylum* derives from the combination of the Greek words *zanthos*, or yellow, and *xylum*, or wood, because of the color of the lumber of plants of this genus.

Prickly Ash or Hercules'-Club   Page 313
Zanthoxylum clava-herculis L.

Form: Deciduous shrub or tree to about 17 m tall with a short, often thorny trunk and rounded crown.

Leaves: Alternate, deciduous, pinnately compound, 10 - 30 cm in overall length, rachis with sharp prickles; leaflets commonly numbering seven to nine, but sometimes numbering to nearly 20, broadly lanceolate, typically inequilateral on either side of the central vein, dark green above, glabrous, 2.5 - 7 cm long, margins crenate.

Flowers: Greenish yellow and borne in long clusters at the ends of branches; appearing in spring and summer.

Fruit: Small, dry, rounded, splitting along only one side when mature.

Distinguishing Marks: Distinguished from *Z. americanum* by having prickles mostly between stem nodes rather than in pairs at stem nodes.

Distribution: Hammocks, wet woods, sand dunes, shell middens, usually near the coast; throughout northern Florida, southward to about Hendry and Dade Counties.

Landscape Use: Potentially a shade tree; the thorns are sharp and irritating to the skin.

Comment: The common name, toothache tree, probably derived from the purported folk use of this plant in alleviating the pain of toothaches in children. Chewing the bark of these plants tends to deaden the tongue and increase the natural flow of saliva and also has the effect of a mild stimulant.

Biscayne Prickly Ash   Photo 251
Zanthoxylum coriaceum A. Rich. in Sagra

Form: Evergreen shrub or tree to about 7 m tall, seedlings usually very thorny with sharp prickles on the branches, older plants usually thornless.

Leaves: Alternate, pinnately compound, 6 - 20 cm in overall length; leaflets usually even pinnate in two to eight pairs, leathery, obovate to elliptic, 2.5 - 6 cm long, 1.5 - 2.5 cm wide, margins entire, apices rounded.

Flowers: Yellow, tiny, borne year-round in long, many-flowered clusters.

Distinguishing Marks: Distinguished as the only member of its genus in Florida with usually even-pinnate leaves.

Distribution: Uncommon to rare in Atlantic coastal hammocks from about Brevard County southward.

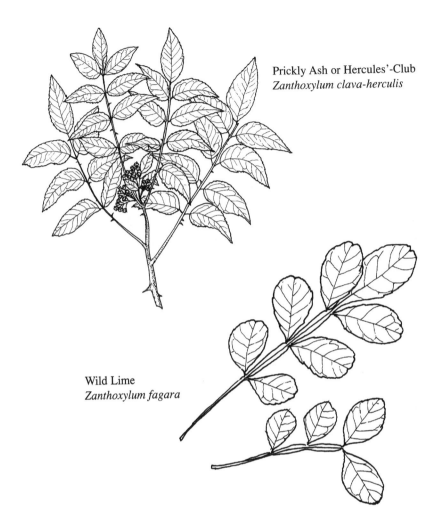

Prickly Ash or Hercules'-Club
Zanthoxylum clava-herculis

Wild Lime
Zanthoxylum fagara

Wild Lime

Page 313

Zanthoxylum fagara (L.) Sarg.

Form: Evergreen shrub or tree to about 10 m tall with sharp spines along the twigs.

Leaves: Alternate, pinnately compound, with a conspicuously winged rachis; leaflets commonly numbering seven to nine but sometimes as many as 15, obovate to ovate, 1 - 3 cm long, 0.5 - 1.5 cm wide, margins crenate on at least the distal half of the leaflet.

Flowers: Yellow green, very small, appearing in spring.

Fruit: A dry, black, shiny seed in a brownish husk, appearing in summer and fall.

Distinguishing Marks: Distinguished from other members of its genus and most other species by the comparatively small leaflets in conjunction with the winged petiole and rachis.

Distribution: Hammocks from about Hernando, Orange, and Brevard Counties southward.

SALICACEAE — WILLOW FAMILY

The willows belong to the family Salicaceae, a widespread association of mostly temperate and north-temperate trees and shrubs, a few of which are found as far north as the edges of the tundra. The male and female flowers of all species are borne on separate individuals.

There are between 400 and 500 species of willows worldwide, all of which are assigned to the genus *Salix*. Florida's members of this extensive family are relatively few in number and exist at the southern limits of the family's more generally northern distribution. There are only five willow species found in Florida, only one of which is classified strictly as a shrub. Of these five, two are common, two are local in occurrence, and one is quite rare. The black willow (*S. nigra* Marsh.), which is a tree, is the only of Florida's species that is not described below.

The genus name *Salix* derives from two Celtic words meaning near water. This name reflects the extreme sensitivity to soil moisture displayed by many willow species. During droughts, willows often conserve energy by becoming dormant and may even lose some of their foliage. When rain returns, however, they recapture their normal vitality and once again put out new leaves. Because of this adaptation, they are also one of the most resilient trees after hurricane-produced defoliation.

Coastal Plain or Carolina Willow
Salix caroliniana Michx.

Photo 252

Form: This is a small, deciduous tree to about 10 m tall in most cases, particularly in the more northern parts of the state; however, in south Florida it is often shrublike, densely vegetated, and bushy.

Leaves: Alternate, simple, lanceolate, variable in size to about 20 cm (typically 6 - 14 cm) long and up to 3.5 cm (typically 1 - 3 cm) wide, about 12 times as long as wide, margins finely toothed, lower surfaces whitish.

Flowers: Male flowers borne in attractive catkins near the ends of branches, each catkin greenish yellow, 2 - 9 cm long, arising in early to midspring with the new leaves.

Fruit: A capsule, typically 4 - 6 mm long but variable.

Distinguishing Marks: Leaves similar in general outline to those of black willow (*S. nigra*, not described here), distinguished from this latter species by being strongly glaucous or grayish-white beneath (rather than green); the ranges of these two plants overlap in the Big Bend from about Walton to Jefferson Counties; specimens found west of Walton County are probably *S. nigra*.

Distribution: Florida's most widely distributed willow; from about Walton County eastward and throughout the rest of the peninsula; often found near flowing water or in very moist areas.

Heart-Leaved Willow
Salix eriocephala Michx.

Page 315, Photo 253

Form: Deciduous shrub or small shrubby tree, sometimes reaching 6 m or so in height in its Florida locations.

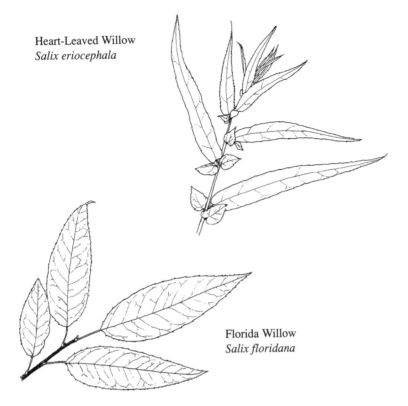

Heart-Leaved Willow
Salix eriocephala

Florida Willow
Salix floridana

Leaves: Alternate, simple, lanceolate, dark green above, pale and silvery gray below, 8 - 15 cm long, 2 - 3 cm wide, margins finely toothed, petioles 5 - 8 mm long; stipules conspicuous, clasping, persistent, rounded, and leaflike.

Flowers: Appearing in spring before the new leaves and borne in conspicuous woolly catkins.

Fruit: A capsule, 7 - 9 mm long.

Distinguishing Marks: Distinguished from other willows with similar leaves by having leaves with cordate or heart-shaped bases in conjunction with comparatively large, rounded, persistent stipules.

Distribution: Wet areas, alluvial woods, along stream banks; found in Florida only in a very few locations in Gadsden and Jackson Counties.

Comment: Listed as endangered by the Florida Department of Agriculture.

Florida Willow

Page 315, Photo 254

Salix floridana Chapm.

Form: Shrub or small deciduous tree to about 4 m tall.

Leaves: Alternate, simple, elliptic, usually widest near the middle, bases broadly rounded, normally 8 - 16 cm long, 3 - 5 cm wide, margins more nearly serrate than finely toothed as in other *Salix* species.

Flowers: Male and female flowers borne in separate catkins.

Fruit: A capsule, 6 - 7 mm long.

Distinguishing Marks: Distinguished from other of Florida's willows by having elliptic to oblong, rather than narrowly lanceolate, leaves, and with more nearly serrate, rather than finely toothed, margins (particularly large-leaved specimens of the much more common *S. caroliniana* may potentially be confused with this species), and by being found mostly near spring runs.

Distribution: Rare and local in wet areas along spring runs of Jefferson, Columbia, Levy, Lake, and perhaps other northeastern counties.

Comment: Listed as threatened by the Florida Department of Agriculture.

Small Pussy Willow, Dwarf Gray Willow, Prairie Willow
Salix humilis Marsh.

Photo 255

Form: Slender, deciduous shrub to about 3 m tall; leaves often held on the stem at an acute angle, hence pointing upward.

Leaves: Alternate, simple, oblanceolate to narrowly spatulate, 1.5 - 10 cm long, 0.5 - 2 cm wide; margins undulate or with obscure teeth (better seen with magnification); lower surfaces conspicuously grayish due to dense pubescence.

Flowers: Borne in globular catkins along naked wood before new leaf growth; male catkins to about 1 cm long, female catkins to about 3.5 cm long; appearing in spring.

Fruit: A capsule, 7 - 12 mm long.

Distinguishing Marks: The erectly held, narrow, oblanceolate leaves with grayish under-surfaces are diagnostic.

Distribution: Ditches, wet roadsides, wet flatwoods, pond margins, bogs; central Panhandle to about the Suwannee River.

SAPINDACEAE — SOAPBERRY FAMILY

The Sapindaceae, or soapberry family, is a large family of about 150 genera and 2,000 species. It is most widely represented in the tropical and subtropical regions of the world. The common name of the family refers primarily to members of the genus *Sapindus*, a collection of about 13 species, three of which are native to the United States. The name derives from the presence of saponin in the soft pulp of the plants' fruits. Solutions made from this pulp produce a lather much like commercially manufactured soap and have been used as detergents in some tropical countries. However, while the several species of *Sapindus* are most often associated with this attribute, saponins are present in all members of the family.

Florida Cupania

Photo 256

Cupania glabra Sw.

Form: Evergreen shrub or small tree to about 15 m tall, with smooth, splotchy, gray and brown, closely striated bark that is very similar to that of the related inkwood (*Exothea paniculata*).

Leaves: Alternate, compound; leaflets numbering 5 to 15, oblong with rounded tips and coarsely toothed margins, 6 - 18 cm long, 2.5 - 8 cm wide, dark shiny green above, typically borne upright along the rachis, thus each pair of leaflets forming the shape of a V.

Flowers: White, borne in long, branched clusters and appearing in the fall.

Fruit: A three-lobed, leathery capsule, 1.2 - 2 cm long.

Distinguishing Marks: Distinguished from soapberry (*Sapindus saponaria*) by lacking a winged rachis, from both Mexican alvaradoa (*Alvaradoa amorphoides*) and bitterbush (*Picramnia pentandra*), which also have pinnately compound leaves, by occurring only in the Keys and by having coarsely toothed leaflets.

Distribution: Common member of the flora of Jamaica, Cuba, and the West Indies but rare in Florida; exclusively in hammocks of the lower Keys, especially Big Pine Key.

Comment: Listed as endangered by the Florida Department of Agriculture.

Varnish Leaf or Florida Hop Bush

Photo 257

Dodonaea viscosa (L.) Jacq.

Form: Low, evergreen shrub or small tree to about 3 m tall, typically a shrub in the pinelands, sometimes a tree in hammocks; bark of mature plants gray and shaggy, exfoliating in strips.

Leaves: Alternate, simple, narrowly to widely obovate and quite variable depending upon the plant's geographic location (see comment below), entire, 2.5 - 15 cm long, 0.5 - 4 cm wide, surfaces yellowish green and sticky, often with a scaly texture and appearing varnished, hence its common name.

Flowers: Yellowish green, borne in small clusters at the tips of leafy branches; appearing summer and fall.

Fruit: A distinctive three-winged and three-locular capsule, 0.6 - 2.5 cm long.

Distinguishing Marks: Most easily recognized by leaf shape in conjunction with the three-winged (or occasionally four-winged) fruit.

Distribution: Hammocks and pinelands; from Hillsborough and Pinellas Counties southward, most common in the southernmost peninsula and the Keys.

Comment: Varnish leaf is an outlier species of a primarily Australian genus. Of the 60 species within the genus, all but five are restricted to the Australian continent. In Florida, varnish leaf displays several different leaf forms. According to Roger Hammer, those in the pine rocklands of the southern mainland have comparatively long, narrow, pointed leaves; those in the Florida Keys have shorter, blunt leaves that often have an indented leaf tip; and those along the coastal mainland and on sand barrier islands, such as Key Biscayne, have leaves that are much larger than either of the other two populations. Those shown in Photo 257 were found on North Key Largo.

Inkwood

Photo 258

Exothea paniculata (Juss.) Radlk.

Form: Sometimes shrublike, more often a small or medium-sized evergreen tree to about 15 m tall.

Leaves: Alternate, compound; leaflets usually four in number (rarely six, typically two on younger plants), entire, 5 - 12.5 cm long, apices rounded or slightly notched, upper surfaces dark, shiny green.

Flowers: White, five petaled, borne in terminal or axillary clusters, appearing January to April.

Fruit: Berrylike, fleshy, red at first, turning purplish black at maturity, 8 - 12 mm in diameter, ripening in June and July.

Distinguishing Marks: Recognized as the only south Florida shrub or tree with pinnately compound leaves and only four leaflets (as opposed to the bipinnately compound leaves with four leaflets of the three leguminous species in the genus *Pithecellobium*).

Distribution: Hammocks and shell mounds; Volusia County southward along the east coast and throughout the southern peninsula and the Keys.

Comment: Inkwood's common name probably derives either from its sap, which turns black upon exposure to the air, or from its black, berrylike fruits which were once crushed to allow the juice to be used as ink.

White Ironwood

Page 318

Hypelate trifoliata Sw.

Form: Evergreen shrub or tree to 13 m in height with smooth, reddish-gray bark.

Leaves: Alternate, palmately compound; leaflets three in number, all arising from the same place on the leaf stalk, 3.5 - 7 cm long, 1.5 - 3.5 cm wide, shiny green above.

Flowers: Small, white, borne in few-flowered, axillary clusters, appearing April through July.

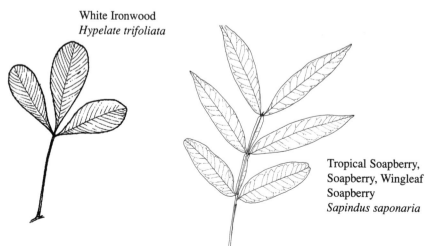

White Ironwood
Hypelate trifoliata

Tropical Soapberry, Soapberry, Wingleaf Soapberry
Sapindus saponaria

Fruit: A rounded, black, fleshy drupe, 8 - 12 mm in diameter.

Distinguishing Marks: Recognized as the only south Florida shrub or tree with palmately trifoliolate leaves.

Distribution: Rare in hammocks of Everglades National Park and the Keys.

Comment: This plant has the distinction of being the sole member of its genus. It is listed as threatened by the Florida Department of Agriculture and is extremely difficult to find in the wild. It generally occurs only in very small populations.

Tropical Soapberry, Soapberry, Wingleaf Soapberry
Sapindus saponaria L.   **Page 318**

Form: Most often a deciduous tree to about 15 m tall; flowering and fruiting when of low, shrublike stature, hence included here.

Leaves: Alternate, compound, with a conspicuously winged rachis; leaflets opposite or sub-opposite, six to eight and typically even in number, lanceolate, 5 - 18 cm long, margins entire.

Flowers: Tiny, white, borne in loosely branched clusters at the tips of branches, appearing from early summer into the fall.

Fruit: Rounded, brown to yellowish, leathery, drupelike, 1 - 2 cm in diameter; seed black and poisonous.

Distinguishing Marks: Distinguished from all other south Florida trees with compound leaves by the combination of winged rachis and eight or less, typically even numbered and pointed, leaflets.

Distribution: Hammocks and coastal scrubby vegetation; Lee County southward and throughout the Keys.

Landscape Use: Sometimes planted as a shade tree in parts of its range; does well in areas near salt water. The fruit of this species is sometimes used as a substitute for soap, and its seeds are sometimes fashioned into attractive necklaces. Though poisonous, the seeds are said to have medicinal properties for treatment of rheumatism. They are also sometimes crushed and used as a fish poison.

Comment: A second soapberry (*S. marginatus* Willd.) is also present but uncommon throughout north Florida and southward to about Lee County. It is quite similar to the present species but generally has more leaflets and lacks wings along the central leaf stalk. The two may be most easily distinguished by geographic range except near Lee County where their ranges coincide. It should be noted that some authorities (Wunderlin, et. al., 1985) have suggested that the two should be treated as a single species.

SAPOTACEAE — SAPODILLA OR SAPOTE FAMILY

The sapodilla or sapote (pronounced sa-POTE-ee) family includes six genera in Florida, most of which are confined to the state's southern counties. Worldwide, the family consists of about 600 species in more than 40 genera, all of which are woody trees or shrubs, and all of which occur primarily in the tropics. Only the genus *Bumelia* is found in the United States outside of peninsular Florida. The family is well known for several tropical dessert fruits, some of which are cultivated in Florida. The sapodilla (*Manilkara zapota* [L.] Royen), marmalade plum (*Pouteria mammosa* [L.] Cronq.), egg fruit (*Pouteria campechiana* H.B.K.), and star apple (*Chrysophyllum cainito* L.) are all grown in the Keys or the southern peninsula.

Species of the genus *Bumelia* appear to be in a state of taxonomic flux. Dr. Loran Anderson, botanist and curator of the herbarium at Florida State University, reports that the new name for the genus should be *Sideroxylon*. According to Anderson (personal communication, 1995),

> Linnaeus established *Sideroxylon* for some African species in 1753. In the second edition of his *Species Plantarum* he described some American species as *Sideroxylon*; Swartz later established the genus *Bumelia* and many botanists followed his position for many years. Pennington [1991] recently did a worldwide overview of the genera of the Sapotaceae and gave convincing argument that characteristics used to separate New World and Old World genera in this complex were not consistent; i.e., no set of characters could convincingly separate *Sideroxylon* and *Bumelia*. With *Sideroxylon* being the older generic name, it had precedence and Pennington made any necessary combinations to transfer those species of *Bumelia* that had never been called *Sideroxylon* into that genus. Most botanists that have reviewed Pennington's work agree with his wider view of *Sideroxylon* to include *Bumelia* (and some other American genera).

Though a new generic name for this genus will likely soon become widely accepted, the genus name *Bumelia* has been used here.

Alachua Buckthorn   Page 321

Bumelia anomala (Sarg.) R. B. Clark

Form: Tardily deciduous shrub, sometimes arborescent, not usually exceeding 3 m tall with thorny, crooked branches typical of many *Bumelia* species; mature shoots of the season with a definite pale-gray or silvery hue.

Leaves: Alternate, simple, entire, elliptic, 5 - 6 cm long, 3 - 4 cm wide, upper surfaces dark green and glabrous, lower surfaces densely covered with silvery pubescence that imparts a conspicuous and distinctive sheen.

Distinguishing Marks: Leaves similar in shape to those of *B. lanuginosa*, distinguished from it and other *Bumelia* by the combination of young stems being glabrous and lower surfaces of leaves being very conspicuously silvery pubescent.

Alachua Buckthorn
Bumelia anomala

Distribution: Rare and restricted to several small populations in Alachua, Marion, and St. Johns Counties, including near Alachua Sink and at Silver River State Park.

Saffron Plum
Bumelia celastrina HBK.

Page 322

Form: Small evergreen shrub or tree to about 6 m tall with slender, spreading branches.
Leaves: Alternate (but borne in fascicles and often appearing opposite), simple, slightly leathery, entire, oblanceolate, 1 - 4 cm long, 0.5 - 3 cm wide, quite variable in size from tree to tree, margins thick, lower surfaces pale, upper surfaces dull green.
Flowers: Small, white, with five petals, borne in clusters; appearing year-round.
Fruit: Black, 10 - 25 mm long, sweet, edible.
Distinguishing Marks: Distinguished from tough bumelia (*B. tenax*) by leaves being glabrous or only sparsely hairy below rather than densely pubescent, from smooth bumelia

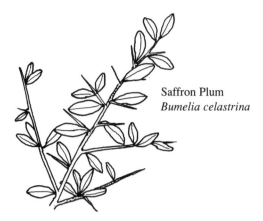

Saffron Plum
Bumelia celastrina

(*B. reclinata*) by having leathery leaves and by occurring in coastal hammocks rather than uplands and pinelands.

Distribution: Coastal hammocks and salt flats of the lower peninsula and the Keys.

Comment: A variety of this species, *B. celastrina* HBK var. *angustifolia* (Nutt.) R. W. Long, is also reported and is distinguished by much smaller leaves and shorter thorns.

Gum Bumelia   Photo 259

Bumelia lanuginosa (Michx.) Pers.

Form: Shrub or small deciduous tree, 6 - 12 m tall with thorny, crooked branches typical of many *Bumelia* species.

Leaves: Alternate but closely clustered, simple, entire, typically oblanceolate, 2 - 8 cm long (sometimes longer), 1 - 4 cm wide, upper surfaces pubescent at first, becoming dark green and shiny, lower surfaces densely pubescent with dull, rusty- (or sometimes whitish-) colored hairs and feltlike to the touch, apices rounded.

Flowers: Small, borne in clusters in the leaf axils; appearing midspring to early summer.

Fruit: A black, fleshy, berry, 6 - 15 mm long.

Distinguishing Marks: Distinguished from other *Bumelia* species by the combination of pubescent stems and copious covering of rusty-brown pubescence on the lower surfaces of leaves.

Distribution: Dry, often sandy, upland woods throughout north Florida and sparingly southward to about Pinellas County.

Buckthorn   Page 323

Bumelia lycioides (L.) Pers.

Form: Small, tardily deciduous shrub or tree, ordinarily to about 9 m tall but potentially reaching heights of 20 m, with thorny, crooked, to slightly zigzag branches typical of many *Bumelia* species.

Leaves: Alternate, simple, entire, oblong-elliptic to elliptic, 8 - 15 cm long, 1 - 5 cm wide,

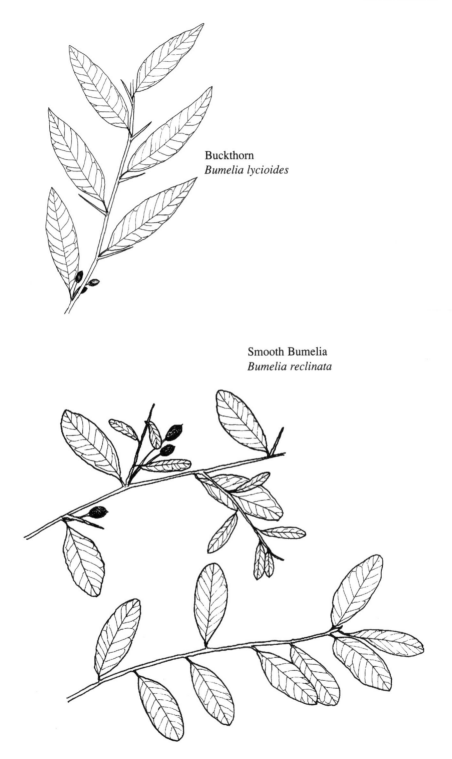

Buckthorn
Bumelia lycioides

Smooth Bumelia
Bumelia reclinata

upper surfaces bright green and glabrous.

Flowers: Small, bell shaped, borne in clusters; appearing mostly in April.

Fruit: A black, egg-shaped berry, 1 - 2 cm long, about 1 cm in diameter.

Distinguishing Marks: Distinguished from other *Bumelia* species by having stems and both leaf surfaces glabrous in conjunction with longer leaves exceeding 8 cm in length; larger leaves look similar to those of sourwood (*Oxydendrum arboreum*) but lack the latter's finely toothed margins.

Distribution: Known predominately from natural silt levees along the eastern bank of the Apalachicola River, and silty areas along the river's western side just south of U. S. 90 and the Jim Woodruff Dam.

Comment: Listed as threatened by the Florida Department of Agriculture.

Smooth Bumelia
Page 323

Bumelia reclinata (Michx.) Vent.

Form: Commonly a deciduous shrub, sometimes treelike in unburned pinelands of southern Florida, reaching heights of 5 m, branches often bearing thorns at the leaf axils, leafy shoots often thorn tipped.

Leaves: Alternate (but sometimes crowded at the tips of leafy shoots and appearing opposite or fascicled), simple, entire, oblanceolate to spatulate, 1 - 6 cm long, 0.4 - 2 cm wide, leaf surfaces glabrous, apices rounded.

Flowers: Small, white, appearing in late spring and early summer and borne in few- to many-flowered clusters.

Fruit: A shiny, black, elongated berry, 5 - 8 mm long.

Distinguishing Marks: Distinguished from other *Bumelia* by stems and upper surfaces of leaves glabrous in combination with the longer leaves usually being much shorter than 7 cm.

Distribution: Bluffs, ravines, and riverbanks; northern and central peninsula, southward generally to Highlands Hammock State Park but also reported from Dade County in Everglades National Park.

Bumelia rufotomentosa Small

Form: Clonal, tardily deciduous shrub, often forming thickets by underground runners; to about 1 m tall but often much shorter, many clones not exceeding about 3 dm tall; young stems with shaggy, rusty-red hairs.

Leaves: Alternate (but often held close together and appearing to be fascicled), elliptic to obovate to spatulate, 1.5 - 6 cm long, 0.5 - 3 cm wide; lower surfaces, especially of new leaves, densely reddish or rusty hairy; lower surfaces of older leaves sometimes with few to no hairs; a few leaves becoming nearly hairless below.

Flowers: Small, white, borne in clusters at the leaf axils.

Fruit: Ovoid, shiny black, 8 - 13 mm long, 8 - 12 mm in diameter.

Distinguishing Marks: This is not an easy plant to identify due to its similarity to at least two other members of the genus. The low stature, shiny and relatively long rusty pubescence of new stems and the lower surfaces of new leaves distinguish this species from many members of its genus. It is similar in some respects to *B. lanuginosa*, but may be most easily distinguished by its size and by the fact that it is often clonal with many low clones. As implied below, less hairy specimens are similar to *B. reclinata*.

Distribution: Sandy ridges and sandy, scrubby woodlands; limited in distribution and found sporadically in north and central Florida.

Comment: Some authorities, including Wunderlin (1982), do not consider this species distinct and place it in the synonymy of *B. reclinata*. As noted in the introduction to the Sapotaceae, above, Pennington's (1991) revision of the family placed all species of *Bumelia* into the genus *Sideroxylon*. This change resulted in the scientific name *Sideroxylon rufotomentosa* for a member of the genus that is not found in the United States. As a result, Herring and Judd (1995) have proposed the name *S. rufohirtum* Herring & Judd for the current species.

Willow Bustic or Bustic

Page 325

Bumelia salicifolia (L.) Sw.

Form: Shrub or small, thornless evergreen tree to about 9 m tall; flowers and fruits arising in clusters along leafless sections of branches.

Leaves: Alternate, simple, lanceolate, 7.5 - 13 cm long, tapering to a distinct petiole; margins entire but often wavy.

Flowers: Tubular, five-petaled, white, fragrant, short lived; appearing most prolifically in spring and early summer.

Fruit: A black, globular to oblong berry, to about 7 mm long.

Distinguishing Marks: Most easily recognized by the flowers and fruit, when present, being borne on the older, leafless portions of the branches and by new growth always being golden pubescent.

Distribution: Common in hammocks and the edges of pinelands; from Martin and Palm Beach Counties southward on the east coast, Fakahatchee Strand State Preserve southward on the west coast, throughout the Keys.

Comment: This plant is also seen listed as *Dipholis salicifolia* (L.) A. DC.

Willow Bustic or Bustic
Bumelia salicifolia

Tough Bumelia
Bumelia tenax

Tough Bumelia

Page 326, Photo 260

Bumelia tenax (L.) Willd.

Form: Thorny, evergreen shrub or small tree to about 8 m tall with reddish-brown, fissured bark.

Leaves: Alternate, simple, entire, oblanceolate, 2 - 7 cm long 0.5 - 3 cm wide; lower surfaces covered with dense, silvery, golden, coppery, or brownish pubescence, often contrasting sharply with the dark green upper surfaces.

Flowers: Small, white, appearing in spring and borne in clusters at the leaf axils.

Fruit: A black berry, inversely egg shaped, 10 - 14 mm long.

Distinguishing Marks: Distinguished from other *Bumelia* with pubescent leaves by pubescence of lower leaf surfaces being densely matted rather than just copious.

Distribution: Coastal dunes and interior scrub across northern Florida and southward to about the central peninsula; more common along the east coast, rather spottily distributed along the Gulf Coast to about Marco Island.

Comment: Small (1933) also described *Bumelia lacuum* Small, a scrub and sand hill species with close affinities to *B. tenax*. He distinguished between the two based upon the pedicel being longer than the fruit in *B. tenax* and shorter than the fruit in *B. lacuum*. Some authorities include this species within the synonymy of *B. tenax*. Others, especially Clark (1944) and Lakela (1963) believe the two are distinct species. Though Clark suggests that the two can be distinguished by the more shrublike habit of *B. lacuum* and the more treelike habit of *B. tenax*, the two are quite similar vegetatively and extremely difficult to separate without the presence of fruit.

Bumelia thornei Cronq.   **Photo 261**

Form: Sparsely to bushy-branched and thorny shrub ranging from about 1.5 to 6 m tall.

Leaves: Alternate, simple, entire, varying from oblanceolate to narrowly elliptic to nearly rounded; 1 - 7 cm long, 0.5 - 2.5 cm wide, with a short petiole; upper surfaces without hairs, lower surfaces loosely woolly hairy with grayish to rusty hairs.

Flowers: Individual flowers very small and inconspicuous, to about 3 mm long.

Fruit: A dull black, rounded berry, 8 - 10 mm long.

Distinguishing Marks: Distinguished from most north Florida wetland shrubs by thorny branches in conjunction with dark green, mostly oblanceolate leaves with woolly-pubescent lower surfaces; seemingly intermediate between *B. reclinata* and *B. lanuginosa*, though perhaps more similar to *B. lanuginosa*, differing from the latter in habitat and by having leaves that are darker green with pubescence of the lower surfaces being less feltlike to the touch and more grayish in color.

Distribution: This plant's main distribution is in Georgia; known in Florida from only two locations in Jackson County; found in drainages and other wet areas, typically where water stands during part of the year.

Comment: Recognized as a candidate for federal listing by the U. S. Fish and Wildlife Service. Named for Dr. Robert F. Thorne, who discovered it at three locations in Georgia in 1947. The plant is described as a much smaller shrub in its Georgia stations (not exceeding about 1.5 m tall) than it appears in at least one of its Florida stations.

Satin Leaf   Photo 262

Chrysophyllum oliviforme L.

Form: Shrub or, more often, a small, handsome evergreen tree to about 9 m tall with reddish-brown bark; branchlets with milky sap.

Leaves: Alternate, simple, oval, entire, 3 - 13 cm long, apices ending in abrupt points, upper surfaces dark green and smooth, lower surfaces covered by dense, velvety, copper-colored pubescence and contrasting sharply with upper surfaces.

Flowers: Tiny, white, with five petals; appearing year-round.

Fruit: A one-seeded berry resembling an olive, up to about 2 cm long and edible.

Distinguishing Marks: Not likely to be confused with any other Florida shrub or tree except, perhaps, for the cultivated and closely related star apple (*C. cainito* L.) which has larger, multiseeded fruits that are 5 - 8 cm in diameter.

Distribution: Hammocks of the Everglades and the Keys; formerly along the coast from about Brevard County southward but now mostly eliminated through poaching and urbanization.

Landscape Use: This plant does well as a free-standing specimen or as a border or background plant along fences; the sharp contrast between the coppery-colored and feltlike lower surfaces of leaves and the dark green color of the upper surfaces is an attractive feature.

Wild Dilly

Photo 263

Manilkara bahamensis (Baker) Lam & Meeuse

Form: Often a low, dense, salt-tolerant evergreen shrub, sometimes a small tree to about 13 m tall.

Leaves: Alternate but crowded near the ends of branches, leathery, dull grayish green, simple, elliptic, entire, 5 - 10 cm long, lower surfaces covered with brownish pubescence, apices conspicuously notched.

Flowers: Yellowish, arising in drooping clusters at the leaf axils; appearing most prolifically in spring and fall.

Fruit: Brownish, globular, to about 4 cm in diameter, edible.

Distinguishing Marks: Most easily recognized by pale, grayish-green leaves clustered near branch tips and brownish, rounded fruit.

Distribution: Common in the coastal zone and along the edges of coastal hammocks of Cape Sable and the Keys.

SAXIFRAGACEAE — SAXIFRAGE FAMILY

This is a family of mostly perennial plants, many of which are shrubby. Several members of the family are used ornamentally, including several species of *Hydrangea* and *Philadelphus* in Florida. The family is quite large and is often divided into smaller subfamilies.

Climbing Hydrangea, Wood Vamp, Cowitch Vine

Page 329

Decumaria barbara L.

Form: Climbing, woody, deciduous vine; ascending the trunks of trees by means of aerial roots arising from the main stem.

Leaves: Opposite, simple, shiny dark green above, predominantly oval to ovate, 10 - 12 cm long, about 6 cm wide; petioles 1 - 3 cm long; margins entire, wavy, or toothed toward the apices.

Flowers: White, small, fragrant, borne in showy clusters at the ends of new shoots; clusters to about 10 cm across; appearing April to June.

Fruit: A ribbed, urn-shaped, greenish-brown capsule, 4 - 5 mm long.

Distinguishing Marks: The opposite, ovate leaves, aerial roots, and showy flower clusters help distinguish this species.

Distribution: Fairly common in swamps, along spring runs, in wet woodlands, and sometimes rich woodlands; throughout northern Florida, southward to the central peninsula.

Landscape Use: Difficult to transplant and probably not readily available from most nurseries; generally requires moist soil and shady conditions.

Climbing Hydrangea, Wood
Vamp, Cowitch Vine
Decumaria barbara

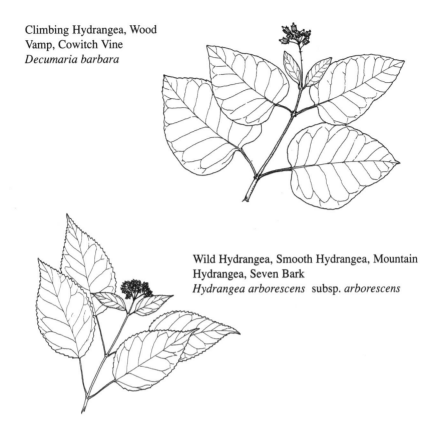

Wild Hydrangea, Smooth Hydrangea, Mountain
Hydrangea, Seven Bark
Hydrangea arborescens subsp. *arborescens*

Wild Hydrangea, Smooth Hydrangea, Mountain Hydrangea, Seven Bark

Page 329

Hydrangea arborescens L. subsp. *arborescens*

Form: Deciduous, understory shrub to about 2 m tall; bark peeling in sheets.

Leaves: Opposite, simple, oval to ovate, 7 - 20 cm long (commonly tending toward the middle of this range), to about 12 cm wide; margins definitely toothed.

Flowers: White, small, borne in showy, conspicuous clusters at the ends of branches; individual clusters 5 - 15 cm across; appearing in summer.

Fruit: A brown, ribbed capsule, 1 - 2 cm long.

Distinguishing Marks: No other low shrub of the central Panhandle has opposite, ovate leaves with long petioles, and such showy flower clusters; flower clusters similar to those of the shrubby dogwoods.

Distribution: Rich woods, bluffs; central Panhandle.

Landscape Use: An easily grown and very attractive species, especially for rich, shady places where a show of white is appropriate; does best in loose, fertile soil.

Comment: As one of its common names suggests, this plant is at the southern limit of its range. It is a well-known summer-flowering species in the southern Appalachians.

Oak-Leaf Hydrangea, Seven Bark, Graybeard
Hydrangea quercifolia

Oak-Leaf Hydrangea, Seven Bark, Graybeard

Hydrangea quercifolia Bartr. **Page 330, Photo 264**

Form: A large, multibranched, sometimes arching, deciduous shrub with peeling, buff- to orange-colored bark.

Leaves: Opposite, simple, yellowish green, to about 30 cm long, unlobed to more commonly with three to seven pointed lobes; margins widely but conspicuously toothed; petioles 10 - 15 cm long.

Flowers: Creamy white, with four large sepals, borne May to June in huge, showy clusters at the ends of branches; individual clusters 15 - 30 cm long.

Fruit: A ribbed, brown capsule.

Distinguishing Marks: The deeply lobed, yellowish-green leaves and showy flowers are diagnostic.

Distribution: Rich woods, calcareous slopes, ravines; from about the Ochlockonee River westward across the Panhandle.

Landscape Use: A very popular, easy-to-grow landscape plant for naturalistic settings or in shady wooded areas. It spreads easily and rapidly once established and blooms best when allowed to receive full morning sun. Its flowers are particularly showy and bring many comments from passersby.

Virginia Willow, Virginia Sweet Spire, Tassel-White, Sweetspire

Page 331

Itea virginica L.

Form: Deciduous (but fairly persistent in south Florida), somewhat vinelike shrub, with slender, arching stems; to about 2 m tall.

Leaves: Alternate, simple, predominantly long-elliptic (but varying considerably in both

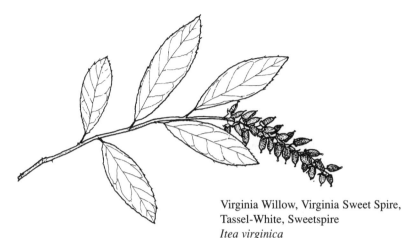

Virginia Willow, Virginia Sweet Spire,
Tassel-White, Sweetspire
Itea virginica

shape and size), typically 5 - 10 cm long, 3 - 4 cm wide; margins finely and minutely toothed, the latter visible without magnification.

Flowers: White, small, with five small petals and sepals; borne in showy, elongated clusters from the ends of the branches; appearing April to June.

Fruit: A hairy, cylindric, two-parted capsule, 2 - 7 mm long, the remains of which hang on the plant nearly the entire year until just before flowering.

Distinguishing Marks: Potentially and often confused with sweet pepperbush (*Clethra alnifolia*), with which it sometimes associates; distinguished by having leaf margins toothed from base to apex rather than predominantly above the middle, and by having mostly elliptic leaves rather than leaves mostly widest above the middle.

Distribution: Common in swamps, wet woods, along stream banks; throughout northern Florida southward to the lower peninsula.

Landscape Use: A very good wetland plant that also does relatively well in rich, drier sites. It spreads easily by underground runners, and new plants transplant easily; little care is required once established. *Itea* is most noticeable during its spring and early summer flowering period. Flowering is best if the plant receives full sun for at least part of the day. The leaves darken and change color in fall and winter.

Summer Dogwood, English Dogwood, Mock-Orange, Syringa
Photo 265
Philadelphus inodorus L.

Form: Arching, multistemmed, deciduous shrub to about 4 m tall.

Leaves: Opposite, simple, predominantly entire (some with very few dentations), oval to elliptic, 4 - 8 cm long, 3 - 4 cm wide; apices mostly long tapering or pointed, sometimes rounded.

Flowers: White, showy, with four spreading petals, similar at a glance to the flowering dogwood (*Cornus florida* L., not described here), hence one of the common names; appearing in late spring and early summer.

Fruit: An erect capsule.

Distinguishing Marks: The dogwoodlike flowers in early summer distinguish the plant.

Distribution: Calcareous hammocks; central Panhandle, predominantly Gadsden and Liberty Counties.

Landscape Use: An often-used species, especially along fences or as background for lower shrubs because of its long, erect, arching branches. It is most prized for its showy flowers and spreads easily once established. Several similar imported species have found popularity in the United States and are also often used in gardens and landscape designs.

Miccosukee Gooseberry
Photo 266

Ribes echinellum (Coville) Rehd.

Form: Low, bushy shrub with erect to spreading branches and sharp-pointed, often forked spines at the leaf nodes; spines to about 1.5 cm long; plant deciduous in summer with new leaf growth in fall.

Leaves: Alternate, simple, with three major lobes, each of which is toothed or minutely lobed, 1.5 - 6 cm wide; petioles 1 - 2 cm long; surfaces of newer leaves pubescent on both sides.

Flowers: Tubular, with five spreading sepals, greenish yellow; borne singly and pendently at the leaf axils; appearing February to March.

Fruit: A spiny, many-seeded berry, 1.5 - 2 cm in diameter.

Distinguishing Marks: The relatively small, palmately three-lobed, pubescent leaves with comparatively long petioles distinguish the species.

Distribution: Moist woods; known only from Jefferson County, Florida and McCormick County, South Carolina.

Comment: Listed as endangered by the Florida Department of Agriculture, and as federally threatened by the U. S. Fish and Wildlife Service. The genus *Ribes* is one of the few genera of the saxifrage family that is known for its economic importance. Though the population of the species represented in Florida is too small to be important, other members of the genus produce commercially valuable gooseberries as well as black, white, and red currants.

SCHISANDRACEAE — STAR VINE FAMILY

This is a small family with only two genera and about 50 species of glabrous, woody or herbaceous vines. Except for *Schisandra glabra*, the family is restricted almost exclusively to Asia and Malaysia. Florida's single species displays a sporadic and limited distribution in the southeastern United States.

Star-Vine, Bay Star Vine, Wild Sarsaparilla, Schisandra

Schisandra glabra (Brickell) Rehd.   **Page 333**

Form: A twining, climbing, or trailing, deciduous vine.

Leaves: Alternate, simple, oval to elliptic, 4 - 12 cm long, 2 - 6 cm wide; margins entire or with a few obscure dentations; petioles relatively long and slender.

Flowers: Greenish white outside, reddish inside, to about 1 cm wide, with five spreading petals; borne singly and pendently from the leaf axils; appearing in June.

Fruit: A red, ellipsoid berry.

Distinguishing Marks: The alternate, elliptic, longer than wide leaves, small pendent flowers, and twining habit distinguish this species in its preferred habitat.

Distribution: Rich woods and bluffs; Panhandle, essentially Jackson and Liberty Counties.

Comment: This is a primitive species that bears close relation to the anise family (Illiciaceae); it is listed as threatened by the Florida Department of Agriculture.

Star-Vine, Bay Star Vine,
Wild Sarsaparilla, Schisandra
Schisandra glabra

SIMAROUBACEAE — QUASSIA FAMILY

The quassia family consists of about 200 species in approximately 30 genera worldwide, most of which occur in the tropics. Only one species in each of three genera is native to southern Florida; only two of these are commonly regarded as shrubby during at least part of their life cycles.

Mexican Alvaradoa or Alvaradoa

Alvaradoa amorphoides Liebm.

Form: Shrub or small to medium-sized evergreen tree to about 15 m tall; fruiting when of shrub stature.

Leaves: Alternate, pinnately compound, 10 - 30 cm long; leaflets numbering to 41 per leaf, elliptic, entire, 1 - 2 cm long, less than 1 cm wide, arranged both alternately and oppositely along the rachis.

Flowers: Male and female flowers borne separately in long, hanging spikes, up to 40 cm long, normally appearing in early winter from about November through December.

Fruit: A compressed, winged, papery or leathery capsule.

Distinguishing Marks: Distinguished from other south Florida shrubs and trees by the combination of compound leaves with small, elliptic leaflets and hairy, jointed twigs; likely to be confused only with the necklace pod (*Sophora tomentosa*), but distinguished from it by occurring primarily within, rather than on the edges of, hammocks; nowhere do these two species occur together.

Distribution: Rare in tropical hammocks of Dade County, not found in the Keys.

Comment: The alvaradoa's precise taxonomic classification is somewhat obscure and has been subject to question. It was once placed with the Sapindaceae, or soapberry family. More recently, it has been shown to be closest in relationship to the genus *Picramnia* and is now generally considered to be part of the quassia family.

Bitterbush   **Page 335**

Picramnia pentandra Sw.

Form: Evergreen shrub, rarely reaching tree stature, potentially to about 6 m tall.

Leaves: Alternate, pinnately compound, 20 - 36 cm long, with or without terminal leaflets; leaflets elliptic to ovate, entire, numbering five to nine, arranged either alternately or oppositely along the rachis, 5 - 10 cm long, 2 - 5 cm wide, apices acuminate.

Flowers: Minute, green with a reddish tinge, less than 3 mm wide, borne in clusters, often appearing in summer from June to August, but appearing other times of the year as well, male and female flowers borne on separate plants.

Fruit: A fleshy berry, borne on slender red stalks, round to elliptic or oblong, 1 - 1.5 cm in diameter, turning from red to black at maturity.

Bitterbush
Picramnia pentandra

Distinguishing Marks: Superficially similar to young specimens of the paradise tree (*Simarouba glauca* DC., not described here) but differing from it by usually having fewer than nine leaflets.
Distribution: Hammocks and sandy soils of Dade County.

SOLANACEAE — POTATO OR NIGHTSHADE FAMILY

The Solanaceae constitute an important collection of food plants, including the potato (*Solanum tuberosum* L.) and the tomato (*Lycopersicum esculentum* Mill.), as well as *Nicotiana tabacum* L., the plant from which cigarette tobacco is made. Many members of the family are poisonous, but some are the source of medicinal drugs. Some authorities believe that the name nightshade derives from folk tales that portrayed members of the family as sinister and loving of the night. Others maintain that the name alludes to the narcotic or sleep-producing properties of certain of the family's berrylike fruits. The genus name *Solanum* derives from the Latin word "solamen," which translates as quieting. The family is probably best known to Florida's plant enthusiasts for the several herbaceous species of ground cherry (*Physalis* spp.) and nightshades (*Solanum* spp.), many of which are low-growing plants that produce attractive and interesting inflorescences.

Cayenne Pepper or Red Pepper   Photo 267
Capsicum annuum L.

Form: Erect herb or shrub to about 2 m tall, with smooth, branching stems.
Leaves: Alternate, entire, dark green, ovate, 1 - 3 cm long, apices acute to acuminate.
Flowers: White, rotate, to about 5 mm long, borne singly in leaf axils; appearing all year.
Fruit: A red, globose to elongated berry, typically borne erect, 8 - 12 mm long, having the appearance of a small pepper; fiery hot to the taste.
Distinguishing Marks: The pepperlike fruit is diagnostic.
Distribution: Hammocks; south Florida and the Keys.
Landscape Use: Often planted for the attractive flowers and fruit.

Day Jessamine   Photo 268
Cestrum diurnum L.

Form: Multi- and sometimes densely branched evergreen shrub to about 2 m tall, with smooth, often arching branches.
Leaves: Alternate, simple, entire, leathery, shiny green, oval or ovate to oblong, 5 - 11 cm long, 2 - 4.5 cm wide.
Flowers: Creamy white, petals recurved; borne in conspicuous clusters near the ends of branches and appearing all year; very fragrant during the day.
Fruit: A shiny, rounded, blue-black berry, 8 - 10 mm in diameter.
Distinguishing Marks: The shiny green leaves, conspicuous flower clusters, and shiny berries help distinguish the species; potentially confused with marlberry (*Ardisia escallonioides*), but having leaves generally shorter than 10 cm.
Distribution: Native of tropical America; escaped from cultivation in south Florida.
Landscape Use: This species has generally been planted as an evergreen shrub in the state's warmer, more tropical regions. It is listed as a Category I pest plant by the Florida Exotic Pest Plant Council, is very invasive, and is not recommended for landscape use.

Comment: The night jessamine (*C. nocturnum* L.) is also escaped in south and south central Florida; it is similar to day jessamine but has erect to spreading, rather than recurved, flower petals, and white fruit. Night jessamine is also a commonly used landscape and ornamental plant. Orange cestrum (*C. aurantiacum* Lindl.), with tubular, orange-yellow flowers, and purple cestrum (*C. elegans* [Brongn.] Schlechtend.), with pendent clusters of purplish flowers are sprawling, vinelike shrubs that are also available from nurseries and used as ornamentals in south Florida.

Christmas Berry or Matrimony Vine   Photo 269
Lycium carolinianum Walt.

Form: Bushy- to sparsely branched, tardily deciduous shrub to about 3 m tall; many of the smaller branches are tipped with thorns.
Leaves: Alternate, simple, without petioles, narrow throughout but wider toward the apex, fleshy and succulent, to about 2.5 cm long; giving off a musky odor when crushed.
Flowers: Blue or lavender to white, usually with four lobes, very attractive; appearing in fall.
Fruit: A shiny, bright red, rounded drupe, 8 - 15 mm long; appearing in winter, hence one of the common names.
Distinguishing Marks: The linear, fleshy leaves, typically blue flowers, and red fruit are diagnostic in the Christmas berry's preferred habitat.
Distribution: Beaches, shell middens, sandy shores, generally near salt or brackish waters; throughout the state's coastal areas, including the Keys.
Comment: The fruit of this species is attractive to birds.

Bahama Nightshade or Canker-Berry   Photo 270
Solanum bahamense L.

Form: An erect shrub to about 2 m tall; main stems hairy; branchlets smooth or prickly.
Leaves: Alternate, simple, lanceolate to oblong, commonly rough to the touch, 6 - 12 cm long; margins entire or wavy.
Flowers: Blue, star shaped with five spreading petals, about 1 cm across when open; borne in clusters with curved stalks.
Fruit: A red, rounded berry, 7 - 8 mm in diameter.
Distinguishing Marks: The blue flowers in conjunction with the curved stalks bearing the flower clusters help distinguish this species from other members of its genus.
Distribution: Hammocks or their edges, roadsides; south Florida and the Keys.
Landscape Use: The several species of *Solanum* described here are sometimes used as shrubs in urban lawns, landscapes, and gardens in the southern parts of the state; they are most prized for their brightly colored fruit.

Nightshade or Twinleaf Nightshade

Photo 271

Solanum diphyllum L.

Form: Unarmed shrub to at least 2 m tall; stems smooth.

Leaves: Alternate, simple, entire, lanceolate to elliptic, 6 - 8 cm long.

Flowers: White, about 1 cm across when open, borne in clusters at the ends of branches; appearing at any time of year.

Fruit: A smooth, rounded, rich-yellow to yellow-orange berry.

Distinguishing Marks: The comparatively short leaves, low stature, and rich-yellow berries distinguish this from the other woody members of the genus.

Distribution: Native to tropical America and sparingly naturalized in southern Florida.

Landscape Use: Listed as a Category II pest plant by the Florida Exotic Pest Plant Council and not recommended for landscape use.

Blodgett's Nightshade or Potato Tree

Photo 272

Solanum donianum Walpers

Form: Bushy-branched shrub to about 2 m tall.

Leaves: Alternate, simple, lanceolate to narrowly elliptic, grayish in color (due to dense, coarse pubescence), typically reflexed and U-shaped upward from the central vein, 5 - 15 cm long; margins entire but wavy.

Flowers: White, star shaped, with five spreading petals and conspicuous yellow stamens, 1 - 1.5 cm wide when open, borne in erect clusters at the ends of branches; appearing all year.

Fruit: Bright-red, rounded berries, borne in conspicuous clusters.

Distinguishing Marks: The coarse pubescence on the flowers and leaves, in conjunction with the commonly white (rarely bluish) flowers help distinguish this species from other woody members of the genus.

Distribution: Hammock edges and roadsides; south Florida and the Keys.

Landscape Use: See *S. bahamense*.

Potato Tree or Mullein Nightshade

Photo 273

Solanum erianthum D.Don

Form: Evergreen shrub or small tree to 5 m tall with thin, warty bark and densely pubescent branches.

Leaves: Alternate, simple, entire, oval to elliptic, light green, 10 - 30 cm long, 4 - 14 cm wide, both surfaces pubescent (the lower copiously so), margins often wavy.

Flowers: Borne in terminal clusters, star shaped with five white petals encircling showy, bright-yellow pollen sacs; appearing all year.

Fruit: Juicy, rounded, yellow, 1 - 2 cm in diameter.

Distinguishing Marks: Easily distinguished by pale-colored, relatively large leaves that are woolly to the touch, copiously covered with star-shaped hairs which require magnification to see clearly, leaves emitting a strong, tarlike odor when crushed; the closely related and similar canker-berry (*S. bahamense*) may be distinguished from the present species by having leaf surfaces that lack the woolly pubescence and are rough to the touch, and by having blue, rather than white, flower petals; the leaves of *S. donianum* are shorter.

Distribution: Thickets, waste places, edges of hammocks; from Brevard County southward on the east coast, Hillsborough County southward on the west coast, throughout the Keys.

Landscape Use: See *S. bahamense*.

Brazilian Nightshade
Solanum seaforthianum Andrews

Form: Woody, trailing vine or sprawling shrub; stems smooth to minutely pubescent (requires magnification) and unarmed.

Leaves: Alternate, pinnately compound, to about 13 cm long, commonly with nine leaflets; leaflets lanceolate with entire margins.

Flowers: Blue to lavender, about 2 cm wide, with five spreading petals, borne in long-stalked clusters; appearing all year.

Fruit: A bright red berry about 1 cm in diameter.

Distinguishing Marks: The compound leaves set this species apart from other woody members of the genus; the flowers identify it as part of the potato family.

Distribution: Well established in hammocks and disturbed sites in southern Florida.

Landscape Use: Typically used as a vine for the attractive flowers and fruit; useful along fences or to hide the sides of small buildings; prefers partial shade but tolerant of a wide range of soil conditions. This is a weedy species that easily escapes cultivation and can become a pest plant.

STAPHYLEACEAE — BLADDERNUT FAMILY
The bladdernut family is a primarily north-temperate collection of trees and shrubs, typically with opposite, compound leaves. The family contains 7 genera and about 50 species.

Bladdernut   **Page 340**
Staphylea trifolia L.

Form: Typically a deciduous shrub, sometimes reaching the stature of a small tree to about 8 m tall.

Leaves: Opposite, compound; leaflets three in number, elliptic, 3 - 10 cm long, 2 - 5 cm wide, margins finely serrate; terminal leaflet borne on a stalk to about 3 cm long.

Flowers: Showy, creamy white, bell shaped, borne in drooping clusters that are 5 - 10 cm long; appearing in June.

Fruit: Three parted, inflated, and bladderlike, similar in appearance to a Japanese lantern, 3 - 6 cm long.

Bladdernut
Staphylea trifolia

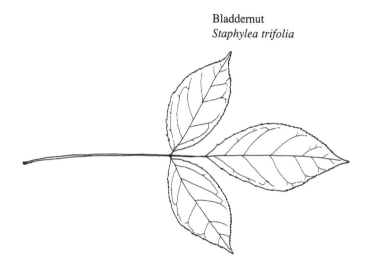

Distinguishing Marks: Leaves similar to those of wafer ash (*Ptelea trifoliata*), but distinguished by being borne opposite rather alternate, by the leaflet margins being finely serrate rather than crenate, and by the terminal leaflet being distinctly stalked.

Distribution: Floodplains and wooded slopes; rarely encountered, confined to rich woodlands along the upper Apalachicola River, a stream that is well known for harboring the southernmost remnants of a typically ice age flora.

Comment: The bladdernut is another of those species that exist in Florida at the extreme southern limits of their ranges. The main part of its distribution extends from northern Georgia to Minnesota, Wisconsin, and Quebec, with only a few scattered localities in the lower elevations of Mississippi and Alabama. The common name of the plant derives from its relatively large, bladderlike fruit pods which mature in the fall following a burst of showy spring flowers. Listed as threatened by the Florida Department of Agriculture. The genus name of this plant derives from the Greek word, *staphyle*, which means "a bunch of grapes."

STERCULIACEAE — STERCULIA FAMILY

The Sterculiaceae constitute a primarily tropical and subtropical family of about 1,000 species contained within approximately 70 genera. Only a single, shrubby member (*Waltheria indica*, which is described below) is found in Florida, and even it is only questionably included here. The Chinese parasol tree (*Firmiana simplex* [L.] W. F. Wright), a nonnative Asian species that was imported in the 1700s, is used sparingly in north Florida and is sporadically naturalized. This latter species sometimes takes on shrubby proportions but is more often thought of as a tree and is not fully described here. It is easily identified by its exceptionally large (to about 30 cm long and wide), deeply three- to seven-lobed leaves, long petioles to about 50 cm, and greenish trunk.

Waltheria or Buffcoat

Photo 274

Waltheria indica L.

Form: Variously described as a much-branched, coarse, subshrub, or shrubby herb; stems erect or reclining; potentially to about 1 m tall.
Leaves: Alternate, simple, ovate, 2 - 7 cm long, surfaces densely pubescent with star-shaped hairs; margins coarsely serrate to dentate.
Flowers: Yellow, small, borne in dense clusters at the leaf axils; petals only 4 - 6 mm long; appearing year-round.
Fruit: A small, hairy capsule about 2 mm long.
Distinguishing Marks: The dense flower clusters with tiny yellow flowers and coarsely serrate to dentate leaves help distinguish the species.
Distribution: Disturbed sites, open pinelands; generally in south-central and southern Florida and the Keys but also reported from the Panhandle and northern Florida.

STYRACACEAE — STORAX FAMILY

This is a family mostly of trees and shrubs that range in temperate regions as well as in the mountains of tropical regions. Members of the family have simple, alternate leaves.

Carolina Silverbell

Page 342

Halesia carolina L.

Form: Large shrub or small deciduous tree usually not exceeding 12 m in height, bark with yellowish to whitish streaks.
Leaves: Alternate, simple, elliptic, entire or finely serrate, 7 - 18 cm long, 3 - 7 cm wide, apices acuminate.
Flowers: White, bell shaped, 1 - 1.5 cm long, with petals fused from their bases to beyond their middles; appearing March and April.
Fruit: Four-winged, 2 - 4 cm long, less than 1.5 cm wide.
Distinguishing Marks: Distinguished from two-winged silverbell (*H. diptera*) by four-winged fruit and more narrowly elliptic leaves, from horse sugar (*Symplocos tinctoria*) by having stellate pubescence on the lower surfaces of leaves.
Distribution: Bluffs, hammocks, and floodplains; from the Panhandle to the north-central peninsula.
Landscape Use: This species and the next are spring-flowering shrubs or trees that make excellent additions to a native plant landscape. Both are fast growing, bear interesting fruit, and display showy leaf color in the fall. Both will also flower when young but become small trees that provide good shading for patios.

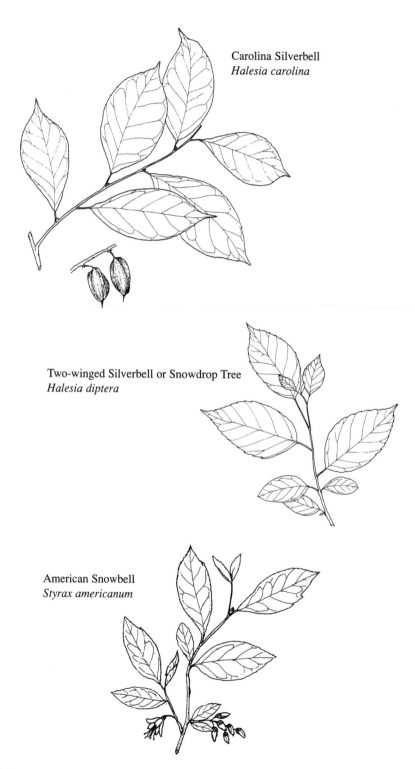

Carolina Silverbell
Halesia carolina

Two-winged Silverbell or Snowdrop Tree
Halesia diptera

American Snowbell
Styrax americanum

Two-winged Silverbell or Snowdrop Tree

Page 342, Photo 275

Halesia diptera Ellis

Form: Large shrub or small, attractive, deciduous tree normally not exceeding 10 m in height.

Leaves: Alternate, simple, unevenly dentate, oval, 6 - 16 cm long, 4 - 10 cm wide, apices abruptly pinched to a point.

Flowers: White, bell shaped, divided nearly to the base, to about 1.5 cm long, hanging in loose, pendant clusters; appearing in March and April.

Fruit: With two large wings.

Distinguishing Marks: Distinguished from Carolina silverbell (*H. carolina*) by two-winged, rather than four-winged, fruit, typically wider leaves, and by the bark lacking the yellowish to whitish streaks characteristic of the latter species.

Distribution: Bluffs, hammocks, and floodplain woodlands; northern Panhandle from about Escambia to Leon Counties.

Landscape Use: See comments for *H. carolina*, above. This species has showier flowers than the previous species.

American Snowbell

Page 342, Photo 276

Styrax americanum Lam.

Form: Deciduous shrub or small tree to about 5 m tall with thin, smooth, dark gray bark; typically displaying larger leaves at the tips of branches and smaller leaves proximally.

Leaves: Alternate, simple, elliptic to obovate, to about 8 cm long, 1 - 4 cm wide, margins very variable from entire to irregularly dentate, apices rounded or tipped with a short point.

Flowers: Normally borne individually in leaf axils, white, with petals typically recurved and spreading, stamens yellow and conspicuous; appearing in March and April.

Fruit: A pubescent capsule that resembles in shape the fruit of the hollies, 6 - 8 mm in diameter.

Distinguishing Marks: Distinguished from big leaf snowbell (*S. grandifolia*) by leaves not usually exceeding 8 cm in length and flowers borne individually.

Distribution: Wet places such as swamps, wet woods, edges of cypress ponds; throughout northern Florida southward to about Charlotte County on the west coast, Brevard County on the east coast.

Landscape Use: The American snowbell is rather nondescript and unnoticeable when not in bloom. At time of flowering, however, its fragrant white flowers make it a wonderful addition to shady, naturalistic landscapes. Though normally found in nature in wet areas, it also does well in rich soil in full sun or partial shade.

Big Leaf Snowbell
Styrax grandifolia

Big Leaf Snowbell

Page 344, Photo 277

Styrax grandifolia Ait.

Form: Deciduous, often multistemmed shrub or small tree not commonly exceeding about 6 m in height with thin, smooth, streaked, dark-brown bark.

Leaves: Alternate, simple, oval to obovate, margins entire to irregularly dentate (especially toward the apices), 6 - 18 cm long, 4 - 15 cm wide.

Flowers: White, borne in racemes, petals often spreading to occasionally recurved; appearing mostly in April.

Fruit: An oval capsule, 7 - 9 mm in diameter.

Distinguishing Marks: Distinguished from American snowbell (*S. americanum*) by leaves usually longer than 8 cm, and by having larger flowers which are borne in racemes.

Distribution: Bluffs, ravines, and well-drained woods; northern Panhandle from about the Ochlockonee River westward.

Landscape Use: Desirable characteristics are like those mentioned for *S. americanum*, above; however, this species also does well in dry, acid soil.

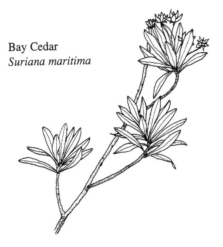

Bay Cedar
Suriana maritima

SURIANACEAE — BAY CEDAR FAMILY

This is a monotypic family, meaning that it has only a single genus and species. This single species was once included within the Simaroubaceae, or quassia family.

Bay Cedar

Page 345, Photo 278

Suriana maritima L.

Form: Typically an evergreen shrub but potentially a small tree to about 5 m tall.

Leaves: Alternate but densely crowded near the tips of branches and branchlets, linear, simple, entire, 1 - 6 cm long, to about 0.6 cm wide, apices rounded.

Flowers: Yellow, borne solitary or in short terminal clusters among the leaves, 1 - 1.5 cm across when open, sepals 6 - 10 mm long, petals 7 - 10 mm long; appearing all year.

Fruit: Dry and nutlike, to about 5 mm long.

Distinguishing Marks: Somewhat similar to sea lavender (*Argusia gnaphalodes*), especially in bark; most easily distinguished by dense clusters of linear, light green to gray-green (rather than silvery-gray) leaves.

Distribution: Strictly coastal, found on beaches and dunes and in sandy thickets; coastal strand from about Brevard and Pinellas Counties southward, including the Keys.

Landscape Use: A good plant for the dry, harsh, salt-rich conditions that exist along the coast from southern Florida throughout the Keys. Also makes an attractive shrub and grows well in inland conditions in southern Florida.

Comment: Bay cedar is one of the first plants to colonize newly stabilized beaches. The plant's scientific name commemorates the French physician and botanist Joseph Donat Surian. The common name derives from the slight cedarlike fragrance of its crushed leaves. The bay cedar's fruit is very buoyant and has the capacity to remain vital for long periods while floating with the ocean currents. It is chiefly this latter factor that accounts for the plant's wide but sporadic distribution along the seashores of both the New and Old World tropics.

SYMPLOCACEAE — SWEETLEAF FAMILY

The Symplocaceae family has only one genus with about 300 species. Most members of the family are found in the warmer parts of the world, including the Americas, Asia, and Australia.

Horse Sugar or Sweetleaf

Symplocos tinctoria (L.) L'Her.

Page 346, Photo 279

Form: A deciduous, understory shrub or small tree to about 10 m tall.

Leaves: Alternate, simple, elliptic, leathery, 5 - 15 cm long, 2 - 6 cm wide, sometimes deformed with whitish, tumorlike growths, upper surfaces dark shiny green, margins mostly entire but sometimes with inconspicuous, blunt teeth; older leaves sweet to the taste, hence the common name.

Flowers: Yellow, fragrant, very conspicuous, borne in rounded clusters along the leafless portions of older twigs; appearing mostly in March and April.

Fruit: A green drupe to about 1 cm in length.

Distinguishing Marks: Distinguished from the Carolina silverbell (*Halesia carolina*) by being evergreen and by lacking the stellate pubescence of the latter species.

Distribution: Often in sand hills and flatwoods, but also ravines, floodplains, and bottomlands; Panhandle and northern Florida southward to about Alachua County.

Landscape Use: This is another of those species that is at its best as a landscape plant when in flower; its dark green, often drooping leaves offer nice greenery during the summer and fall, but its interesting blossoms, which appear in early spring, draw the most attention.

Comment: This plant is called horse sugar because horses, cattle, and white-tailed deer browse on its sweet-tasting leaves.

Horse Sugar or Sweetleaf
Symplocos tinctoria

TAMARICACEAE — TAMARISK FAMILY

The Tamaricaceae is a small group of less than 100 species in four genera. Only the genus *Tamarix* is found in the United States. Most *Tamarix* species are native to Europe, Africa, and Asia, but a few species have become naturalized in North America. Members of the genus are usually used for ornamental purposes, but are sometimes planted as windbreaks in deserts or coastal regions because they are extremely tolerant of salt and drought. Most species have small, alternate, scalelike leaves and white, pink, or rose-colored flowers.

Tamarisk, French Tamarisk, Salt-Cedar
Tamarix gallica L.

Form: Spreading, deciduous shrub or small tree.
Leaves: Alternate, minute, scalelike, simple, entire, feathery, delicate, variously described as gray green or silvery blue.
Flowers: Tiny, pink or white, borne in compact racemes at the tips of leafy branches; appearing in early- and midsummer.
Fruit: A dry capsule, 4 - 5 mm long.
Distinguishing Marks: Distinguished by its minute, scalelike leaves.
Distribution: Nonnative and introduced from Europe but now established on beaches and in dry coastal areas; reported in Florida along beaches in Franklin County and the northeast Florida coast.
Landscape Use: Though it is not often used, this salt-tolerant, drought-resistent species would be excellent along Florida's coastal strand and is well adapted for erosion control on sand dunes.

THEACEAE — TEA FAMILY

The Theaceae, or tea family, is composed primarily of tropical and subtropical species, only a few of which are native to North America. This is the same family that includes the horticulturally important camellias as well as the plant from which commercially made tea is produced. Members of the family are well known for their showy flowers and captivating aroma.

Silky-Camellia   Photo 280
Stewartia malacodendron L.

Form: Usually a deciduous shrub with several stems, sometimes a small tree to about 6 m tall.
Leaves: Alternate, elliptic, growing in two ranks along the stems but sometimes appearing clustered near the tip of branchlets, 5 - 10 cm long, 3 - 5 cm wide, margins minutely serrate and ciliate.

Flowers: Rotate, showy, to about 8 cm wide when fully open, with five white petals that are somewhat crinkled at their edges and encircle a mass of purple filaments, appearing in April and May.

Fruit: A woody capsule, 1 - 3 cm long.

Distinguishing Marks: Most easily distinguished by the attractive flowers, the silky white pubescence along the central vein on the lower surface of young leaves, and the tiny hairs that line the minutely serrated leaf edges.

Distribution: Restricted in Florida to ravine slopes in the Panhandle.

Landscape Use: Though beautiful, this plant is difficult to grow and not easily cultivated. However, for gifted and patient gardeners (it takes several years for specimens to bloom), it can become the most beautiful plant in the yard during its flowering time. The plant should not be over watered and, due to its protected status and difficulty to transplant, it should never be removed from the wild. It seems to do best in high shade and well-drained, rich soil. However, individual plants seem to either "like" or "dislike" their locations. Those that dislike their situation never seem to develop into outstanding specimens.

Comment: When in full bloom, this is one of Florida's most arresting and beautiful plants. Listed as endangered by the Florida Department of Agriculture.

THEOPHRASTACEAE — JOEWOOD FAMILY

The Theophrastaceae, or Joewood family, is a small family of only four genera and 60 to 100 species. Most members of the family are found in the American tropics and Hawaii. About half of these species fall into the genus *Jacquinia*. This genus includes about 30 shrubs and small trees. A single species, *J. keyensis*, is native to the United States but is found only in extreme southern Florida and the Keys. However, a second species, *J. arborea* Vahl, is now established in the Keys. Both the scientific and common names of the genus are in honor of the Austrian botanist, Nicholas Joseph Jacquin.

Joewood
Jacquinia keyensis Mez.

Page 349

Form: Evergreen shrub or small tree to about 6 m tall, with thin, blue-gray bark.

Leaves: Alternate on lower portion of branches, clustered in multileaved whorls near the ends of branches, simple, thick, leathery (but rather brittle), 2 - 8 cm long, 1.5 - 3.5 cm wide, margins entire and often rolled under, upper surfaces yellowish-green, apices often notched.

Flowers: White to pale yellow, funnel shaped, fragrant; appearing all year.

Fruit: A rounded, yellow to orange-red berry, 8 - 10 mm in diameter.

Distinguishing Marks: The small brown spots on the light tan stem help to differentiate this species from others with notched, thickish leaves.

Distribution: Coastal scrub of the Florida Keys and extreme tip of the southern peninsula.

Landscape Use: This is an excellent native for coastal areas but may require special attention and fertilization while becoming established. Since it is a listed species it should not be removed from the wild, except in situations where development will destroy a population. In

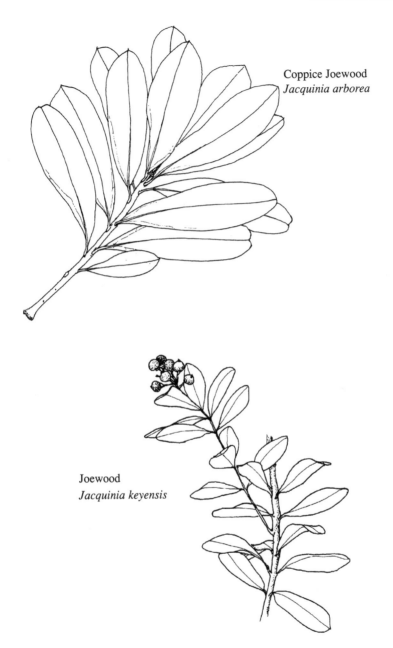

Coppice Joewood
Jacquinia arborea

Joewood
Jacquinia keyensis

the latter case, extreme care must be taken to insure the success of the transplanted specimens. Stephen Mullins offers an excellent summary of the steps for moving joewood in his article for the summer 1993 issue of *The Palmetto*.

Comment: Listed as threatened by the Florida Department of Agriculture; the nonnative *J. arborea* Vahl (pictured above) has been reported within John Pennekamp Coral Reef State Park on Key Largo.

THYMELAEACEAE — MEZERON FAMILY

The Thymelaeaceae is a temperate and tropical family (especially Africa) composed mostly of shrubs with a few trees, vines, and herbs. It is probably best known for the horticulturally important genus *Daphne*. Only a single genus with a single species is native to Florida.

Leatherwood

Page 350, Photo 281

Dirca palustris L.

Form: A widely branched, deciduous shrub to about 2.5 m tall (or a little more); stems jointed, very flexible, somewhat soft and leathery to the touch.

Leaves: Alternate, simple, entire, oval to elliptic or obovate, 5 - 9 cm long, 3 - 6 cm wide; apices blunt.

Flowers: Yellowish, tubular, small, borne with the new leaves in very early spring and easily overlooked as new foliage; see Photo 281.

Fruit: A greenish-yellow, ellipsoid berry, 5 - 6 mm long.

Distinguishing Marks: The jointed, pliable, leathery stems and distinctive flowers are diagnostic.

Distribution: Uncommon and local on rich, wooded ravines and slopes; primarily restricted to the central Panhandle, especially near the upper Apalachicola River.

Comment: Though restricted in distribution in Florida and commonly described as infrequent across much of its range outside Florida, *D. palustris* is not listed on either the state or federal lists of protected species. Nevertheless, it is tracked by the Florida Natural Areas Inventory, which ranks it as "apparently secure globally" but as "either very rare and local throughout its range (21-100 occurrences or less than 10,000 individuals) or found locally in a restricted range or vulnerable to extinction of other factors" in Florida (FNAI, 1995).

Leatherwood
Dirca palustris

TURNERACEAE — TURNERA FAMILY

This is a small family of mostly herbs and subshrubs and a few small trees. Most members of the family have alternate, toothed leaves, and attractive flowers. The single member of the family described below is an introduced species. The perennial native wildflower piriqueta (*Piriqueta caroliniana* [Walt.] Urban), which blooms from spring to fall and is frequent throughout much of Florida, is the state's only native member of the family.

Yellow Alder
Turnera ulmifolia L.

Photo 282

Form: Aromatic shrub or erect herb to about 7 dm tall; stems with soft, longish pubescence.
Leaves: Alternate, simple, broadly lanceolate to oblong, 3 - 10 cm long, 2 - 5 cm wide; apices pinched to a point; bases rounded to wedge shaped; margins mostly conspicuously toothed.
Flowers: Yellow, conspicuous, with five, often overlapping, petals, each 1 - 3 cm long, 1 - 3 cm wide, petals sometimes with a brown spot at the base; flowers borne sessile or near sessile, opening during the day but closing in late afternoon; appearing all year.
Fruit: A densely pubescent capsule to about 8 mm long and 1 cm wide.
Distinguishing Marks: The bright-yellow, stalkless flowers and broadly lanceolate, dentate leaves help distinguish the species.
Distribution: Native to tropical America; escaped in disturbed sites and hammocks; south Florida, the Keys, and at least one location in Hillsborough County.
Landscape Use: Most often used ornamentally for its bright-yellow flowers.

ULMACEAE — ELM FAMILY

The Ulmaceae is a worldwide family of 15 genera and approximately 200 species, mostly of temperate regions. Members of the family have small, inconspicuous flowers and two-ranked leaves. Four of the family's genera occur in the United States, all of which are represented in Florida. These genera include *Ulmus*, or the true elms; *Celtis*, which is made up of the hackberries or sugarberries; *Planera*, a monotypic genus that occurs only in the southeastern United States; and *Trema*, one of the family's few tropical genera and the only U. S. member of the family confined strictly to southern Florida. Fossil data indicate that the elm family has ancient origins, perhaps as far back as 25 million years, and was once much more widespread in distribution.

Iguana Hackberry
Celtis iguanaea (Jacq.) Sarg.

Form: Spiny, spreading, often climbing shrub, 1 - 3 m tall.
Leaves: Alternate, simple, ovate or oblong to elliptic, 3.5 - 12 cm long, to about 2 cm wide;

upper surfaces smooth to the touch; margins entire to conspicuously serrate above the middle.

Flowers: Greenish yellow, small, 3 - 4 mm wide, borne in branched clusters and appearing in spring.

Fruit: A rounded, slightly four-angled, orange to red drupe, 8 - 12 mm long.

Distinguishing Marks: Distinguished from *C. pallida* by larger leaves with upper surfaces smooth to the touch.

Distribution: Very rare and endemic to shell mounds of southern Florida; known in the United States only from Collier and Lee Counties.

Comment: Listed as endangered by the Florida Department of Agriculture. The fruits of all three of the hackberries described here are eaten by wildlife. The fruits are fleshy, brightly colored, and ripen in the fall. A wide variety of birds as well as raccoons and squirrels use them.

Spiny Hackberry or Desert Hackberry Page 353
Celtis pallida Torr.

Form: Shrub with spreading branches; armed at the leaf nodes with pairs of sharp, straight spines; spines to about 2.5 cm long.

Leaves: Alternate, simple, ovate, usually less than 2.5 cm long but some to about 3 cm, to about 2 cm wide; upper surfaces slightly rough to the touch.

Flowers: Inconspicuous, borne in branched clusters and appearing in spring.

Fruit: A fleshy, nearly rounded, glabrous, sweet, orange, red, or yellow drupe; 5 - 8 mm in diameter.

Distinguishing Marks: The small, scabrid leaves and thorny branches help distinguish the species.

Distribution: Rare and restricted in Florida to a few shell mounds in Lee County.

Comment: Listed as endangered by the Florida Department of Agriculture. This plant is native to the arid southwest, hence the name desert hackberry. It is one of few such plants to become established in the much more humid southeast. The specific epithet, *pallida*, derives from the root word pallid, or pale, and refers to the color of the plant's branches. The proposed state champion for this plant was discovered by Dick Workman along the Shell Mound Trail boardwalk at Ding Darling National Wildlife Refuge near Ft. Myers. This latter specimen is about 7 m tall, about 8 cm in diameter, and has a crown spread of nearly 11 m.

Georgia or Dwarf Hackberry Page 353
Celtis tenuifolia Nutt.

Form: Normally a scraggly deciduous shrub, sometimes to 10 m tall.

Leaves: Alternate, entire or serrate, triangle shaped, 2.5 - 7 cm long, 1.5 - 4.5 cm wide, widest near the base, bases rounded or truncate, upper surfaces rough to the touch; the two lowermost lateral leaf veins arising with, and being nearly equal in size with, the central leaf vein.

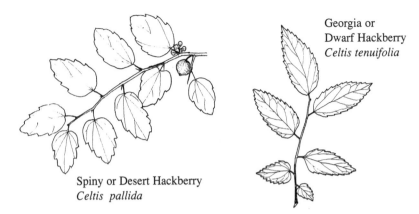

Georgia or
Dwarf Hackberry
Celtis tenuifolia

Spiny or Desert Hackberry
Celtis pallida

Flowers: Tiny, borne singly or in small clusters along the branchlets; appearing in spring.

Fruit: Orange to reddish, globular, 5 - 8 mm in diameter.

Distinguishing Marks: Leaves similar in overall outline to sugarberry (*C. laevigata* Willd.), a tree-sized plant which is not described here; distinguished from it by being darker, dull green above, by being less tapered toward the apices, and by having leaf surfaces that are slightly rough to the touch rather than smooth.

Distribution: Sporadic in northern Florida, predominantly along the upper Apalachicola River and the northern portions of Walton and Holmes Counties.

Planer Tree or Water Elm Page 354

Planera aquatica Walt. ex Gmel.

Form: Large, arching shrub or small deciduous tree to about 18 m tall, trunk often short with scaly and flaky, grayish-brown outer bark and reddish inner bark, branches spreading.

Leaves: Alternate, simple, typically ovate, two ranked along the branch, 2 - 8.5 cm long, 2 - 4 cm wide, upper surfaces dark green, bases rounded, apices tapering to a point, margins serrate.

Flowers: Small, borne in dense clusters at the leaf axils; appearing February to March.

Fruit: A soft, burrlike drupe, to 1 cm in diameter.

Distinguishing Marks: Most easily recognized by the combination of two-ranked and serrated leaves, scaly bark, and wetland habitat; potentially confused with eastern hophornbeam (*Ostrya virginiana*, [Mill.] K. Koch) and ironwood (*Carpinus caroliniana* Walt.), both of which are trees that are not described here; distinguished from both by lacking doubly serrated leaf margins.

Distribution: Riverbanks, backwaters, and oxbow lakes in a wide band across the northernmost border of the state from about Union, Alachua, and Dixie Counties westward; it is especially abundant along the courses of major rivers such as the Apalachicola, Choctawhatchee, and Suwannee, as well as in the deeper reaches of San Felasco Hammock State Preserve near Gainesville.

Comment: This plant is named for German botanist Johann Jacob Planer and is the only living representative of its genus.

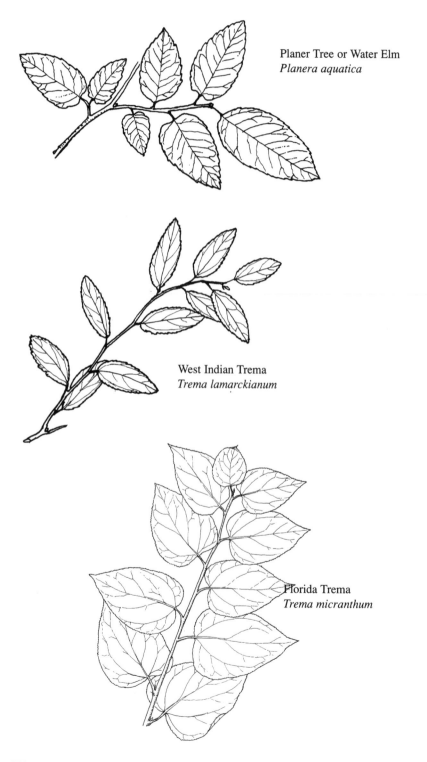

Planer Tree or Water Elm
Planera aquatica

West Indian Trema
Trema lamarckianum

Florida Trema
Trema micranthum

West Indian Trema

Page 354

Trema lamarckianum (R. & S.) Blume

Form: Large shrub, or small, shrublike evergreen tree to about 6 m tall.

Leaves: Alternate, simple, two ranked, lanceolate, usually not exceeding 5 cm in length, hairy and rough to the touch on both surfaces, margins finely toothed.

Flowers: Small and greenish; appearing all year.

Fruit: Pink, rounded, crowded around the leaf axils, measuring about 3 mm in diameter.

Distinguishing Marks: Distinguished from *T. micranthum* by smaller leaves that are rough to the touch on both the upper and lower surfaces.

Distribution: Uncommon at the southernmost tip of the peninsula, more plentiful in the Keys.

Florida Trema

Page 354

Trema micranthum (L.) Blume

Form: Large shrub or small to medium-sized evergreen tree to about 8 m tall, with smooth, light brown bark and long, horizontally spreading branches.

Leaves: Alternate, simple, broadly lanceolate, 6 - 15 cm long, two ranked, margins finely toothed.

Flowers: Small, greenish yellow to whitish, borne in the leaf axils; appearing year-round.

Fruit: Round, orange, 2 - 3 mm in diameter.

Distinguishing Marks: Most easily distinguished from other south Florida species by serrated, two-ranked leaves in conjunction with flowers and fruits, which are evident during much of the year; distinguished from *T. lamarckianum* by leaves being larger and rough to the touch only on the upper surfaces.

Distribution: From about the Broward/Palm Beach County line southward on the east coast, Pinellas County (where it is rare) southward on the west coast, throughout the Keys.

VERBENACEAE — VERVAIN FAMILY

The Verbenaceae is a large family of about 75 genera and more than 3,000 species. It is probably best known for its shrubby and herbaceous species, many of which are widespread components of Florida's flora. However, the family also encompasses a variety of economically and horticulturally important shrubs and trees. The teak (*Tectona grandis* L.f.), which is prized for the beauty of its wood, is the family's most famous and valuable tree, and lemon verbena (*Lippia citriodora* [Lam.] HBK) is cultivated as a source of oils used in perfume manufacture. Many of the family's members, including several of those described below, are highly regarded for their horticultural utility and have become naturalized in many parts of the world.

Beautyberry, Beautybush, American Beautyberry, French Mulberry

Photo 283

Callicarpa americana L.

Form: Multibranched deciduous shrub to about 2 m tall; young stems with star-shaped hairs, lower stems light brown.

Leaves: Opposite, simple, ovate, 7 - 15 cm long, 3 - 10 cm wide, aromatic when bruised; both surfaces of young leaves and lower surfaces of older leaves covered with star-shaped hairs; margins crenate to serrate from a little below the middle to the apices.

Flowers: Pink, small, borne in short-stalked to sessile clusters at the leaf axils; appearing in late spring and early summer.

Fruit: A small, magenta to rich-purple (very rarely white), rounded drupe; borne in conspicuous clusters at the leaf axils; appearing mostly in late summer and fall.

Distinguishing Marks: The distinctive fruit is diagnostic.

Distribution: Common in pinelands, hammock margins, well-drained woods, wooded road edges; throughout the state, including the Keys.

Landscape Use: The abundant fruit, for which the plant is most enjoyed in the garden, is also attractive to wildlife, especially birds. However, bees are drawn to its delicate pink flowers. The plant is easily propagated from seed or cuttings and is a good addition to a naturalized bed, or massed with other native shrubs. It fruits best in full sun, but also thrives in shade. According to H. W. Martin in an article for *The Palmetto*, the beautyberry's tolerance of many conditions and ease of transplantation and propagation make it a good candidate for reclamation and restoration projects.

Comment: The name *Callicarpa* derives from the Greek and means "bearing beautiful fruit", a fitting name for this common plant.

Fiddlewood

Photo 284

Citharexylum fruticosum L.

Form: Evergreen shrub or, more typically, a small, slender tree to about 12 m tall with smooth, light brown bark and square twigs.

Leaves: Opposite, simple, predominately elliptic to obovate but variable, leathery, thick, 5 - 17 cm long, 1 - 6 cm wide, upper surfaces shiny, yellow green and pubescent, lower surfaces dull, margins entire (or rarely toothed on younger branchlets), petioles and midribs orange to pinkish, midribs especially so toward the leaf base.

Flowers: White, fragrant, tubular, borne in terminal or lateral racemes 5 - 30 cm in length, each flower to about 1.2 m long; appearing any time of the year.

Fruit: A rounded, red-brown drupe, 8 - 12 mm in diameter.

Distinguishing Marks: Most easily recognized by opposite, shiny leaves with orange midribs and borne on square twigs.

Distribution: Hammocks and pinelands from Brevard and Manatee Counties southward and throughout the Keys.

Comment: The fiddlewood's common name is somewhat misleading and has apparently resulted from the corruption of similar words from separate languages. The French colonial name for members of this genus was "bois fidele," which literally translates as reliable or trustworthy wood, an accolade that likely refers to the tree's strength and toughness. The French word "fidele" was apparently misinterpreted as fiddle by the English, and the name has stayed with the plant. There is no history that the wood from this tree has ever been used in the manufacture of violins.

Java Glorybower, Clerodendrum, Java Shrub Photo 285
Clerodendrum speciosissimum Van Geert

Form: Shrub or small tree to about 4 m tall.

Leaves: Opposite, ovate to heart shaped, densely pubescent, to about 30 cm long; margins entire or, more commonly, toothed.

Flowers: Scarlet, 2 - 3 cm long, with five petals; borne in conspicuous, multibranched, long-stalked clusters; clusters to about 40 cm long; appearing summer and fall.

Fruit: A rounded drupe.

Distinguishing Marks: The showy clusters of scarlet flowers in conjunction with the relatively large, densely pubescent leaves are distinctive.

Distribution: Native to Java and Ceylon but escaped from cultivation in Florida, mostly in disturbed sites; south Florida and the Keys.

Landscape Use: Prized mostly for the large, red, showy flower clusters and the extended flowering period.

Comment: This species is one of several members of its genus that are regularly used as ornamentals in Florida, and sometimes the south, but have escaped from cultivation. Others include: glorybower (*C. fragrans* R. Br.) which has fragrant white, rose, or bluish-tinged flowers and large deltoid leaves which are 9 - 25 cm long; turk's cap or tube flower (*C. indicum* [L.] Kuntze), illustrated below, which has long, white, narrowly tubular flowers 10 - 14 cm long, and whorled, lanceolate leaves 12 - 13 cm long; glorybower (*C. bungei* Steud.), which is very similar to *C. speciosissimum*, but with smaller, white to pinkish flowers; and bleeding heart (*C. thomsoniae* Balf.), a vigorous, evergreen, twining vine to about 7 m long,

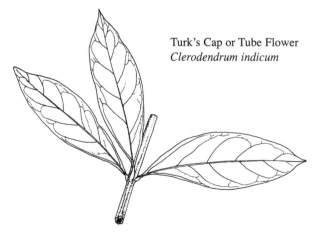

Turk's Cap or Tube Flower
Clerodendrum indicum

with crimson petals and white sepals (see Photo 286). The latter species has been in cultivation since at least 1861, the year in which it was introduced into Great Britain. Though many species of *Clerodendrum* are used ornamentally statewide, they are sporadically escaped in disturbed sites only in the southern part of the state.

Golden Dewdrop, Pigeon Berry, Sky Flower   Photos 287, 288
Duranta repens L.

Form: Evergreen shrub or small tree, sometimes vinelike, to about 6 m tall with light- to dark-gray bark; sometimes somewhat spiny, sometimes not at all spiny.
Leaves: Opposite, simple, ovate to elliptic, 2.5 - 7.5 cm long, upper and lower surfaces dull light green, apices short pointed, margins entire or serrate.
Flowers: Tubular, light blue to purple to white with five, spreading petals, to about 1.3 cm across, borne in terminal or lateral racemes to 15 cm long; appearing year-round, especially in the southern parts of the state, perhaps having a more restricted blooming period in the north.
Fruit: A rounded, yellow drupe borne in hanging clusters, to about 1.3 cm in diameter.
Distinguishing Marks: The bright-yellow fruit and blue to purple flowers, which may appear on the plant at the same time, are distinctive.
Distribution: Purportedly native to the Keys but more likely an introduced ornamental; available from commercial nurseries and used as a landscape plant primarily in southern Florida but also farther north.
Landscape Use: Though the fruits of this species are poisonous to humans, they are relished by birds. The plant is easy to cultivate, requires little care once established, is used as a street tree in the warmer parts of the state, and as a shrub in the more northern parts. It also makes a good hedge or solitary specimen plant in the lawn. The flowers and fruit are often borne at the same time.
Comment: The plant's common name derives from its bright-yellow fruit.

Lantana or Shrub Verbena   Photos 289
Lantana camara L.

Form: An erect, deciduous, multibranched shrub to about 2 m tall; herbaceous portions of the stem with bristly hairs and rough to the touch.
Leaves: Opposite, simple, ovate, 2 - 15 cm long, 2 - 6 cm wide, giving off a rank odor when crushed; margins crenate or with blunt teeth; surfaces covered with bristly hairs and rough to the touch; petioles to about 2 cm long.
Flowers: Multicolored and colorful, pink, yellow, orange, and white; borne in dense, conspicuous, stalked clusters; appearing from late spring to fall.
Fruit: Green at first, turning dark blue, borne in conspicuous clusters.
Distinguishing Marks: The multicolored flowers in conjunction with the rough-to-the-touch aromatic leaves are distinctive.

Distribution: Native to tropical America but now common in pinelands, open woods, disturbed sites, coastal areas; throughout the state, including the Keys.

Landscape Use: Though listed as a Category I pest plant by the Florida Exotic Pest Plant Council, this species remains a very popular landscape and garden plant, primarily for the beauty of the flowers, but also for their attractiveness to several species of butterflies. Homeowners and landscape gardeners should avoid this plant due to its weedy nature.

Comment: Green fruits of this plant are very poisonous and reported to be lethal if ingested. The leaves are poisonous to livestock. Though generally considered nonnative, this plant was commented on by William Bartram in his visits to Florida in the late 1700s.

Florida Lantana
Lantana depressa Small

Form: Multibranched shrub with prostrate to reclining branches; to about 1.1 m tall.

Leaves: Opposite, simple, ovate to elliptic, 1 - 7 cm long; margins toothed.

Flowers: Bright yellow, borne in dense clusters; appearing year-round.

Fruit: A drupe, 3 - 5 mm in diameter.

Distinguishing Marks: Similar in form to *L. camara*, except shorter in stature, with smaller leaves, and with bright yellow flowers.

Distribution: There are three varieties of *L. depressa* in Florida. *L. depressa* Small var. *depressa* is endemic to south Florida pinelands, especially in the everglades; *L. depressa* Small var. *floridana* (Mold.) R. Sanders occurs up the east coast from the Miami area to Duval and Flagler Counties, including on Little Talbot Island north of Jacksonville; *L. depressa* var. *sanibelensis* R. Sanders occurs along the west coast from about Cape Sable through Lee County and Sanibel Island to Levy County (Sanders, 1987). No varieties of this species occur in the Keys.

Comment: Recognized as a candidate for federal listing by the U. S. Fish and Wildlife Service; listed as endangered by the Florida Department of Agriculture. Though this plant has yellow flowers, it is not the same plant as that seen lining many walkways and garden borders and that is commonly referred to as "Lantana Gold".

Wild Lantana, White Sage, White Lantana   Photos 290
Lantana involucrata L.

Form: Multibranched, shrub to about 2 m tall; bark of stems yellowish.

Leaves: Opposite, simple, oval, pale green, 1 - 4 cm long; surfaces minutely hairy and rough to the touch; margins crenate or toothed.

Flowers: White, sometimes with a bluish or lavender tint, borne in dense, small, but conspicuous, stalked clusters; appearing any time of year.

Fruit: A small, purple drupe, 3 - 4 mm in diameter.

Distinguishing Marks: The small, pale-green leaves and white flower clusters are distinctive.

Distribution: Hammocks, pinelands, mostly near the coast; south Florida and the Keys.

Landscape Use: This is a hardy, bushy plant that does well in full sun; it may be planted as an individual shrub or massed along fences or backgrounds.

Lantana microcephala A. Rich.

Form: An erect shrub with pale gray to whitish stems.
Leaves: Opposite, simple, narrowly lanceolate to elliptic, 3 - 6 cm long; margins serrate; surfaces pubescent.
Flowers: Small, borne in short-stalked clusters at the leaf axils; appearing year-round.
Fruit: A tiny nutlet.
Distinguishing Marks: The axillary, rather than terminal, flower clusters distinguish this species from others in the genus.
Distribution: Rare along hammock margins in Dade County; only a few populations of this species are extant.

Trailing Lantana, Polecat Geranium, Weeping Lantana
Lantana montevidensis (Spreng.) Briq.   **Photo 291**

Form: A vinelike shrub with trailing or decumbent, pubescent stems; to about 2 m tall.
Leaves: Opposite, simple, ovate, 2 - 3 cm long, aromatic when crushed; surfaces pubescent and rough to the touch; margins serrate.
Flowers: Rose lilac in color, borne in dense clusters to about 3 cm wide; appearing spring through fall in north Florida, nearly all year in more tropical parts of the state.
Fruit: Small, rounded, metallic-black, fleshy drupe to about 5 mm long.
Distinguishing Marks: Leaves similar to other members of the genus; the vinelike stature, reclining branches, and rose-lilac flowers distinguish it.
Distribution: Native to South America but naturalized in Florida in pinelands, along roadsides, and other disturbed sites; statewide but mostly in south Florida; only locally naturalized in limited regions of the Panhandle.
Landscape Use: Tolerates dry sites; most often used where a trailing vine is appropriate, such as on slopes or along low fences.

Bastard Teak   **Page 361**
Premna odorata Blanco

Form: Large shrub or small tree with pubescent stems (typically described as a tree in Taiwan and the Philippines, where it is native).
Leaves: Opposite, simple, ovate to oblong, 10 - 12 cm long, 6 - 7 cm wide; margins entire or finely toothed; apices acutely pointed.
Flowers: Greenish white, borne in branched clusters.
Fruit: A small, rounded, dark-purple drupe, about 4 mm across.
Distinguishing Marks: The large leaves and very fragrant flowers borne in large clusters help distinguish the species.
Distribution: Native to Taiwan, escaped from cultivation in southernmost Florida.

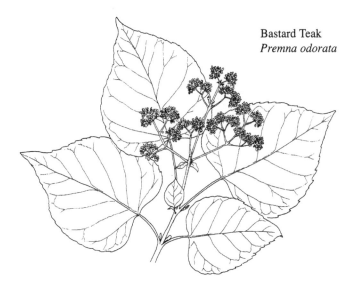

Bastard Teak
Premna odorata

Landscape Use: An attractive, large, bushy shrub with showy flower clusters; used as an isolated specimen plant, or massed against fences.

Jamaica Porterweed or Blue Porterweed   Page 362
Stachytarpheta jamaicensis (L.) Vahl

Form: Typically a low, decumbent shrub that appears at first glance to be an herb; usually not taller than about 6 dm, potentially to about 1 m; stems angled.

Leaves: Opposite, simple, ovate to broadly lanceolate, dark green, 2 - 8 cm long; margins distinctly toothed.

Flowers: Blue, small, about 8 mm across; opening in the morning and closing during the hottest part of the day; borne in cylindrical, quill-like spikes 10 - 15 cm long; appearing year-round.

Distinguishing Marks: The small, blue flowers on cylindrical spikes are diagnostic.

Distribution: Shell mounds, beaches, disturbed sites, dry sandy sites; along the coast from about Hillsborough County southward, throughout south Florida and the Keys.

Comment: According to Roger Hammer (1995), there are at least two species of *Stachytarpheta* in Florida: the native species described above and the nonnative *S. urticifolia* (Salisb.) Sims (sometimes seen spelled *S. urticaefolia*). Hammer holds that it is the latter plant that is sold and used extensively as a landscape plant, especially in southern Florida. This latter plant is a 1 - 2 m tall, woody shrub with violet to purple flowers that are similar to those of the native species (Photo 292). *S. urticifolia* may be distinguished from *S. jamaicensis* by the distinctively impressed veins on the upper surfaces of the leaves which give an overall quilted appearance to the leaf blade, by the more numerous and outward pointing marginal teeth (averaging about 38 as opposed to about 24 per leaf, according to

Hammer), and by the more robust growth habit. *S. urticifolia* is easily cultivated in a variety of soils, including dry sandy areas, and may even be used as a pot plant or in summer gardens in north Florida. It is also becoming a well-established exotic in southern Florida.

Jamaica Porterweed or
Blue Porterweed
Stachytarpheta jamaicensis

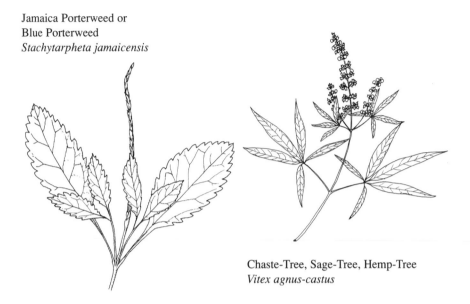

Chaste-Tree, Sage-Tree, Hemp-Tree
Vitex agnus-castus

Chaste-Tree, Sage-Tree, Hemp-Tree   Page 362

Vitex agnus-castus L.

Form: A bushy-branched, strongly aromatic, deciduous shrub or small tree with densely pubescent twigs.

Leaves: Opposite, simple, palmately compound with three to nine (usually five) leaflets; leaflets grayish green, lanceolate, varying in length, to about 10 cm long, 3 cm wide; petioles 1.5 - 7.5 cm long.

Flowers: Lavender to white, borne in conspicuous, branched clusters at the ends of branches; cluster 12 - 18 cm long overall; flowers appearing in summer.

Fruit: A small, hard, dry, rounded drupe with four seeds.

Distinguishing Marks: The opposite, palmate leaves with lanceolate leaflets of varying lengths are distinctive.

Distribution: Native to southern Europe, used as an ornamental but occasionally naturalized in northern Florida.

Landscape Use: Valued as a fragrant, summer-flowering tree or shrub.

Comment: At least two other species of *Vitex* occur in Florida. Vitex (*V. trifolia* L. f.), a native of Asia which is used ornamentally in central and southern Florida, has also escaped from cultivation and may be even more widely established in some locations than the present species; it may be distinguished by its variegated, trifoliolate leaves and conspicuously branched clusters of blue flowers. *V. negundo* L., a native of China, has also been reported as locally escaped in Florida (Wunderlin, et. al., 1988).

VITACEAE — GRAPE FAMILY

This is a family of climbing vines, mostly of the world's tropical and subtropical regions. The family includes five genera and nearly 600 species. Several members of the family, particularly *Vitis vinifera* L., are well known for their fruit, which is the source of wines, jellies, raisins, and currants. A few of the family's genera, especially *Vitis*, are still not well worked out taxonomically and can be quite confusing to identify in the field.

Pepper-Vine
Page 363

Ampelopsis arborea (L.) Koehne

Form: A woody vine; usually climbing by tendrils.

Leaves: Alternate, bipinnately compound, with many leaflets, 15 - 20 cm long overall; leaflets ovate, 1 - 7 cm long, with deeply toothed margins.

Flowers: Small, greenish, appearing in spring.

Fruit: Rounded, shiny-black to dark-purplish berry, to about 1.5 cm in diameter.

Distinguishing Marks: The vinelike habit and bipinnate leaves with coarsely toothed leaflets are diagnostic.

Distribution: Common in wet woods, hammocks, low areas, stream banks, floodplains; throughout most of state southward to the southern peninsula.

Landscape Use: This is an easy-to-grow, fast-growing, climbing vine with very attractive foliage; it has a tendency to spread rapidly if not monitored and kept under control.

Comment: There are about 30 species of *Ampelopsis* worldwide; most are from China or eastern Asia. Almost all of these species are used ornamentally, including the two that are native to the United States.

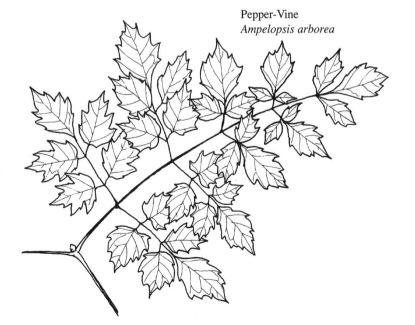

Pepper-Vine
Ampelopsis arborea

Raccoon-Grape

Page 365

Ampelopsis cordata Michx.

Form: Deciduous, woody vine; climbing by means of tendrils.
Leaves: Alternate, simple, ovate, sometimes with two, poorly defined lobes, to about 9 cm long and wide, distinctly grapelike in appearance; margins coarsely and distinctly toothed; bases truncate; petioles long and conspicuous.
Flowers: Small, green, petals to about 3 mm long; appearing in May.
Fruit: A blue berry at maturity, passing through stages of green, rose, and purple as it matures; 5 - 10 mm in diameter; borne in branched clusters, unlike those of the several species of *Vitis*.
Distinguishing Marks: Distinguished from members of the genus *Vitis*, with which it is most similar, by slicing off the outer bark of a twig to examine the innermost tissue (the pith); species of *Ampelopsis* have a white pith, those of *Vitis* have a brown pith.
Distribution: Wet woods, stream banks, floodplains; mostly along the Apalachicola River in the central Panhandle.

Possum Grape

Page 365

Cissus sicyoides L.

Form: A flexible woody vine.
Leaves: Alternate, simple, ovate to heart shaped, predominantly densely pubescent, 2 - 16 cm long; margins serrate, sometimes coarsely so; bases heart shaped.
Flowers: Yellowish green, with four sepals and four petals, borne in stalked, branched clusters; appearing any time of year but mostly spring through fall.
Fruit: A rounded, black, one-seeded berry, about 1 cm in diameter.
Distinguishing Marks: The heart-shaped leaves with serrate margins distinguish this species from other members of its family; the grapelike fruit in conjunction with the heart-shaped leaves helps distinguish it from other south Florida species.
Distribution: Hammocks, low woods; south and south-central Florida.
Landscape Use: Several species of *Cissus* are used ornamentally in Florida, most often as climbing vines on trellises or as a ground cover.

Marine Vine, Marine Ivy, Sorrel Vine

Page 365

Cissus trifoliata L.

Form: A warty, deciduous, climbing vine, older stems woody; to about 10 m long.
Leaves: Alternate, simple to three lobed or trifoliolate, somewhat succulent or at least fleshy, to about 8 cm both long and wide; leaflets ovate to oblong and with toothed margins; tendrils long, unbranched, and borne opposite some of the leaves.
Flowers: Greenish, creamy yellow, whitish, or purplish; cuplike with four short, spreading petals; appearing late summer.

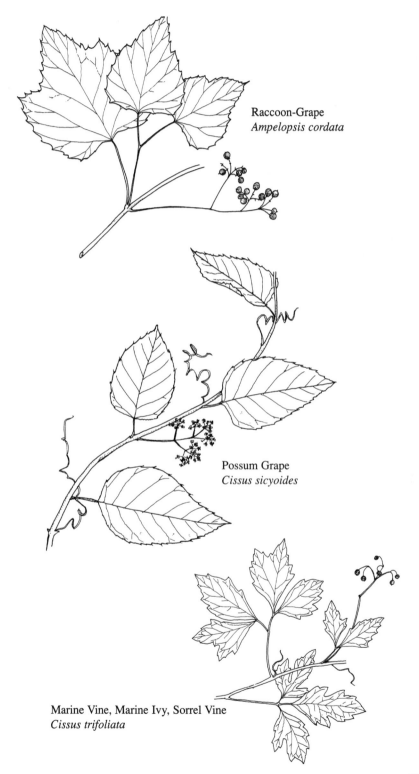

Raccoon-Grape
Ampelopsis cordata

Possum Grape
Cissus sicyoides

Marine Vine, Marine Ivy, Sorrel Vine
Cissus trifoliata

Fruit: An egg-shaped berry (reminiscent of a small pepper), green at first but becoming bluish-black, 6 - 8 mm long.

Distinguishing Marks: The three-lobed to trifoliolate fleshy leaves are distinctive.

Distribution: Dunes, shell mounds, coastal hammocks; mostly central and southern Florida and the Keys, sporadic along the Gulf Coast in north Florida, particularly near Apalachicola.

Landscape Use: See comment for *C. sicyoides*, above. This plant is sometimes seen listed by its synonym, *C. incisa* (Nutt.) Desmoul.

Virginia Creeper or Woodbine
Page 366

Parthenocissus quinquefolia (L.) Planch.

Form: Deciduous, woody, climbing vine; climbing by means of small, adhesive dilations on the tendrils; often climbing high into trees or along the walls of buildings.

Leaves: Alternate, palmately compound, typically with five leaflets (sometimes with three or four); leaflets varying in shape on various parts of the plant, from lanceolate or oblanceolate to obovate, with toothed to doubly toothed margins; leaflets to about 18 cm long, 5 cm wide; petioles conspicuous, 15 - 20 cm long.

Flowers: Small, reddish, borne in few- to many-branched clusters; appearing in spring.

Fruit: A rounded, blue to black berry, 8 - 9 mm in diameter; somewhat flattened at the apex.

Distinguishing Marks: Easily distinguished by its viney habit in conjunction with its compound leaves with five leaflets; it is often confused with poison oak (*Toxicodendron toxicarium*) and poison ivy (*T. radicans*) but is easily distinguished; the latter two species have only three leaflets.

Distribution: Various kinds of sites, including both uplands and lowlands, throughout the state; native to the U. S. from New England to Florida and west to Mexico.

Virginia Creeper or Woodbine
Parthenocissus quinquefolia

Landscape Use: This rapidly growing, climbing vine is excellent for trellises or fences. It is prized for its brilliant scarlet and crimson fall color and for the attractiveness of its fruit to wildlife. It will also trail along the ground and may be used as a ground cover but its fast growth requires monitoring to keep it in check. The adhesive tips on its tendrils can leave a difficult-to-remove residue from wood and brick where the plant has become attached.

Summer Grape
Photo 293

Vitis aestivalis Michx.

Form: High-climbing deciduous vine with divided tendrils and rounded branchlets.

Leaves: Alternate, simple, varying in size to about 15 cm long, heart shaped in overall outline, often with three to five lobes, deeply cordate at their bases; lower surfaces typically whitish and generally pubescent, the pubescence sometimes obscuring the whitish cast; margins coarsely toothed; petioles about as long as the blade.

Flowers: Small, borne in branched clusters 5 - 16 cm long; appearing spring and summer.

Fruit: A berry, 5 - 12 mm in diameter, changing from green to black as it matures, often with a whitish coating.

Distinguishing Marks: The divided tendrils, whitish and pubescent undersurfaces of the leaves, and whitish cast of the berries distinguish this species from other members of the genus.

Distribution: Common in well-drained woods, scrub, dunes; throughout northern and southern Florida.

Landscape Use: Does well on arbors and trellises; provides an excellent wildlife food.

Comment: In general, the several species of grapes found in Florida are easily identified to genus by the characteristic grapelike shape of their leaves. They tend to have individually inconspicuous flowers but very conspicuous fruit. Though generally similar in appearance and seemingly confusing at first glance, they can usually be readily identified by close observation of a number of characters as detailed in the several descriptions offered here.

Sweet Winter Grape or Downy Grape
Photo 294

Vitis cinerea (Engelm. ex Gray) Millardet

Form: High-climbing deciduous vine with angled branchlets and divided tendrils.

Leaves: Alternate, simple, heart shaped with cordate bases, unlobed to three lobed, to about 15 cm long; margins crenate to toothed; undersurfaces with whitish hairs, but not with an overall whitish cast (as in *V. aestivalis*); petioles about as long as the blades.

Flowers: Small, borne in branched clusters.

Fruit: A black berry at maturity, 4 - 9 mm in diameter, without a whitish cast (as in *V. aestivalis*).

Distinguishing Marks: The distinctly angled branchlets and whitish pubescence (as opposed to a whitish cast in the previous species) on the undersurfaces of the leaves distinguish this species from the other members of its genus; most easily confused with *V. aestivalis*, differing in habitat and as mentioned above.

Distribution: There are two varieties of this species. *V. cinerea* (Engelm. ex Gray) Millardet var. *cinerea* is uncommon in lowland woods and floodplains of the central Panhandle and has been recorded only from Wakulla, Jackson, and Washington Counties; *V. cinerea* var. *floridana* Munson (also called Simpson's grape), which is found in the same kinds of habitats, is more common and ranges throughout northern Florida.

Red Grape, Cat Grape, Catbird Grape
Vitis palmata Vahl

Form: High-climbing vine with forked tendrils; stems reddish to purplish red when young, reddish brown at maturity.
Leaves: Alternate, simple, ovate to heart shaped in overall outline, predominantly deeply lobed with three to five lobes; apices of lobes predominantly long tapering and pointed at the tip; margins serrate to coarsely dentate; petioles slightly shorter than the leaf blades.
Flowers: Small, individually inconspicuous, borne in branched clusters 6 - 15 cm long.
Fruit: A rounded, bluish-black to black berry, 5 - 8 mm in diameter.
Distinguishing Marks: Most easily distinguished from the other members of the genus by the young (first year) branchlets being rounded (not angled) and purplish red throughout, and by the leaves being at least three lobed and lacking a whitish cast below.
Distribution: Restricted in Florida primarily to the floodplain of the Apalachicola River.

Muscadine or Bullace   Page 369, Photos 295, 296
Vitis rotundifolia Michx.

Form: High-climbing vine with unbranched tendrils.
Leaves: Alternate, simple, generally heart shaped in overall outline, about as wide as long; upper surfaces without hairs, lower surface with or without hairs but not with a whitish cast; margins predominantly dentate, but sometimes the tips of the teeth rounded rather than pointed; petioles about as long as the leaf blades.
Flowers: Small, individually inconspicuous, borne in branched clusters 3 - 8 cm long; appearing from spring to early summer.
Fruit: A berry, predominantly black to purplish, sometimes golden green (at such times often referred to as scuppernongs), 1 - 2.5 cm in diameter.
Distinguishing Marks: This species can be distinguished from all other members of the genus by its unbranched tendrils; most easily confused with *V. vulpina*.
Distribution: Common in well-drained uplands but ranging widely in habitat, including lowland woods and floodplains; throughout northern Florida and southward to the southernmost peninsula.
Landscape Use: Easily grown on trellises and arbors; often naturally present in wooded suburban yards. The yellow autumn foliage of this species is quite attractive, especially after the passage of unseasonably early cold fronts.
Comment: As described here, *V. rotundifolia* also includes what some list as *V. munsoniana* Simpson ex Munson. This latter species has noticeably smaller fruit (averaging 5 - 9 mm in

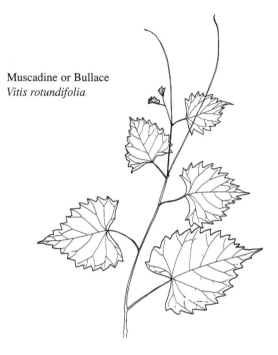

Muscadine or Bullace
Vitis rotundifolia

diameter) and smaller leaves, but is otherwise indistinct. The latter species is listed as southern fox grape by Wunderlin (1982), who reports it as a common component in several habitats in central Florida. It is also well known in wetland areas of the central Panhandle as well as in a variety of habitats in the northeastern parts of the state.

Calusa Grape
Vitis shuttleworhtii House

Form: High-climbing vine with rounded, hairy stems (more so when young) and two- to three-branched tendrils.

Leaves: Alternate, simple, nearly rounded in outline, predominantly unlobed but sometimes with three to five lobes, lobes typically shallow on leaves of mature stems, more deeply cut on leaves of new shoots; margins entire or with blunt teeth; lower surfaces densely white to rusty tomentose; bases heart shaped or truncate; petioles about half as long as the blade and densely hairy.

Flowers: Small, individually inconspicuous, borne in branched clusters 4 - 12 cm long; appearing in spring.

Fruit: A nearly rounded, dark red to purplish-black berry, 8 - 18 mm in diameter.

Distinguishing Marks: The dense, white to rusty pubescence on the lower surfaces of the leaves distinguishes this species from other members of its genus in southern Florida; the leaf stalk being about one-half to three-quarters the length of the blade offers another clue to this species' identity.

Distribution: Hammocks, low woods, mixed woods; endemic to the Florida peninsula from about Marion, Volusia, and Citrus Counties southward.

Winter Grape, Frost Grape, Chicken Grape   Page 370
Vitis vulpina L.

Form: High-climbing vine with mostly rounded, greenish-gray to brown (sometimes reddish above) stems and forked tendrils.

Leaves: Alternate, simple, broadly ovate to heart shaped in overall outline; margins coarsely dentate and unlobed to sometimes three lobed; lobing mostly shallow on leaves of mature, climbing stems; bases heart shaped; lower surfaces green, without a whitish cast, and with little to no pubescence; petioles about as long as the leaf blades.

Flowers: Small, individually inconspicuous, borne in branched clusters 10 - 17 cm long; appearing in spring.

Fruit: A nearly rounded, black berry, 5 - 10 mm in diameter.

Distinguishing Marks: Leaves most like those of *V. rotundifolia*; the current species is distinguished from the latter by having forked, rather than unforked, tendrils; distinguished from other members of the genus by the combination of rounded, grayish-green to brown stems, and the lower surfaces of the leaves being green and lacking a whitish cast.

Distribution: Mixed upland woods, hammocks and their borders; throughout northern Florida and southward to the southernmost peninsula.

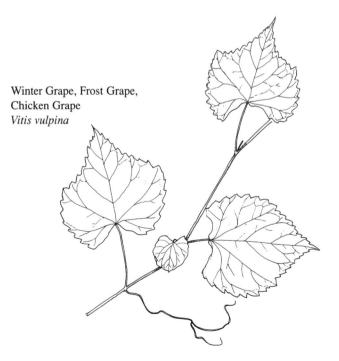

Winter Grape, Frost Grape,
Chicken Grape
Vitis vulpina

ZYGOPHYLLACEAE — CALTROP FAMILY

The caltrop family consists of a little more than 20 genera and about 160 species, mostly of the tropics and subtropics. Many members of the family thrive in dry, salt-rich habitats, especially near the coast. The single species described below, which is one of only a few members of the family found in Florida, is one of the Sunshine State's most historic plants.

Lignum Vitae, Holywood, Tree of Life   Photo 297
Guaiacum sanctum L.

Form: Short, essentially evergreen shrub or tree to about 10 m tall with chalky white bark and a gnarled trunk; twigs light gray and enlarged at the nodes.

Leaves: Opposite, pinnately compound to about 10 cm long overall; leaflets elliptic to obovate in three to four pairs, the lower pair being largest, dark green, 2 - 3 cm long, less than 2 cm wide, inequilateral on either side of the central vein (particularly toward the leaf base), apices tipped with a small point, each pair of leaflets sometimes folding together during the hottest part of the day (and then said to be sleeping).

Flowers: Radially symmetrical with five blue petals, about 2.5 cm wide and borne in clusters; appearing primarily in spring.

Fruit: A bright, orange-yellow capsule which splits open to expose bright red seeds; to about 2 cm long.

Distinguishing Marks: Most easily recognized by its even-compound leaves with small leaflets, and by each leaflet bearing a small tooth at its apex.

Distribution: Found only in tropical hammocks of the Keys, particularly on Lignumvitae Key State Botanical Site; once somewhat more common than today but now found in limited numbers and considered endangered in the state.

Landscape Use: An often-used landscape plant in the Keys; valued for its dense foliage, delicate blue flowers, and historical significance. As might be expected from its dense wood, it is slow growing.

Comment: The lignum vitae is a plant of significant historical importance. Its wood is very dense, very strong, has a heavy resin content, and is extremely resistant to decay and to attack by insects. Its sap also dries very slowly which allows the wood to retain its elasticity. This unique set of characteristics has made it very useful in applications calling for self-lubricating wood products and immunity to water damage. The wood was used in the early shipbuilding trade for bearings, propeller shafts, pins, hubs, pulleys, and a variety of other small parts. Other historical uses include the fabrication of mallets, bowling balls, caster wheels, false teeth, and other such items. Hinges made from lignum vitae served the locks of the Erie Canal for over 100 years. Lignum vitae literally means "wood of life", and reflects a long-held belief that the plant's timber exhibits powerful medicinal properties. The plant was discovered during the early explorations of the New World. From the beginning of the 1500s large quantities were shipped back to Europe. For over 200 years the plant was the source of a popular drug used as a remedy for syphilis and other venereal diseases, and its heartwood became a sought-after product. The wood was sold by the pound for exorbitant prices, making it a lucrative commodity. As a result, much of its population has now been decimated by commercial exploitation, and the plant is listed as an endangered species by the Florida Department of Agriculture.

BIBLIOGRAPHY

Abrahamson, Warren G. 1995. Habitat Distribution and Competitive Neighborhoods of two Florida Palmettos. *Bulletin of the Torrey Botanical Club*, 122(1):1-14.

Adams, C. D. 1972. *Flowering Plants of Jamaica*. University of the West Indies: Jamaica.

Alexander, Taylor R. 1968. *Acacia choriophylla*, A Tree New to Florida. *Quarterly Journal of the Florida Academy of Sciences*, 31(3):197-198.

Anderson, Loran C. 1985. *Forestiera godfreyi* (Oleaceae), A New Species From Florida and South Carolina. *Sida*, 11:1-5.

Anderson, Loran C. 1986. Noteworthy Plants from North Florida. II. *Sida*, 11(4):379-384.

Anderson, Loran C. 1988. Noteworthy Plants from North Florida. III. *Sida*, 13(1):93-100.

Argus, George W. 1986. The Genus *Salix* (Salicaceae) in the Southeastern United States. *Systematic Botany Monographs*, 9:1-170.

Ashe, W. W. 1929. A New Oak from Florida. *Rhodora*, 31: 79-80.

Associated Press. 1995. Price soars for 'aphrodisiac' palmetto berry. *The Orlando Sentinel*, September 26.

Austin, Daniel. 1979. Studies of the Florida Convolvulaceae—Key to Genera. *Florida Scientist*, 42(4):214-216.

Austin, Daniel. 1979. Studies of the Florida Convolvulaceae—II. *Merremia*. *Florida Scientist*, 42(4):216-222.

Austin, Daniel. undated. *Coastal Park Plant Guide: A Pocket Guide to the Native Trees, Shrubs, & Vines of Boca Raton's Hammock and Mangrove Parklands*. Boca Raton, FL: City of Boca Raton Dept. of Parks and Recreation.

Austin, Daniel. 1991. *Coastal Dune Plants: The Common Plants of Southeast Florida's Ocean-Side Communities*. Boca Raton, FL: Gumbo Limbo Nature Center of South Palm Beach County, Inc.

Austin, Daniel. 1993. *Scrub Plant Guide: A Pocket Guide to the Common Plants of Southern Florida's Scrub Community*. Boca Raton, FL: Gumbo Limbo Nature Center of South Palm Beach County, Inc.

Bailey, L. H. 1963. *How Plants Get Their Names*. Mineola, NY: Dover Publications, Inc.

Bell, C. Ritchie and Brian J. Taylor. 1982. *Florida Wildflowers and Roadside Plants*. Chapel Hill, NC: Laurel Hill Press.

Bir, Richard E. 1992. *Growing and Propagating Showy Native Woody Plants*. Chapel Hill, NC: University of North Carolina Press.

Blombery, A. M. 1967. *A Guide to Native Australian Plants*. Sydney, Australia: Angus and Robertson, Ltd.

Bogle, A. Linn. 1974. The Genera of Nyctaginaceae in the Southeastern United States, *Journal of the Arnold Arboretum*, 55:1-37.

Bridges, Edwin L. and Steve Orzell. 1989. *Lindera subcoriacea* (Lauraceae) New to Alabama. *Phytologia*, 67(3):214-216.

Brizicky, George K. 1962. The Genera of Rutaceae in the Southeastern United States. *Journal of the Arnold Arboretum*, 43:1-22.

Brizicky, George K. 1962. The Genera of Simaroubaceae and Burseraceae in the Southeastern United States. *Journal of the Arnold Arboretum*, 43:173-186.

Brizicky, George K. 1962. The Genera of Anacardiaceae in the Southeastern United States. *Journal of the Arnold Arboretum*, 43:359-375.

Brizicky, George K. 1963. The Genera of Sapindales in the Southeastern United States. *Journal of the Arnold Arboretum*, 44:462-501.

Brizicky, George K. 1964. The Genera of Celastrales in the Southeastern United States. *Journal of the Arnold Arboretum*, 45:206-234.

Brizicky, George K. 1964. The Genera of Rhamnaceae in the Southeastern United States. *Journal of the Arnold Arboretum*, 45:439-463.

Brizicky, George K. 1966. The Goodeniaceae in the Southeastern United States. *Journal of the Arnold Arboretum*, 47:293-300.

Burckhalter, Robert E. 1992. The Genus *Nyssa* (Cornaceae) in North America: A Revision. *Sida*, 15(2):323-342.

Campbell, Rob. 1995. Here Today .... *Tillandsia, The Newsletter of the Dade County Chapter of the Florida Native Plant Society*, Nov-Dec:4.

Carlton, Jedfrey M. 1975. *A Guide to Common Salt Marsh and Mangrove Vegetation*. Florida Marine Research Publications, No. 6. St. Petersburg, FL: Florida Department of Natural Resources.

Channell, R. B. and C. E. Wood, Jr. 1962. The Leitneriaceae in the Southeastern United States. *Journal of the Arnold Arboretum*, 43:435-438.

Chapman, A. W. 1885. *Torreya taxifolia*, Arnott. A Reminiscence. *Botanical Gazette*, 10(4):251-254.

Christman, Steven P. and Walter S. Judd. 1990. Notes on Plants Endemic to Florida Scrub. *Florida Scientist*, 53(1):52-73.

Clancy, Keith E. and Michael J. Sullivan. 1990. Distribution of the Needle Palm, *Rhapidophyllum hystrix*. *Castanea*, 55(1):31-39.

Clark, Robert B. 1942. A Revision of the Genus *Bumelia* in the United States. *Annals of the Missouri Botanical Garden*, 29:155-182.

Clewell, Andre F. 1985. *Guide to the Vascular Plants of the Florida Panhandle*. Tallahassee: University Presses of Florida, Florida State University Press.

Clewell, Andre F. 1986. *Natural Setting and Vegetation of the Florida Panhandle*. Mobile, AL: U.S. Army Corps of Engineers.

Clewell, Andre F. 1971. *The Vegetation of the Apalachicola National Forest: An Ecological Perspective*. Tallahassee: Unpublished manuscript prepared under contract 38-2249, U. S. Department of Agriculture, U. S. Forest Service.

Corner, E. J. H. 1964. *The Life of Plants*. New York: World Publishing Co.

Delaney, Kris R., Richard P. Wunderlin, and Bruce E. Hansen. 1989. Rediscovery of *Ziziphus celata* (Rhamnaceae). *Sida*, 13(3):325-330.

DePhilipps, R. 1969. Parasitism in *Ximenia* (Olacaceae). *Rhodora*, 71:439-443.

Duncan, Wilbur H. and Marion B. Duncan. 1988. *Trees of the Southeastern United States*. Athens, GA: University of Georgia Press.

Eisner, Thomas, Kevin D. McCormick, Makoto Sakaino, Maria Eisner, Scott R. Smedley, Daniel J. Aneshansley, Mark Deyrup, Ronald L. Myers, and Jerrold Meinwald. 1990. Chemical Defense of a Rare Mint Plant. *Chemoecology*, 1:30-37.

Elias, Thomas S. 1971. The Genera of Myricaceae in the Southeastern United States. *Journal of the Arnold Arboretum*, 52:305-318.

Elias, Thomas S. 1974. The Genera of Mimosoideae (Leguminosae) in the Southeastern United States. *Journal of the Arnold Arboretum*, 55:67-118.

Ernst, Wallace R. 1963. The Genera of Hamamelidaceae and Platanaceae in the Southeastern United States. *Journal of the Arnold Arboretum*, 44:193-210.

Ernst, Wallace R. 1964. The Genera of Berberidaceae, Lardizabalaceae, and Menispermaceae in the Southeastern United States. *Journal of the Arnold Arboretum*, 45: 1-35.

Eyde, Richard H. 1966. The Nyssaceae in the Southeastern United States. *Journal of the Arnold Arboretum*, 47:117-125.

Ferguson, I. K. 1966. The Genera of Caprifoliaceae in the Southeastern United States. *Journal of the Arnold Arboretum*, 47:33-59.

Ferguson, I. K. 1966. Notes on the Nomenclature of *Cornus. Journal of the Arnold Arboretum*, 47:100-105.

Ferguson, I. K. 1966. The Cornaceae in the Southeastern United States. *Journal of the Arnold Arboretum*, 47:106-116.

Fernald, M. L. 1950. *Gray's Manual of Botany*. New York: D. Van Nostrand Company.

Florida Natural Areas Inventory. October 1995. *Tracking Lists of Special Plants and Lichens, Invertebrates, Vertebrates, and Natural Communities.*

Furlow, John J. 1990. The Genera of Betulaceae in the Southeastern United State. *Journal of the Arnold Arboretum*, 71:1-67.

Gentry, Alwyn H. 1993. *A Field Guide to the Families of Woody Plants of Northwest South America (Columbia, Ecuador, Peru)*. Washington, DC: Conservation International.

Gledhill, D. 1989. *The Names of Plants, Second Edition*. Cambridge: Cambridge University Press.

Godfrey, Robert K. 1988. *Trees, Shrubs, and Woody Vines of Northern Florida and Adjacent Georgia and Alabama*. Athens, GA: University of Georgia Press.

Godfrey, Robert K., and Jean W. Wooten. 1979. *Aquatic and Wetland Plants of Southeastern United States. Monocotyledons*. Athens: University of Georgia Press.

Godfrey, Robert K., and Jean W. Wooten. 1981. *Aquatic and Wetland Plants of Southeastern United States. Dicotyledons*. Athens: University of Georgia Press.

Graham, Shirley A. 1964. The Genera of Lythraceae in the Southeastern United States. *Journal of the Arnold Arboretum*, 45:235-250.

Graham, Shirley A. 1966. The Genera of Araliaceae in the Southeastern United States. *Journal of the Arnold Arboretum*, 47:126-136.

Graham, Shirley A. and C. E. Wood, Jr. 1965. The Genera of Polygonaceae in the Southeastern United States. *Journal of the Arnold Arboretum*, 46:91-121.

Hall, David W. 1993. *Illustrated Plants of Florida and the Coastal Plain*. Gainesville, FL: Maupin House Publishing.

Hammer, Roger. 1995. The So-Called Porterweeds. *Tillandsia, The Newsletter of the Dade Chapter of the Florida Native Plant Society*, Jul-Aug:2-3.

Hammer, Roger. 1995. The Coontie and the Atala Hairstreak. *The Palmetto*, 15(4):3-5.

Hardin, James W. 1972. Studies of the Southeastern United States Flora. III. Magnoliaceae and Illiciaceae. *Journal of the Elisa Mitchell Society*, 87:30-32.

Hawkes, Alex D. 1965. *Guide to Plants of the Everglades National Park*. Coral Gables, FL: Tropic Isle Publishers, Inc.

Herring, Brenda J. And Walter S. Judd. 1995. A Floristic Study of Ichetucknee Springs state Park, Suwannee and Columbia Counties, Florida. *Castanea*. 60(4):318-369.

Hickey, Michael and Clive King. 1988. *100 Families of Flowering Plants*, Second Edition. New York: Cambridge University Press.

Howard, Richard A. 1958. A History of the Genus Coccoloba in Cultivation. *Baileya*, 6:204-212.

Huegel, Craig. 1993. Hawthorns. *The Palmetto*, 13(2):4-5.

Hume, H. H. 1953. *Hollies*. New York: The Macmillan Co.

Isley, Duane. 1969. Legumes of the United States: I. Native Acacia. *Sida*, 3(6):365-386.

Isely, Duane. 1990. *Vascular Flora of the Southeastern United States, Volume 3, Part 2, Leguminosae (Fabaceae)*. University of North Carolina Press: Chapel Hill, NC.

Johnson, Ann F. and Warren G. Abrahamson. 1982. *Quercus inopina*: A Species to be Recognized from South-central Florida. *Bulletin of the Torrey Botanical Club*, 109(3):392-395.

Judd, Walter S. and David W. Hall. 1984. A New Species of *Ziziphus* (Rhamnaceae) from Florida. *Rhodora*, 86:381-387.

Kral, Robert. 1960. A Revision of Asimina and Deeringothamnus (Annonaceae). *Brittonia*, 12:233-278.

Kral, Robert. 1983. *A Report On Some Rare, Threatened, or Endangered Forest-Related Vascular Plants of The South*. 2 vols. Atlanta: USDA Forest Service, Technical Publication R8-TP 2.

Kral, Robert. 1991. A New Species of *Conradina* (Lamiaceae) From Northeastern Peninsular Florida. *Sida*, 14(3): 391-398.

Krezdorn, A. H., Albert A. Will, Eric V. Golby, Lewis Maxwell. 1991. *Florida Fruit*. Tampa: Lewis S. Maxwell, Publisher.

Kruckoff, B. A. and R. C. Barneby. 1974. Conspectus of Species of the Genus *Erythrina*. *Lloydia*, 37:332-459.

Kuijt, Job. 1982. The Viscaceae in the Southeastern United States. *Journal of the Arnold Arboretum*, 63:401-410.

Kunkel, Gunther. 1978. *Flowering Trees in Subtropical Gardens*. The Hague: Dr. W. Junk b.v., Publishers.

Lakela, Olga. 1963. The Identity of *Bumelia lacuum* Small. *Rhodora*, 65:280-282.

Lakela, Olga and Richard P. Wunderlin. 1980. *Trees of Central Florida*. Miami: Banyan Press.

Lance, Ronald. 1995. *The Hawthorns of the Southeastern United States*. Fletcher, NC: published by the author.

Lippincott, Carol. 1992. Return of the Native: Restoring Sargent's Cherry Palm on the Florida Keys. *Fairchild Tropical Garden Bulletin*, 47(1):12-21.

Little, Elbert. L., Jr. and F. W. Wadsworth. 1964. *Common Trees of Puerto Rico and the Virgin Islands*. Agricultural Handbook 249, Washington, D.C.: U.S. Department of Agriculture.

Little, Elbert L. Jr., R. O. Woodbury, and F. H. Wadsworth. 1974. *Trees of Puerto Rico and the Virgin Islands*. Vol. 2, Agriculture Handbook 449, Washington D.C.: U.S. Department of Agriculture.

Long, R. W. and Olga Lakela. 1976. *A Flora of Tropical Florida*. Miami: Banyan Books.

Lyrene, Paul. 1995. In Defense of *Vacinium elliottii*. *The Palmetto*, 15(4):9-11.

Martin, H. W. 1994. More on Beautyberry. *The Palmetto*, 14(1):5-6.

Martin, Laura C. 1992. *The Folklore of Trees and Shrubs*. Old Saybrook, Connecticut: The Globe Pequot Press.

McCormick, Kevin D., Mark A. Deyrup, Eric S. Menges, Susan R. Wallace, Jerrold Meinwald, and Thomas Eisner. 1993. Relevance of Chemistry to Conservation of Isolated Populations: The Case of Volatile Leaf Components of *Dicerandra* Mints. *Proceedings of the National Academy of Sciences, USA*, 90:7701-7705.

Mell, C. D. 1922. The Early Uses of Yaupon. *American Forestry*, 28:531.

Menninger, Edwin A. 1970. *Flowering Vines of the World: An Enclyclopedia of Climbing Plants*. Hearthside Press: New York.

Miller, R. F. 1975. The Deciduous Magnolias of West Florida. *Rhodora*, 77:64-75.

Mullins, Stephen. 1993. Moving Joewood Trees. *The Palmetto*, 13(2): 8-9.

Nellis, David. 1994. *Seashore Plants of South Florida and the Caribbean*. Sarasota, FL: Pineapple Press.

Odenwald, Neil and James Turner. 1987. *Identification, Selection and Use of Southern Plants for Landscape Design*. Baton Rouge: Claitor's Publishing Division.

Peattie, Donald C. 1950. *A Natural History of Trees of Eastern and Central North America*. Boston: Houghton Mifflin Company, 1950.

Pennington, T. D. 1991. *The Genera of Sapotaceae*. New York: Royal Botanic Gardens and New York Botanical Gardens.

Pennington, Terrence D., Brian T. Styles, and D. A. H. Taylor. 1981. *Flora Neotropica: Meliaceae*. Monograph 28. New York: New York Botanical Garden.

Petrides, George A. 1986. *A Field Guide to Trees and Shrubs, 2nd Ed*. Boston: Houghton Mifflin.

Phipps, J. B. 1988. Re-Assessment of *Crataegus flava* Aiton and Its Nomenclatural Implications for the *Crataegus* Serial Name *Flavae* (Loud.) Rehd. and Its Sectional Equivalent. *Taxon*, 37(1):108-113.

Phipps, J. B. 1988. Crataegus (Maloideae, Rosaceae) of the Southeastern United States, I. Introduction and Series Aestivales. *Journal of the Arnold Arboretum*, 69:401-431.

Porter, Duncan M. 1972. The Genera of Zygophyllaceae in the Southeastern United States. *Journal of the Arnold Arboretum*, 53:531-552.

Prance, Ghillean T. 1970. The Genera of Chrysobalanaceae in the Southeastern United States. *Journal of the Arnold Arboretum*, 51:521-528.

Price, R. A. 1990. The Genera of Taxaceae in the Southeastern United States. *Journal of the Arnold Arboretum*, 71:69-91.

Race, Tammera. 1994. Update on *Ziziphus celata*: the Persistent Species. *Plant Conservation*, 8(2):1.

Robertson, Kenneth R. 1972. The Malpighiaceae in the Southeastern United States. *Journal of the Arnold Arboretum*, 53:101-112.

Robertson, Kenneth R. 1974. The Genera of Rosaceae in the Southeastern United States. *Journal of the Arnold Arboretum*, 55:303-332.

Robertson, Kenneth R. 1974. The Genera of Rosaceae in the Southeastern United States. *Journal of the Arnold Arboretum*, 55:611-662.

Robertson, Kenneth R. 1982. The Genera of Olacaceae in the Southeastern United States. *Journal of the Arnold Arboretum*, 63:387-399.

Rogers, David J. and Constance Rogers. 1991. *Woody Ornamentals for Deep South Gardens*. Pensacola, FL: University of West Florida Press.

Rogers, George K. 1982. The Bataceae in the Southeastern United States. *Journal of the Arnold Arboretum*, 63:375-386.

Sanders, Roger W. 1987. Identity of *Lantana depressa* and *L. ovatifolia* (Verbenaceae) of Florida and the Bahamas. *Systematic Botany*, 12(1):44-60.

Schwartz, Mark W. and Sharon M. Hermann. 1993. The Continuing Population Decline of *Torreya taxifolia* Arn. *Bulletin of the Torrey Botanical Club*, 120:275-286.

Scurlock, J. Paul. 1987. *Native Trees and Shrubs of the Florida Keys*. Bethel Park, PA: Laurel Press.

Shinners, Lloyd H. 1962. Synopsis of Conradina (Labiatae). *Sida*, 1(2): 84-88.

Shinners, Lloyd H. 1962. Synopsis of Dicerandra (Labiatae). *Sida*, 1(2): 89-91.

Shinners, Lloyd H. 1962. Vegetative Key to Woody Labiatae of The Southeastern Coastal Plain. *Sida*, 1(2): 92-93.

Small, John K. 1913. *Flora of the Southeastern United States*. 2nd edition. Published by the author.

Small, John K. 1927. A New Nyssa from Florida. *Torreya*, 27:92-93.

Small, John K. 1933. *Manual of the Southeastern Flora*. Lancaster, PA: The Science Press.

Spongberg, Stephen. 1971. The Staphyleaceae in the Southeastern United States. *Journal of the Arnold Arboretum*, 52:196-203.

Stern, William L., George K. Brizicky, and Francisco N. Tamolang. 1963. The Woods and Flora of the Florida Keys: Capparaceae. *Contributions from the United States National Herbarium*, 34(2).

Sternberg, Guy and Jim Wilson. 1995. *Landscaping with Native Trees*. Shelburne, VT: Chapters Publishing, Ltd.

Steyermark, Julian A. 1949. Lindera melissaefolia. *Rhodora*, 51:153-162.

Taylor, Walter Kingsley. 1992. *The Guide to Florida Wildflowers*. Dallas: Taylor Publishing Co.

Tomlinson, P. B. 1986. *The Botany of Mangroves*. Cambridge: Cambridge University Press.

Tomlinson, P. B. 1980. *The Biology of Trees Native to Tropical Florida*. Allston, MA: Bound and Printed by the Harvard University Printing Office.

Van Doren, Mark (ed). 1955. *Travels of William Bartram*. New York: Dover Publications, Inc.

Vander Kloet, S. P. 1980. The Taxonomy of the Highbush Blueberry, *Vaccinium corymbosum*. *Canadian Journal of Botany*, 58:1187-1201.

Wagner, Warren L., Darral R. Herbst, and S. H. Sohmer. 1990. *Manual of the Flowering Plants of Hawaii, Vol. 2*. Honolulu: U. of Hawaii Press.

Ward, Daniel B. 1967. *Acacia macracantha*, A Tree New to Florida and the United States. *Brittonia*, 19:283-284.

Ward, Daniel B. 1978. *Rare and Endangered Biota of Florida. Volume 5. Plants*. Gainesville: University Presses of Florida.

Ward, Daniel B. and James R. Burkhalter. 1977. Rediscovery of Small's Acacia in Florida. *Florida Scientist*, 40(3):267-270.

Watkins, John V. and Thomas J. Sheehan. 1975. *Florida Landscape Plants, Revised Edition*. Gainesville, FL: The University Presses of Florida.

Webster, Grady L. 1967. The Genera of Euphorbiaceae in the Southeastern United States. *Journal of the Arnold Arboretum*, 48: 303-430.

Wilson, Kenneth A. 1960. The Genera of Convolvulaceae in the Southeastern United States. *Journal of the Arnold Arboretum*, 41:298-317.

Wilson, Kenneth A. 1960. The Genera of Myrtaceae in the Southeastern United States. *Journal of the Arnold Arboretum*, 41:270-278.

Wilson, Kenneth A. and Carroll E. Wood. 1959. The Genera of Oleaceae in the Southeastern United States. *Journal of the Arnold Arboretum*, 40:369-384.

Wofford, B. Eugene. 1983. A New *Lindera* (Lauraceae) from North America. *Journal of the Arnold Arboretum*, 64:325-331.

Wood, Carroll E., Jr. 1958. The Genera of the Woody Ranales in the Southeastern United States. *Journal of the Arnold Arboretum*, 39:296-346.

Wood, Carroll E., Jr. 1961. The Genera of Ericaceae in the Southeastern United States. *Journal of the Arnold Arboretum*, 42:10-80.

Wood, Carroll. E., Jr. and R. B. Channell. 1960. The Genera of the Ebenales in the Southeastern United States. *Journal of the Arnold Arboretum*, 41:1-35.

Wunderlin, Richard P. 1982. *Guide to the Vascular Plants of Central Florida*. Gainesville, FL: University Presses of Florida.

Wunderlin, Richard P. and James E. Poppleton. 1977. The Florida Species of *Ilex* (Aquifoliaceae). *Florida Scientist*, 40 (1977) 7-21.

Wunderlin, R. P., B. F. Hansen, and D. W. Hall. 1985. The Vascular Flora of Central Florida: Taxonomic and Nomenclatural Changes, Additional Taxa. *Sida*, 11(2):232-244.

Wunderlin, R. P., B. F. Hansen, and D. W. Hall. 1988. The Vascular Flora of Central Florida: Taxonomic and Nomenclatural Changes, Additional Taxa, II. *Sida*, 13(1):83-91.

Wurdack, John J. and Robert Kral. 1982. The Genera of the Melastomataceae in the Southeastern United States. *Journal of the Arnold Arboretum*, 63:429-439.

Zona, Scott. 1985. A New Species of *Sabal* (Palmae) from Florida. *Brittonia*, 37(4):366-368.

Zona, Scott. 1994. Beautyberry, An Under-used Native. *The Palmetto*, 14(1): 3-4.

Zona, Scott and Walter S. Judd. 1986. *Sabal etonia* (Palmae): Systematics, Distribution, Ecology, and Comparisons to Other Florida Scrub Endemics. *Sida*, 11(4):417-427.

INDEX TO COMMON NAMES

Note: Illustrations are indicated by boldface type. CP refers to the color photographs between pages 202 and 203.

Here are some other books from Pineapple Press on related topics. For a complete catalog, write to Pineapple Press, P.O. Box 3889, Sarasota, Florida 34230, or call (800) 746-3275. Or visit our website at www.pineapplepress.com.

The Art of South Florida Gardening by Harold Songdahl and Coralee Leon. Gardening advice specifically written for the unique conditions of south Florida. This practical, comprehensive guide, written with humor and know-how, will teach you how to outsmart the soil, protect against pests and weather, and select the right trees and shrubs for Florida's climate. ISBN 1-56164-088-3 (pb)

Exotic Foods: A Kitchen and Garden Guide by Marian Van Atta. Take advantage of year-round warm weather and grow fruit trees, exotic vegetables, and rare delights such as Surinam cherry. Discover tips to keep your garden free of pests and producing for years. Includes a wealth of delicious and nutritious recipes for drinks, main courses, desserts, relishes, jams, and jellies. ISBN 1-56164-215-0 (pb)

The Ferns of Florida by Gil Nelson. The first field guide in 25 years to treat Florida's amazing variety of ferns. Includes color plates with more than 200 images, notes on each species' growth form and habit, general remarks about its botanical and common names, unique characteristics, garden use, and history in Florida. ISBN 1-56164-193-6 (hb); 1-56164-197-9 (pb)

Gardening in the Coastal South by Marie Harrison. A Master Gardener discusses coastal gardening considerations such as salt tolerance; environmental issues such as pesticide use, beneficial insects, and exotic invasives; and specific issues such as gardening for butterflies and birds. Color photos and charming pen-and-ink illustrations round out the text, which covers perennials, herbs, shrubs and small trees, vines, and edible flowers. ISBN 1-56164-274-6 (pb)

Guide to the Gardens of Florida by Lilly Pinkas. This comprehensive guide to Florida's gardens includes detailed information about featured species and garden facilities as well as directions, hours of operation, and admission fees. Learn the history and unique offerings of each garden, what plants to see and the best time of year to see them.

Traveling outside of Florida? Check out *Guide to the Gardens of Georgia* and *Guide to the Gardens of South Carolina* by the same author. Florida ISBN 1-56164-169-3 (pb); Georgia ISBN 1-56164-198-7 (pb); South Carolina ISBN 1-56164-251-7 (pb)

Landscaping in Florida by Mac Perry. A photo idea book packed with irresistible ideas for inviting entryways, patios, pools, walkways, and more. Over 200 photos and eight pages of color photos, plus charts of plant materials by region, condition of soil and sunlight, and purpose. ISBN 1-56164-057-3 (pb)

Ornamental Tropical Shrubs by Amanda Jarrett. Stunning color photos and full information profile for 83 shrubs including country of origin, drought and salt tolerance, growth rate and suitable soils, preferred sun exposure, mature size and form, flowers and fruits, potential insect and disease problems, and more. ISBN 1-56164-289-4 (hb); 1-56164-275-4 (pb)

Poisonous Plants and Animals of Florida and the Caribbean by David W. Nellis. An illustrated guide to the characteristics, symptoms, and treatments for over 300 species of poisonous plants and toxic animals. ISBN 1-56164-111-1 (hb); 1-56164-113-8 (pb)

Seashore Plants of South Florida and the Caribbean by David W. Nellis. A full-color guide to the flora of nearshore environments, including complete characteristics of each plant as well as ornamental, medicinal, ecological, and other aspects. Suitable for backyard gardeners and serious naturalists. ISBN 1-56164-026-3 (hb); 1-56164-056-5 (pb)

The Trees of Florida by Gil Nelson. The first comprehensive guide to Florida's amazing variety of tree species, this book serves as both a reference and a field guide. ISBN 1-56164-053-0 (hb); 1-56164-055-7 (pb)